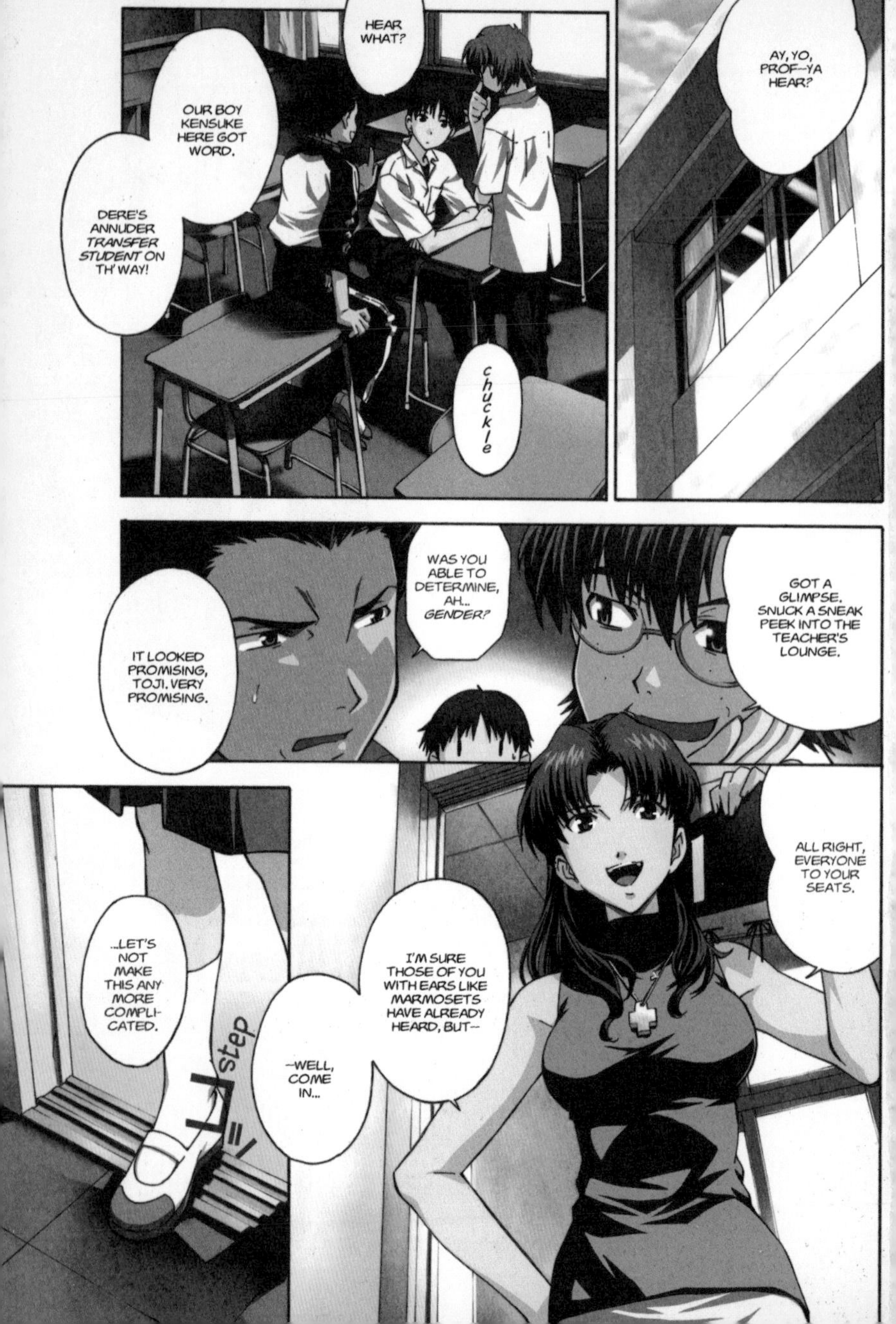
AY, YO, PROF--YA HEAR?
HEAR WHAT?
OUR BOY KENSUKE HERE GOT WORD.
DERE'S ANNUDER *TRANSFER STUDENT* ON TH' WAY!
chuckle
GOT A GLIMPSE. SNUCK A SNEAK PEEK INTO THE TEACHER'S LOUNGE.
WAS YOU ABLE TO DETERMINE, AH... *GENDER?*
IT LOOKED PROMISING, TOJI. VERY PROMISING.
ALL RIGHT, EVERYONE TO YOUR SEATS.
I'M SURE THOSE OF YOU WITH EARS LIKE MARMOSETS HAVE ALREADY HEARD, BUT--
--WELL, COME IN...
...LET'S NOT MAKE THIS ANY MORE COMPLI-CATED.
step

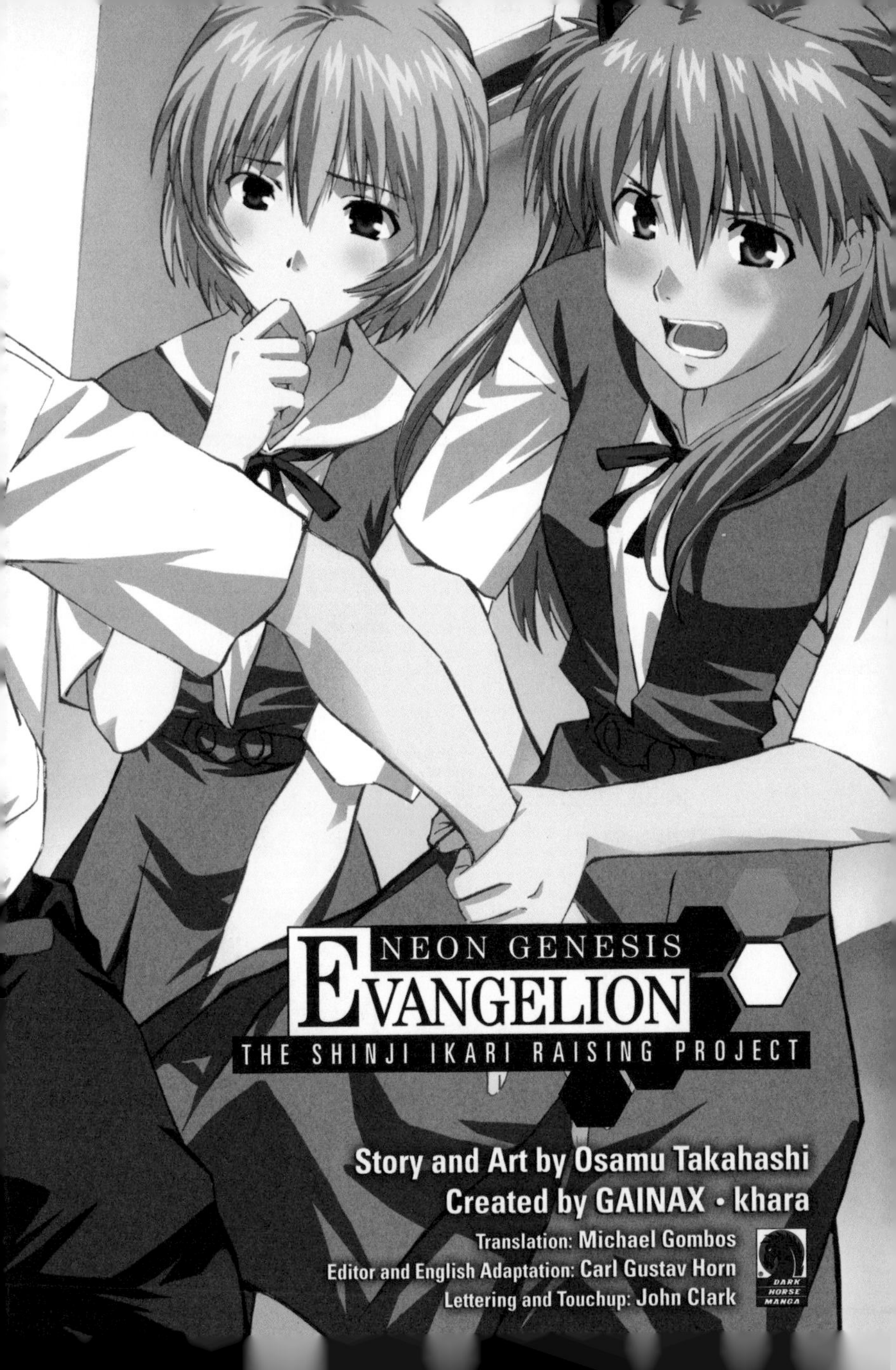

NEON GENESIS EVANGELION

THE SHINJI IKARI RAISING PROJECT

Story and Art by Osamu Takahashi

Created by GAINAX • khara

Translation: Michael Gombos

Editor and English Adaptation: Carl Gustav Horn

Lettering and Touchup: John Clark

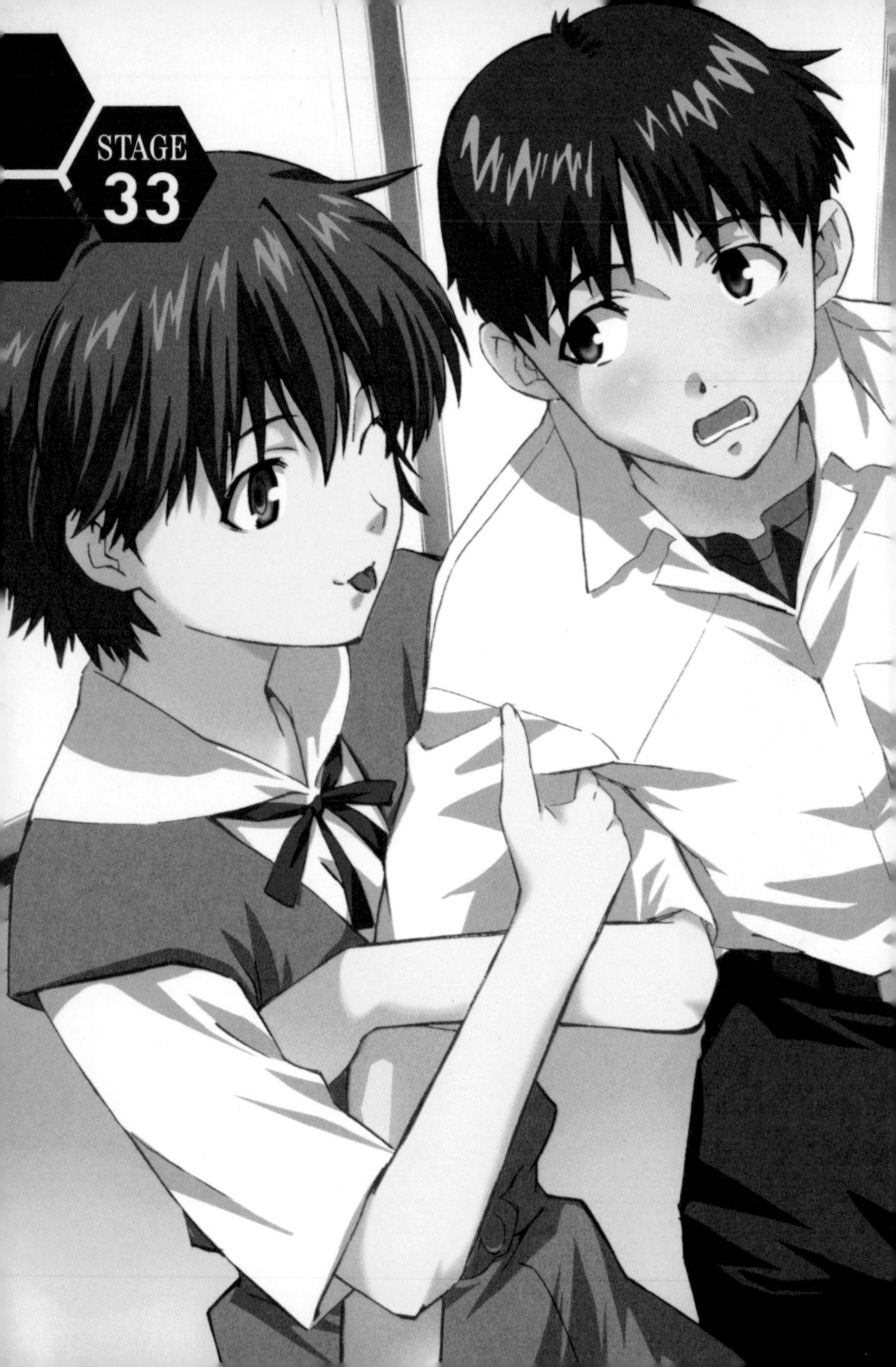
STAGE
33

CONTENTS

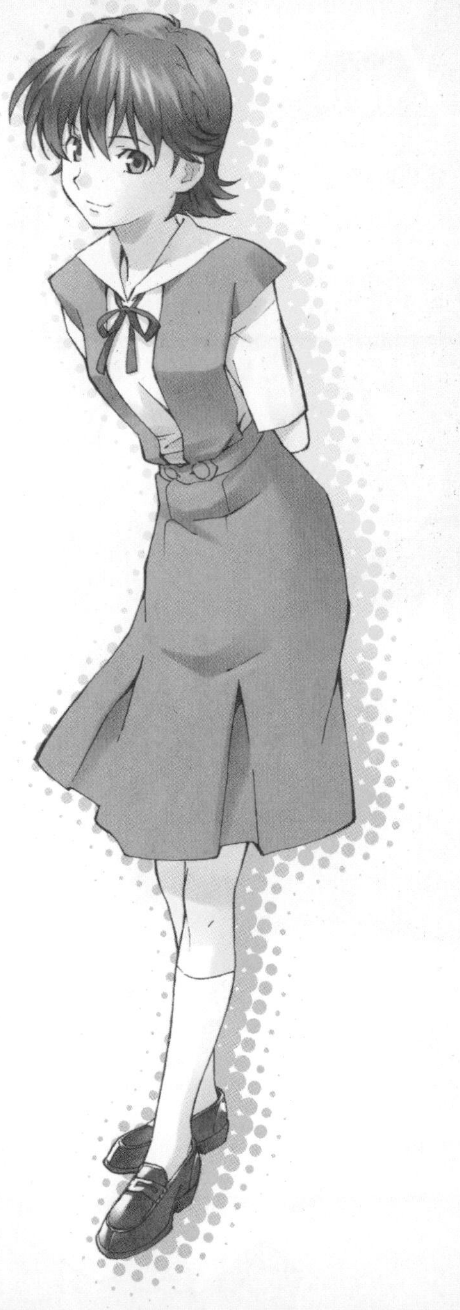

NEON GENESIS EVANGELION

THE SHINJI IKARI RAISING PROJECT

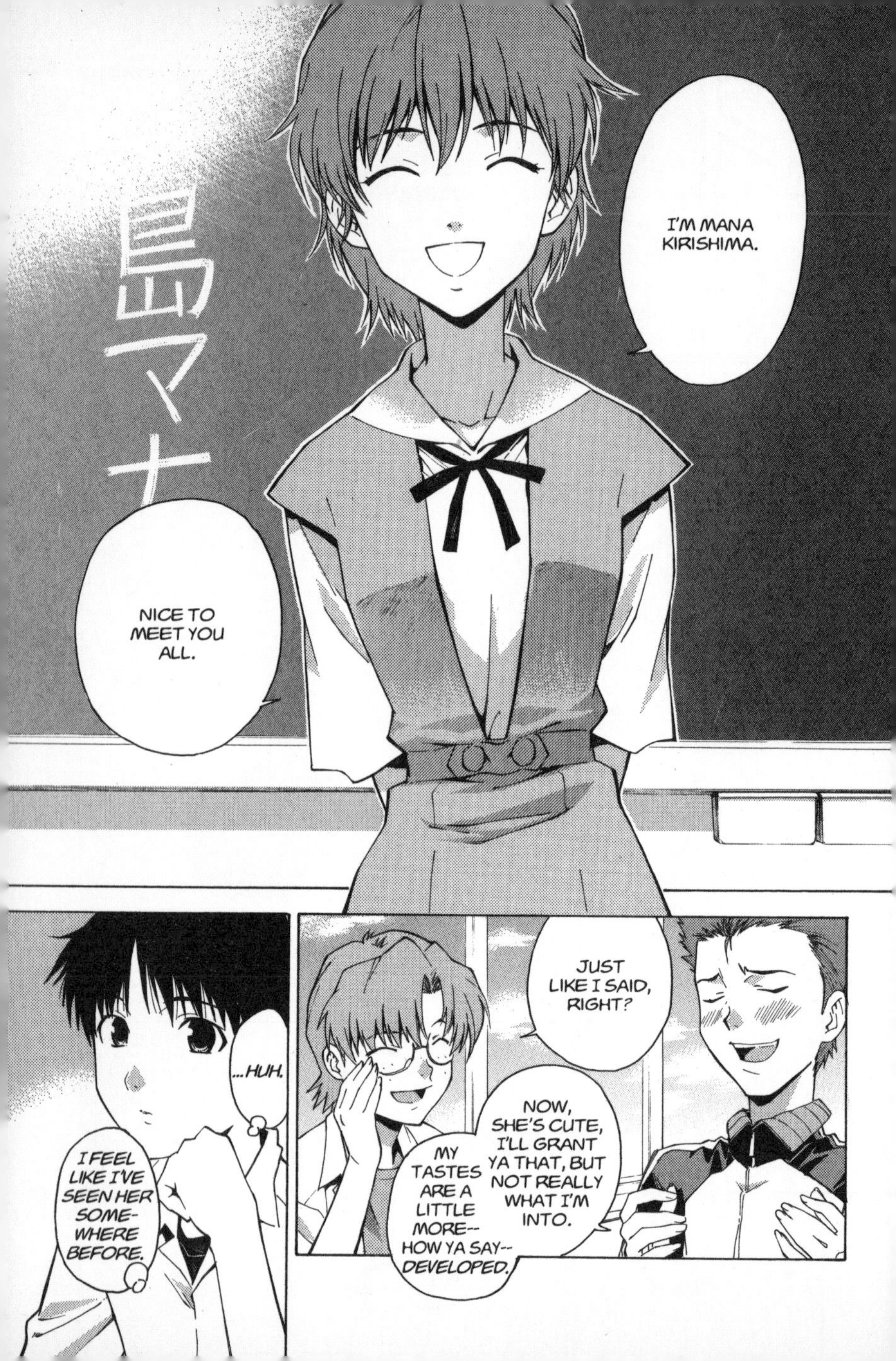
I'M MANA KIRISHIMA.
島マナ
NICE TO MEET YOU ALL.
JUST LIKE I SAID, RIGHT?
NOW, SHE'S CUTE, I'LL GRANT YA THAT, BUT NOT REALLY WHAT I'M INTO.
MY TASTES ARE A LITTLE MORE-- HOW YA SAY-- DEVELOPED.
...HUH.
I FEEL LIKE I'VE SEEN HER SOME-WHERE BEFORE.

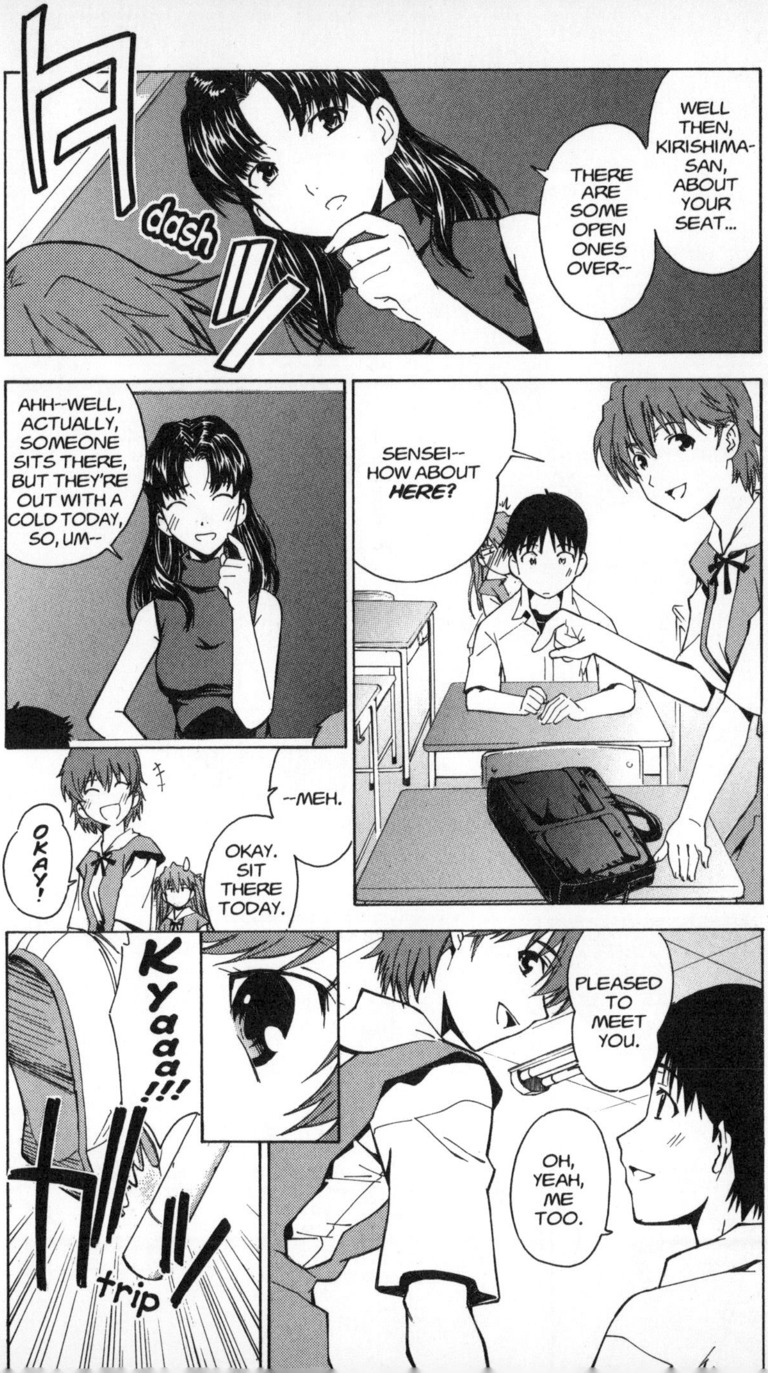
WELL THEN, KIRISHIMA-SAN, ABOUT YOUR SEAT...
THERE ARE SOME OPEN ONES OVER--
dash
SENSEI-- HOW ABOUT *HERE?*
AHH--WELL, ACTUALLY, SOMEONE SITS THERE, BUT THEY'RE OUT WITH A COLD TODAY, SO, UM--
--MEH.
OKAY. SIT THERE TODAY.
OKAY!
PLEASED TO MEET YOU.
OH, YEAH, ME TOO.
Kyaaa!!!
trip

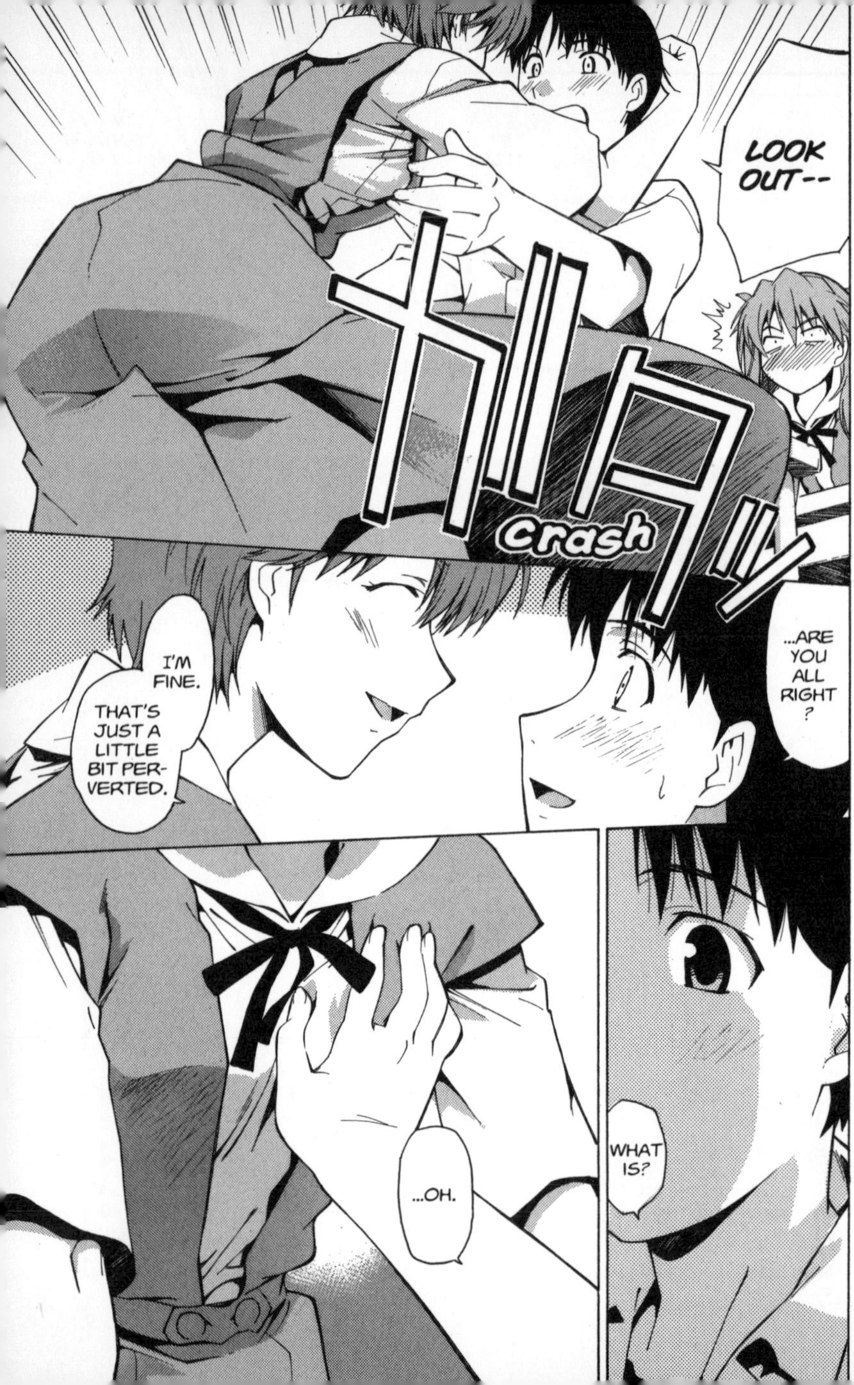
LOOK OUT--
ガタッ
Crash
...ARE YOU ALL RIGHT?
I'M FINE.
THAT'S JUST A LITTLE BIT PERVERTED.
WHAT IS?
...OH.

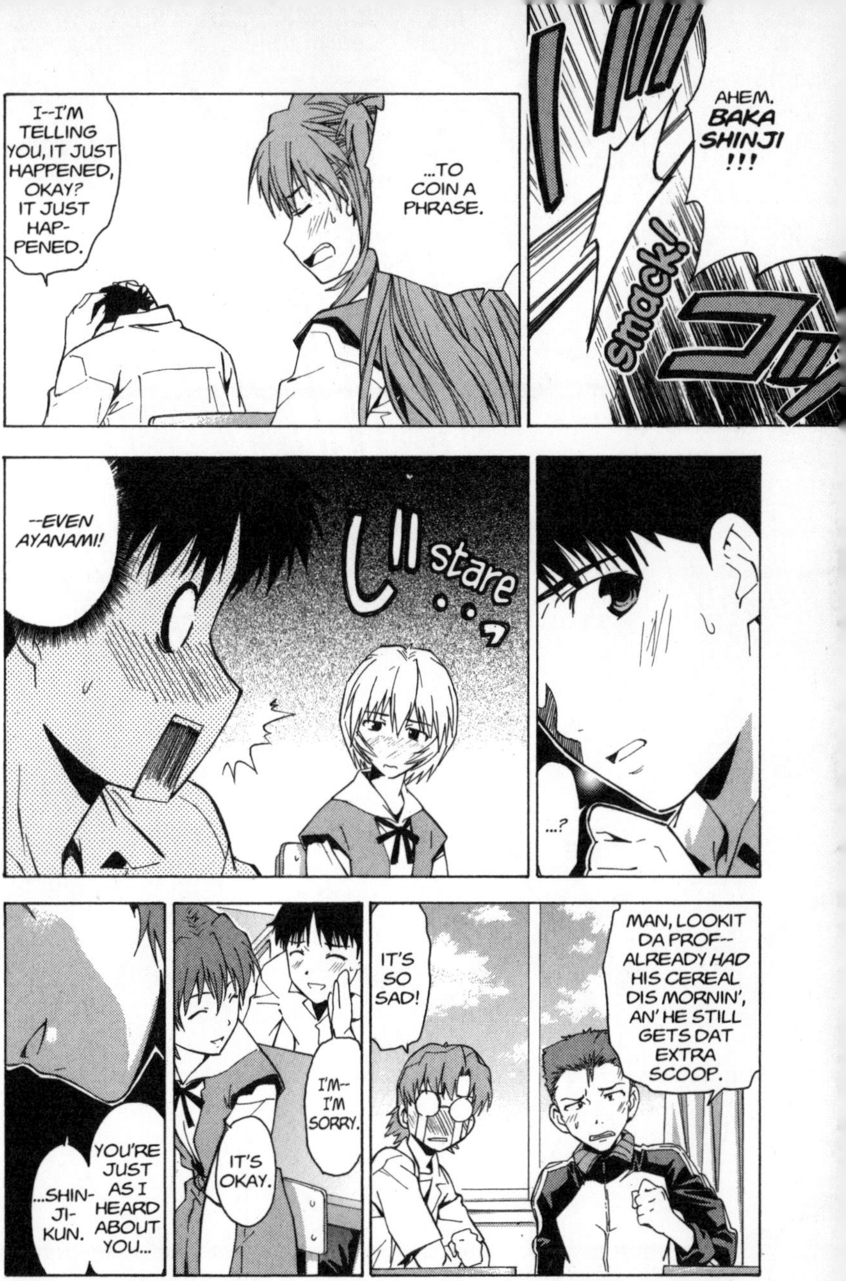
AHEM. BAKA SHINJI!!!
smack!
...TO COIN A PHRASE.
I--I'M TELLING YOU, IT JUST HAPPENED, OKAY? IT JUST HAP-PENED.
...?
--EVEN AYANAMI!
stare...
MAN, LOOKIT DA PROF-- ALREADY HAD HIS CEREAL DIS MORNIN', AN' HE STILL GETS DAT EXTRA SCOOP.
IT'S SO SAD!
I'M-- I'M SORRY.
IT'S OKAY.
YOU'RE JUST AS I HEARD ABOUT YOU...
...SHIN-JI-KUN.

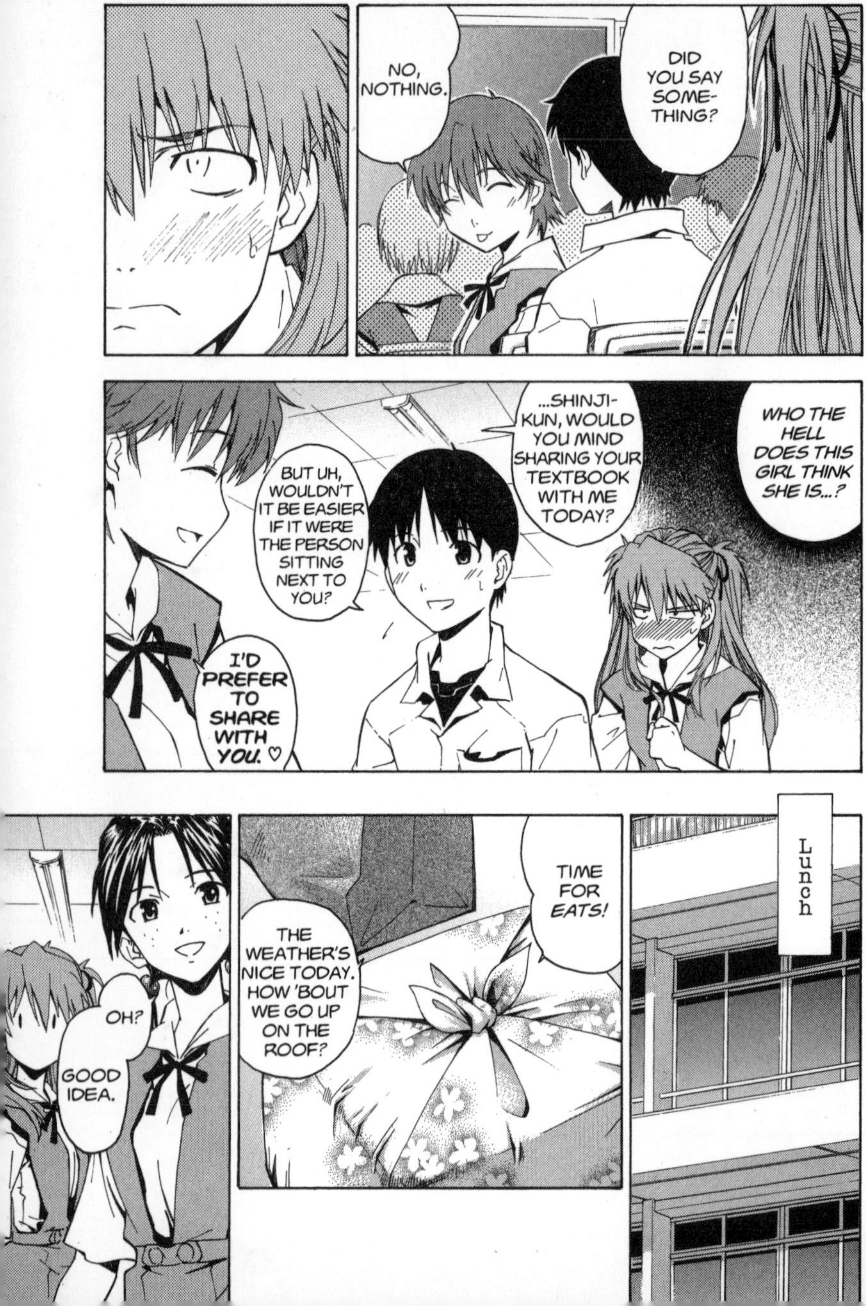
DID YOU SAY SOMETHING?
NO, NOTHING.
WHO THE HELL DOES THIS GIRL THINK SHE IS...?
...SHINJI-KUN, WOULD YOU MIND SHARING YOUR TEXTBOOK WITH ME TODAY?
BUT UH, WOULDN'T IT BE EASIER IF IT WERE THE PERSON SITTING NEXT TO YOU?
I'D PREFER TO SHARE WITH YOU. ♡
Lunch
TIME FOR EATS!
THE WEATHER'S NICE TODAY. HOW 'BOUT WE GO UP ON THE ROOF?
OH? GOOD IDEA.

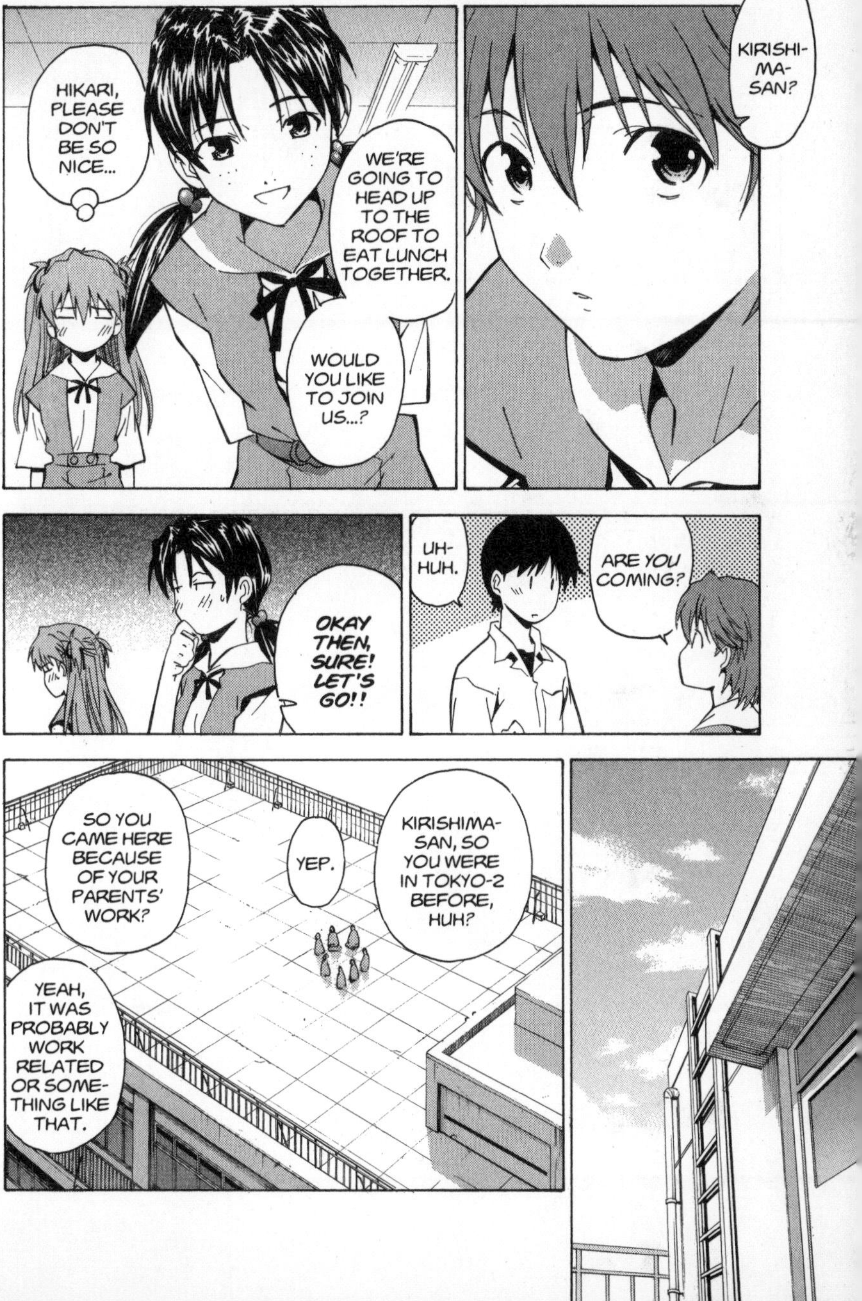
KIRISHIMA-SAN?
WE'RE GOING TO HEAD UP TO THE ROOF TO EAT LUNCH TOGETHER.
WOULD YOU LIKE TO JOIN US...?
HIKARI, PLEASE DON'T BE SO NICE...
ARE YOU COMING?
UH-HUH.
OKAY THEN, SURE! LET'S GO!!
KIRISHIMA-SAN, SO YOU WERE IN TOKYO-2 BEFORE, HUH?
YEP.
SO YOU CAME HERE BECAUSE OF YOUR PARENTS' WORK?
YEAH, IT WAS PROBABLY WORK RELATED OR SOMETHING LIKE THAT.

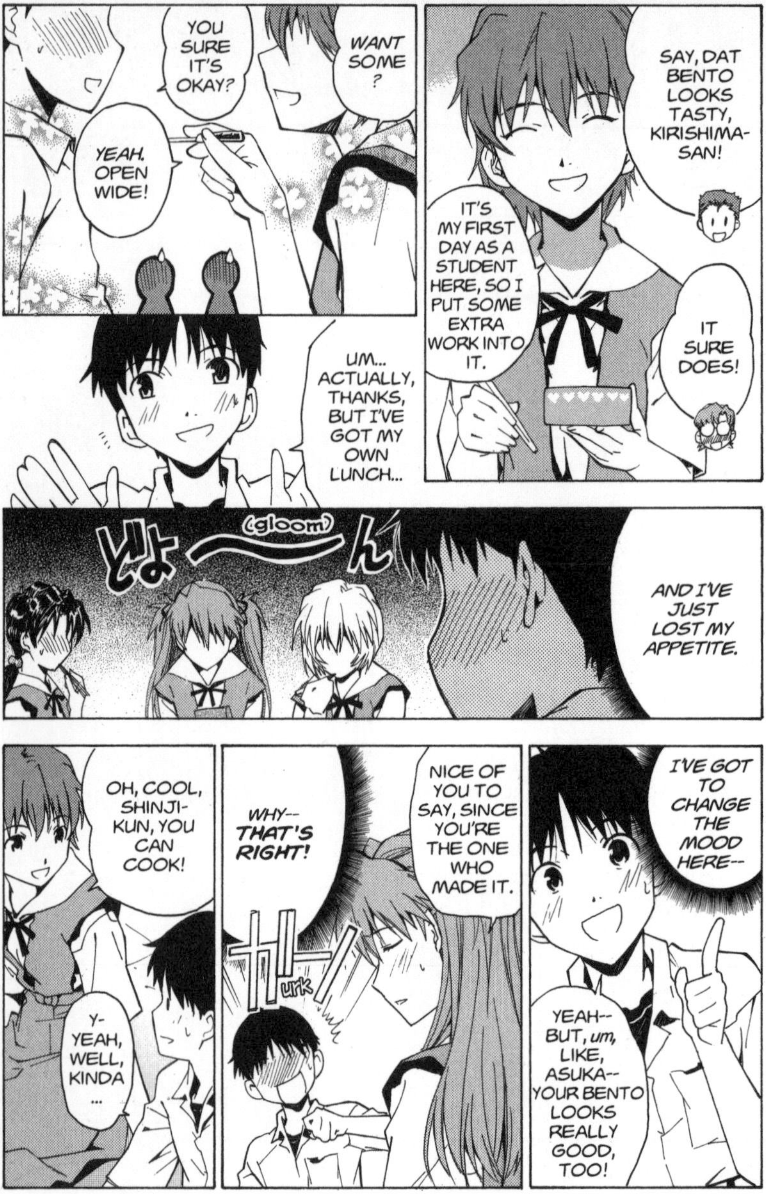
SAY, DAT BENTO LOOKS TASTY, KIRISHIMA-SAN!
IT'S MY FIRST DAY AS A STUDENT HERE, SO I PUT SOME EXTRA WORK INTO IT.
IT SURE DOES!
WANT SOME?
YOU SURE IT'S OKAY?
YEAH. OPEN WIDE!
UM... ACTUALLY, THANKS, BUT I'VE GOT MY OWN LUNCH...
AND I'VE JUST LOST MY APPETITE.
どよーん
(gloom)
I'VE GOT TO CHANGE THE MOOD HERE--
YEAH-- BUT, *um,* LIKE, ASUKA-- YOUR BENTO LOOKS REALLY GOOD, TOO!
NICE OF YOU TO SAY, SINCE YOU'RE THE ONE WHO MADE IT.
WHY-- ***THAT'S RIGHT!***
カーン
urk
OH, COOL, SHINJI-KUN, YOU CAN COOK!
Y-YEAH, WELL, KINDA ...

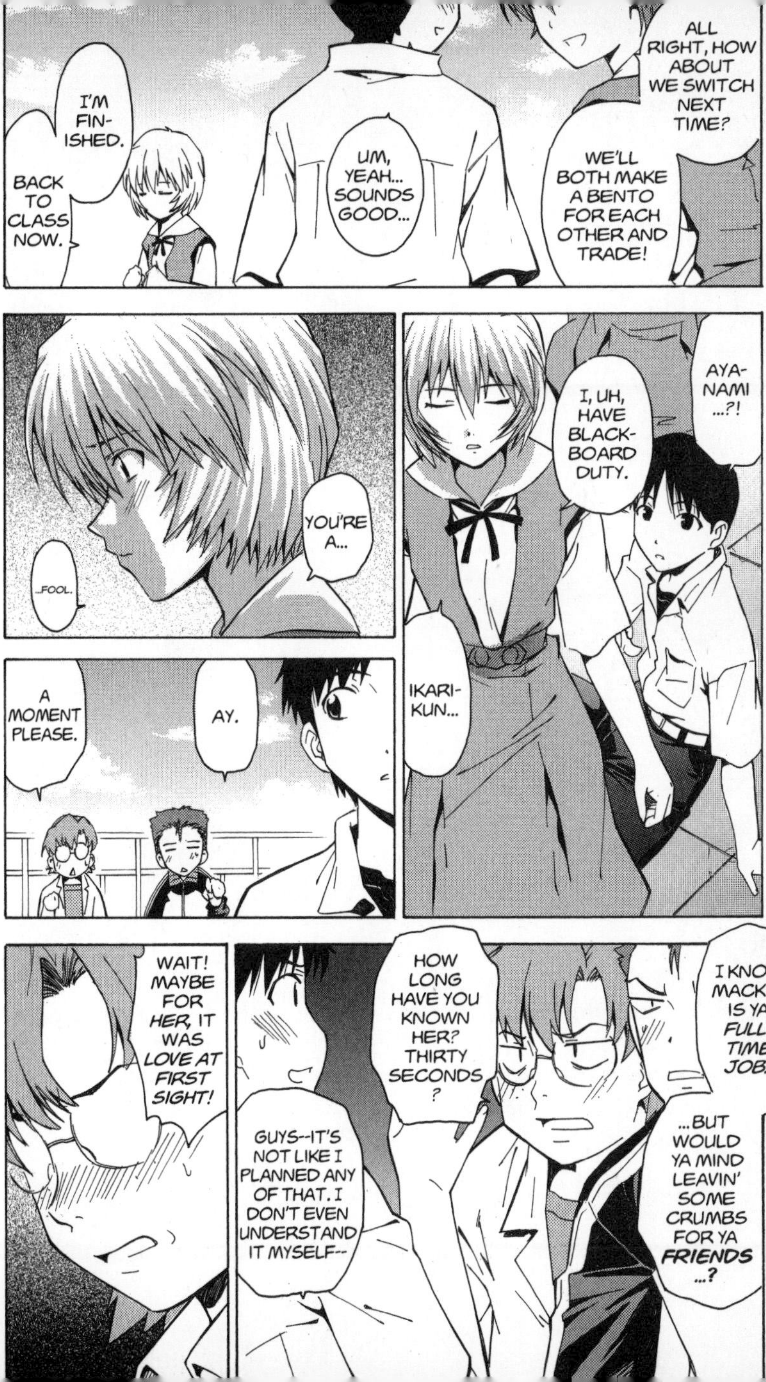
ALL RIGHT, HOW ABOUT WE SWITCH NEXT TIME?
WE'LL BOTH MAKE A BENTO FOR EACH OTHER AND TRADE!
UM, YEAH... SOUNDS GOOD...
I'M FIN-ISHED.
BACK TO CLASS NOW.
AYA-NAMI ...?!
I, UH, HAVE BLACK-BOARD DUTY.
IKARI-KUN...
YOU'RE A...
...FOOL.
AY.
A MOMENT PLEASE.
I KNOW MACKIN' IS YA *FULL-TIME* JOB...
...BUT WOULD YA MIND LEAVIN' SOME CRUMBS FOR YA **FRIENDS** ...?
HOW LONG HAVE YOU KNOWN HER? THIRTY SECONDS?
GUYS--IT'S NOT LIKE I PLANNED ANY OF THAT. I DON'T EVEN UNDERSTAND IT MYSELF--
WAIT! MAYBE FOR *HER*, IT WAS *LOVE AT FIRST SIGHT!*

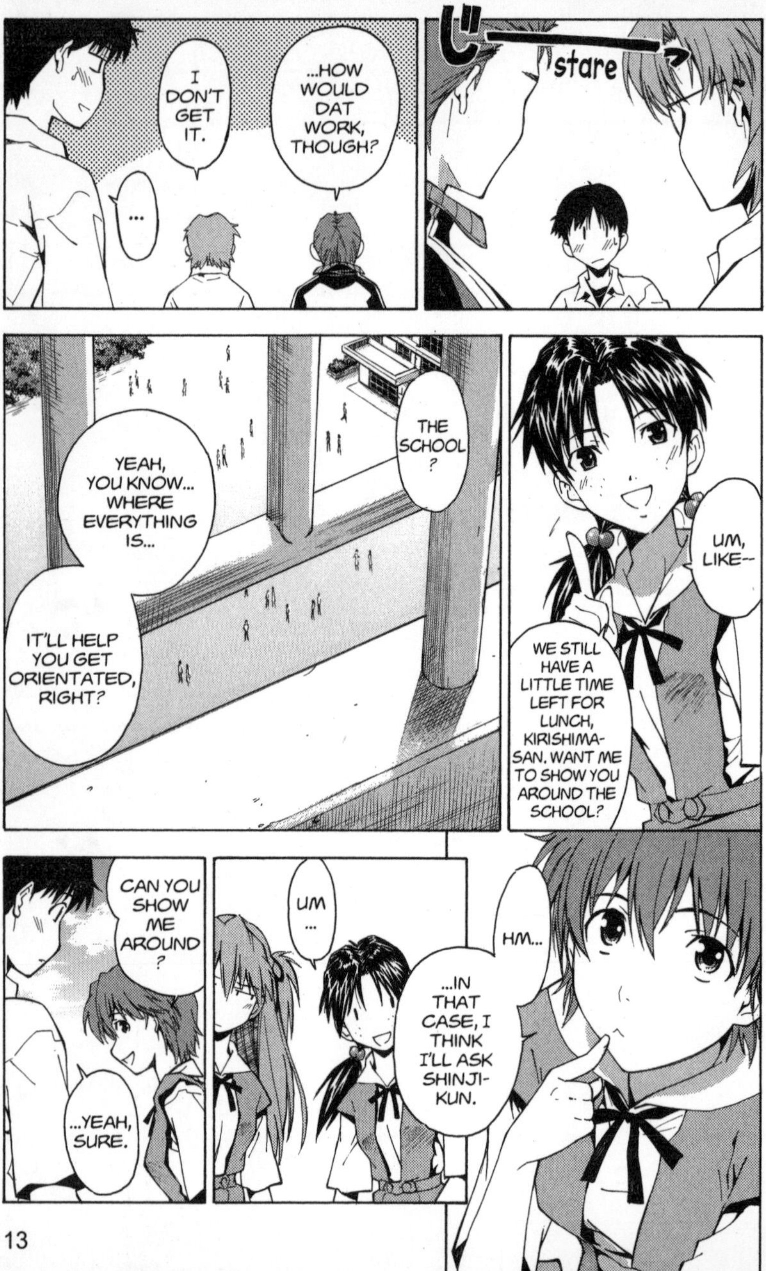
じー
stare
...HOW WOULD DAT WORK, THOUGH?
I DON'T GET IT.
...
UM, LIKE--
WE STILL HAVE A LITTLE TIME LEFT FOR LUNCH, KIRISHIMA-SAN. WANT ME TO SHOW YOU AROUND THE SCHOOL?
THE SCHOOL?
YEAH, YOU KNOW... WHERE EVERYTHING IS...
IT'LL HELP YOU GET ORIENTATED, RIGHT?
HM...
...IN THAT CASE, I THINK I'LL ASK SHINJI-KUN.
UM ...
CAN YOU SHOW ME AROUND?
...YEAH, SURE.

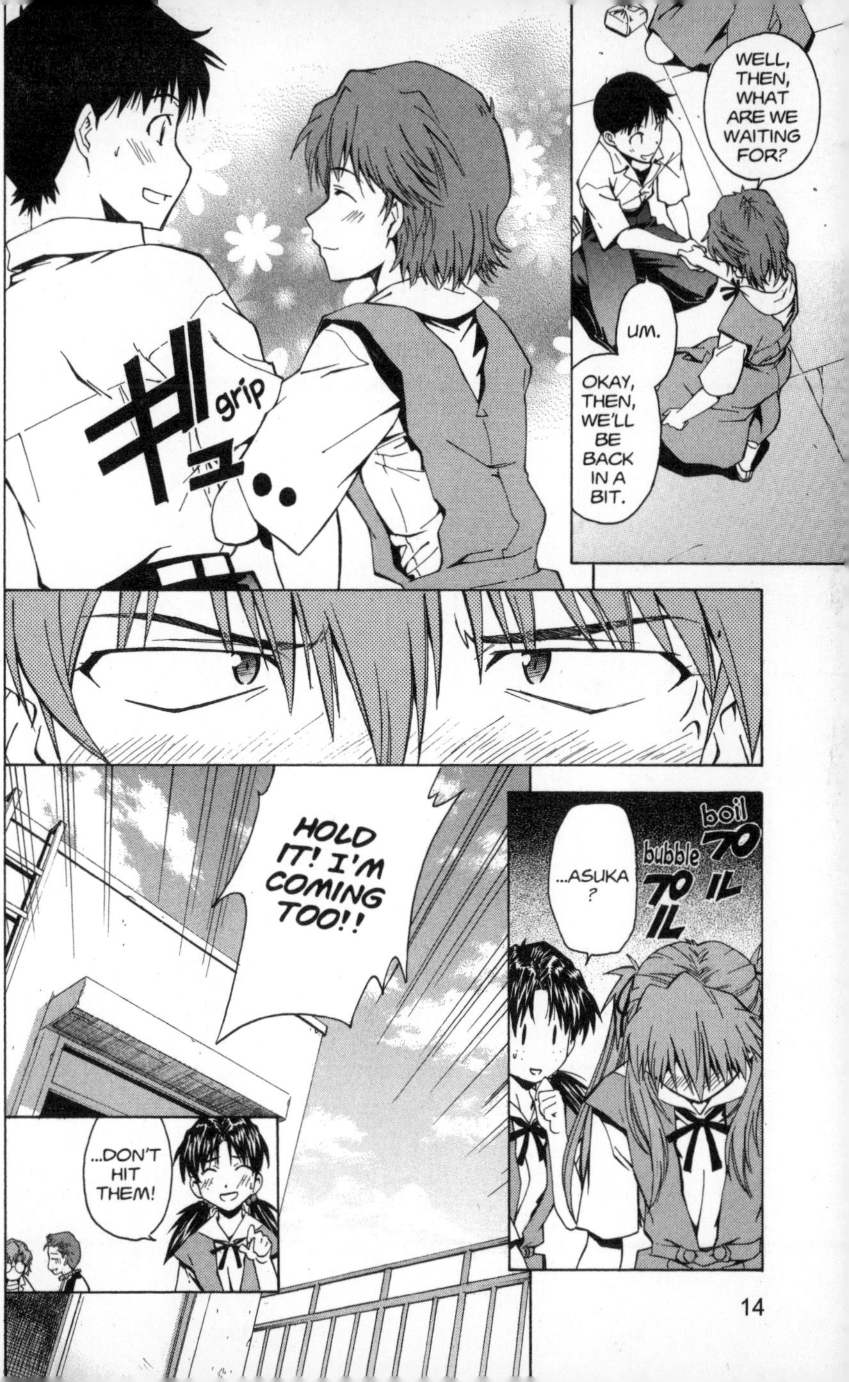
WELL, THEN, WHAT ARE WE WAITING FOR?
UM.
OKAY, THEN, WE'LL BE BACK IN A BIT.
grip
ギュ
boil
プル
bubble
プル
...ASUKA?
HOLD IT! I'M COMING TOO!!
...DON'T HIT THEM!

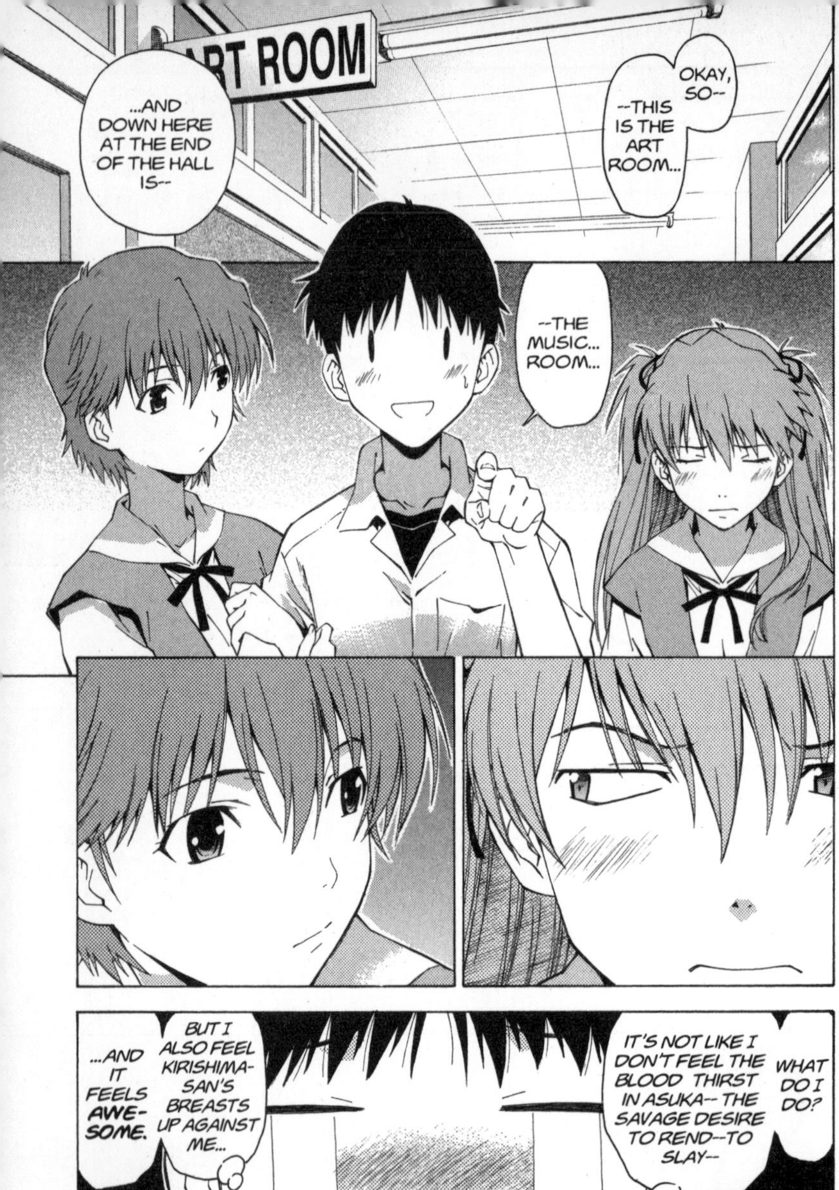
ART ROOM
OKAY, SO--
--THIS IS THE ART ROOM...
...AND DOWN HERE AT THE END OF THE HALL IS--
--THE MUSIC... ROOM...
WHAT DO I DO?
IT'S NOT LIKE I DON'T FEEL THE BLOOD THIRST IN ASUKA-- THE SAVAGE DESIRE TO REND--TO SLAY--
BUT I ALSO FEEL KIRISHIMA-SAN'S BREASTS UP AGAINST ME...
...AND IT FEELS **AWE-SOME.**

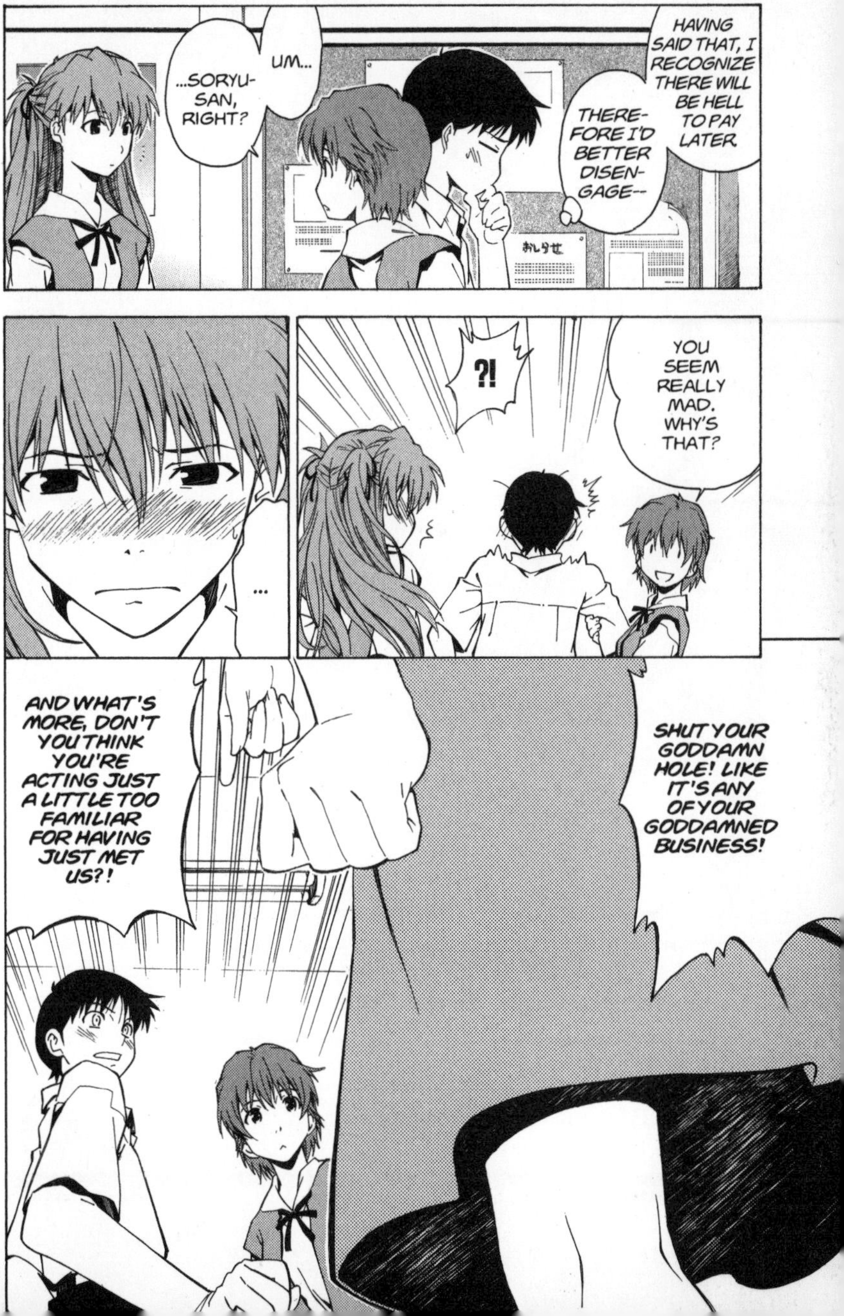

HAVING SAID THAT, I RECOGNIZE THERE WILL BE HELL TO PAY LATER.
THERE-FORE I'D BETTER DISEN-GAGE--
UM...
...SORYU-SAN, RIGHT?
おしらせ
YOU SEEM REALLY MAD. WHY'S THAT?
?!
...
SHUT YOUR GODDAMN HOLE! LIKE IT'S ANY OF YOUR GODDAMNED BUSINESS!
AND WHAT'S MORE, DON'T YOU THINK YOU'RE ACTING JUST A LITTLE TOO FAMILIAR FOR HAVING JUST MET US?!

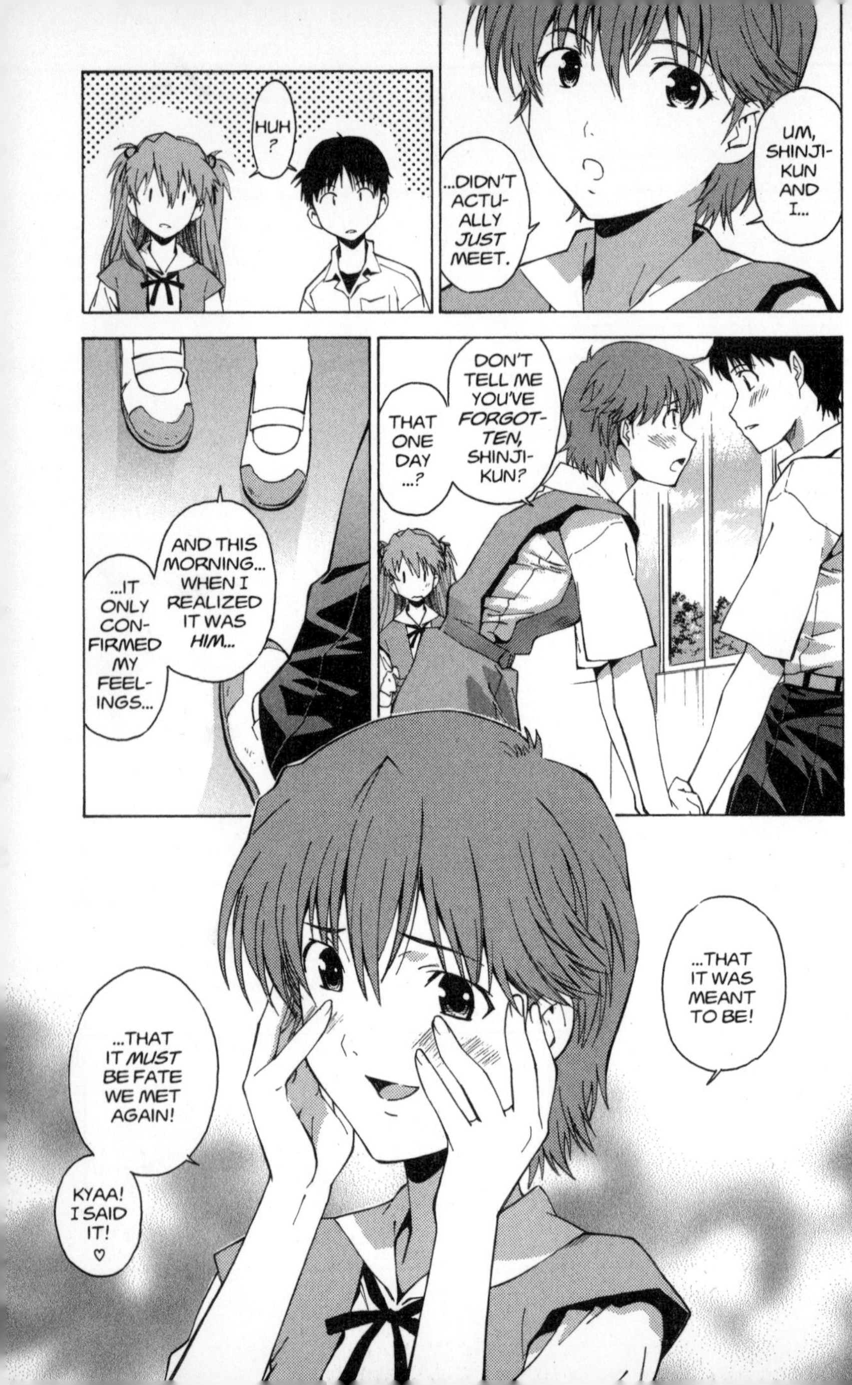
UM, SHINJI-KUN AND I...
...DIDN'T ACTUALLY *JUST* MEET.
HUH?
DON'T TELL ME YOU'VE *FORGOTTEN*, SHINJI-KUN?
THAT ONE DAY ...?
AND THIS MORNING... WHEN I REALIZED IT WAS *HIM*...
...IT ONLY CONFIRMED MY FEELINGS...
...THAT IT WAS MEANT TO BE!
...THAT IT *MUST* BE FATE WE MET AGAIN!
KYAA! I SAID IT! ♡

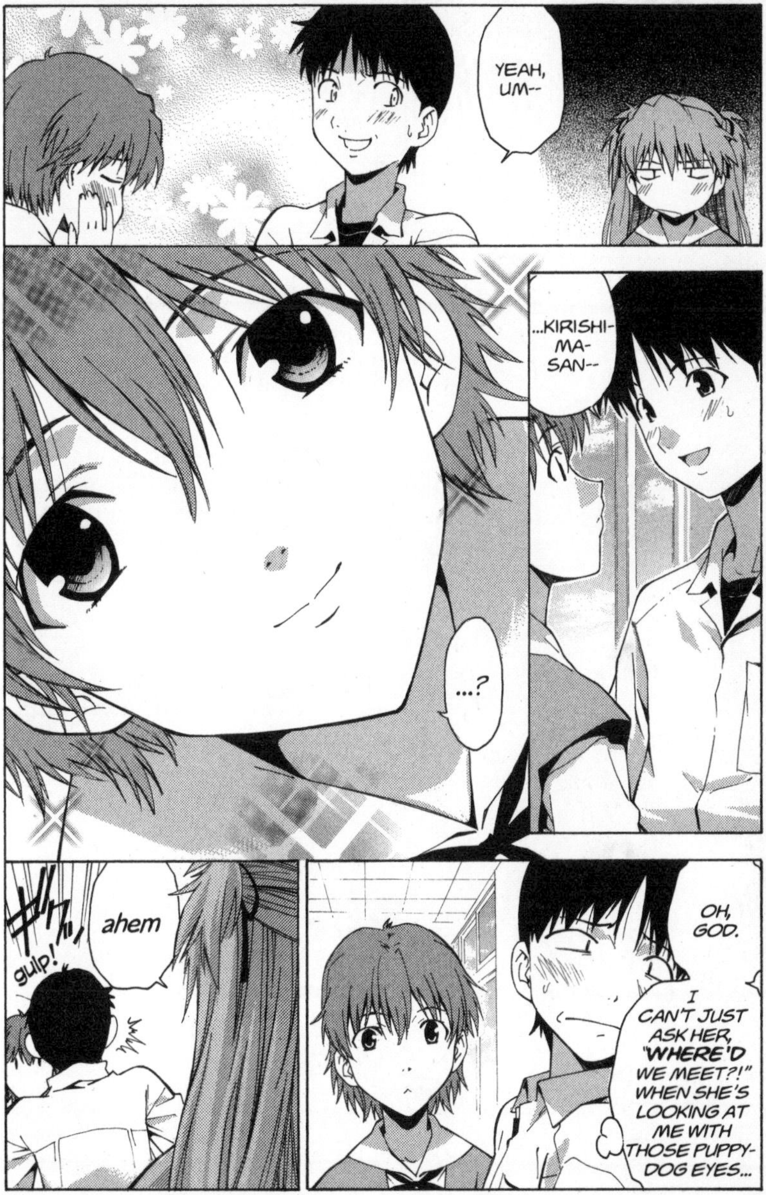
YEAH, UM--
...KIRISHI-MA-SAN--
...?
OH, GOD.
I CAN'T JUST ASK HER, "WHERE'D WE MEET?!" WHEN SHE'S LOOKING AT ME WITH THOSE PUPPY-DOG EYES...
ahem
gulp!

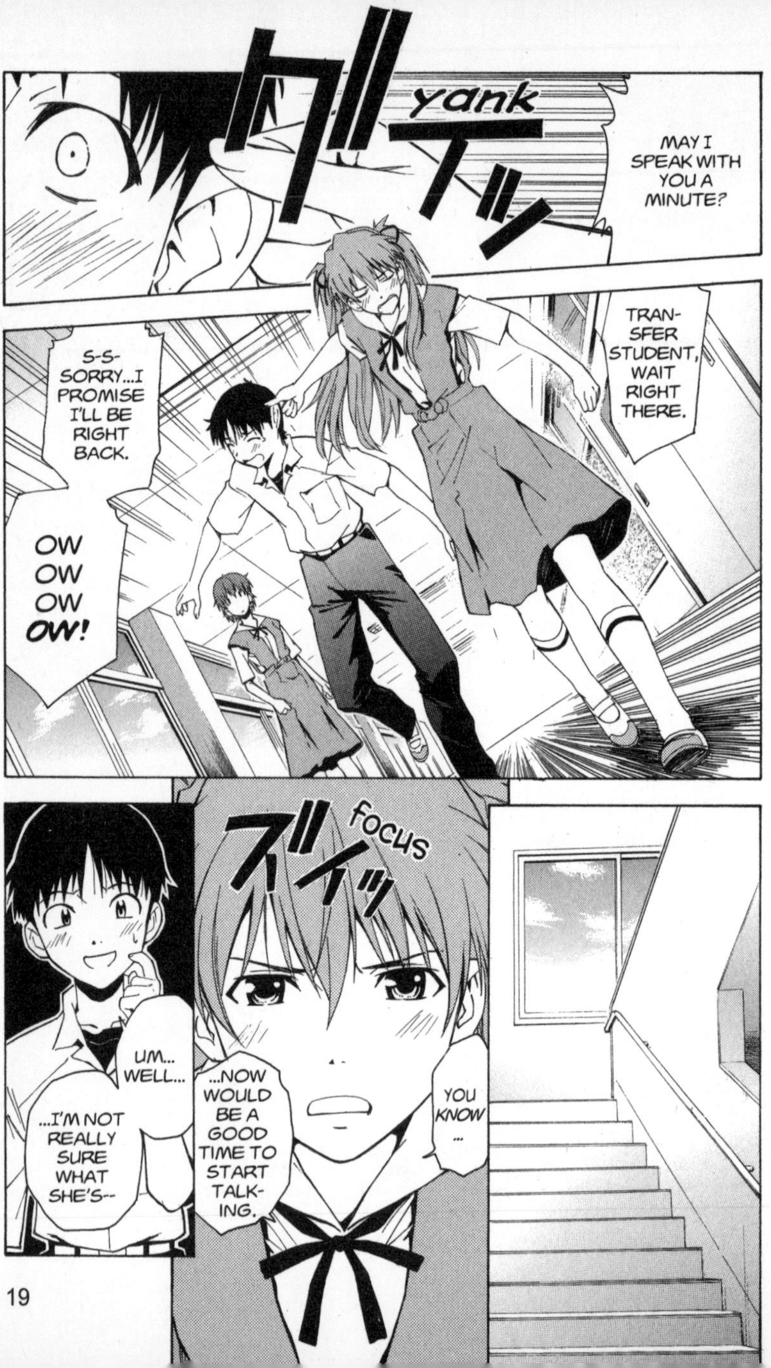
MAY I SPEAK WITH YOU A MINUTE?
yank
TRAN-SFER STUDENT, WAIT RIGHT THERE.
S-S-SORRY...I PROMISE I'LL BE RIGHT BACK.
OW OW OW OW!
focus
YOU KNOW ...
...NOW WOULD BE A GOOD TIME TO START TALK-ING.
UM... WELL...
...I'M NOT REALLY SURE WHAT SHE'S--

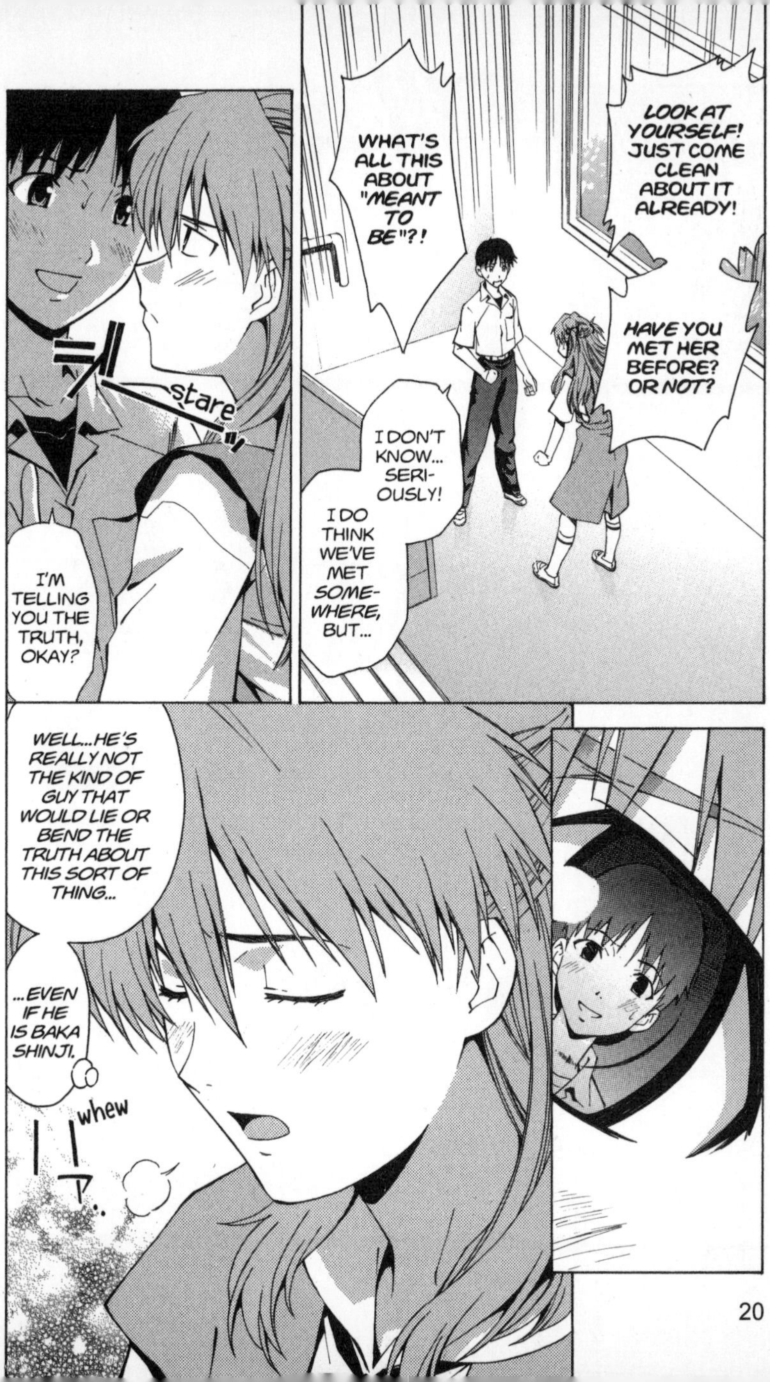
LOOK AT YOURSELF! JUST COME CLEAN ABOUT IT ALREADY!
WHAT'S ALL THIS ABOUT "MEANT TO BE"?!
HAVE YOU MET HER BEFORE? OR NOT?
I DON'T KNOW... SERI-OUSLY!
I DO THINK WE'VE MET SOME-WHERE, BUT...
stare
I'M TELLING YOU THE TRUTH, OKAY?
WELL...HE'S REALLY NOT THE KIND OF GUY THAT WOULD LIE OR BEND THE TRUTH ABOUT THIS SORT OF THING...
...EVEN IF HE IS BAKA SHINJI.
whew

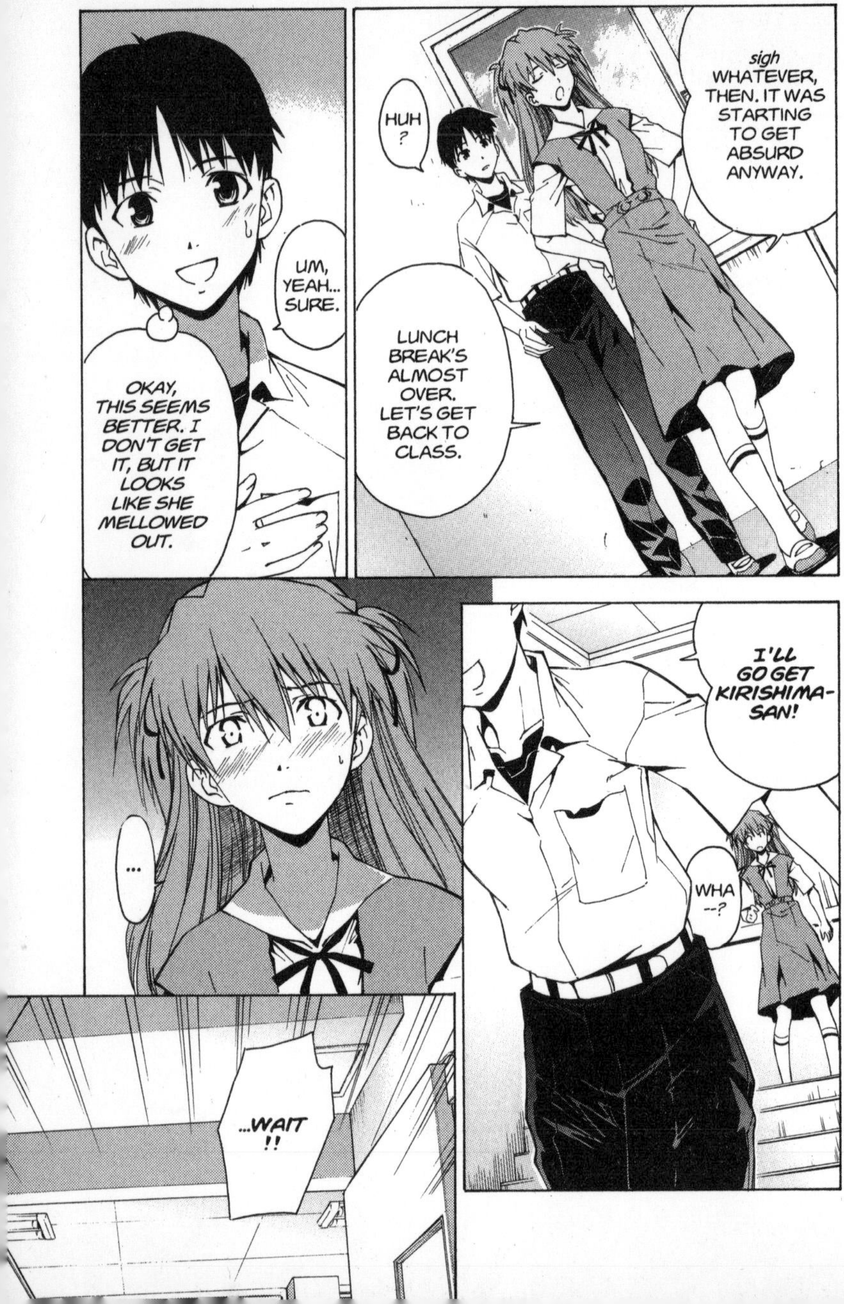
sigh WHATEVER, THEN. IT WAS STARTING TO GET ABSURD ANYWAY.
HUH ?
LUNCH BREAK'S ALMOST OVER. LET'S GET BACK TO CLASS.
UM, YEAH... SURE.
OKAY, THIS SEEMS BETTER. I DON'T GET IT, BUT IT LOOKS LIKE SHE MELLOWED OUT.
I'LL GO GET KIRISHIMA-SAN!
WHA --?
...
...WAIT !!

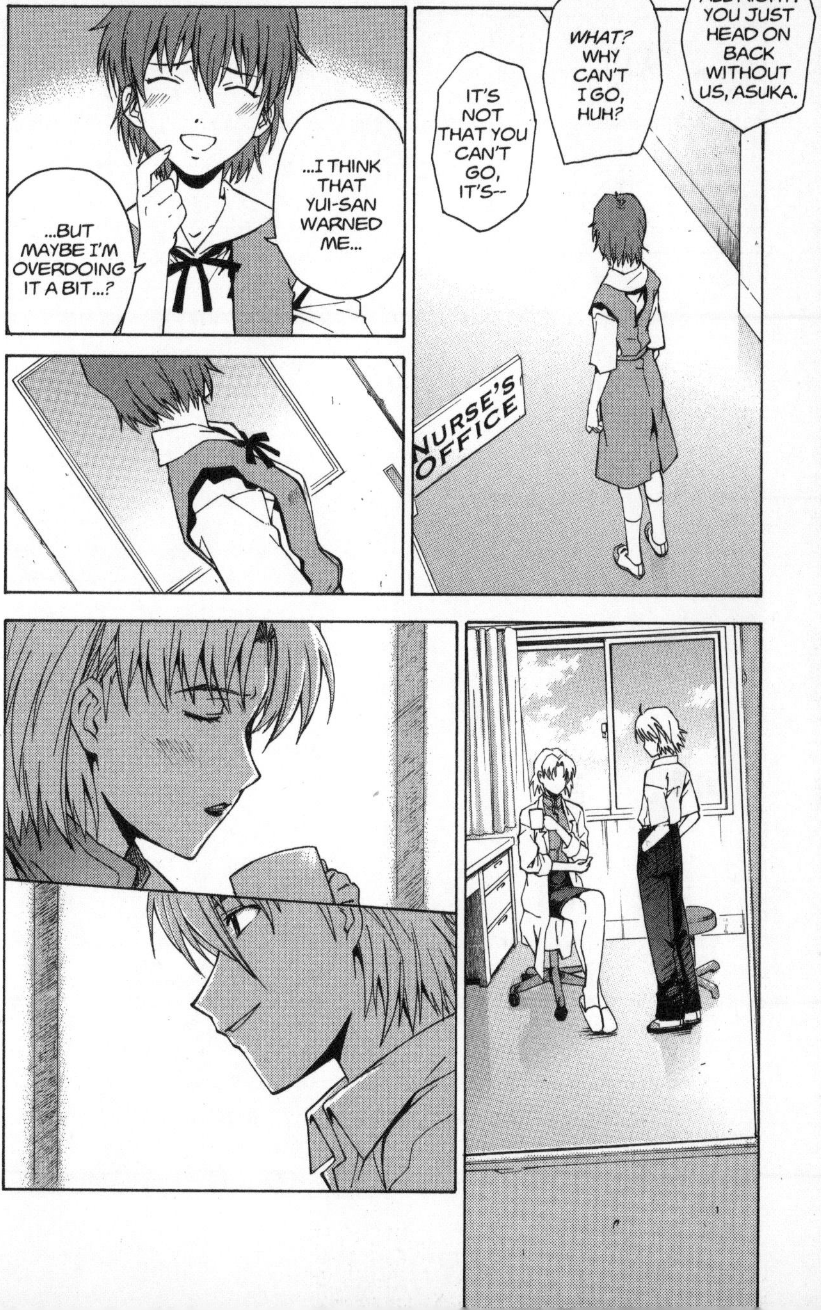
I'LL BE ALL RIGHT. YOU JUST HEAD ON BACK WITHOUT US, ASUKA.
WHAT? WHY CAN'T I GO, HUH?
IT'S NOT THAT YOU CAN'T GO, IT'S--
NURSE'S OFFICE
...I THINK THAT YUI-SAN WARNED ME...
...BUT MAYBE I'M OVERDOING IT A BIT...?

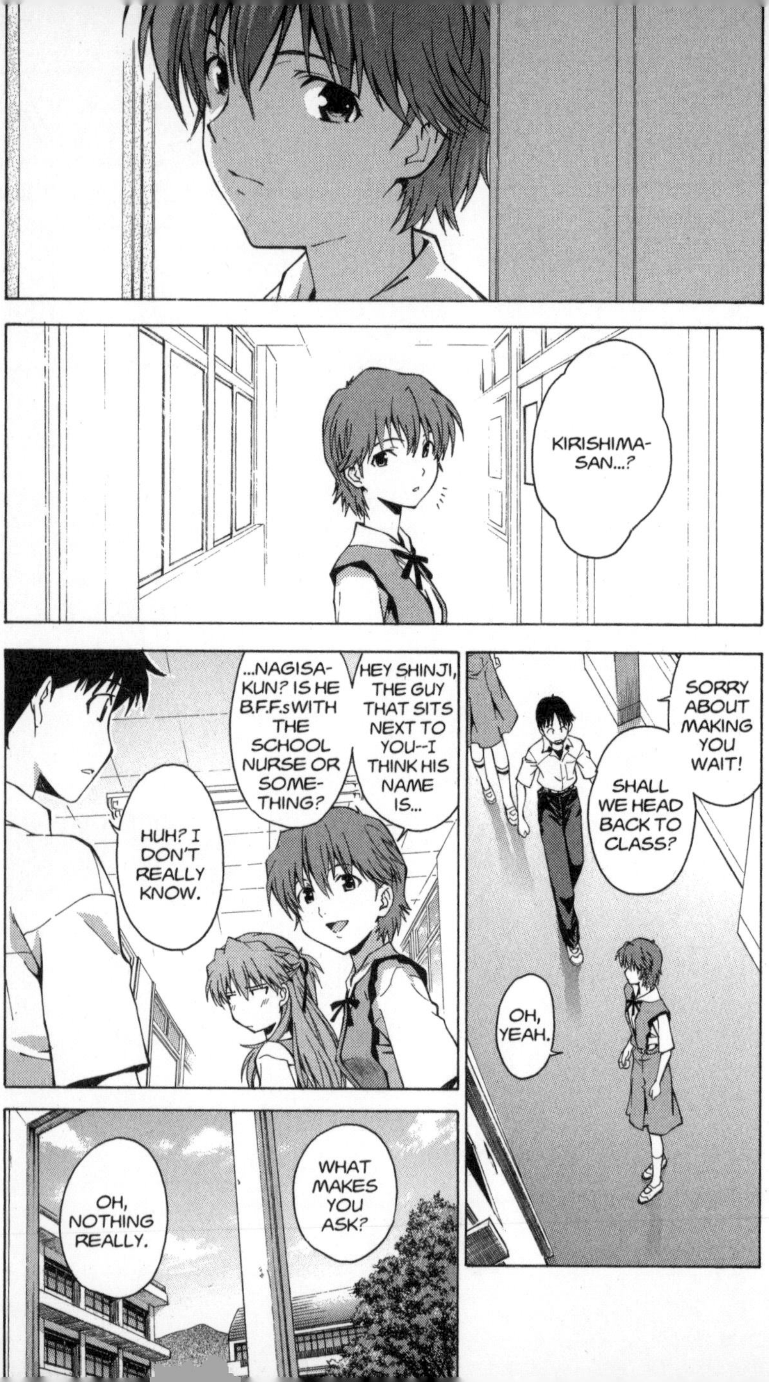
KIRISHIMA-SAN...?
SORRY ABOUT MAKING YOU WAIT!
SHALL WE HEAD BACK TO CLASS?
OH, YEAH.
HEY SHINJI, THE GUY THAT SITS NEXT TO YOU--I THINK HIS NAME IS...
...NAGISA-KUN? IS HE B.F.F.s WITH THE SCHOOL NURSE OR SOMETHING?
HUH? I DON'T REALLY KNOW.
WHAT MAKES YOU ASK?
OH, NOTHING REALLY.

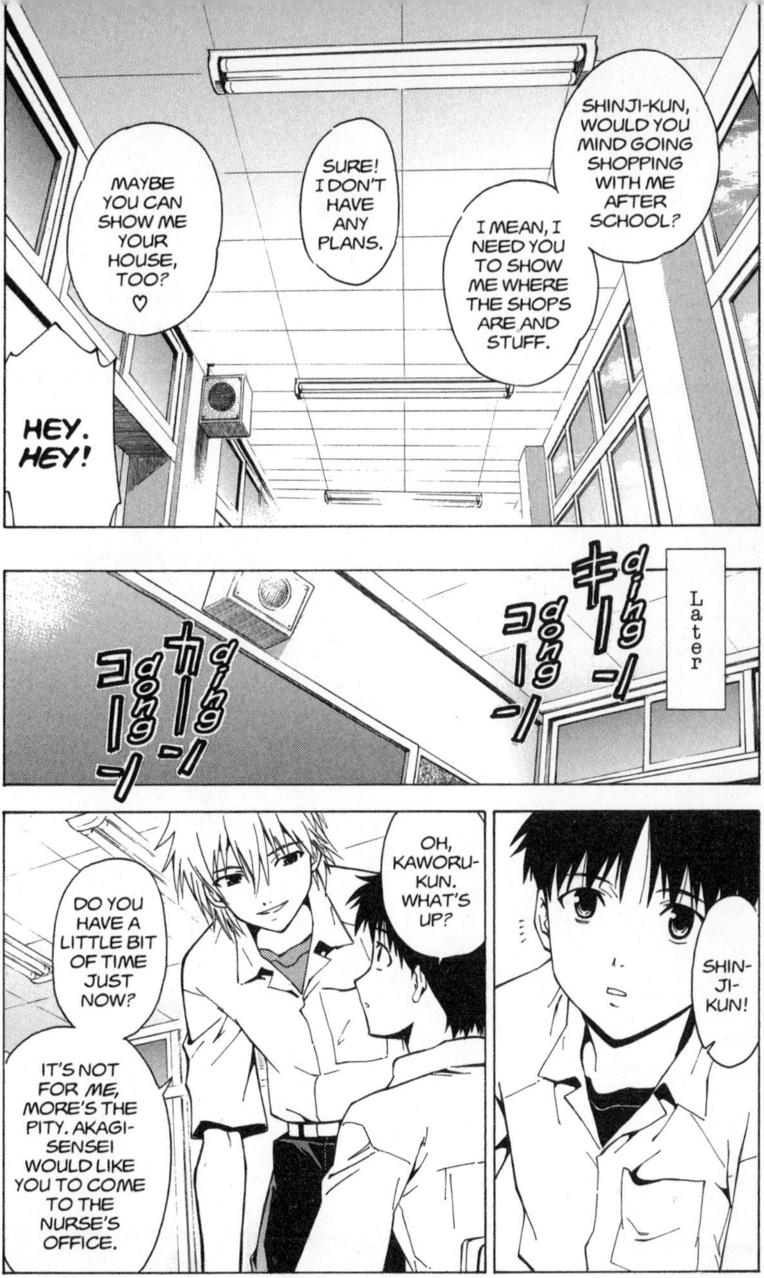
SHINJI-KUN, WOULD YOU MIND GOING SHOPPING WITH ME AFTER SCHOOL?
I MEAN, I NEED YOU TO SHOW ME WHERE THE SHOPS ARE AND STUFF.
SURE! I DON'T HAVE ANY PLANS.
MAYBE YOU CAN SHOW ME YOUR HOUSE, TOO? ♡
HEY. HEY!
Later
ding dong
ding dong
SHINJI-KUN!
OH, KAWORU-KUN. WHAT'S UP?
DO YOU HAVE A LITTLE BIT OF TIME JUST NOW?
IT'S NOT FOR *ME*, MORE'S THE PITY. AKAGI-SENSEI WOULD LIKE YOU TO COME TO THE NURSE'S OFFICE.

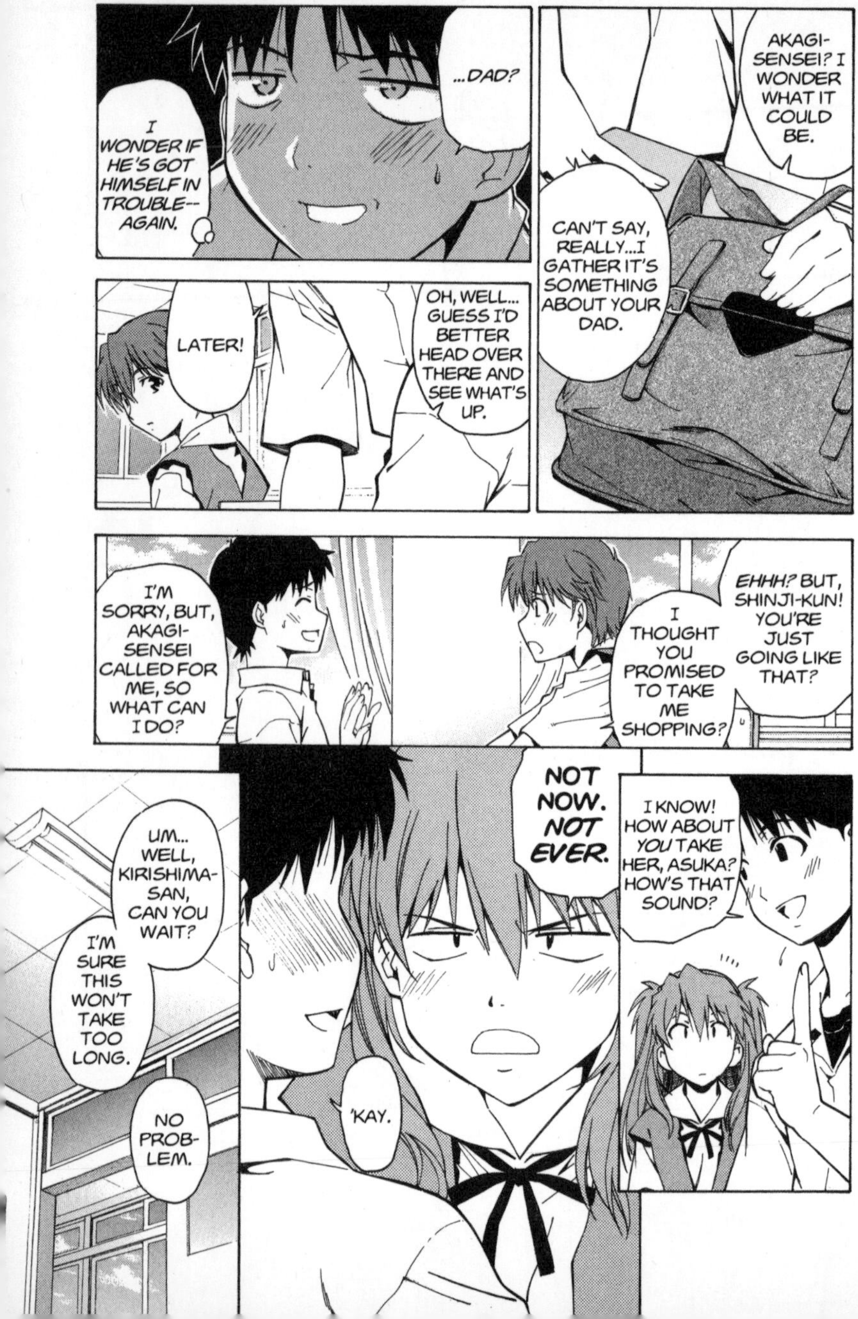
AKAGI-SENSEI? I WONDER WHAT IT COULD BE.
CAN'T SAY, REALLY...I GATHER IT'S SOMETHING ABOUT YOUR DAD.
...DAD?
I WONDER IF HE'S GOT HIMSELF IN TROUBLE--AGAIN.
OH, WELL... GUESS I'D BETTER HEAD OVER THERE AND SEE WHAT'S UP.
LATER!
EHHH? BUT, SHINJI-KUN! YOU'RE JUST GOING LIKE THAT?
I THOUGHT YOU PROMISED TO TAKE ME SHOPPING?
I'M SORRY, BUT, AKAGI-SENSEI CALLED FOR ME, SO WHAT CAN I DO?
I KNOW! HOW ABOUT *YOU* TAKE HER, ASUKA? HOW'S THAT SOUND?
NOT NOW. *NOT EVER.*
'KAY.
UM... WELL, KIRISHIMA-SAN, CAN YOU WAIT?
I'M SURE THIS WON'T TAKE TOO LONG.
NO PROBLEM.

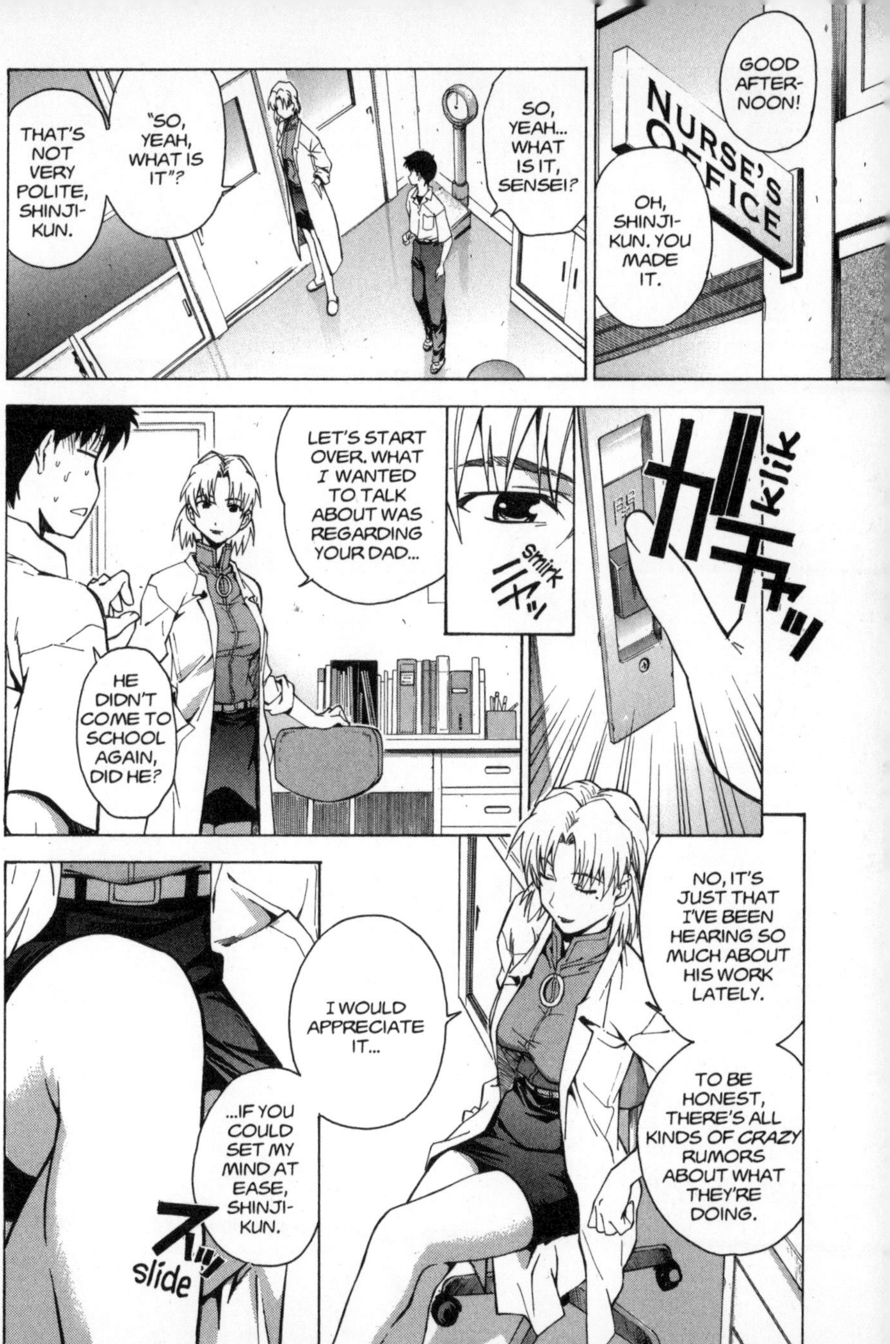

GOOD AFTERNOON!
NURSE'S OFFICE
OH, SHINJI-KUN. YOU MADE IT.
SO, YEAH... WHAT IS IT, SENSEI?
"SO, YEAH, WHAT IS IT"?
THAT'S NOT VERY POLITE, SHINJI-KUN.
ガチャッ
klik
ニヤッ
smirk
LET'S START OVER. WHAT *I* WANTED TO TALK ABOUT WAS REGARDING YOUR DAD...
HE DIDN'T COME TO SCHOOL AGAIN, DID HE?
NO, IT'S JUST THAT I'VE BEEN HEARING SO MUCH ABOUT HIS WORK LATELY.
TO BE HONEST, THERE'S ALL KINDS OF *CRAZY* RUMORS ABOUT WHAT THEY'RE DOING.
I WOULD APPRECIATE IT...
...IF YOU COULD SET MY MIND AT EASE, SHINJI-KUN.
スッ
slide

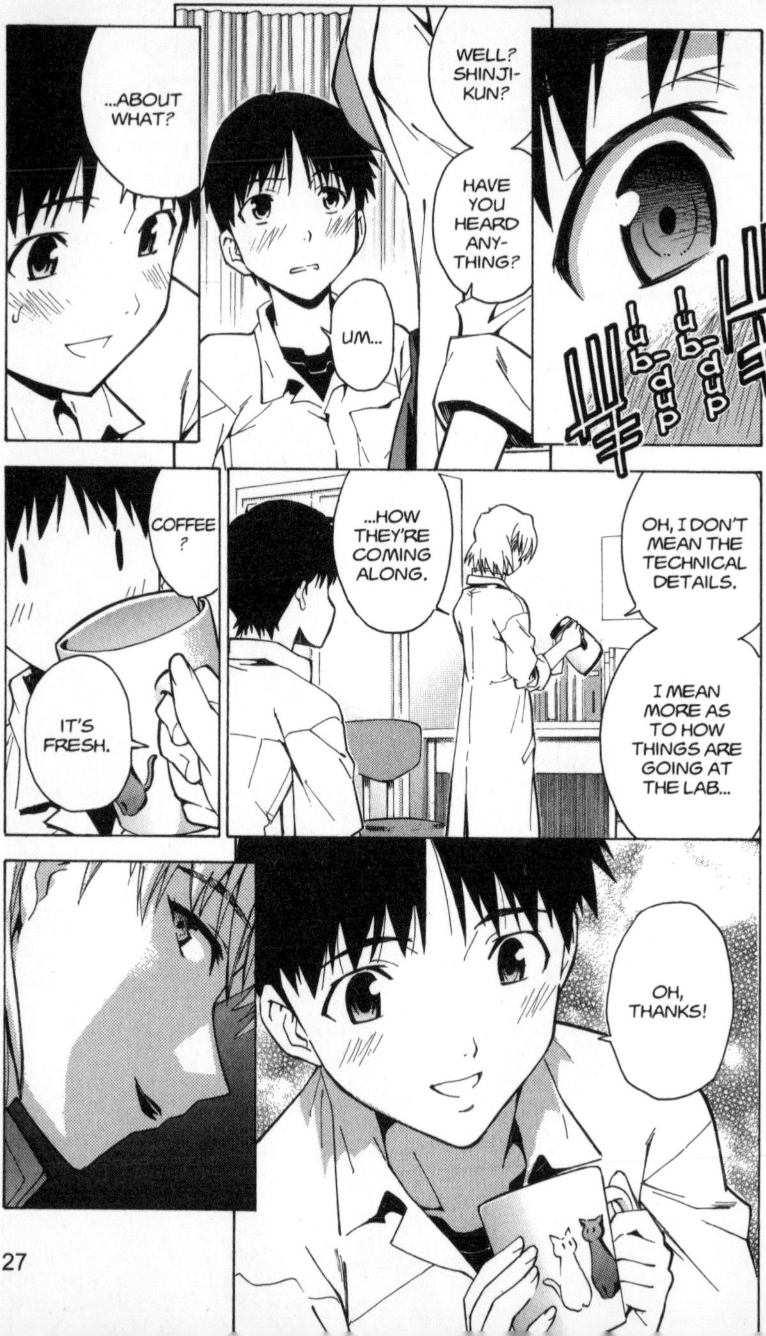
WELL? SHINJI-KUN?
HAVE YOU HEARD ANYTHING?
UM...
...ABOUT WHAT?
OH, I DON'T MEAN THE TECHNICAL DETAILS.
I MEAN MORE AS TO HOW THINGS ARE GOING AT THE LAB...
...HOW THEY'RE COMING ALONG.
COFFEE?
IT'S FRESH.
OH, THANKS!

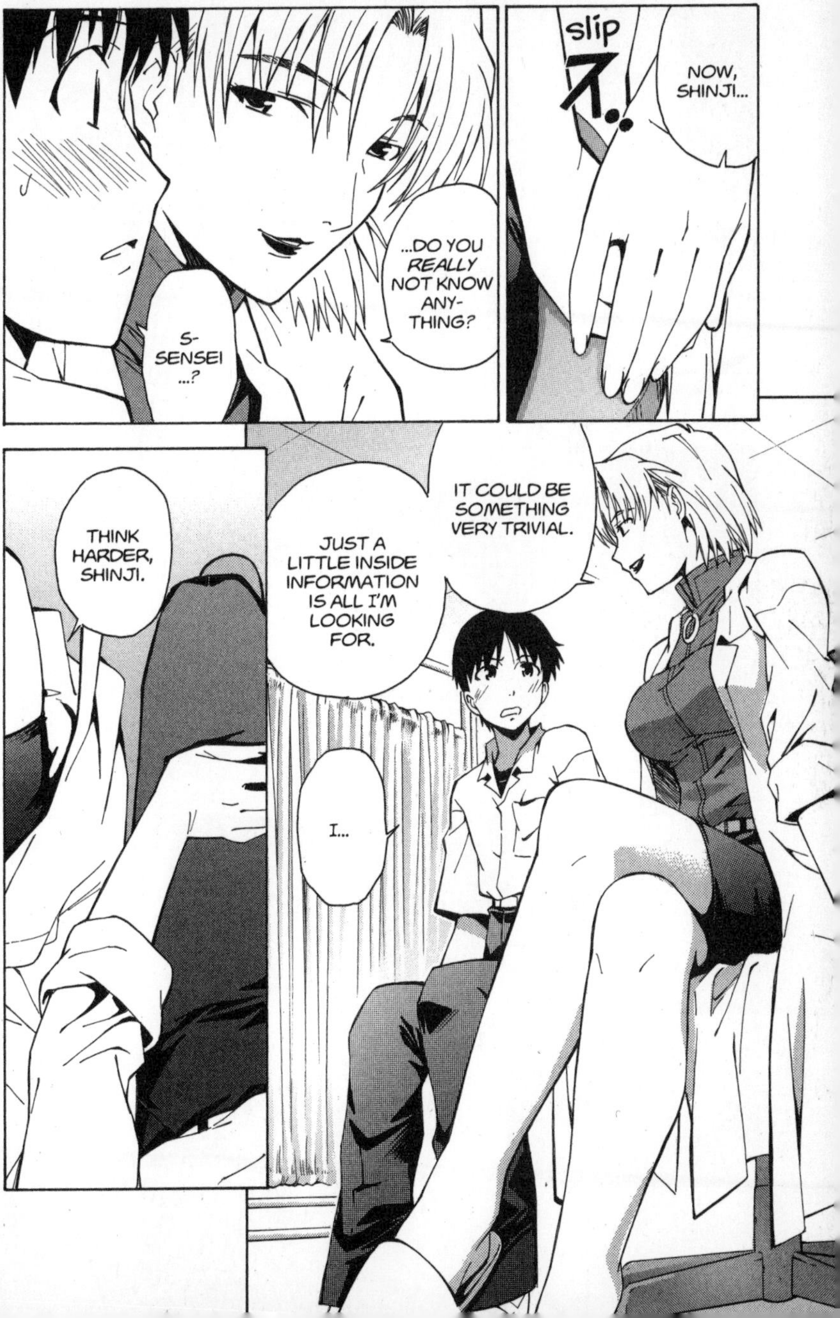
slip
ス..!
NOW, SHINJI...
...DO YOU REALLY NOT KNOW ANY-THING?
S-SENSEI ...?
IT COULD BE SOMETHING VERY TRIVIAL.
JUST A LITTLE INSIDE INFORMATION IS ALL I'M LOOKING FOR.
I...
THINK HARDER, SHINJI.

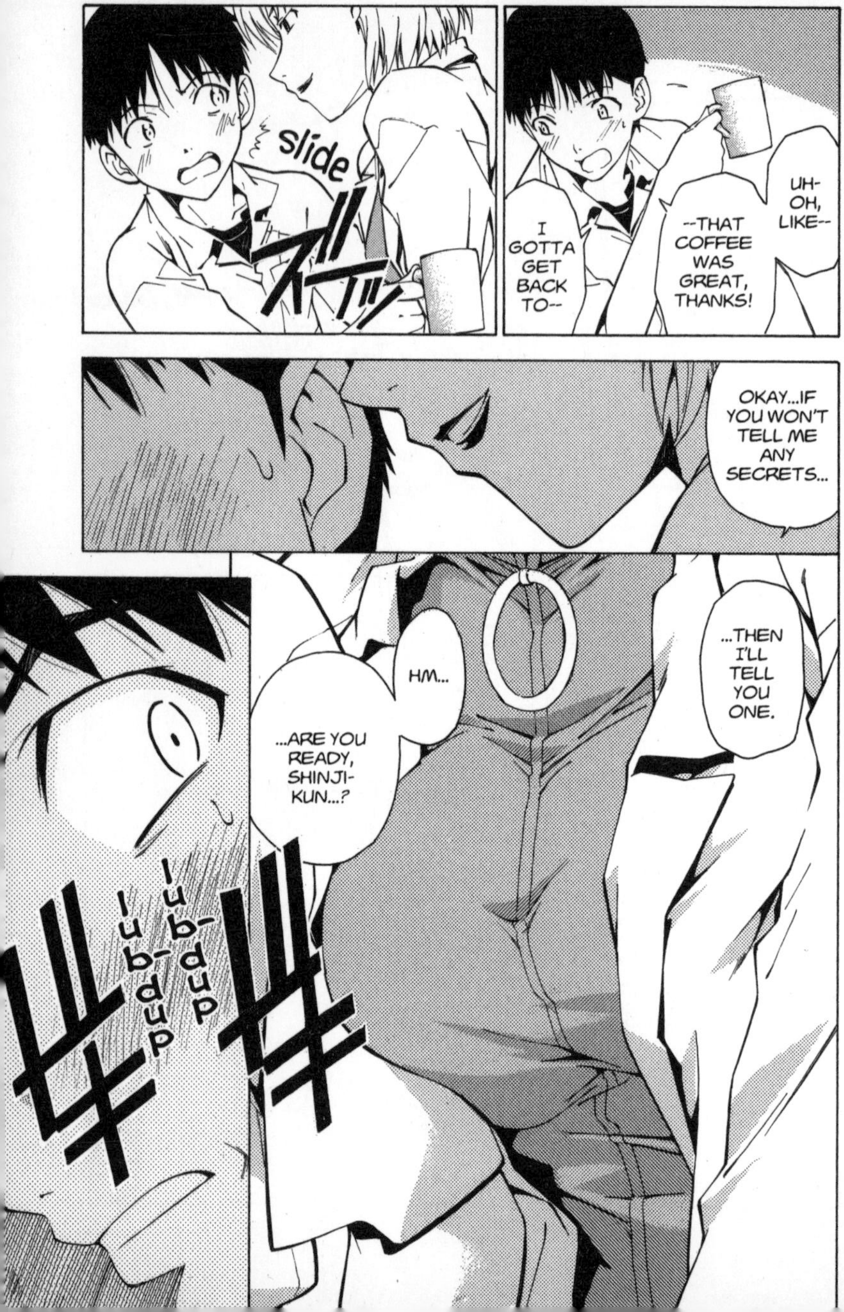
UH-OH, LIKE--
--THAT COFFEE WAS GREAT, THANKS!
I GOTTA GET BACK TO--
slide
OKAY...IF YOU WON'T TELL ME ANY SECRETS...
...THEN I'LL TELL YOU ONE.
HM...
...ARE YOU READY, SHINJI-KUN...?
lub-dup
lub-dup

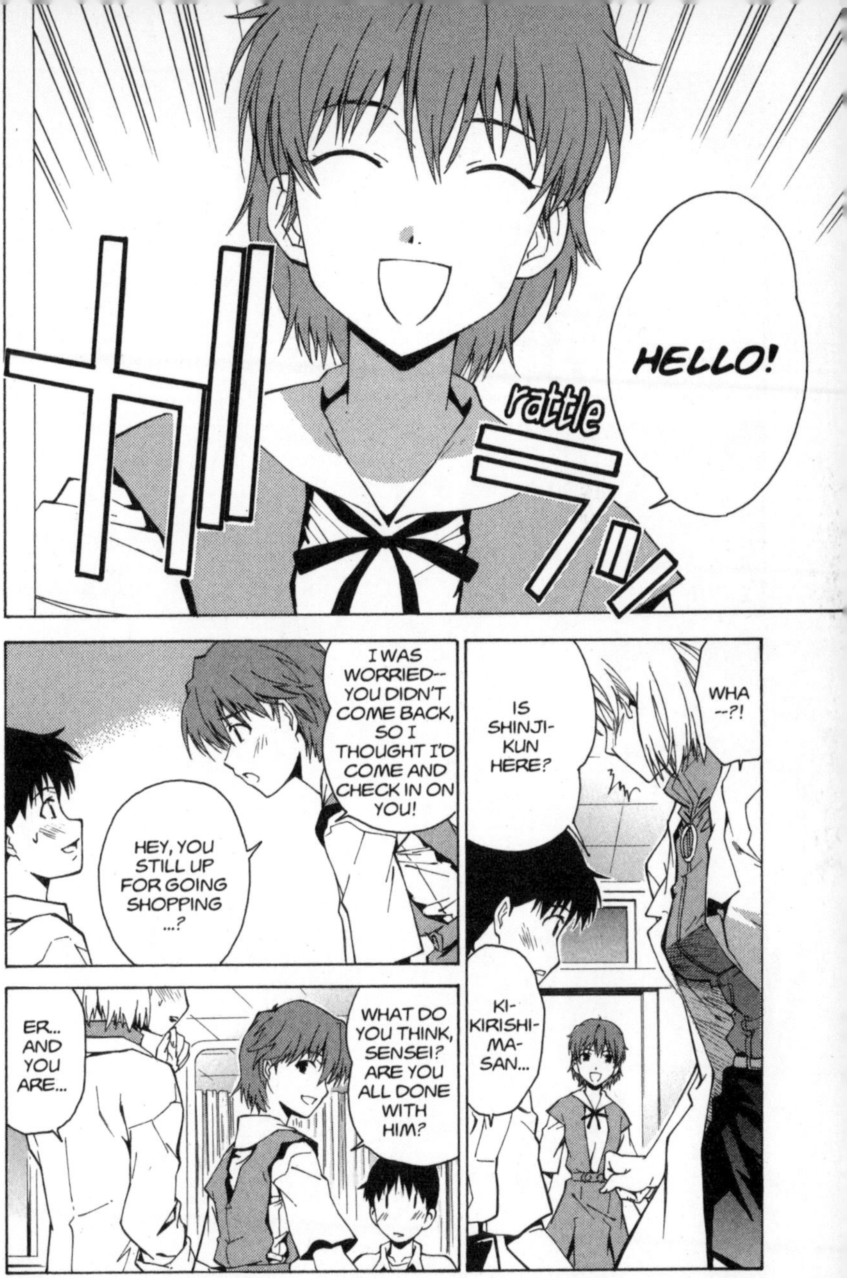
HELLO!
rattle
WHA --?!
IS SHINJI-KUN HERE?
I WAS WORRIED-- YOU DIDN'T COME BACK, SO I THOUGHT I'D COME AND CHECK IN ON YOU!
HEY, YOU STILL UP FOR GOING SHOPPING ...?
KI-KIRISHIMA-SAN...
WHAT DO YOU THINK, SENSEI? ARE YOU ALL DONE WITH HIM?
ER... AND YOU ARE...

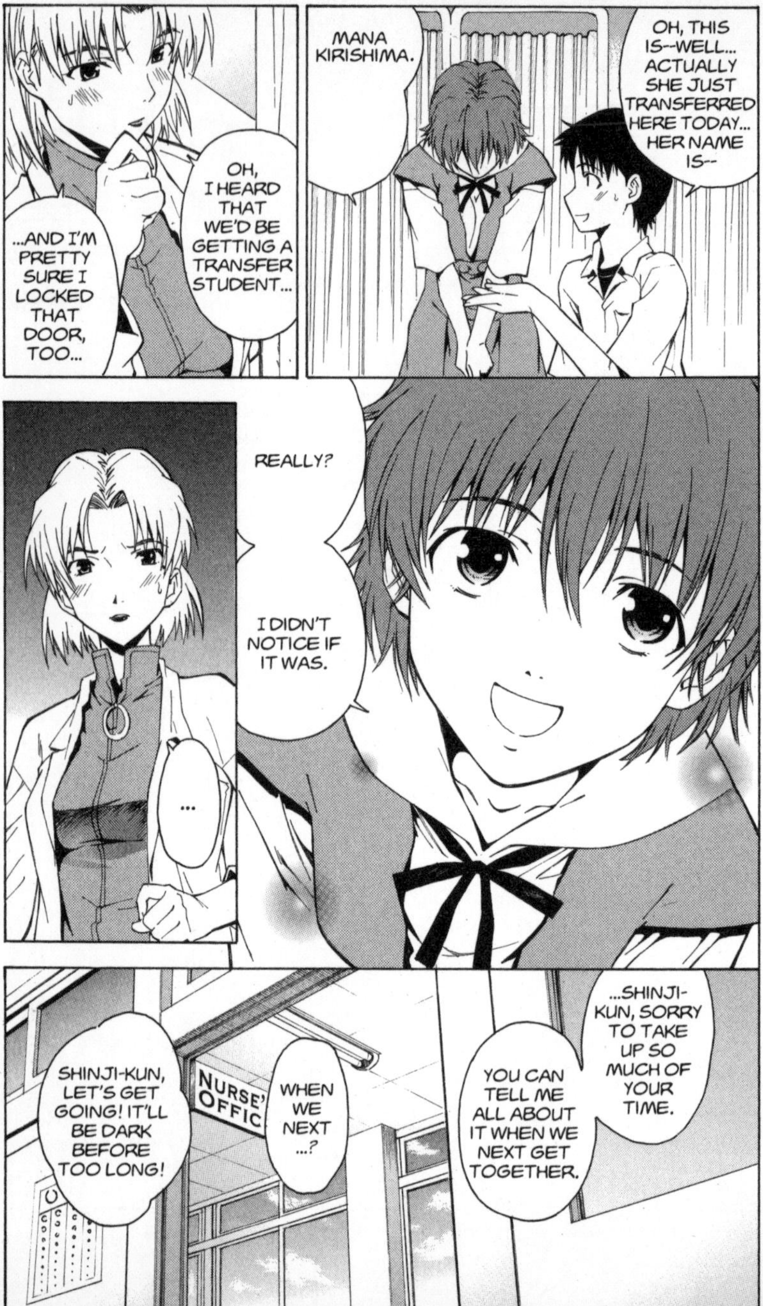
OH, THIS IS--WELL... ACTUALLY SHE JUST TRANSFERRED HERE TODAY... HER NAME IS--
MANA KIRISHIMA.
OH, I HEARD THAT WE'D BE GETTING A TRANSFER STUDENT...
...AND I'M PRETTY SURE I LOCKED THAT DOOR, TOO...
REALLY?
I DIDN'T NOTICE IF IT WAS.
...
...SHINJI-KUN, SORRY TO TAKE UP SO MUCH OF YOUR TIME.
YOU CAN TELL ME ALL ABOUT IT WHEN WE NEXT GET TOGETHER.
WHEN WE NEXT ...?
NURSE' OFFIC
SHINJI-KUN, LET'S GET GOING! IT'LL BE DARK BEFORE TOO LONG!

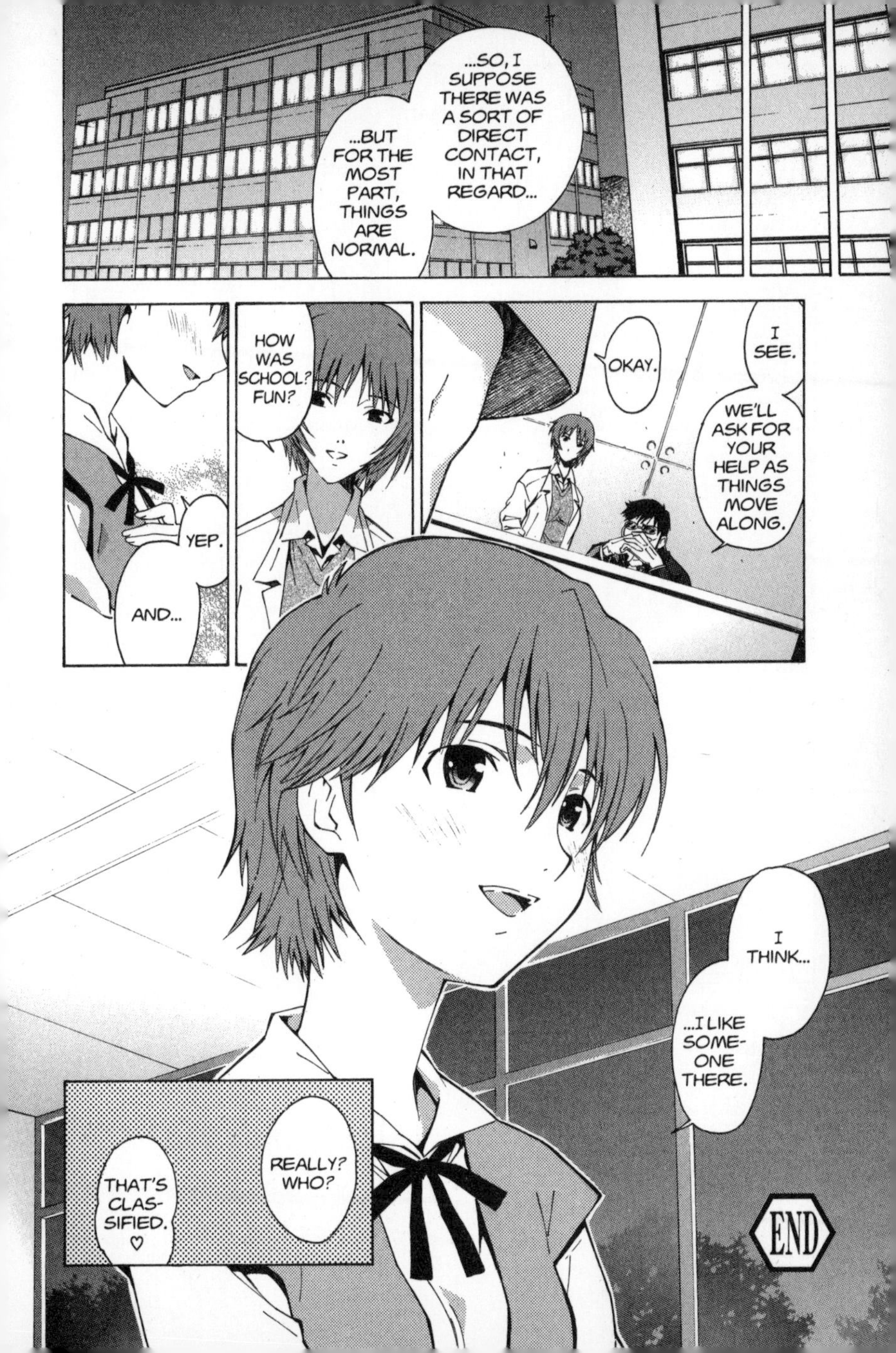
...SO, I SUPPOSE THERE WAS A SORT OF DIRECT CONTACT, IN THAT REGARD...
...BUT FOR THE MOST PART, THINGS ARE NORMAL.
I SEE.
WE'LL ASK FOR YOUR HELP AS THINGS MOVE ALONG.
OKAY.
HOW WAS SCHOOL? FUN?
YEP.
AND...
I THINK...
...I LIKE SOME-ONE THERE.
REALLY? WHO?
THAT'S CLAS-SIFIED. ♡
END

NEON GENESIS
EVANGELION
THE SHINJI IKARI RAISING PROJECT

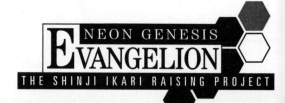

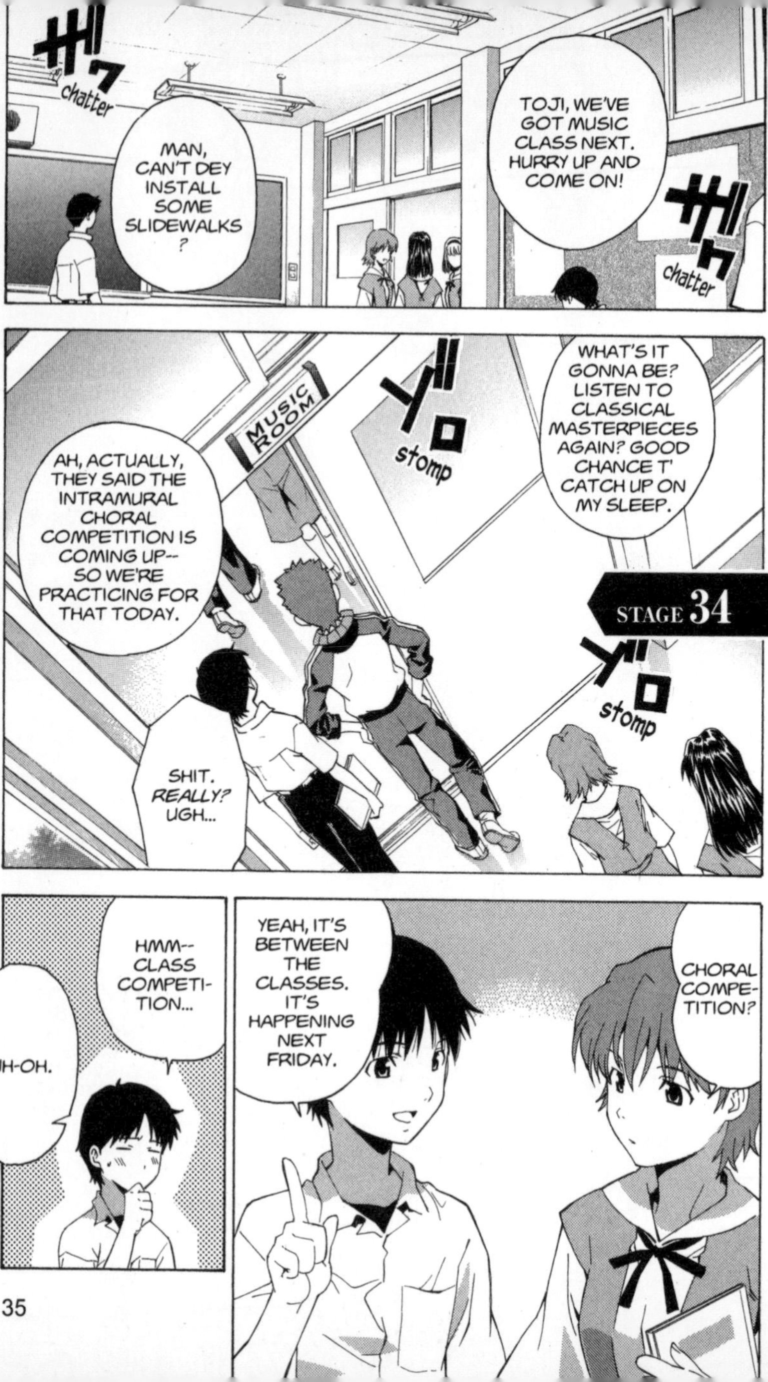
TOJI, WE'VE GOT MUSIC CLASS NEXT. HURRY UP AND COME ON!
chatter
chatter
MAN, CAN'T DEY INSTALL SOME SLIDEWALKS?
WHAT'S IT GONNA BE? LISTEN TO CLASSICAL MASTERPIECES AGAIN? GOOD CHANCE T' CATCH UP ON MY SLEEP.
stomp
MUSIC ROOM
AH, ACTUALLY, THEY SAID THE INTRAMURAL CHORAL COMPETITION IS COMING UP-- SO WE'RE PRACTICING FOR THAT TODAY.
STAGE 34
stomp
SHIT. *REALLY?* UGH...
CHORAL COMPETITION?
YEAH, IT'S BETWEEN THE CLASSES. IT'S HAPPENING NEXT FRIDAY.
HMM-- CLASS COMPETITION...
...UH-OH.

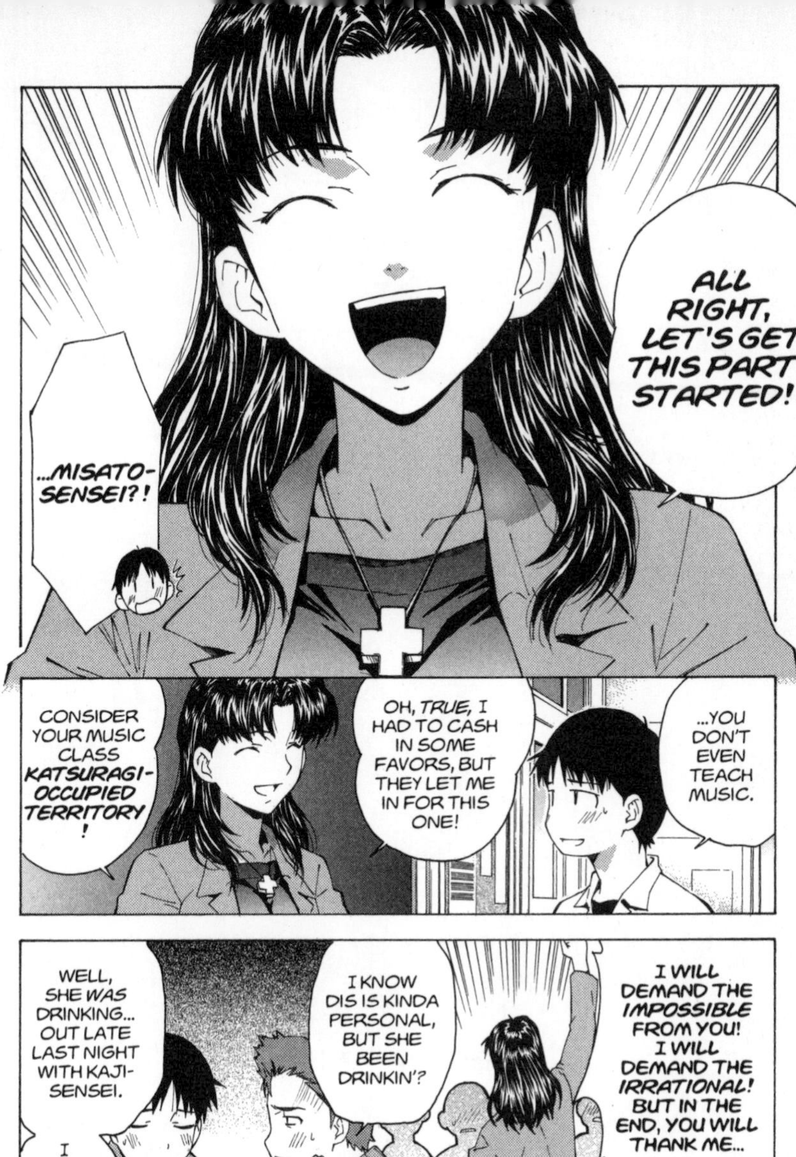
ALL RIGHT, LET'S GET THIS PARTY STARTED!!
...MISATO-SENSEI?!
...YOU DON'T EVEN TEACH MUSIC.
OH, *TRUE*, I HAD TO CASH IN SOME FAVORS, BUT THEY LET ME IN FOR THIS ONE!
CONSIDER YOUR MUSIC CLASS **KATSURAGI-OCCUPIED TERRITORY!**
I WILL DEMAND THE *IMPOSSIBLE* FROM YOU! I WILL DEMAND THE *IRRATIONAL!* BUT IN THE END, YOU WILL THANK ME...
I KNOW DIS IS KINDA PERSONAL, BUT SHE BEEN DRINKIN'?
WELL, SHE *WAS* DRINKING... OUT LATE LAST NIGHT WITH KAJI-SENSEI.
I BELIEVE WE ARE PAWNS IN THIS GAME.

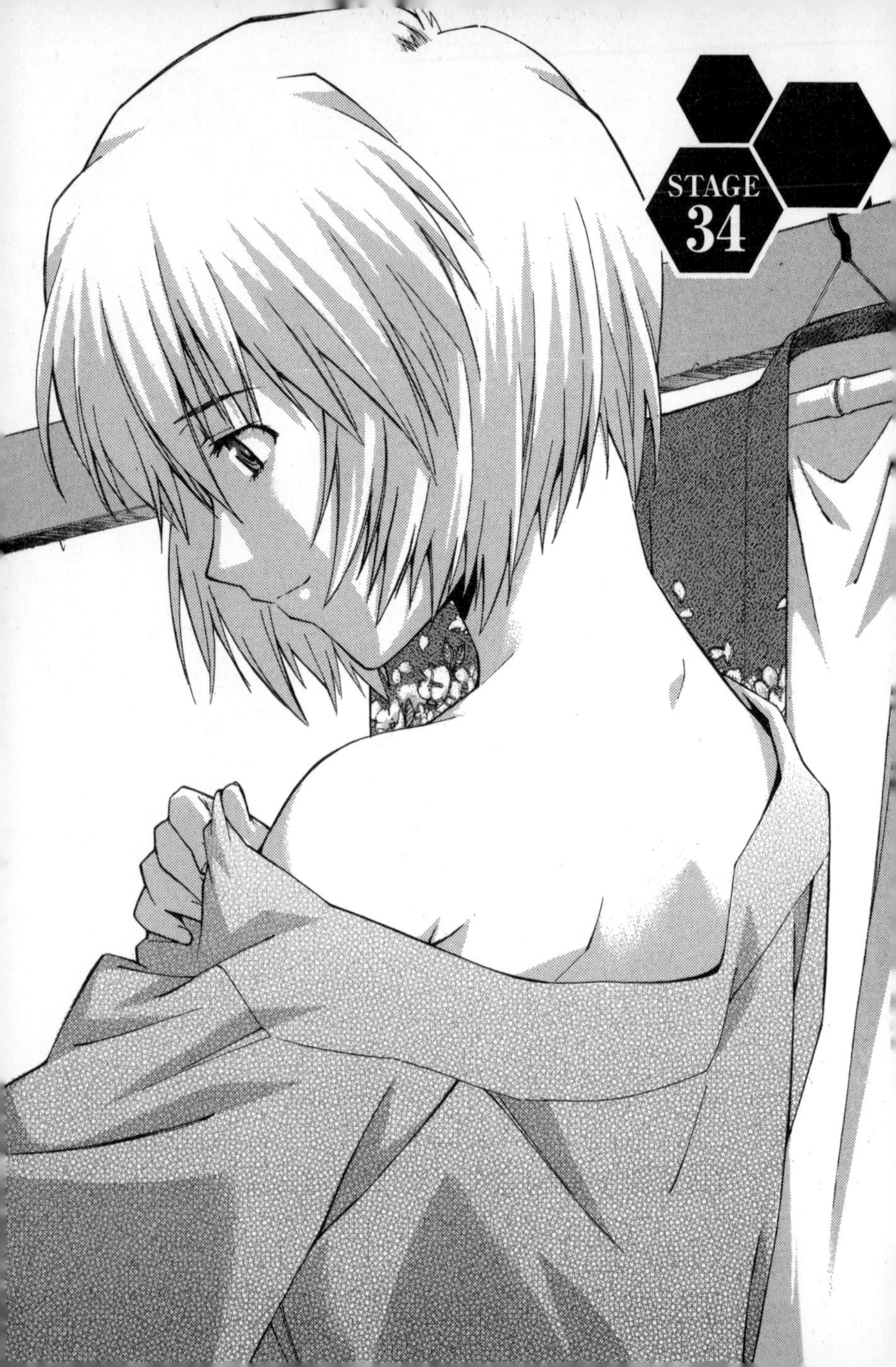
STAGE
34

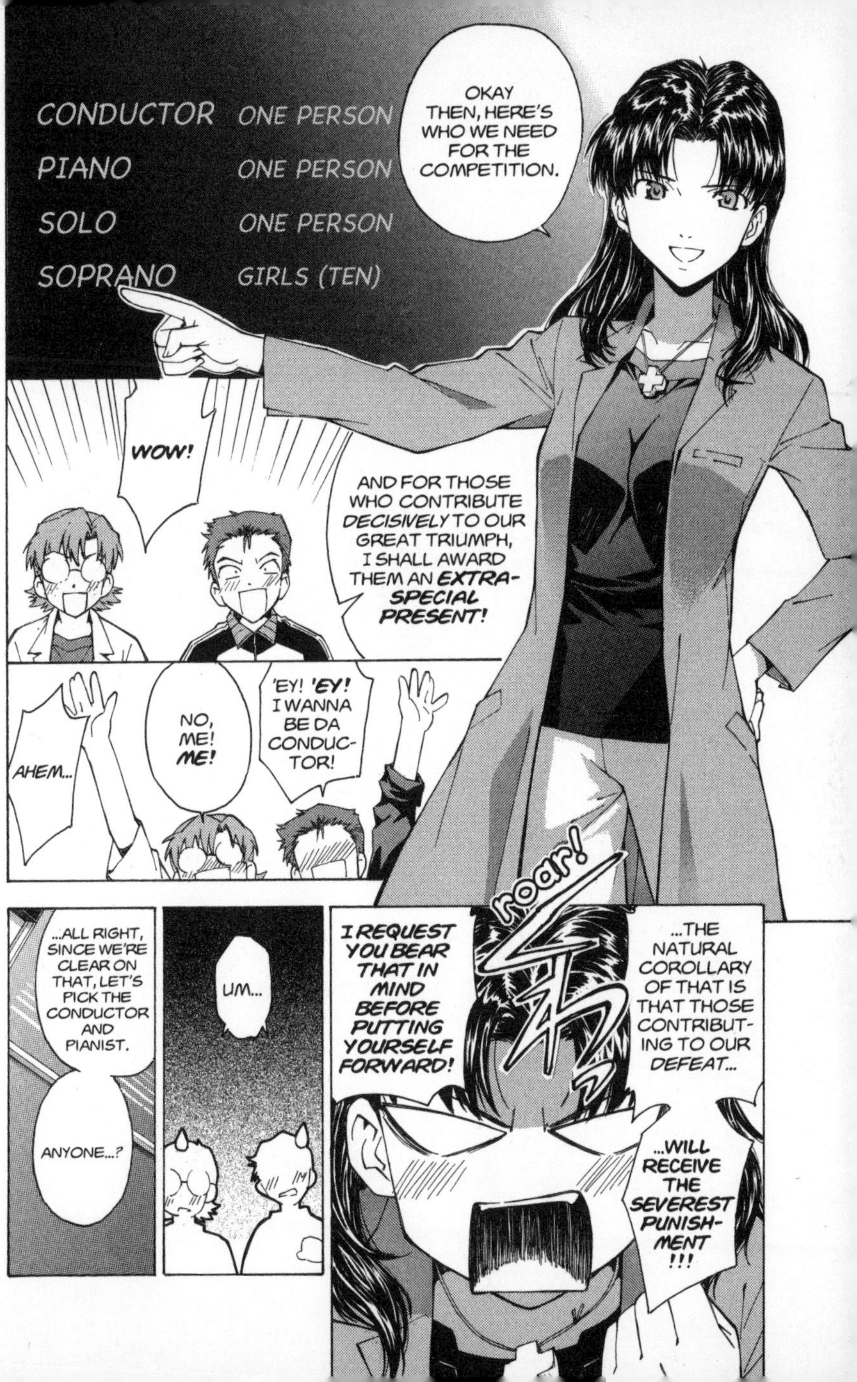
CONDUCTOR ONE PERSON
PIANO ONE PERSON
SOLO ONE PERSON
SOPRANO GIRLS (TEN)
OKAY THEN, HERE'S WHO WE NEED FOR THE COMPETITION.
AND FOR THOSE WHO CONTRIBUTE DECISIVELY TO OUR GREAT TRIUMPH, I SHALL AWARD THEM AN EXTRA-SPECIAL PRESENT!
WOW!
'EY! 'EY! I WANNA BE DA CONDUC-TOR!
NO, ME! ME!
AHEM...
...THE NATURAL COROLLARY OF THAT IS THAT THOSE CONTRIBUT-ING TO OUR DEFEAT...
...WILL RECEIVE THE SEVEREST PUNISH-MENT!!!
roar!
I REQUEST YOU BEAR THAT IN MIND BEFORE PUTTING YOURSELF FORWARD!
UM...
...ALL RIGHT, SINCE WE'RE CLEAR ON THAT, LET'S PICK THE CONDUCTOR AND PIANIST.
ANYONE...?

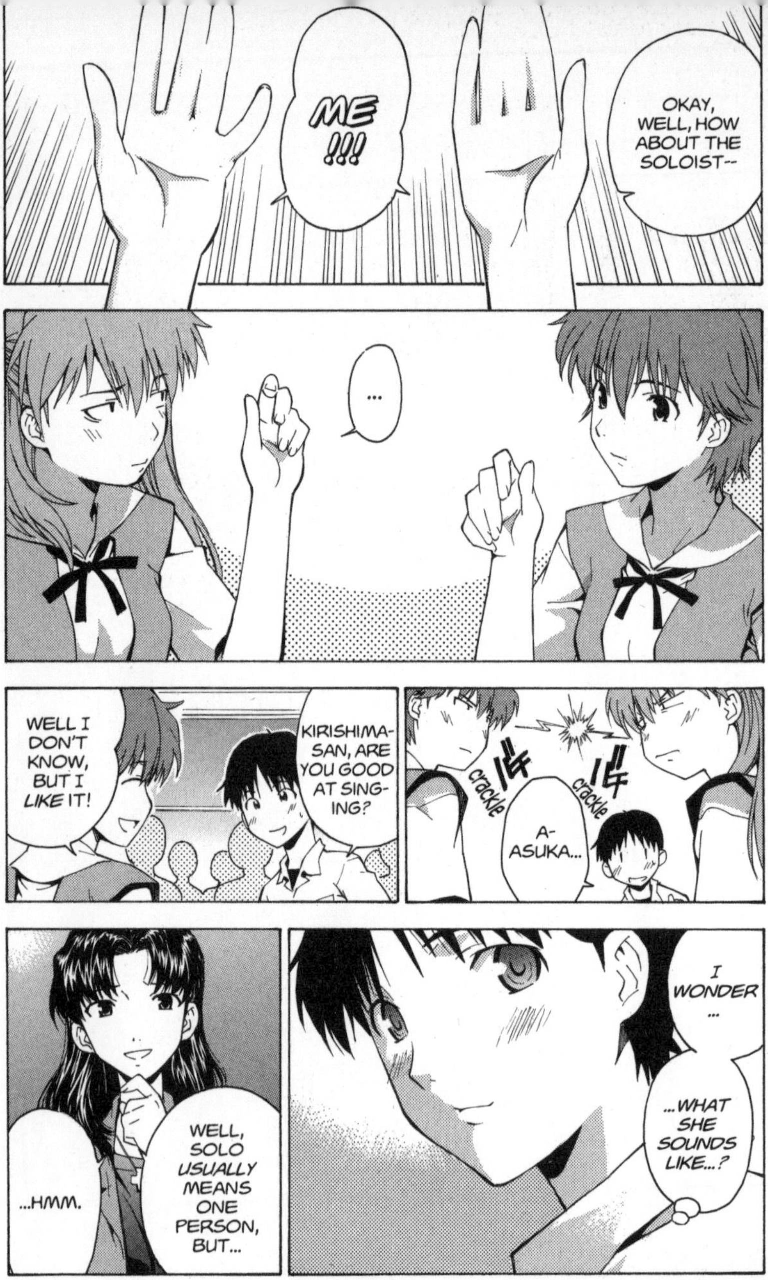
OKAY, WELL, HOW ABOUT THE SOLOIST--
ME !!!
...
crackle
crackle
A- ASUKA...
KIRISHIMA-SAN, ARE YOU GOOD AT SING-ING?
WELL I DON'T KNOW, BUT I *LIKE* IT!
I WONDER ...
...WHAT SHE SOUNDS LIKE...?
WELL, SOLO *USUALLY* MEANS ONE PERSON, BUT...
...HMM.

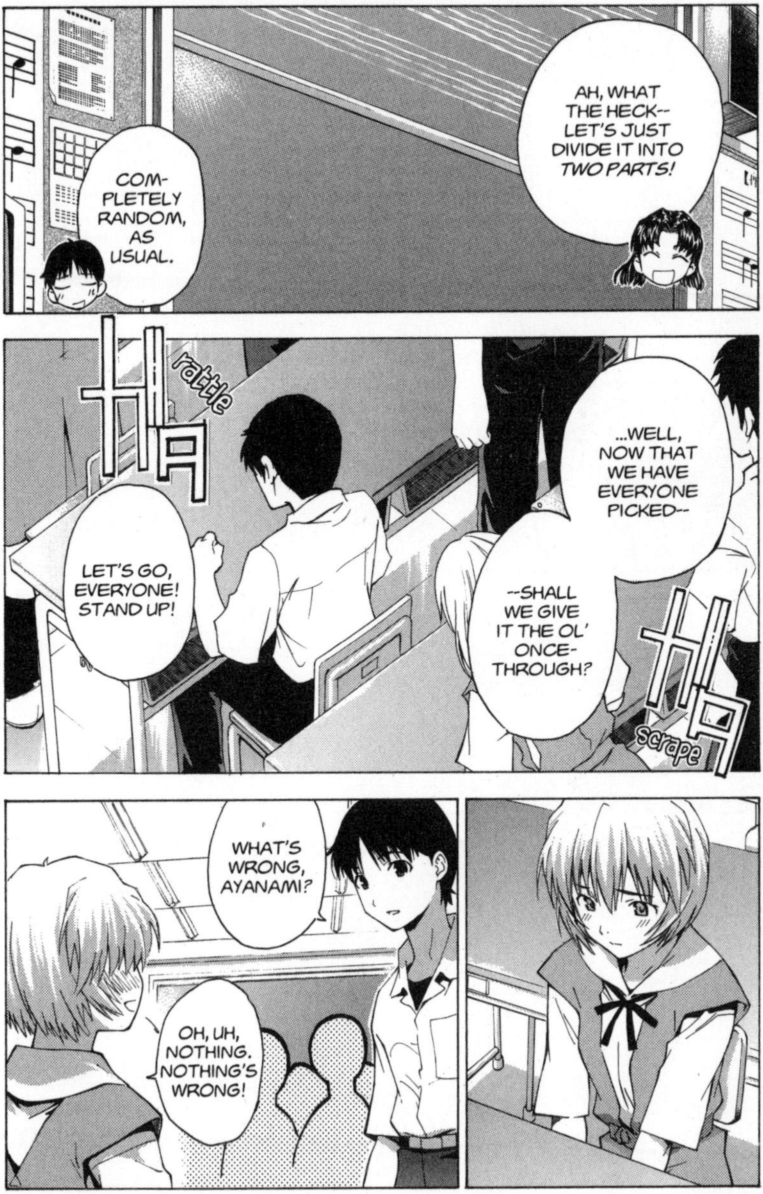
AH, WHAT THE HECK-- LET'S JUST DIVIDE IT INTO *TWO PARTS!*
COM- PLETELY RANDOM, AS USUAL.
...WELL, NOW THAT WE HAVE EVERYONE PICKED--
--SHALL WE GIVE IT THE OL' ONCE- THROUGH?
ガタ
scrape
ガタ
rattle
LET'S GO, EVERYONE! STAND UP!
WHAT'S WRONG, AYANAMI?
OH, UH, NOTHING. NOTHING'S WRONG!

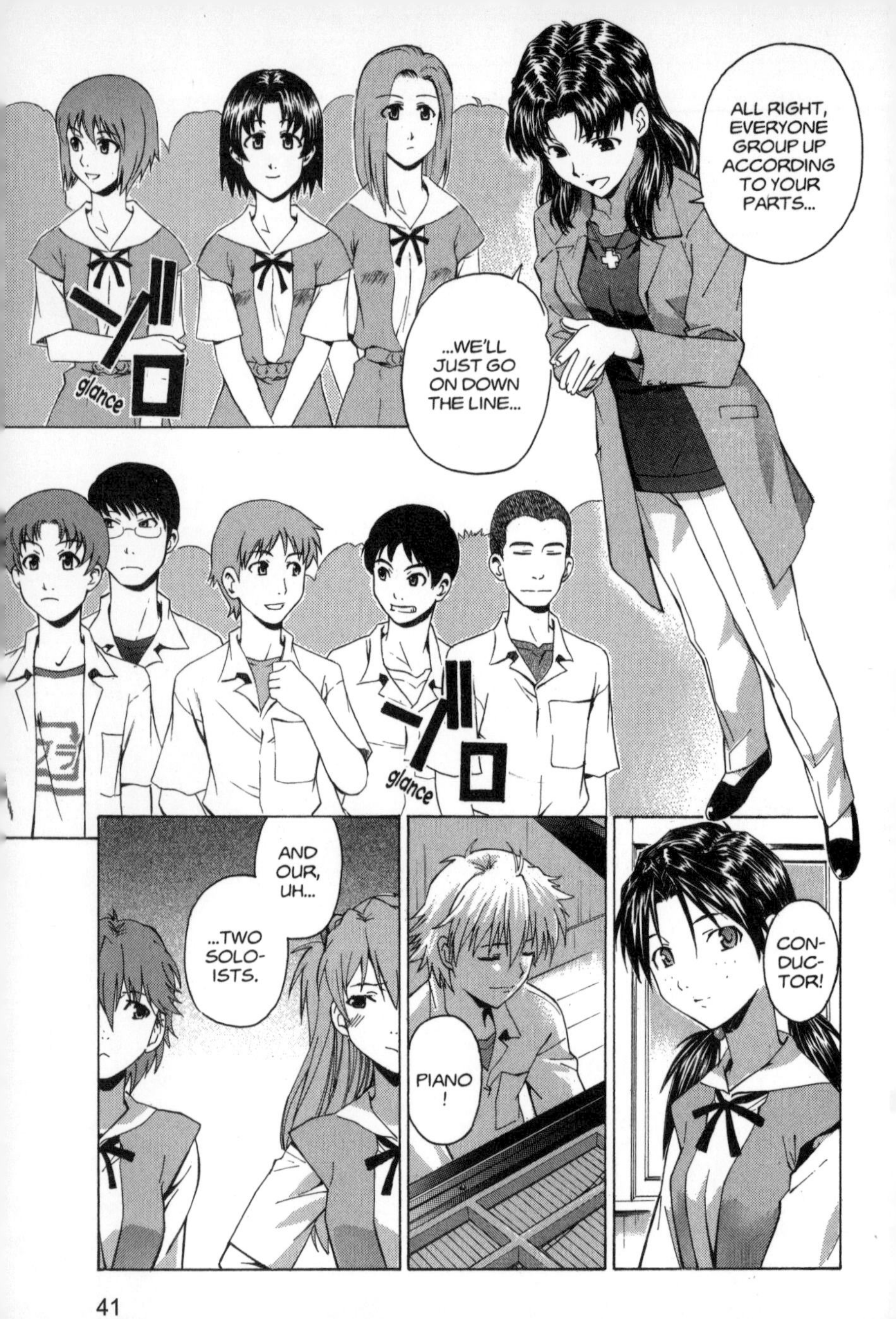
ALL RIGHT, EVERYONE GROUP UP ACCORDING TO YOUR PARTS...
...WE'LL JUST GO ON DOWN THE LINE...
glance
glance
CON-DUC-TOR!
PIANO!
AND OUR, UH...
...TWO SOLO-ISTS.

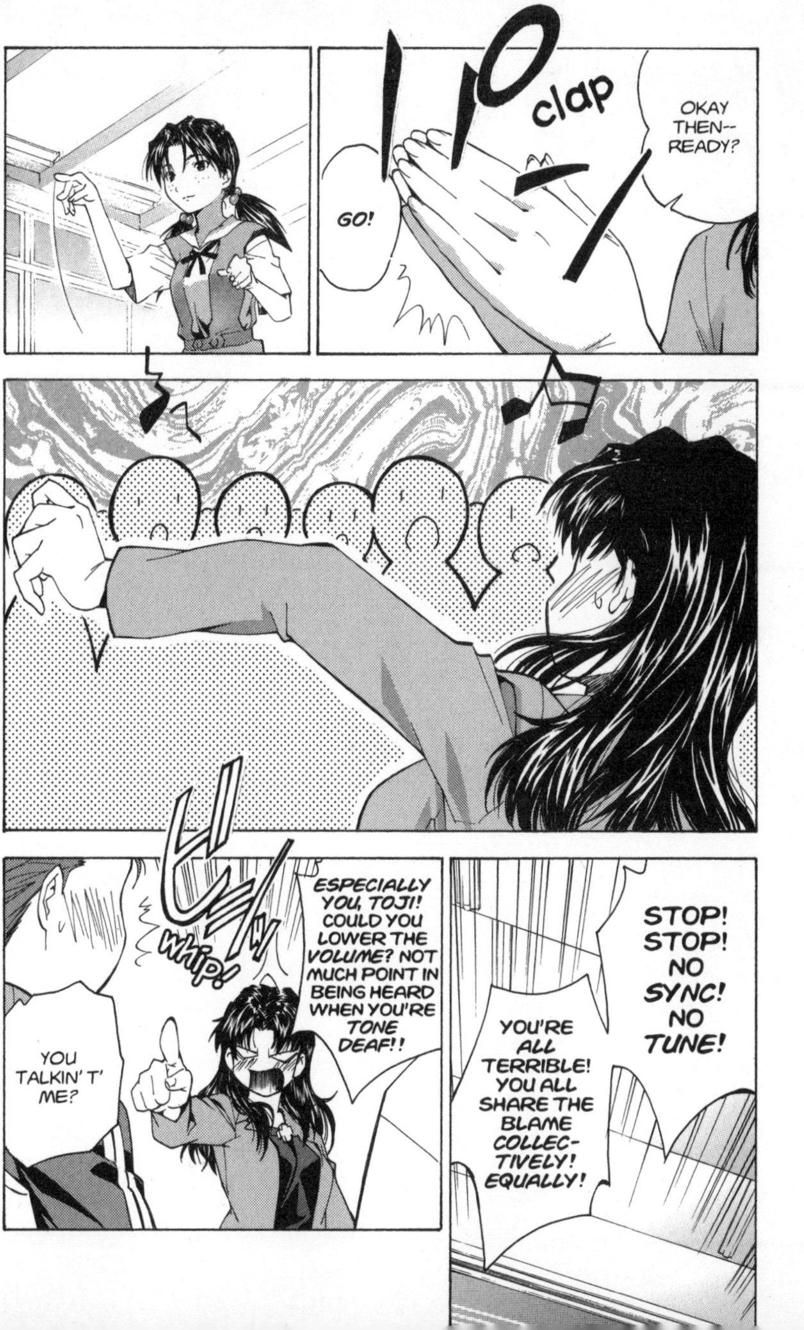
OKAY THEN-- READY?
clap
GO!
STOP! STOP! NO SYNC! NO TUNE!
YOU'RE ALL TERRIBLE! YOU ALL SHARE THE BLAME COLLECTIVELY! EQUALLY!
whip!
ESPECIALLY YOU, TOJI! COULD YOU LOWER THE VOLUME? NOT MUCH POINT IN BEING HEARD WHEN YOU'RE TONE DEAF!!
YOU TALKIN' T' ME?

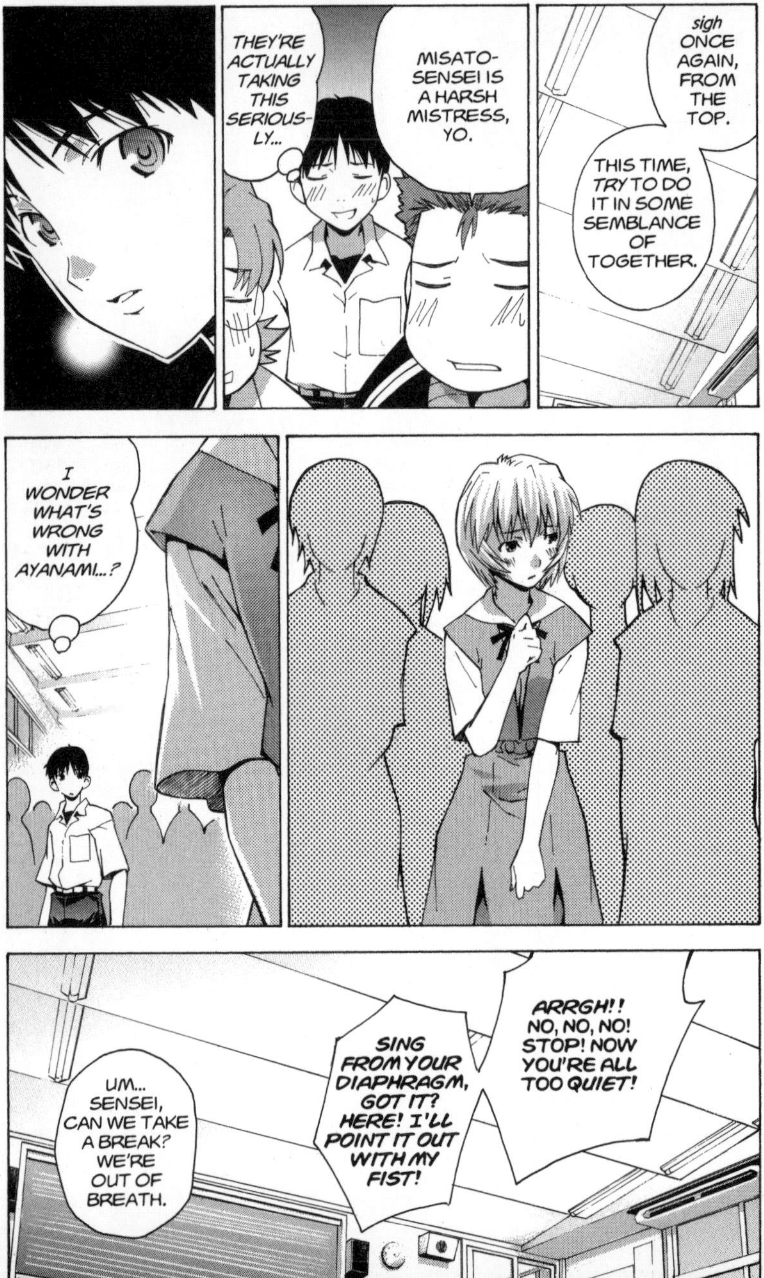
sigh ONCE AGAIN, FROM THE TOP.
THIS TIME, TRY TO DO IT IN SOME SEMBLANCE OF TOGETHER.
MISATO-SENSEI IS A HARSH MISTRESS, YO.
THEY'RE ACTUALLY TAKING THIS SERIOUS-LY...
I WONDER WHAT'S WRONG WITH AYANAMI...?
ARRGH!! NO, NO, NO! STOP! NOW YOU'RE ALL TOO QUIET!
SING FROM YOUR DIAPHRAGM, GOT IT? HERE! I'LL POINT IT OUT WITH MY FIST!
UM... SENSEI, CAN WE TAKE A BREAK? WE'RE OUT OF BREATH.

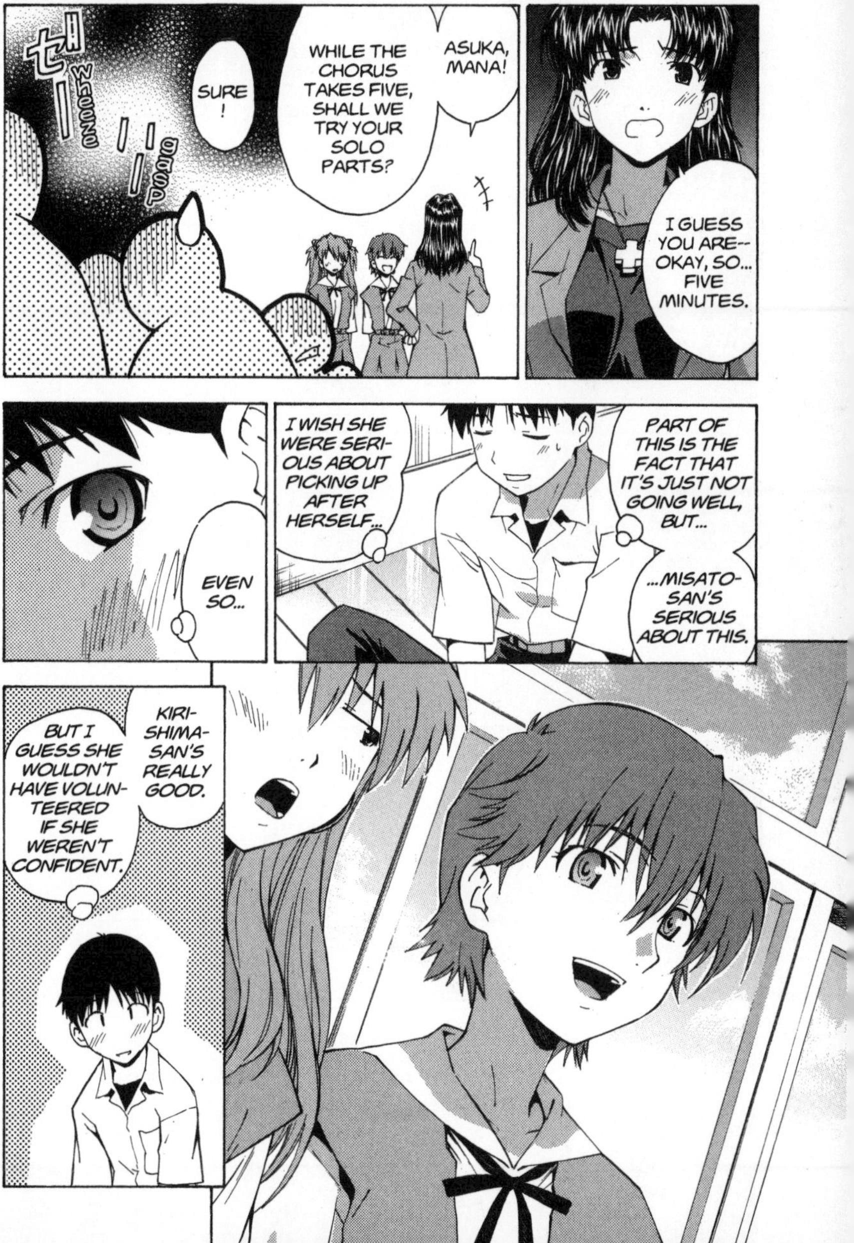
I GUESS YOU ARE-- OKAY, SO... FIVE MINUTES.
ASUKA, MANA!
WHILE THE CHORUS TAKES FIVE, SHALL WE TRY YOUR SOLO PARTS?
SURE!
wheeze
gasp
PART OF THIS IS THE FACT THAT IT'S JUST NOT GOING WELL, BUT...
...MISATO-SAN'S SERIOUS ABOUT THIS.
I WISH SHE WERE SERIOUS ABOUT PICKING UP AFTER HERSELF...
EVEN SO...
KIRISHIMA-SAN'S REALLY GOOD.
BUT I GUESS SHE WOULDN'T HAVE VOLUNTEERED IF SHE WEREN'T CONFIDENT.

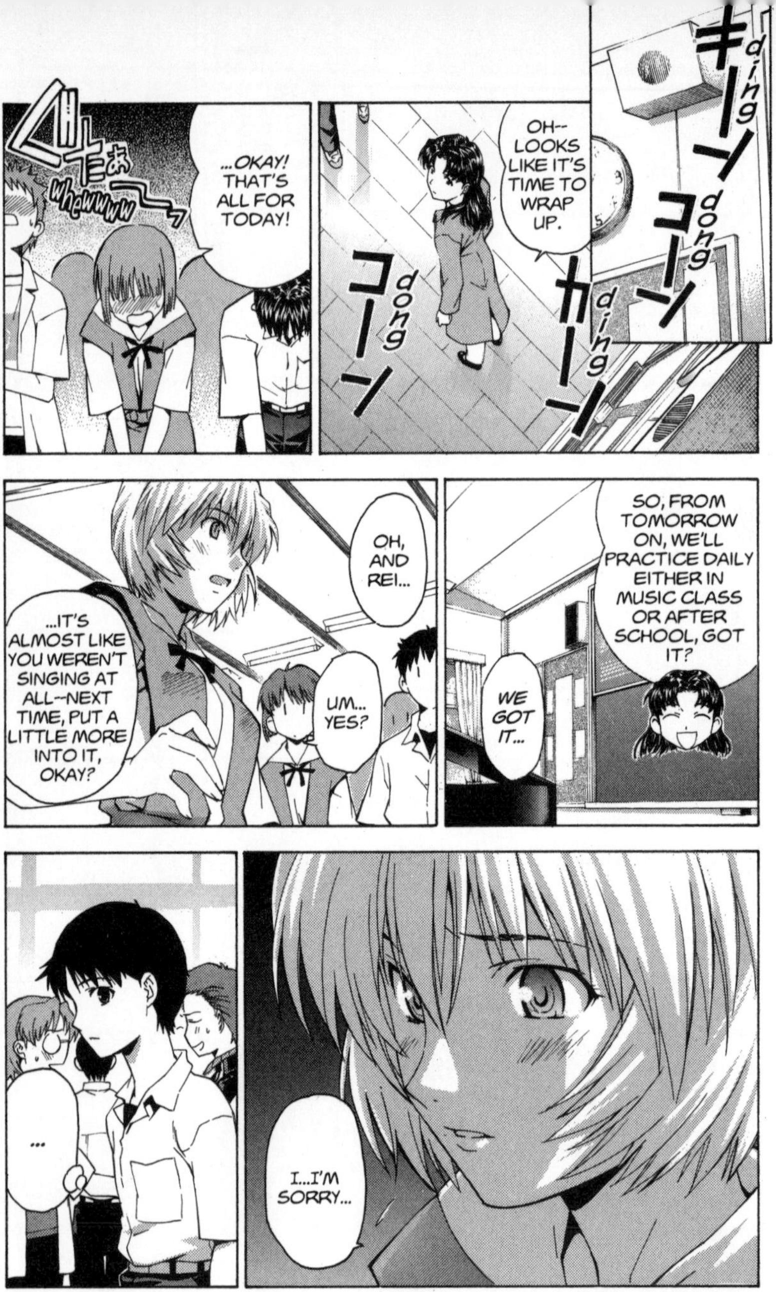
キーン ding
コーン dong
カーン ding
コーン dong
OH-- LOOKS LIKE IT'S TIME TO WRAP UP.
...OKAY! THAT'S ALL FOR TODAY!
whewwww
SO, FROM TOMORROW ON, WE'LL PRACTICE DAILY EITHER IN MUSIC CLASS OR AFTER SCHOOL, GOT IT?
WE GOT IT...
OH, AND REI...
UM... YES?
...IT'S ALMOST LIKE YOU WEREN'T SINGING AT ALL--NEXT TIME, PUT A LITTLE MORE INTO IT, OKAY?
I...I'M SORRY...
...

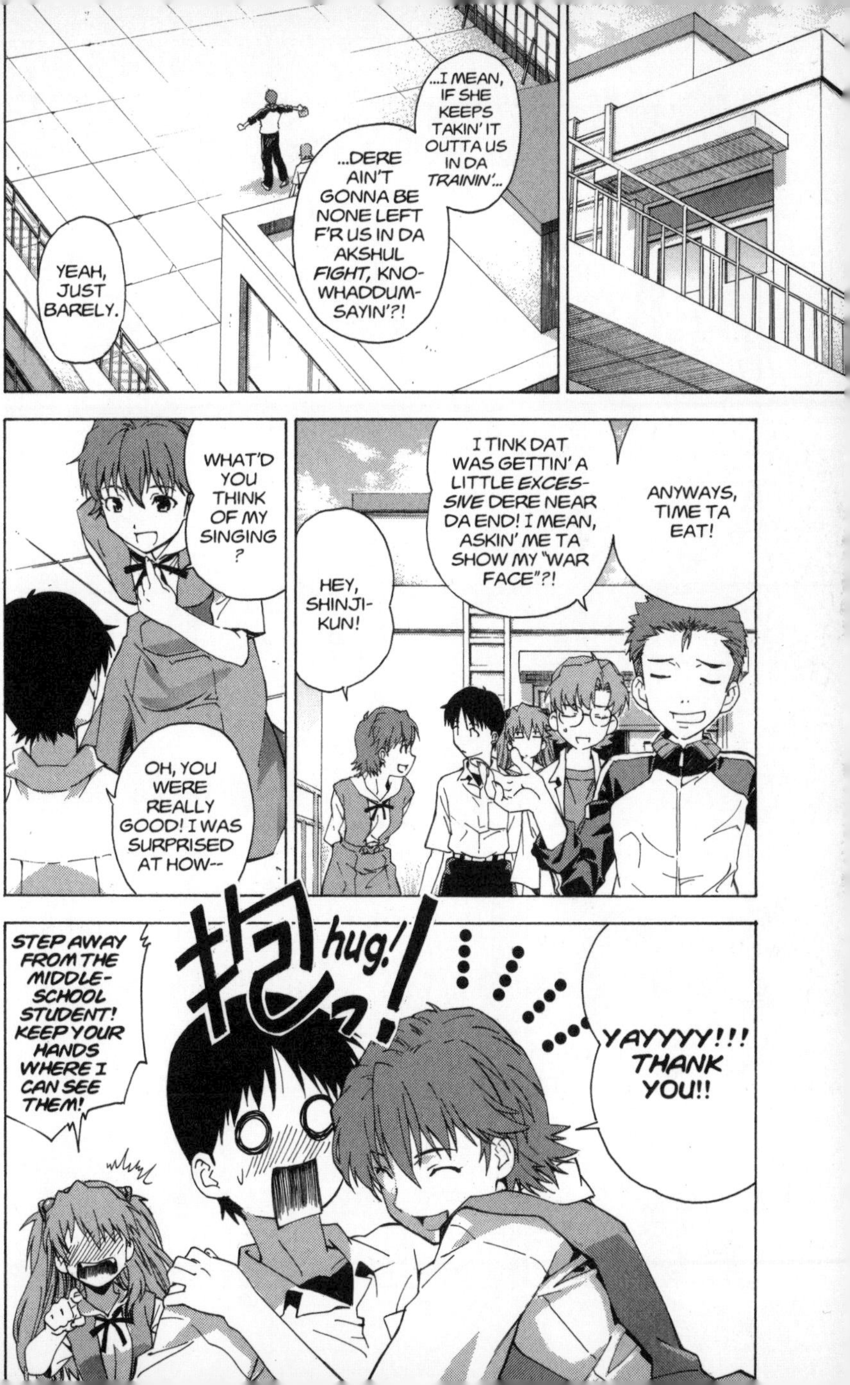
...I MEAN, IF SHE KEEPS TAKIN' IT OUTTA US IN DA *TRAININ'*...
...DERE AIN'T GONNA BE NONE LEFT F'R US IN DA AKSHUL *FIGHT*, KNO-WHADDUM-SAYIN'?!
YEAH, JUST BARELY.
ANYWAYS, TIME TA EAT!
I TINK DAT WAS GETTIN' A LITTLE *EXCESSIVE* DERE NEAR DA END! I MEAN, ASKIN' ME TA SHOW MY "WAR FACE"?!
HEY, SHINJI-KUN!
WHAT'D YOU THINK OF MY SINGING?
OH, YOU WERE REALLY GOOD! I WAS SURPRISED AT HOW--
YAYYYY!!! THANK YOU!!
......
hug!
STEP AWAY FROM THE MIDDLE-SCHOOL STUDENT! KEEP YOUR HANDS WHERE I CAN SEE THEM!

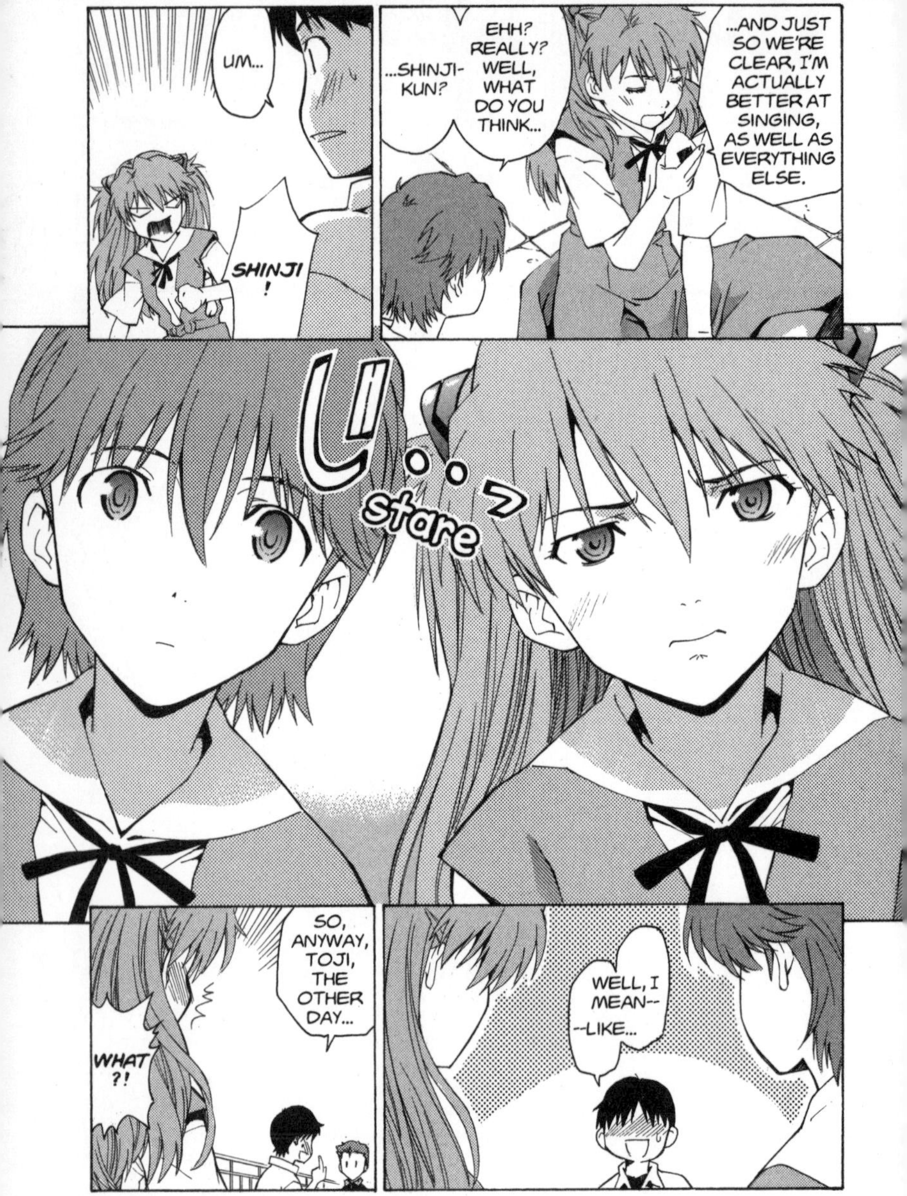
...AND JUST SO WE'RE CLEAR, I'M ACTUALLY BETTER AT SINGING, AS WELL AS EVERYTHING ELSE.
EHH? REALLY? WELL, WHAT DO YOU THINK...
...SHINJI-KUN?
UM...
SHINJI!
stare
WELL, I MEAN--
--LIKE...
SO, ANYWAY, TOJI, THE OTHER DAY...
WHAT?!

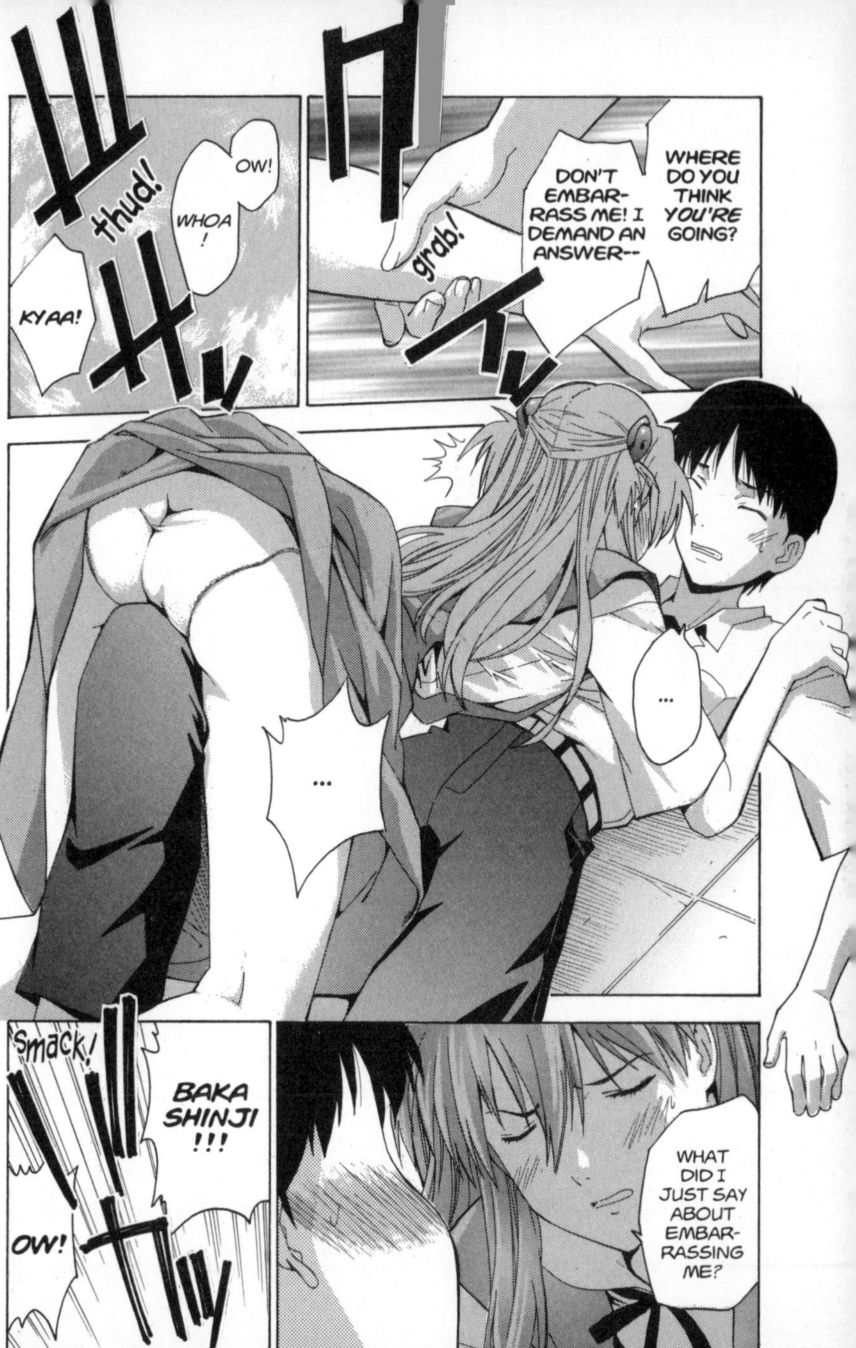
WHERE DO YOU THINK YOU'RE GOING?
DON'T EMBAR-RASS ME! I DEMAND AN ANSWER--
grab!
OW!
WHOA!
thud!
KYAA!
...
...
WHAT DID I JUST SAY ABOUT EMBAR-RASSING ME?
Smack!
BAKA SHINJI!!!
OW!

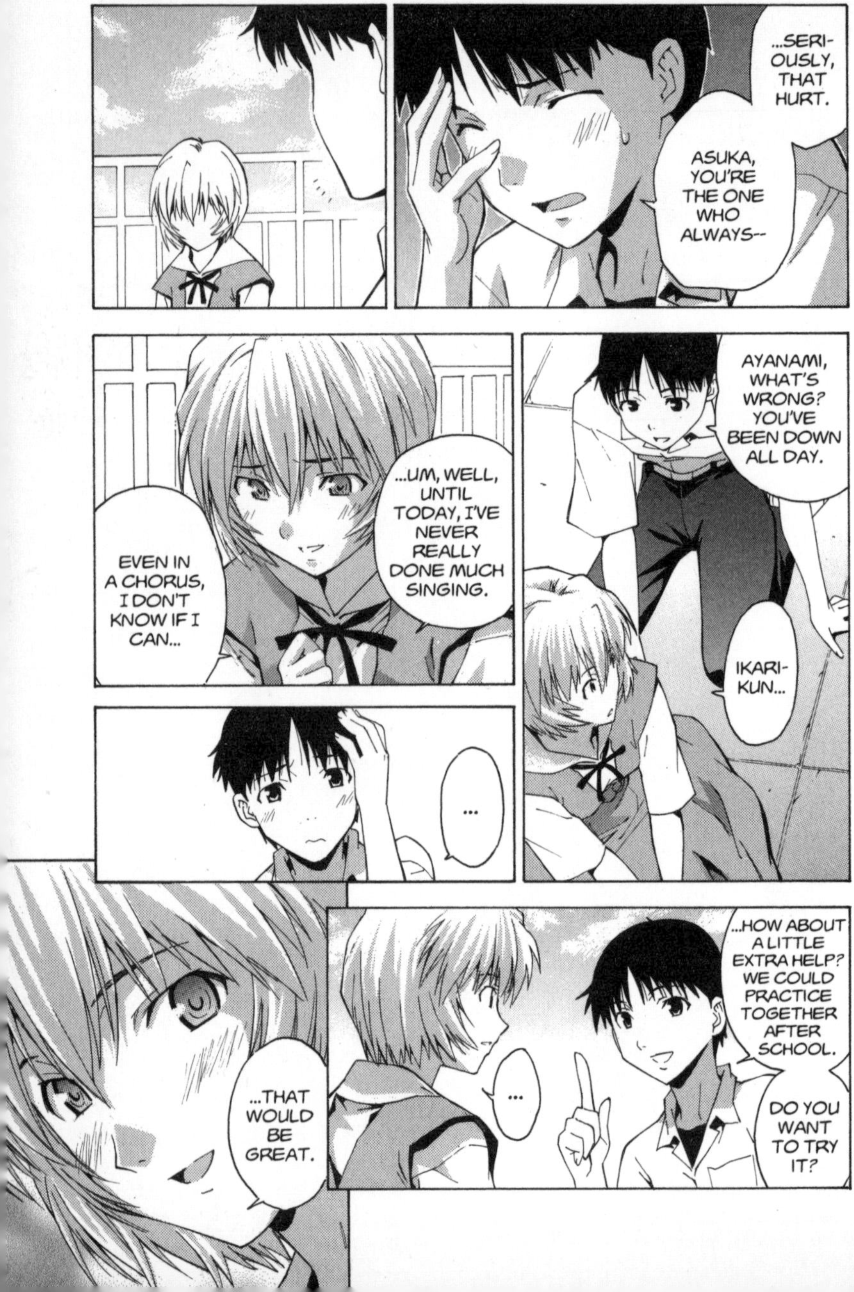
...SERI-OUSLY, THAT HURT.
ASUKA, YOU'RE THE ONE WHO ALWAYS--
AYANAMI, WHAT'S WRONG? YOU'VE BEEN DOWN ALL DAY.
IKARI-KUN...
...UM, WELL, UNTIL TODAY, I'VE NEVER REALLY DONE MUCH SINGING.
EVEN IN A CHORUS, I DON'T KNOW IF I CAN...
...
...HOW ABOUT A LITTLE EXTRA HELP? WE COULD PRACTICE TOGETHER AFTER SCHOOL.
DO YOU WANT TO TRY IT?
...
...THAT WOULD BE GREAT.

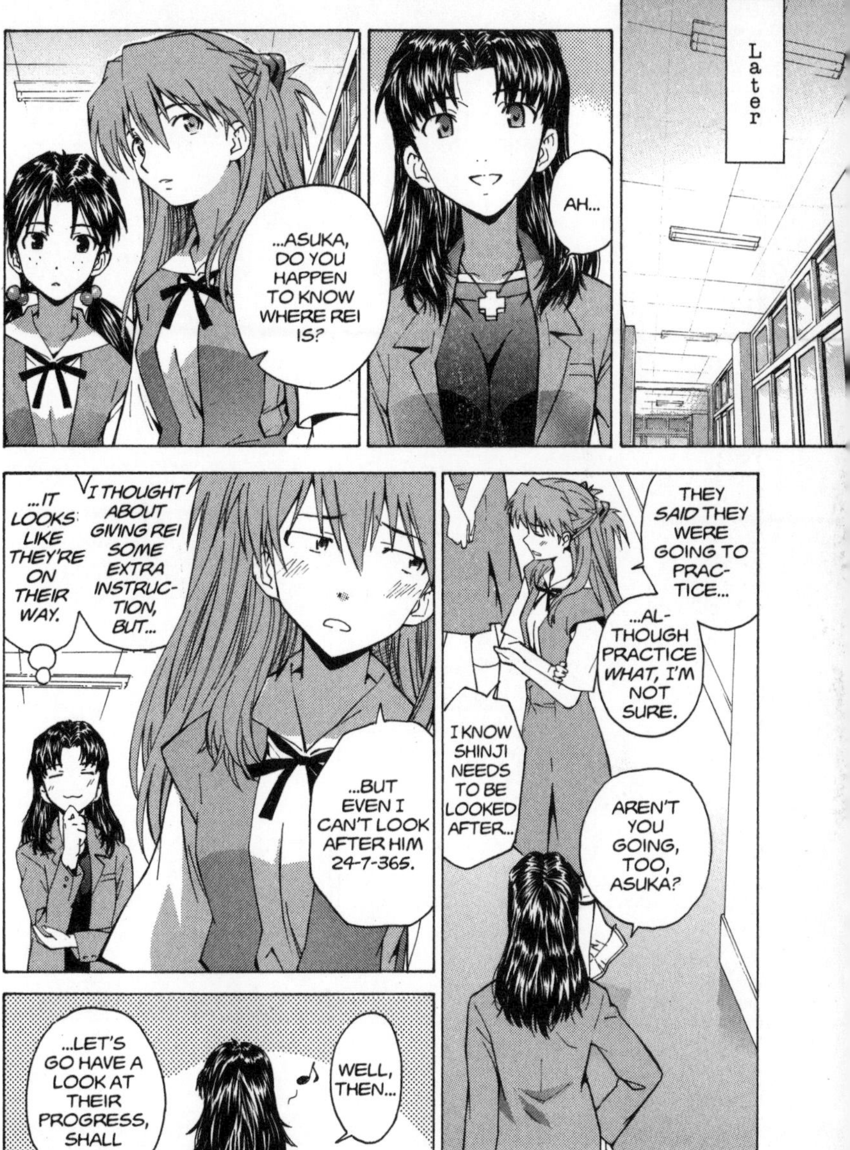
Later
AH...
...ASUKA, DO YOU HAPPEN TO KNOW WHERE REI IS?
THEY *SAID* THEY WERE GOING TO PRACTICE...
...ALTHOUGH PRACTICE *WHAT*, I'M NOT SURE.
I KNOW SHINJI NEEDS TO BE LOOKED AFTER...
AREN'T YOU GOING, TOO, ASUKA?
I THOUGHT ABOUT GIVING REI SOME EXTRA INSTRUCTION, BUT...
...IT LOOKS LIKE THEY'RE ON THEIR WAY.
...BUT EVEN I CAN'T LOOK AFTER HIM 24-7-365.
WELL, THEN...
...LET'S GO HAVE A LOOK AT THEIR PROGRESS, SHALL WE?

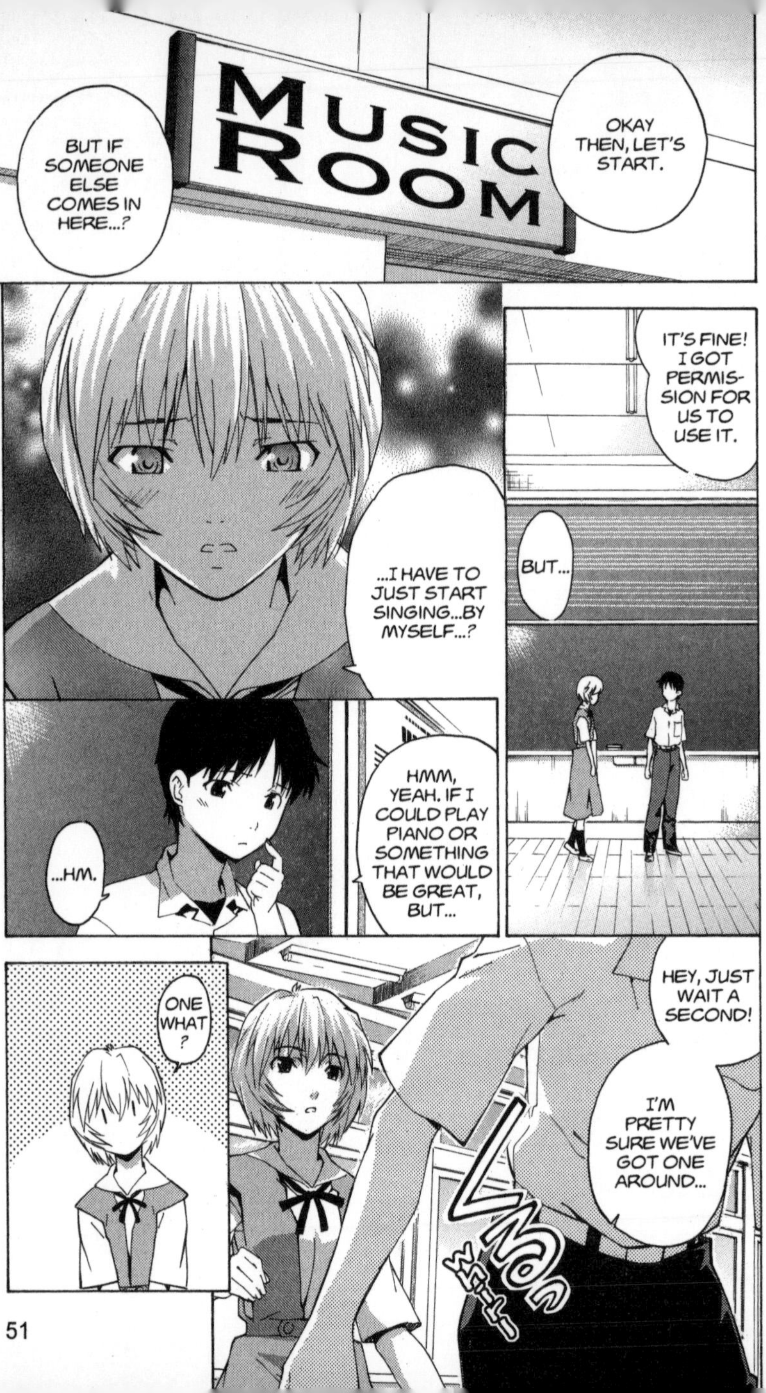
MUSIC ROOM
OKAY THEN, LET'S START.
BUT IF SOMEONE ELSE COMES IN HERE...?
IT'S FINE! I GOT PERMIS-SION FOR US TO USE IT.
BUT...
...I HAVE TO JUST START SINGING...BY MYSELF...?
HMM, YEAH. IF I COULD PLAY PIANO OR SOMETHING THAT WOULD BE GREAT, BUT...
...HM.
HEY, JUST WAIT A SECOND!
I'M PRETTY SURE WE'VE GOT ONE AROUND...
VMOO
ONE WHAT?

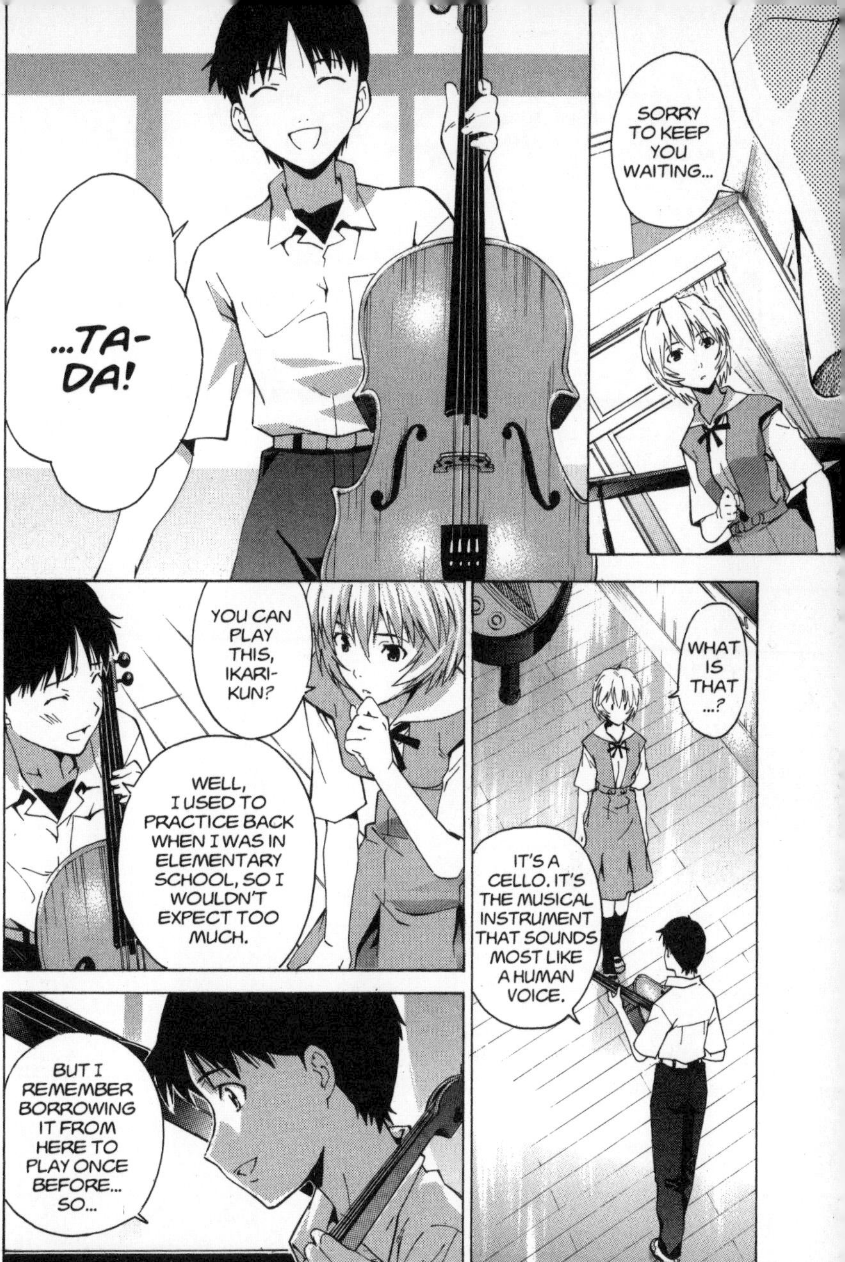
SORRY TO KEEP YOU WAITING...
...TA-DA!
WHAT IS THAT ...?
IT'S A CELLO. IT'S THE MUSICAL INSTRUMENT THAT SOUNDS MOST LIKE A HUMAN VOICE.
YOU CAN PLAY THIS, IKARI-KUN?
WELL, I USED TO PRACTICE BACK WHEN I WAS IN ELEMENTARY SCHOOL, SO I WOULDN'T EXPECT TOO MUCH.
BUT I REMEMBER BORROWING IT FROM HERE TO PLAY ONCE BEFORE... SO...

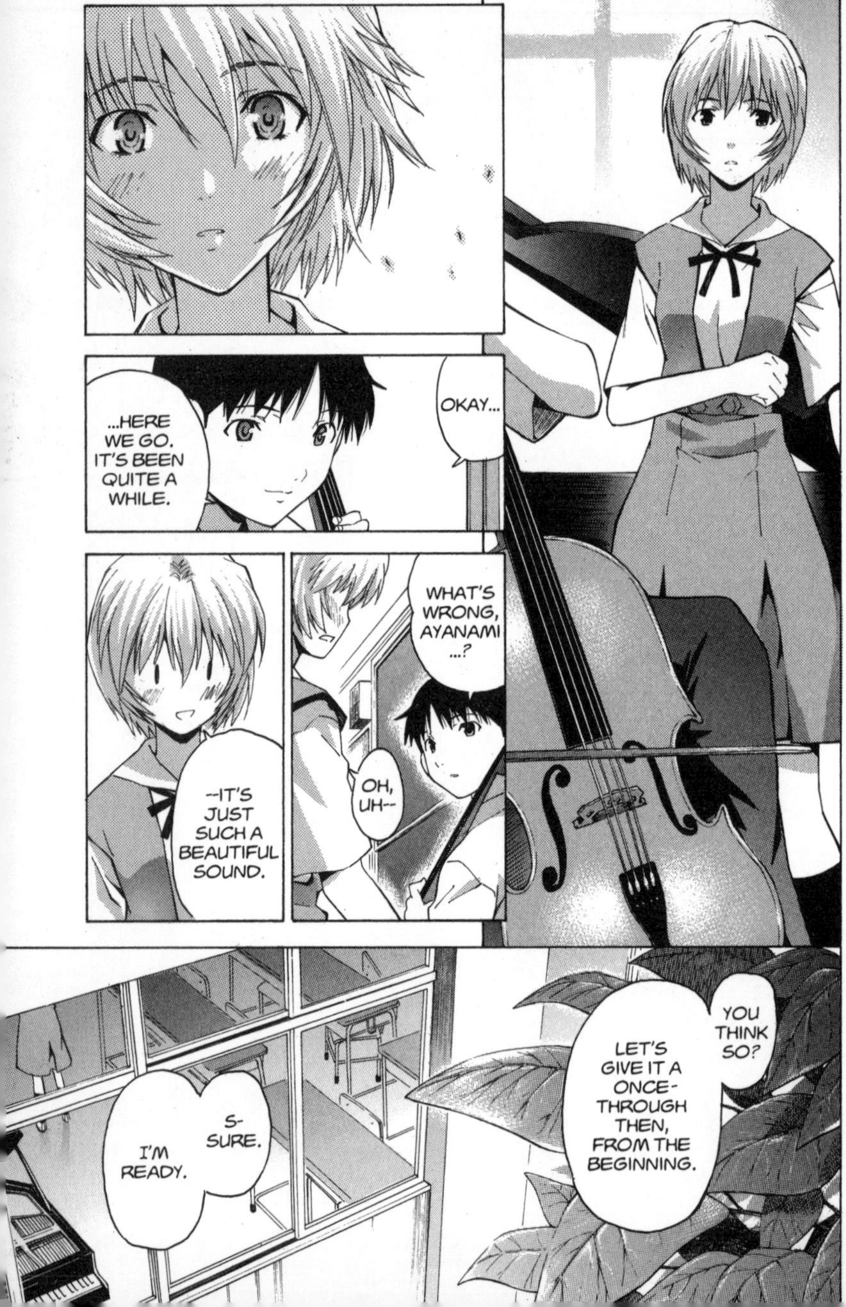
OKAY...
...HERE WE GO. IT'S BEEN QUITE A WHILE.
WHAT'S WRONG, AYANAMI ...?
OH, UH--
--IT'S JUST SUCH A BEAUTIFUL SOUND.
YOU THINK SO?
LET'S GIVE IT A ONCE-THROUGH THEN, FROM THE BEGINNING.
S- SURE.
I'M READY.

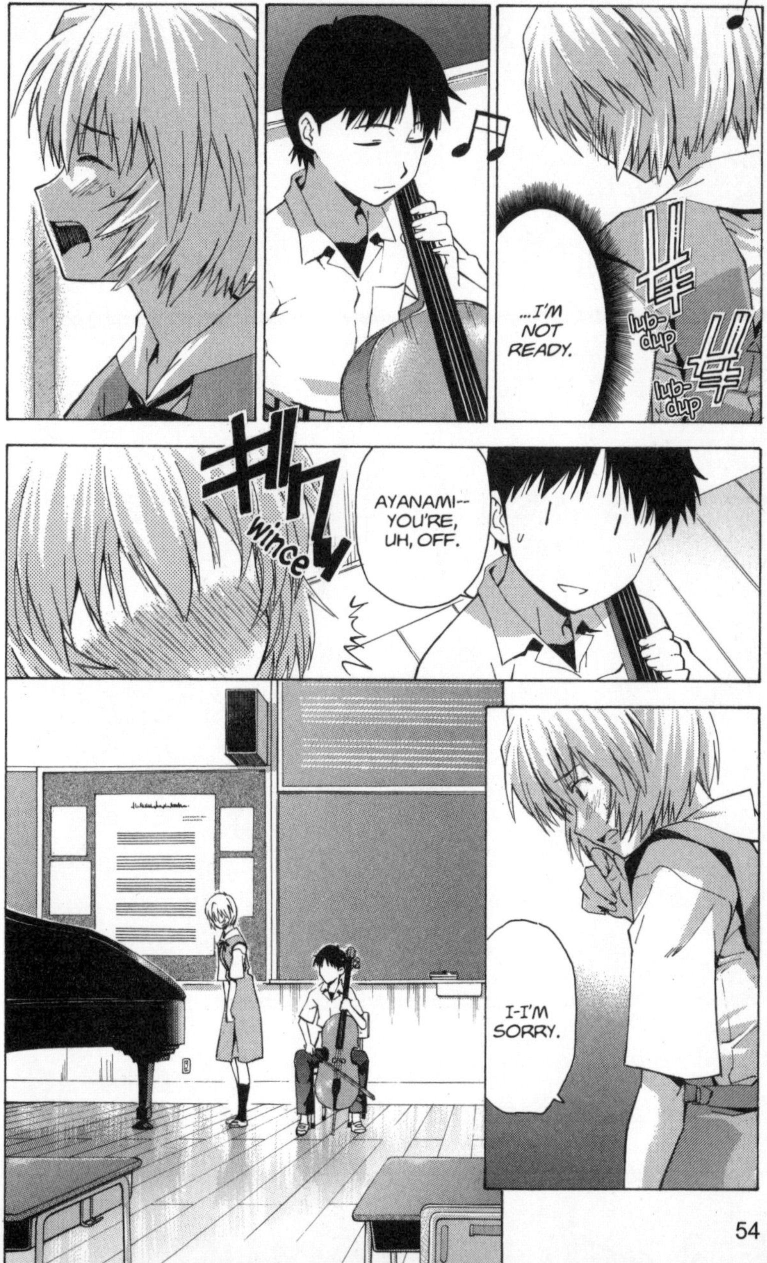
lub-dup
lub-dup
...I'M NOT READY.
AYANAMI-- YOU'RE, UH, OFF.
wince
I-I'M SORRY.

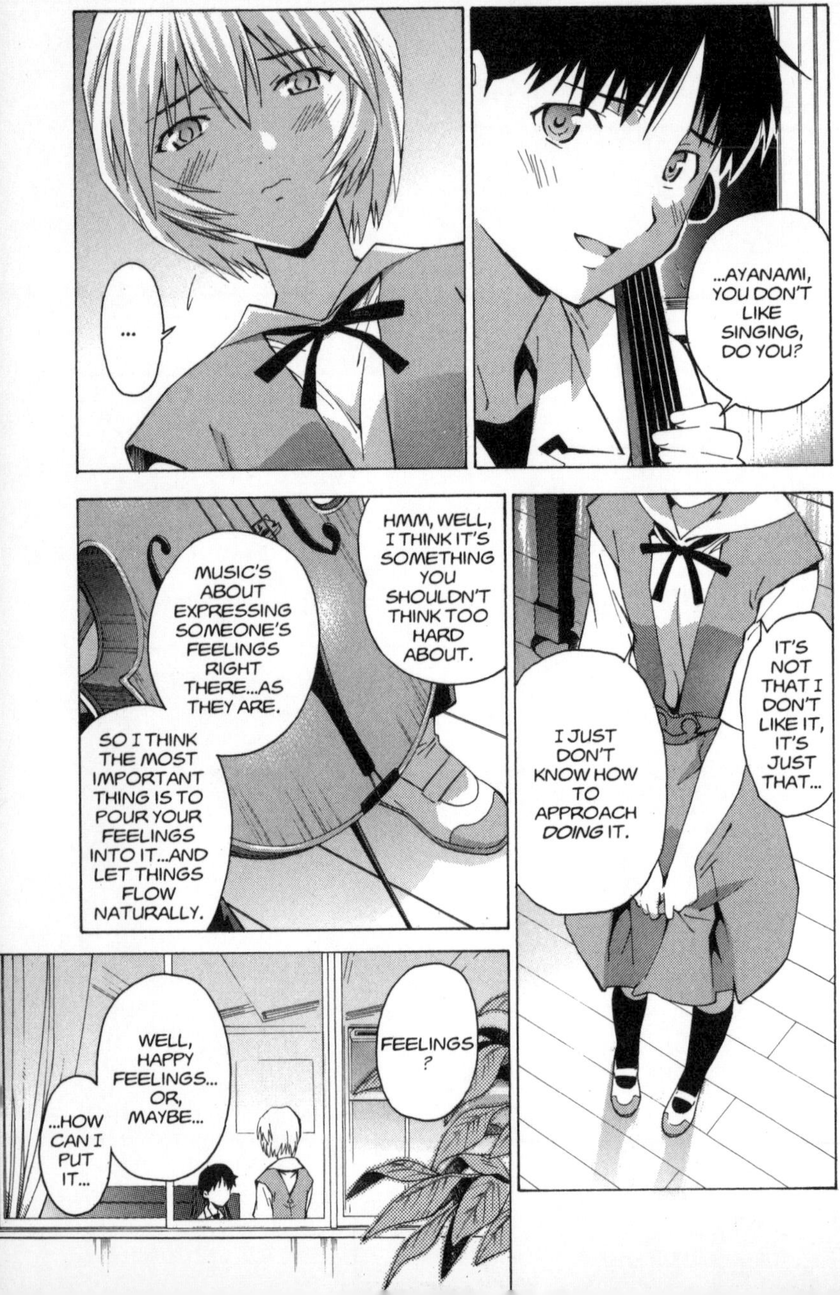
...AYANAMI, YOU DON'T LIKE SINGING, DO YOU?
...
IT'S NOT THAT I DON'T LIKE IT, IT'S JUST THAT...
I JUST DON'T KNOW HOW TO APPROACH *DOING* IT.
HMM, WELL, I THINK IT'S SOMETHING YOU SHOULDN'T THINK TOO HARD ABOUT.
MUSIC'S ABOUT EXPRESSING SOMEONE'S FEELINGS RIGHT THERE...AS THEY ARE.
SO I THINK THE MOST IMPORTANT THING IS TO POUR YOUR FEELINGS INTO IT...AND LET THINGS FLOW NATURALLY.
FEELINGS?
WELL, HAPPY FEELINGS... OR, MAYBE...
...HOW CAN I PUT IT...

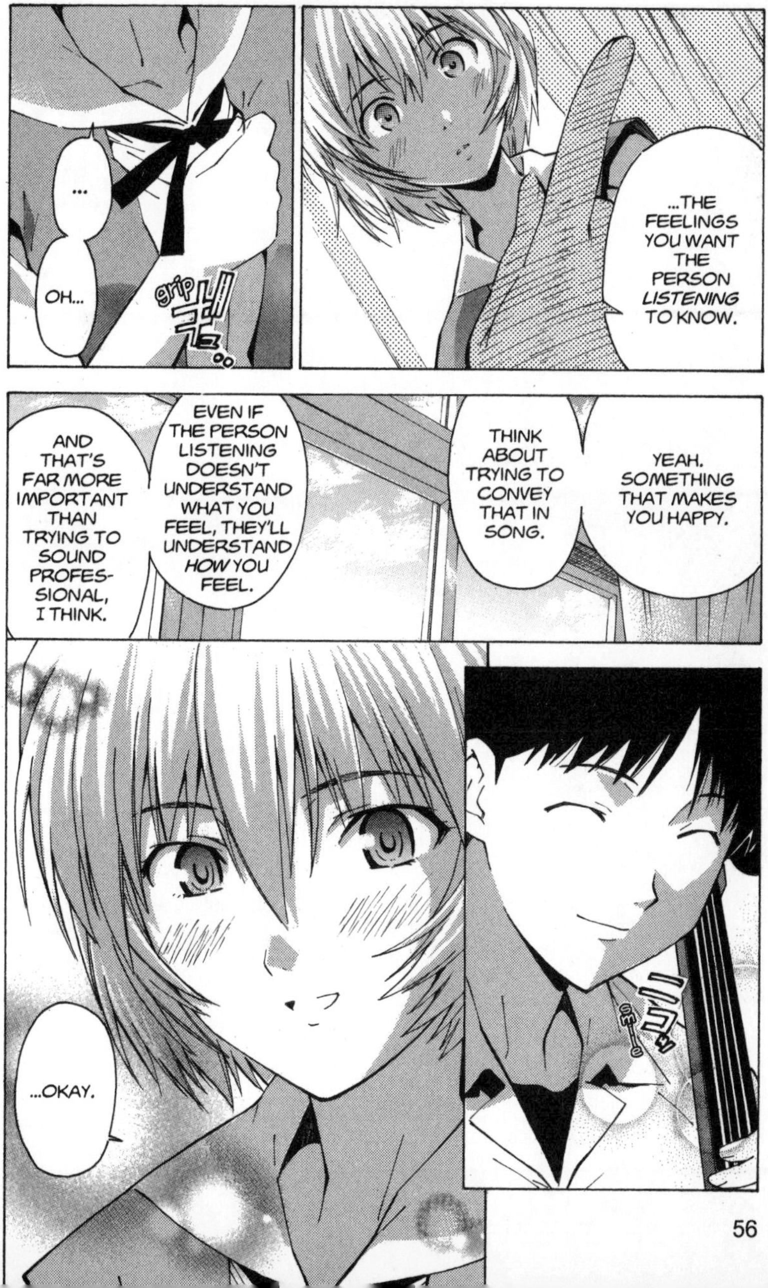
...THE FEELINGS YOU WANT THE PERSON *LISTENING* TO KNOW.
...
OH...
grip
YEAH. SOMETHING THAT MAKES YOU HAPPY.
THINK ABOUT TRYING TO CONVEY THAT IN SONG.
EVEN IF THE PERSON LISTENING DOESN'T UNDERSTAND WHAT YOU FEEL, THEY'LL UNDERSTAND *HOW* YOU FEEL.
AND THAT'S FAR MORE IMPORTANT THAN TRYING TO SOUND PROFES-SIONAL, I THINK.
smile
...OKAY.

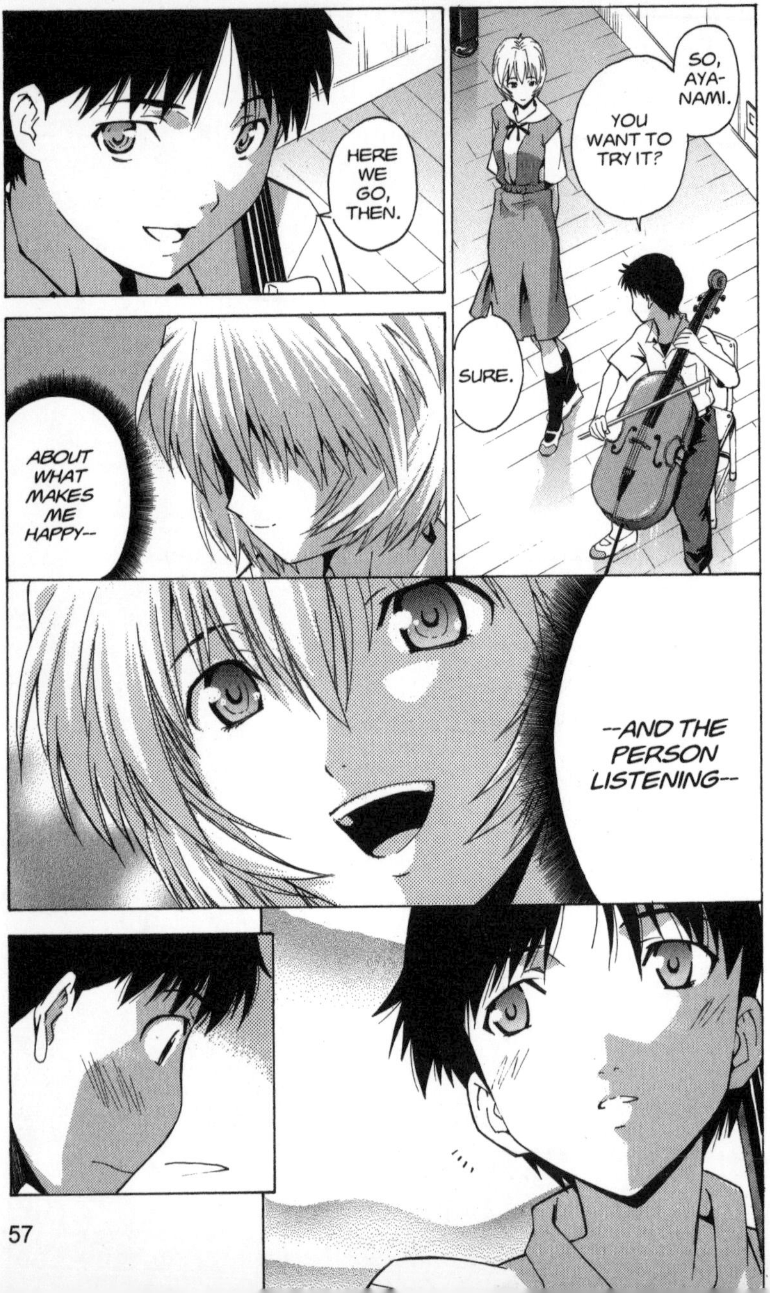
SO, AYA-NAMI.
YOU WANT TO TRY IT?
SURE.
HERE WE GO, THEN.
ABOUT WHAT MAKES ME HAPPY--
--AND THE PERSON LISTENING--

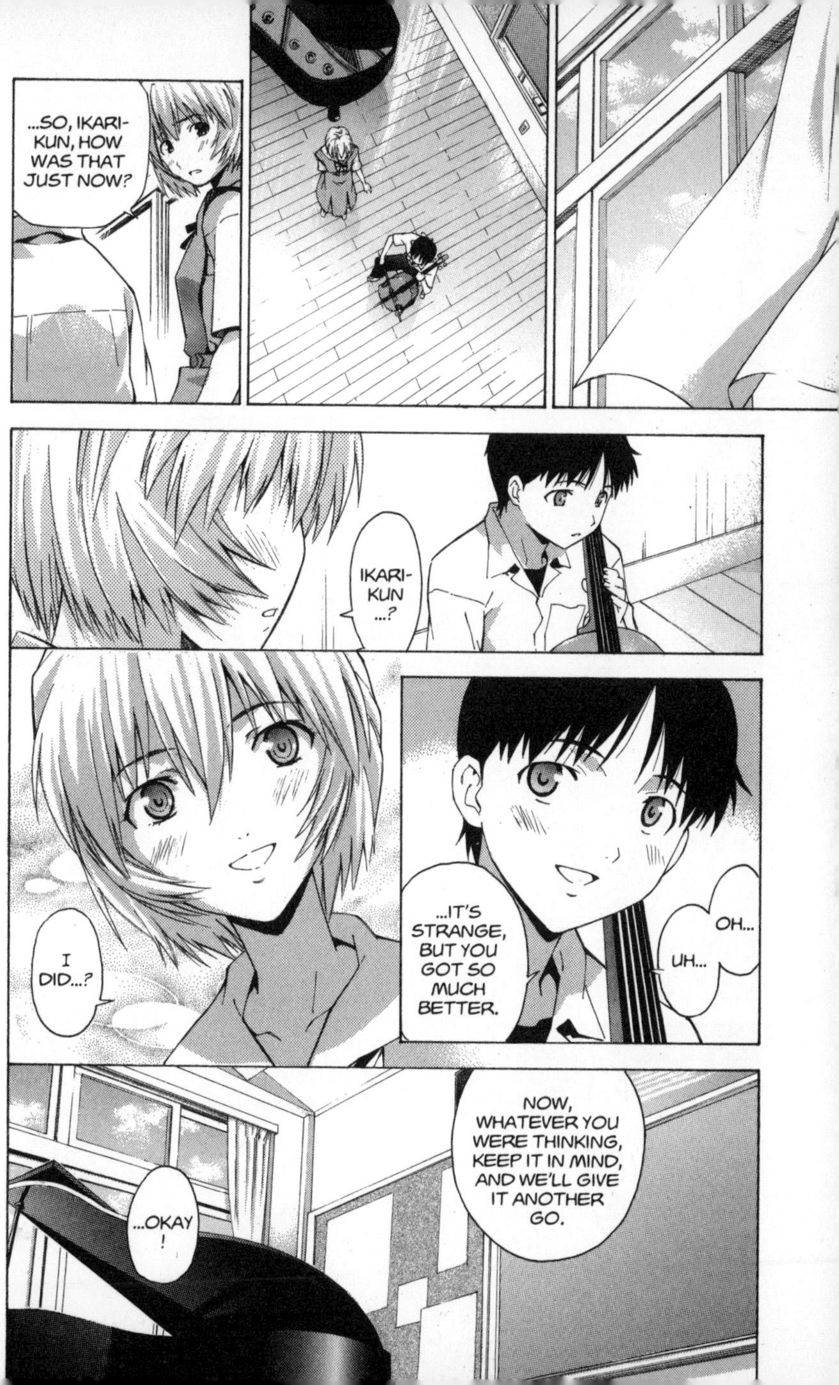
...SO, IKARI-KUN, HOW WAS THAT JUST NOW?
IKARI-KUN ...?
OH...
UH...
...IT'S STRANGE, BUT YOU GOT SO MUCH BETTER.
I DID...?
NOW, WHATEVER YOU WERE THINKING, KEEP IT IN MIND, AND WE'LL GIVE IT ANOTHER GO.
...OKAY!

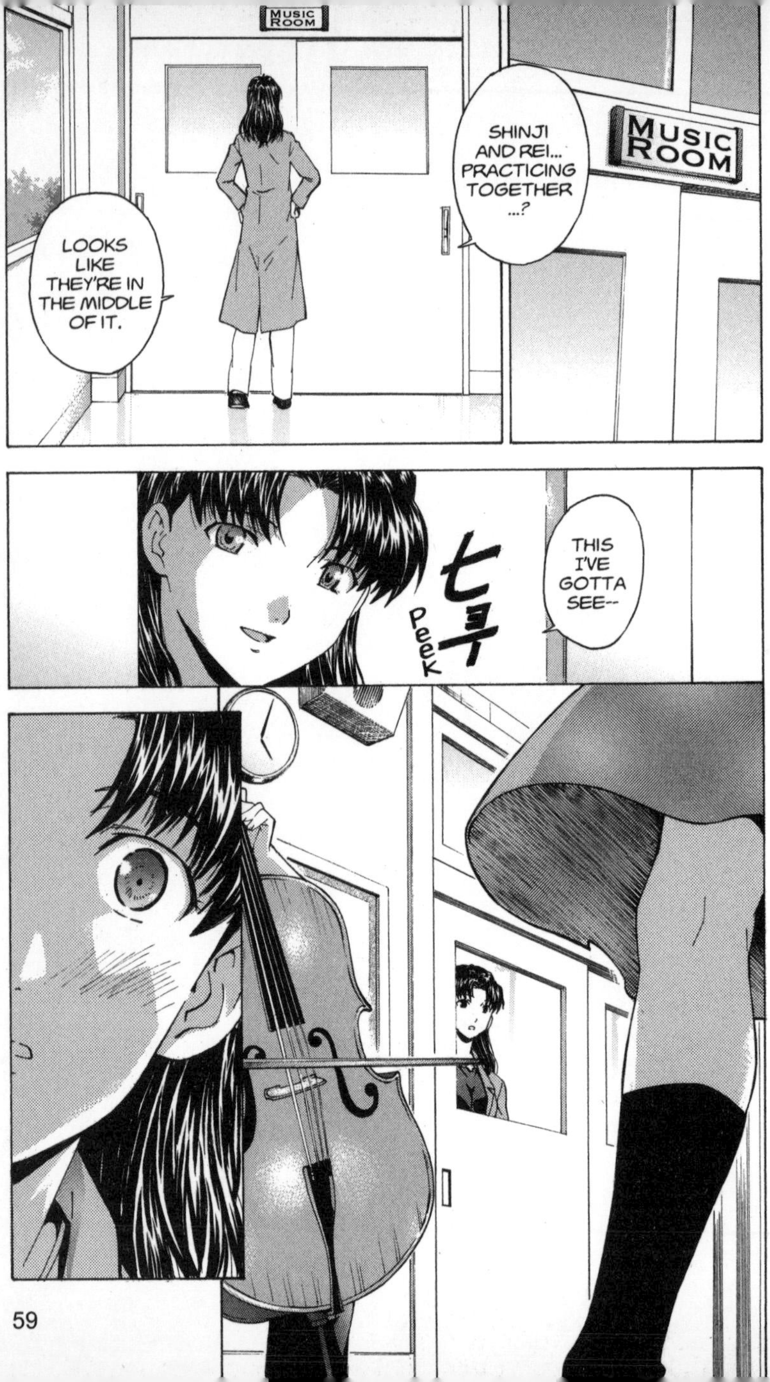
MUSIC ROOM
SHINJI AND REI... PRACTICING TOGETHER ...?
MUSIC ROOM
LOOKS LIKE THEY'RE IN THE MIDDLE OF IT.
THIS I'VE GOTTA SEE--
Peek

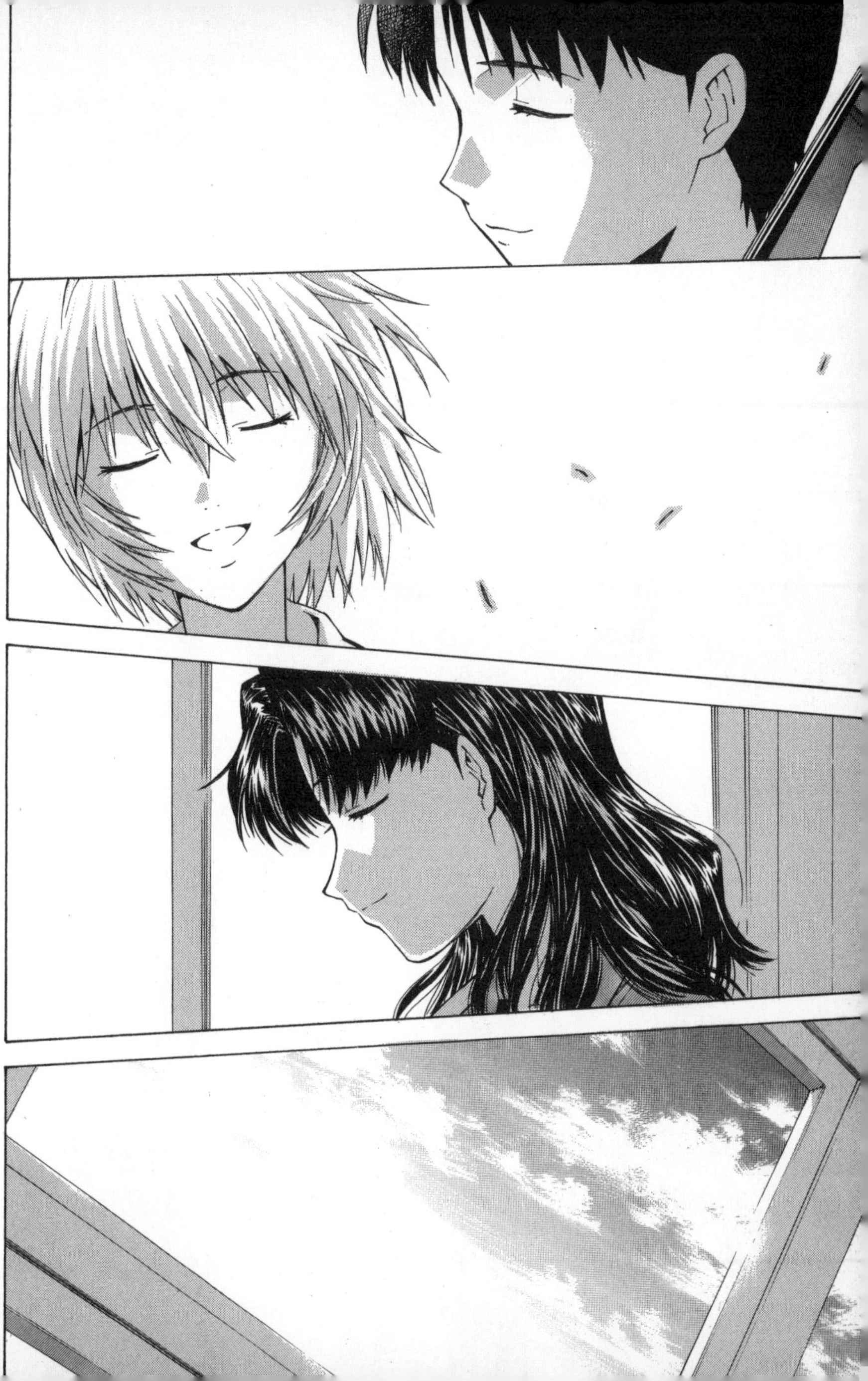

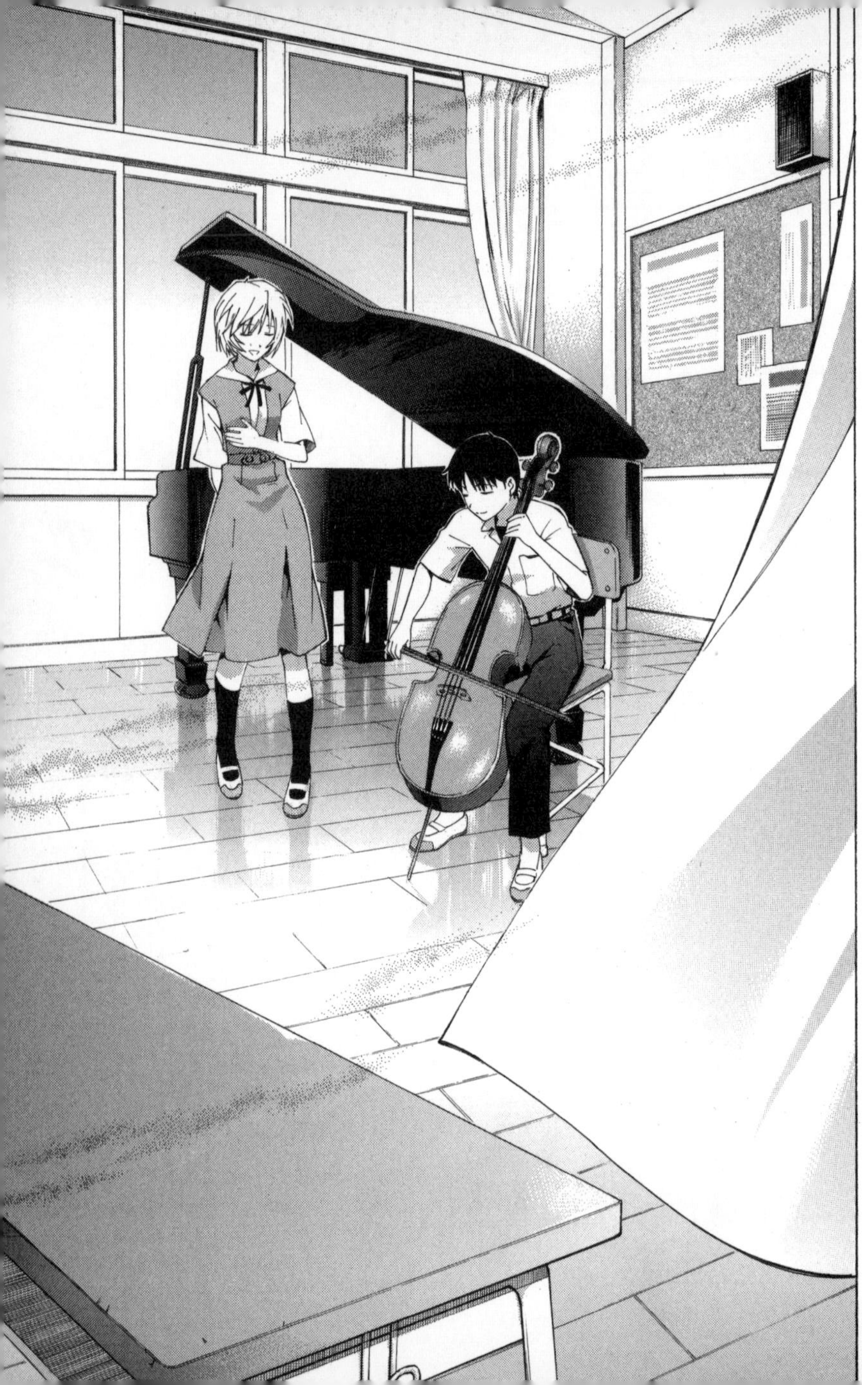

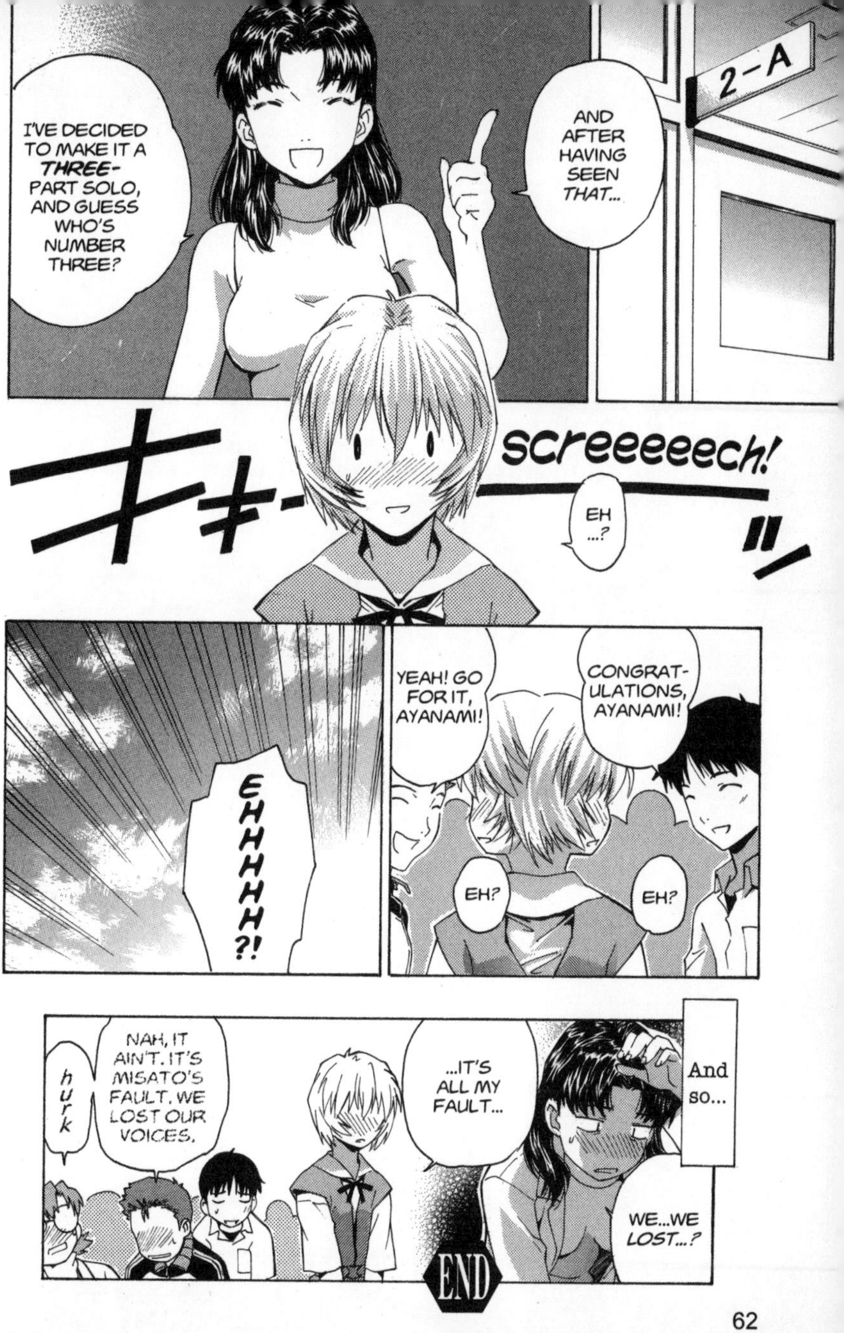
2-A
AND AFTER HAVING SEEN THAT...
I'VE DECIDED TO MAKE IT A THREE-PART SOLO, AND GUESS WHO'S NUMBER THREE?
screeeeeech!
EH ...?
CONGRAT-ULATIONS, AYANAMI!
YEAH! GO FOR IT, AYANAMI!
EH?
EH?
EHHHHHH?!
And so...
WE...WE LOST...?
...IT'S ALL MY FAULT...
NAH, IT AIN'T. IT'S MISATO'S FAULT. WE LOST OUR VOICES.
hurk
END

NEON GENESIS
EVANGELION
THE SHINJI IKARI RAISING PROJECT

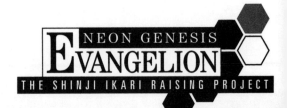

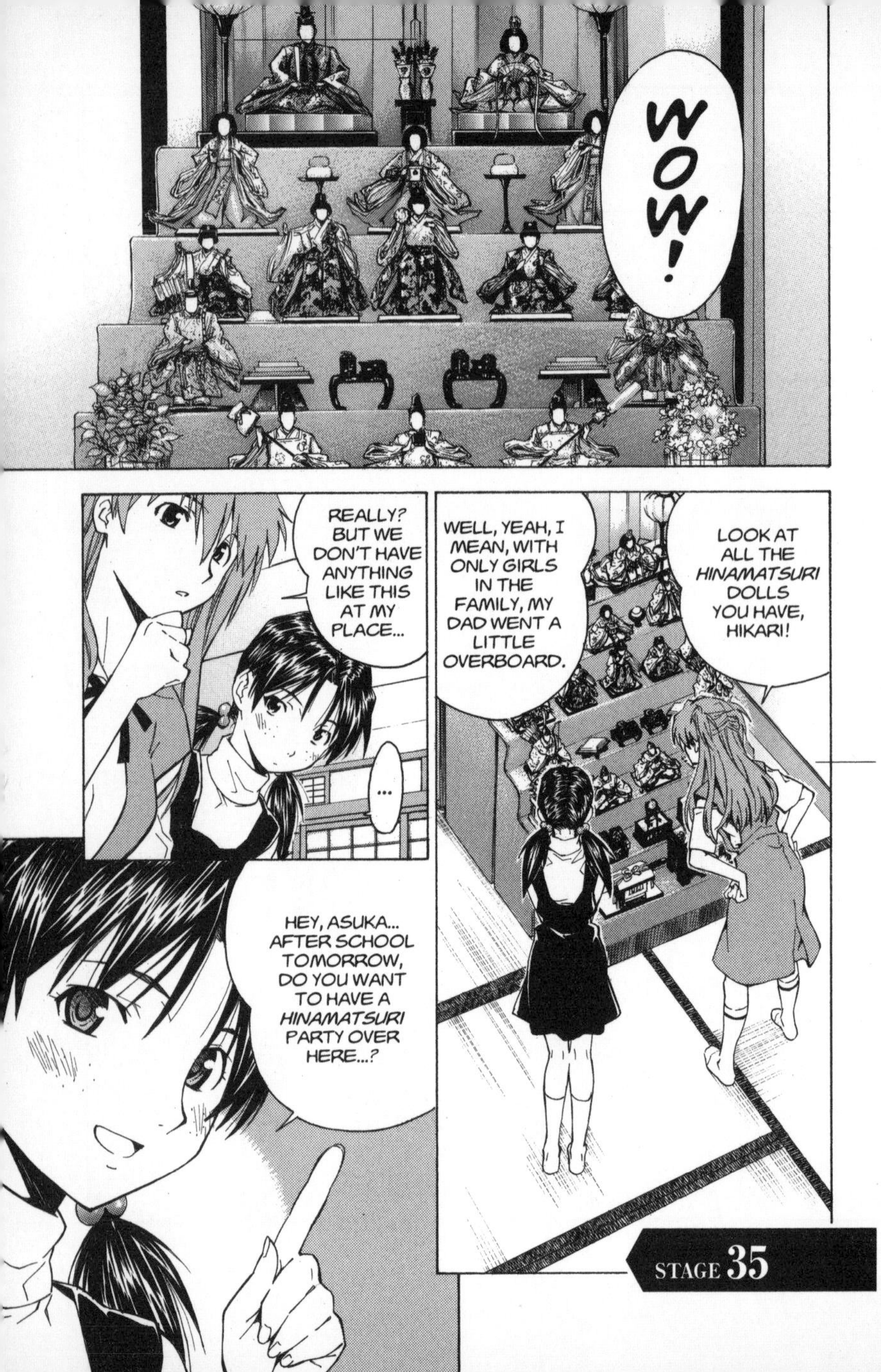
WOW!
LOOK AT ALL THE *HINAMATSURI* DOLLS YOU HAVE, HIKARI!
WELL, YEAH, I MEAN, WITH ONLY GIRLS IN THE FAMILY, MY DAD WENT A LITTLE OVERBOARD.
REALLY? BUT WE DON'T HAVE ANYTHING LIKE THIS AT MY PLACE...
...
HEY, ASUKA... AFTER SCHOOL TOMORROW, DO YOU WANT TO HAVE A *HINAMATSURI* PARTY OVER HERE...?
STAGE 35

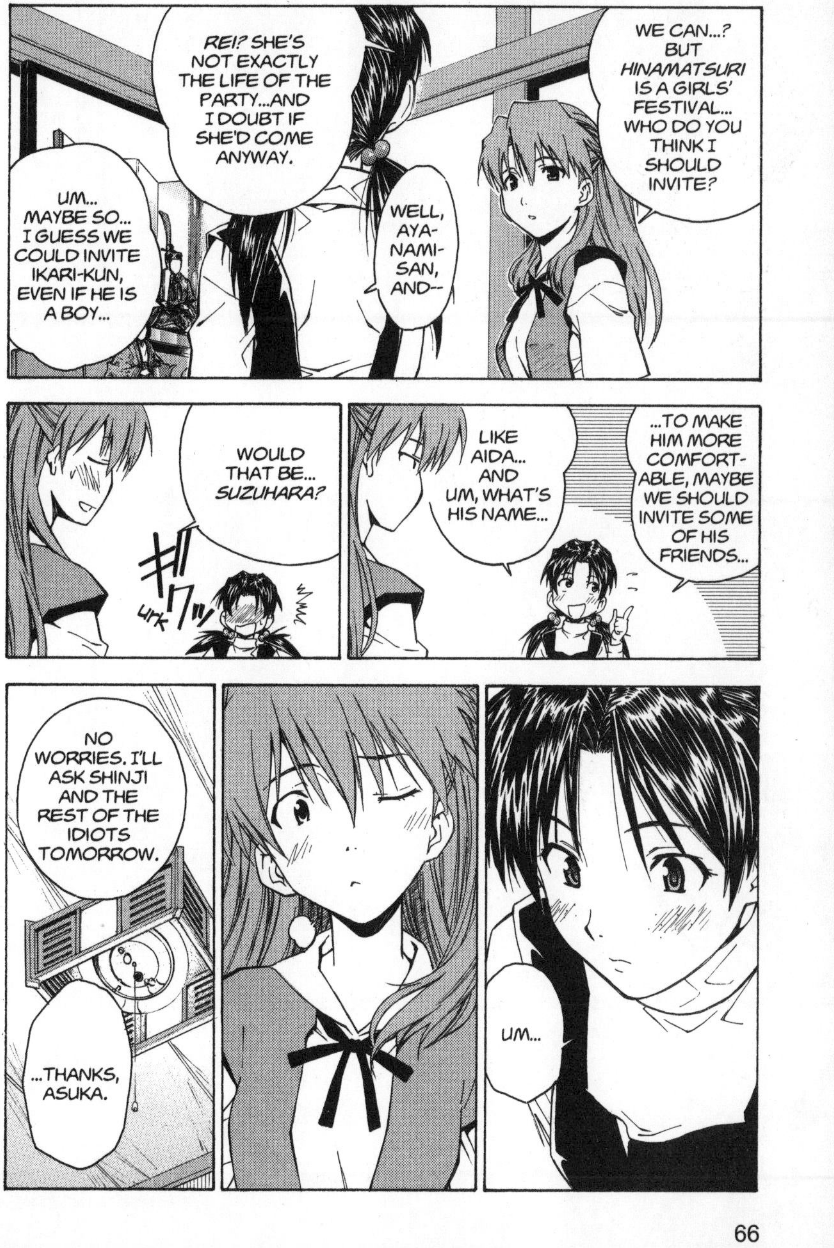
WE CAN...? BUT *HINAMATSURI* IS A GIRLS' FESTIVAL... WHO DO YOU THINK I SHOULD INVITE?
WELL, AYA-NAMI-SAN, AND--
REI? SHE'S NOT EXACTLY THE LIFE OF THE PARTY...AND I DOUBT IF SHE'D COME ANYWAY.
UM... MAYBE SO... I GUESS WE COULD INVITE IKARI-KUN, EVEN IF HE IS A BOY...
...TO MAKE HIM MORE COMFORT-ABLE, MAYBE WE SHOULD INVITE SOME OF HIS FRIENDS...
LIKE AIDA... AND UM, WHAT'S HIS NAME...
WOULD THAT BE... *SUZUHARA?*
ギクッ
urk
UM...
NO WORRIES. I'LL ASK SHINJI AND THE REST OF THE IDIOTS TOMORROW.
...THANKS, ASUKA.

STAGE 35

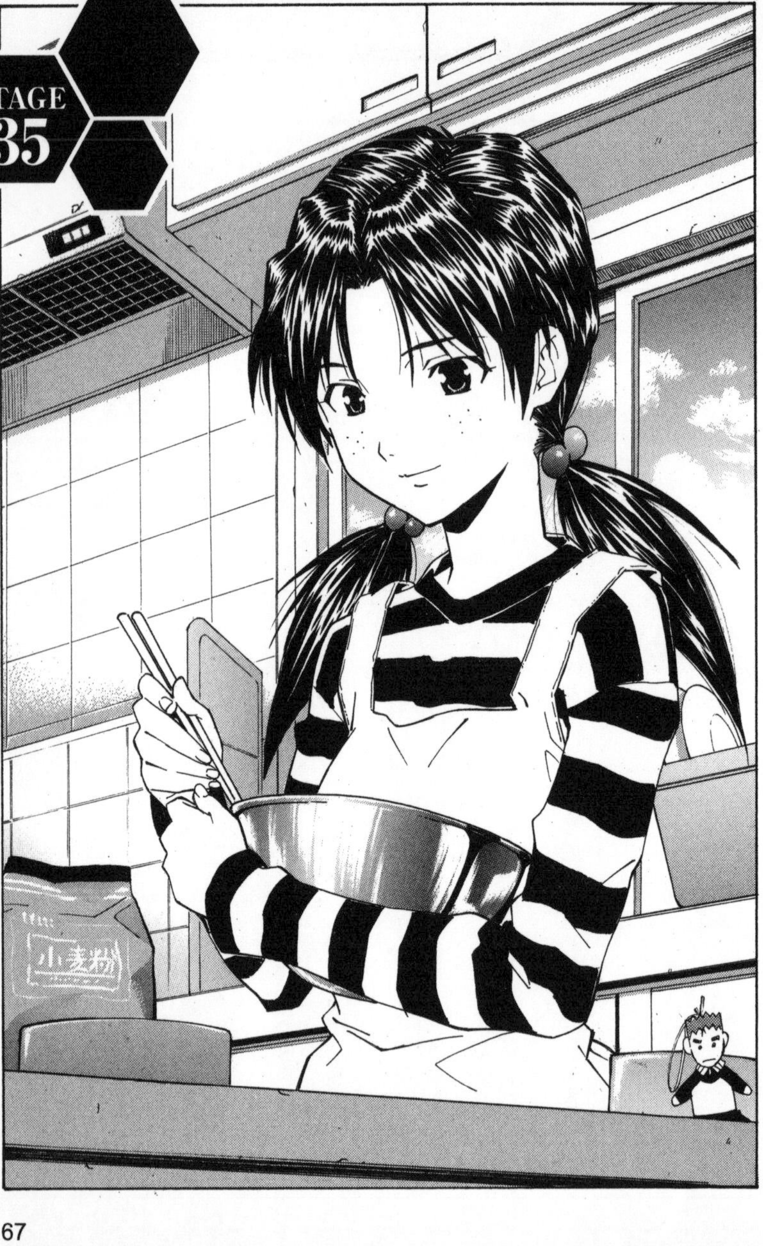
小麦粉

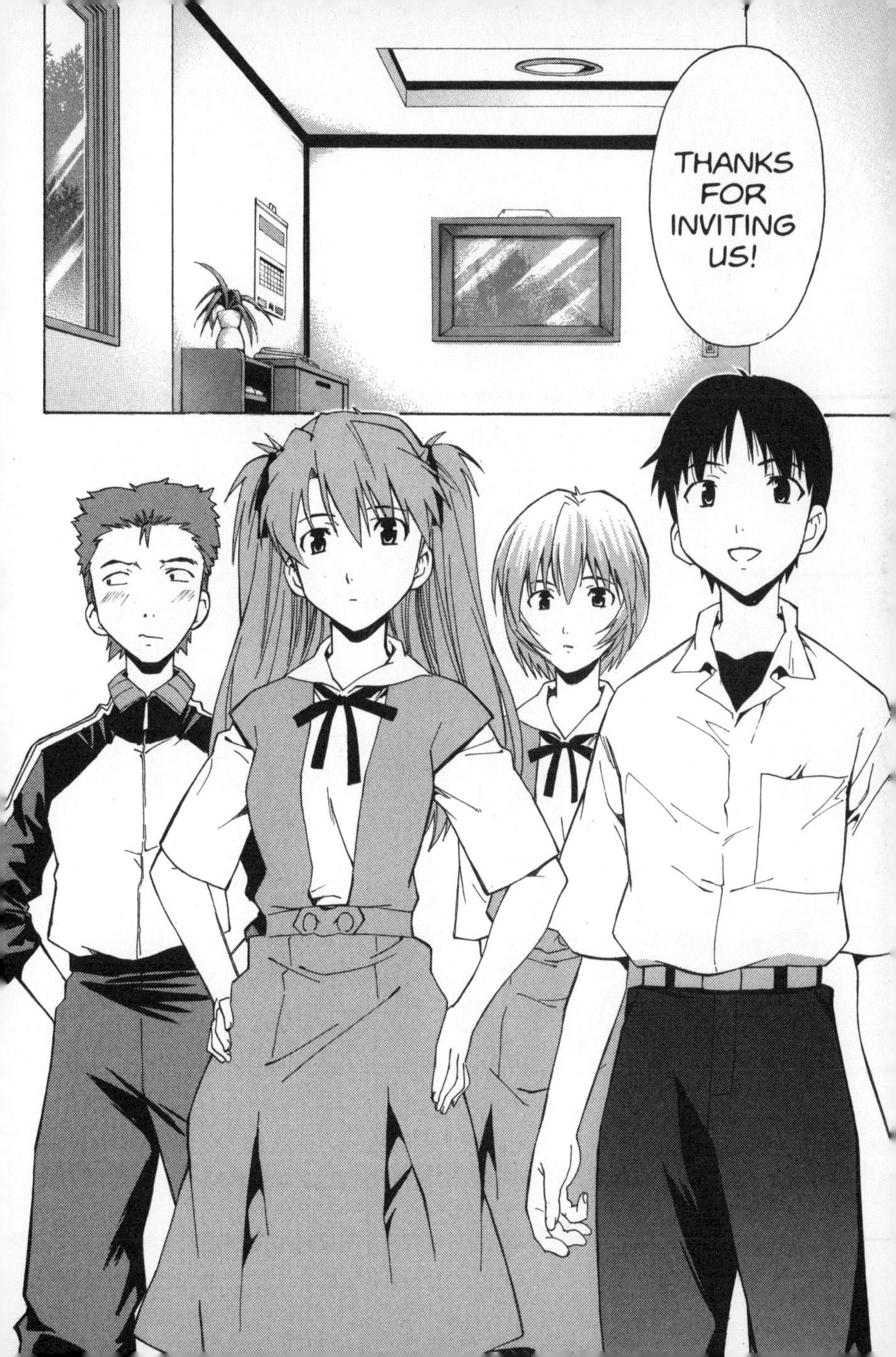
THANKS FOR INVITING US!

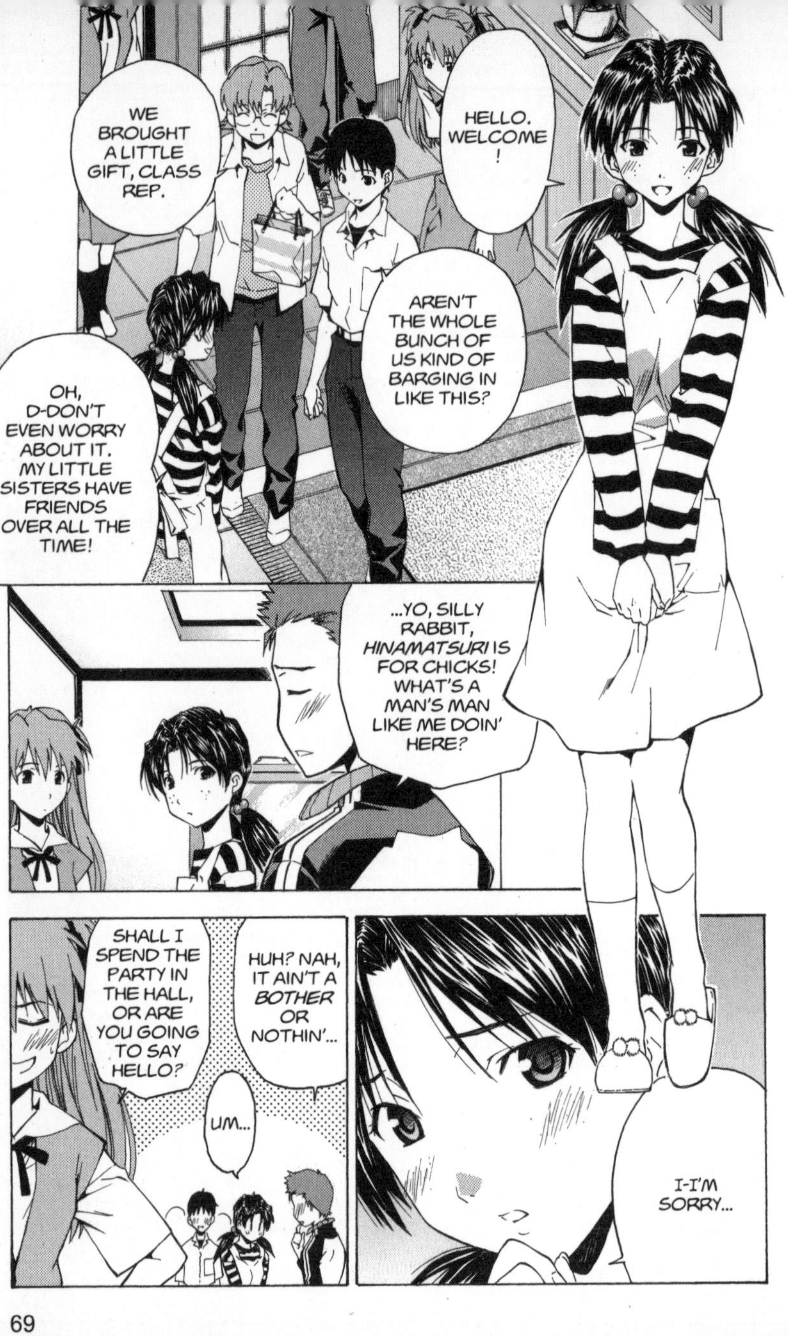
HELLO. WELCOME!
WE BROUGHT A LITTLE GIFT, CLASS REP.
AREN'T THE WHOLE BUNCH OF US KIND OF BARGING IN LIKE THIS?
OH, D-DON'T EVEN WORRY ABOUT IT. MY LITTLE SISTERS HAVE FRIENDS OVER ALL THE TIME!
...YO, SILLY RABBIT, *HINAMATSURI* IS FOR CHICKS! WHAT'S A MAN'S MAN LIKE ME DOIN' HERE?
I-I'M SORRY...
HUH? NAH, IT AIN'T A *BOTHER* OR NOTHIN'...
SHALL I SPEND THE PARTY IN THE HALL, OR ARE YOU GOING TO SAY HELLO?
UM...

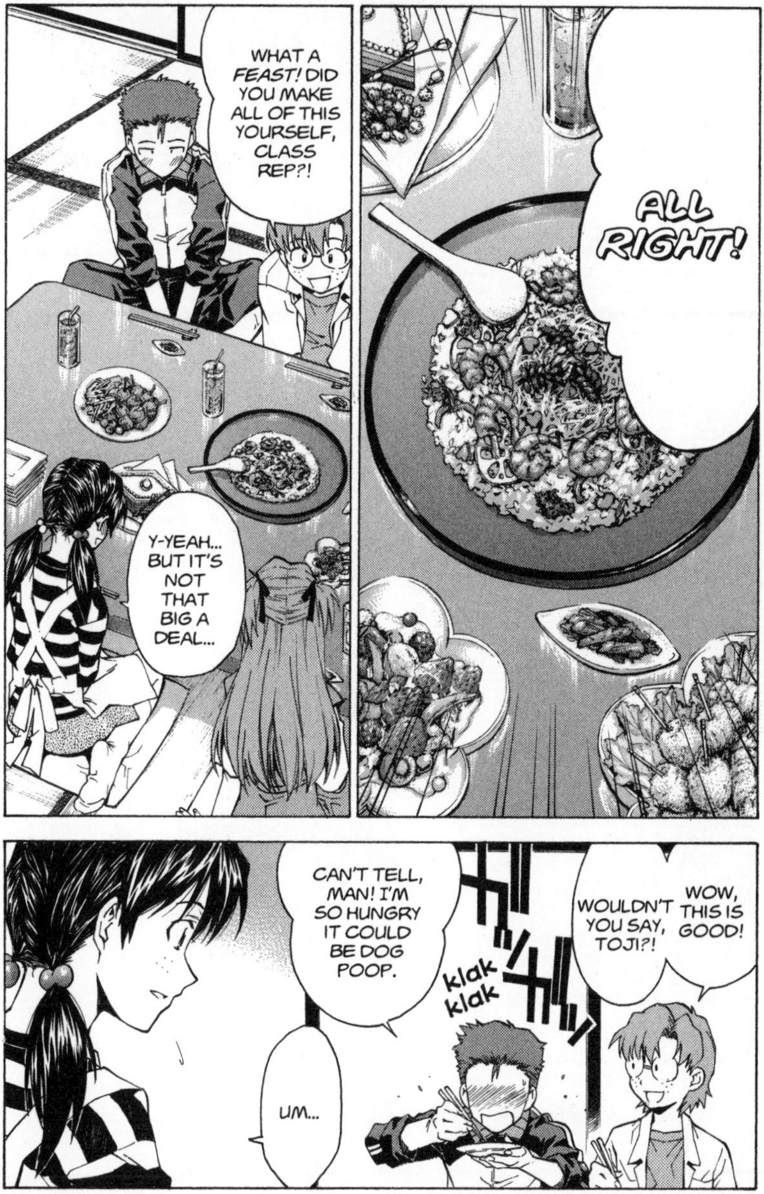
ALL RIGHT!
WHAT A FEAST! DID YOU MAKE ALL OF THIS YOURSELF, CLASS REP?!
Y-YEAH... BUT IT'S NOT THAT BIG A DEAL...
WOW, THIS IS GOOD!
WOULDN'T YOU SAY, TOJI?!
klak klak
CAN'T TELL, MAN! I'M SO HUNGRY IT COULD BE DOG POOP.
UM...

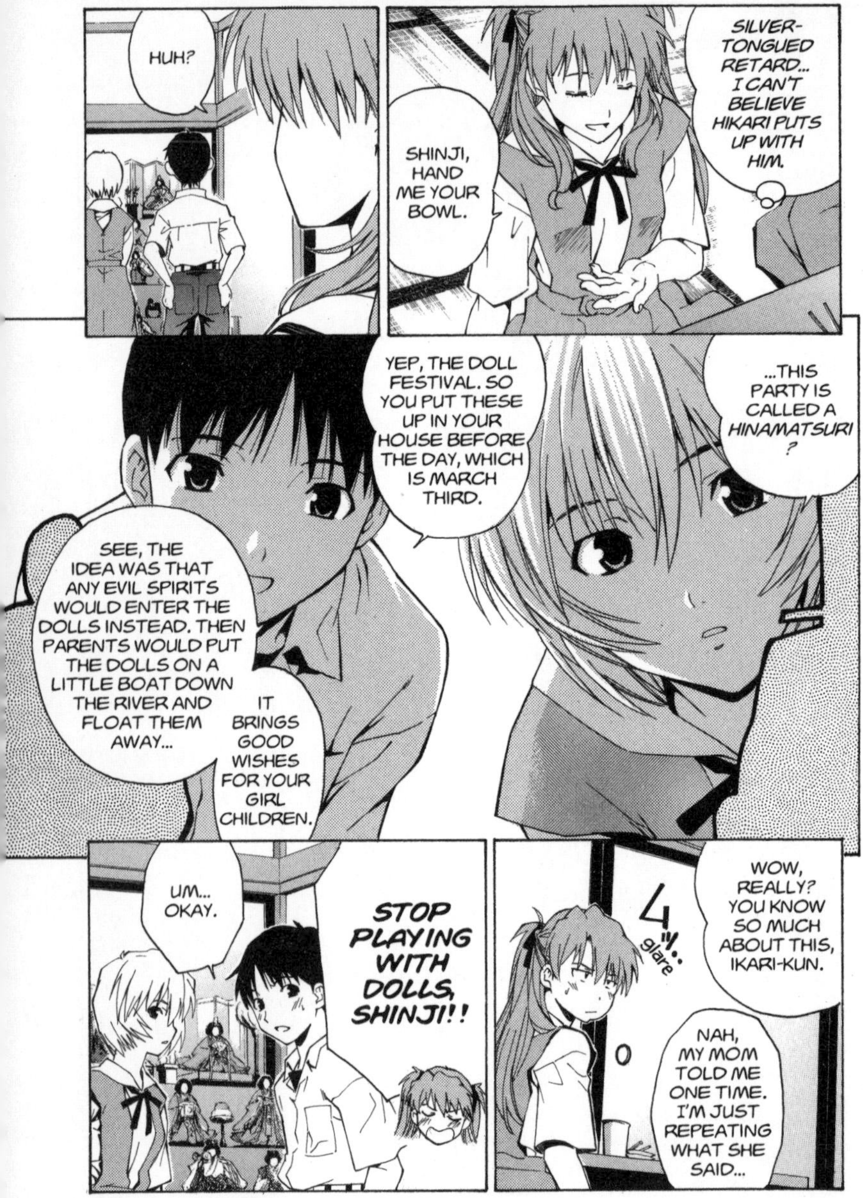
SILVER-TONGUED RETARD... I CAN'T BELIEVE HIKARI PUTS UP WITH HIM.
SHINJI, HAND ME YOUR BOWL.
HUH?
...THIS PARTY IS CALLED A HINAMATSURI?
YEP, THE DOLL FESTIVAL. SO YOU PUT THESE UP IN YOUR HOUSE BEFORE THE DAY, WHICH IS MARCH THIRD.
SEE, THE IDEA WAS THAT ANY EVIL SPIRITS WOULD ENTER THE DOLLS INSTEAD. THEN PARENTS WOULD PUT THE DOLLS ON A LITTLE BOAT DOWN THE RIVER AND FLOAT THEM AWAY...
IT BRINGS GOOD WISHES FOR YOUR GIRL CHILDREN.
WOW, REALLY? YOU KNOW SO MUCH ABOUT THIS, IKARI-KUN.
glare
NAH, MY MOM TOLD ME ONE TIME. I'M JUST REPEATING WHAT SHE SAID...
STOP PLAYING WITH DOLLS, SHINJI!!
UM... OKAY.

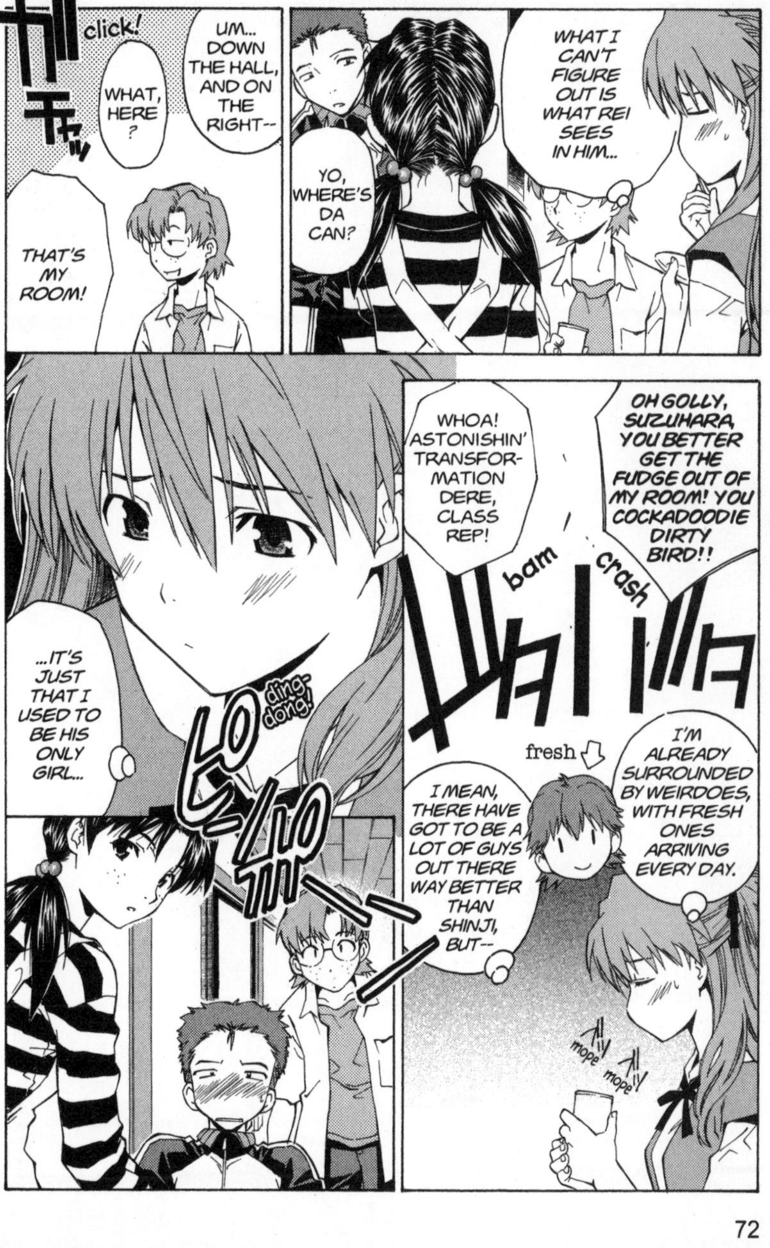
WHAT I CAN'T FIGURE OUT IS WHAT REI SEES IN HIM...
YO, WHERE'S DA CAN?
UM... DOWN THE HALL, AND ON THE RIGHT--
click!
WHAT, HERE?
THAT'S MY ROOM!
OH GOLLY, SUZUHARA, YOU BETTER GET THE FUDGE OUT OF MY ROOM! YOU COCKADOODIE DIRTY BIRD!!
WHOA! ASTONISHIN' TRANSFORMATION DERE, CLASS REP!
crash
bam
I'M ALREADY SURROUNDED BY WEIRDOES, WITH FRESH ONES ARRIVING EVERY DAY.
fresh
I MEAN, THERE HAVE GOT TO BE A LOT OF GUYS OUT THERE WAY BETTER THAN SHINJI, BUT--
mope
mope
...IT'S JUST THAT I USED TO BE HIS ONLY GIRL...
ding-dong!

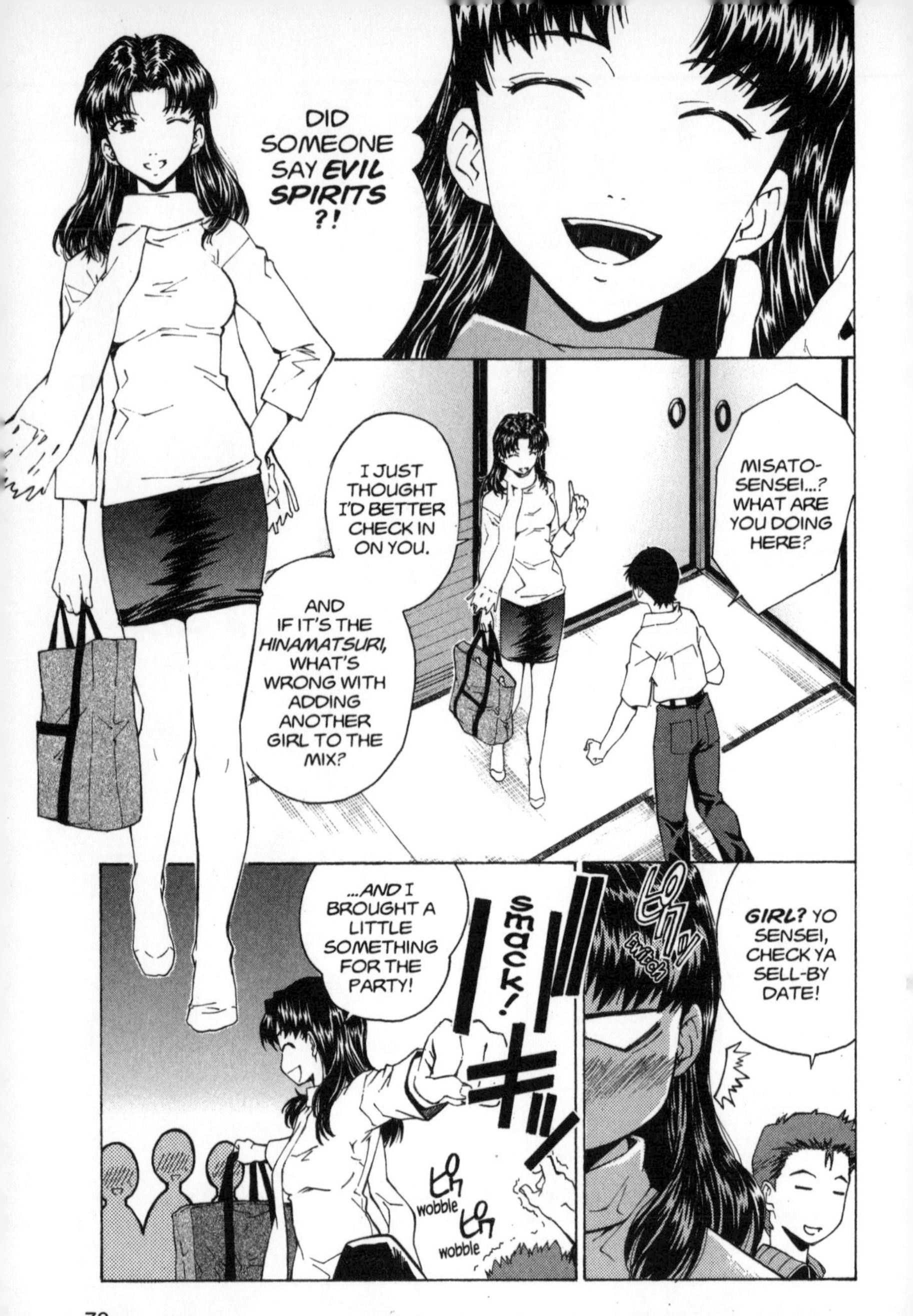
DID SOMEONE SAY EVIL SPIRITS?!
MISATO-SENSEI...? WHAT ARE YOU DOING HERE?
I JUST THOUGHT I'D BETTER CHECK IN ON YOU.
AND IF IT'S THE HINAMATSURI, WHAT'S WRONG WITH ADDING ANOTHER GIRL TO THE MIX?
GIRL? YO SENSEI, CHECK YA SELL-BY DATE!
twitch
...AND I BROUGHT A LITTLE SOMETHING FOR THE PARTY!
smack!
wobble
wobble

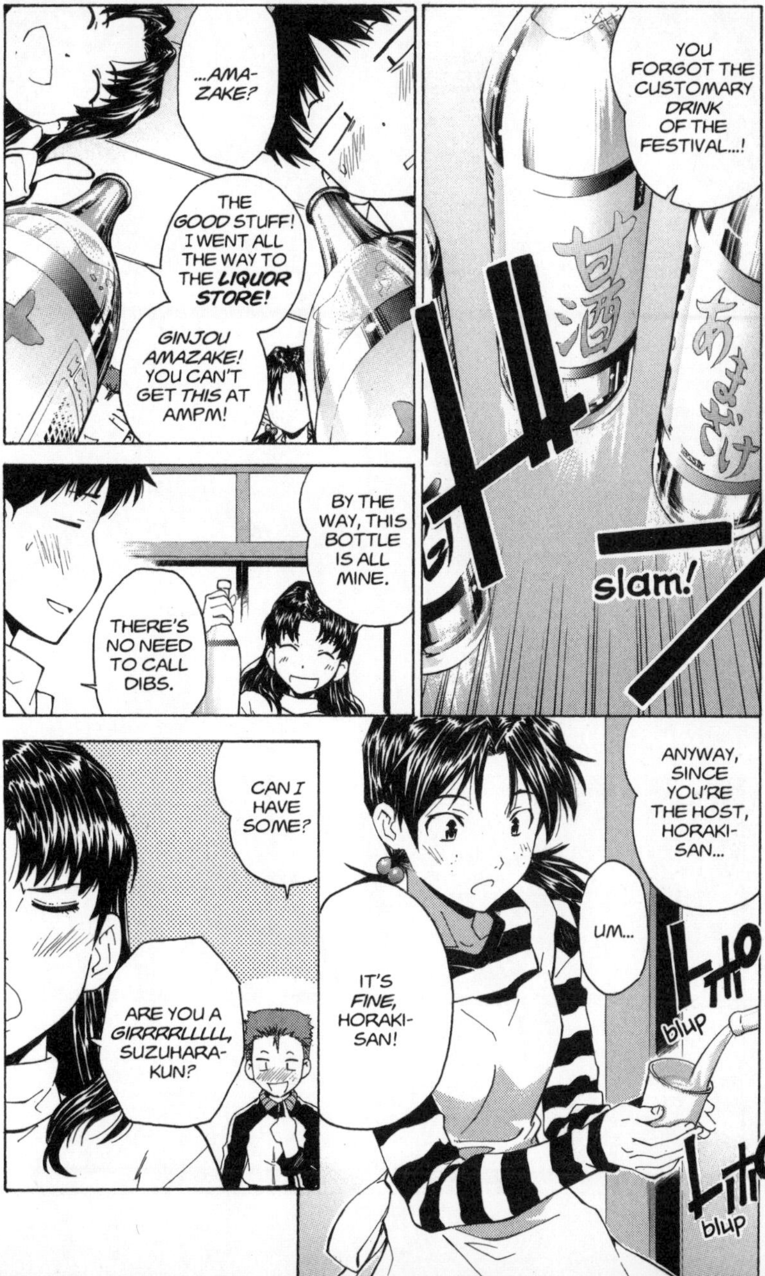

YOU FORGOT THE CUSTOMARY DRINK OF THE FESTIVAL...!
甘酒
あまざけ
slam!
...AMA-ZAKE?
THE GOOD STUFF! I WENT ALL THE WAY TO THE LIQUOR STORE!
GINJOU AMAZAKE! YOU CAN'T GET THIS AT AMPM!
BY THE WAY, THIS BOTTLE IS ALL MINE.
THERE'S NO NEED TO CALL DIBS.
ANYWAY, SINCE YOU'RE THE HOST, HORAKI-SAN...
UM...
IT'S FINE, HORAKI-SAN!
blup
blup
CAN I HAVE SOME?
ARE YOU A GIRRRRLLLLL, SUZUHARA-KUN?

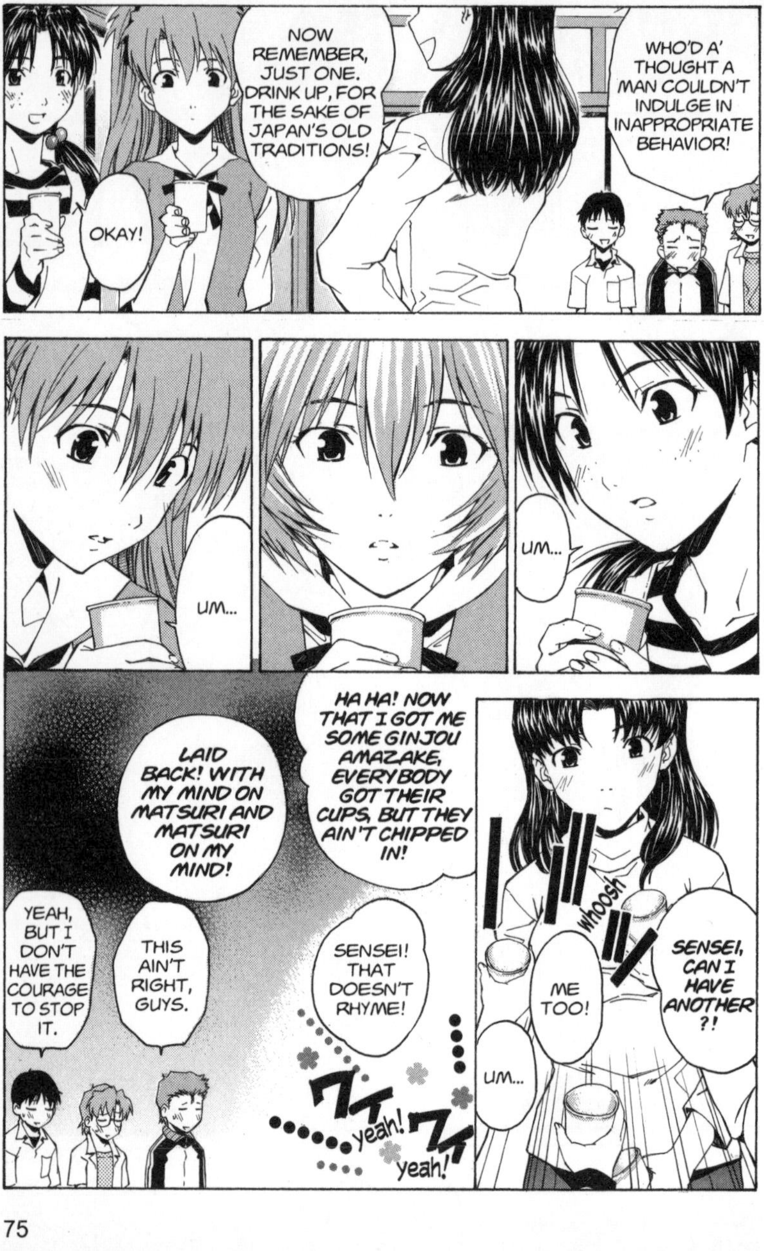

WHO'D A' THOUGHT A MAN COULDN'T INDULGE IN INAPPROPRIATE BEHAVIOR!
NOW REMEMBER, JUST ONE. DRINK UP, FOR THE SAKE OF JAPAN'S OLD TRADITIONS!
OKAY!
UM...
UM...
whoosh
SENSEI, CAN I HAVE ANOTHER?!
ME TOO!
UM...
HA HA! NOW THAT I GOT ME SOME GINJOU AMAZAKE, EVERYBODY GOT THEIR CUPS, BUT THEY AIN'T CHIPPED IN!
LAID BACK! WITH MY MIND ON MATSURI AND MATSURI ON MY MIND!
SENSEI! THAT DOESN'T RHYME!
ワイ yeah!
ワイ yeah!
THIS AIN'T RIGHT, GUYS.
YEAH, BUT I DON'T HAVE THE COURAGE TO STOP IT.

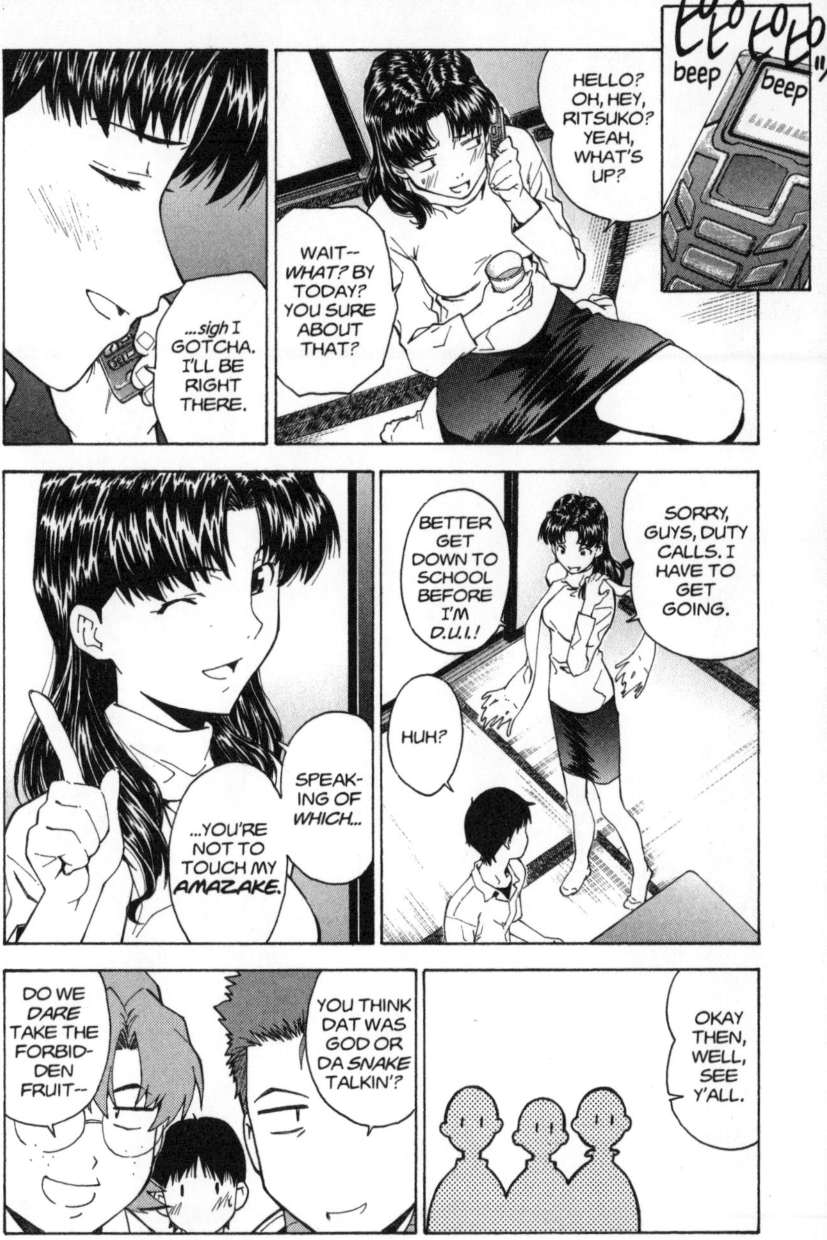

beep beep
HELLO? OH, HEY, RITSUKO? YEAH, WHAT'S UP?
WAIT-- *WHAT?* BY TODAY? YOU SURE ABOUT THAT?
...*sigh* I GOTCHA. I'LL BE RIGHT THERE.
SORRY, GUYS, DUTY CALLS. I HAVE TO GET GOING.
BETTER GET DOWN TO SCHOOL BEFORE I'M *D.U.I.!*
HUH?
SPEAK-ING OF *WHICH...*
...YOU'RE NOT TO TOUCH MY ***AMAZAKE.***
OKAY THEN, WELL, SEE Y'ALL.
YOU THINK DAT WAS GOD OR DA *SNAKE* TALKIN'?
DO WE *DARE* TAKE THE FORBID-DEN FRUIT--

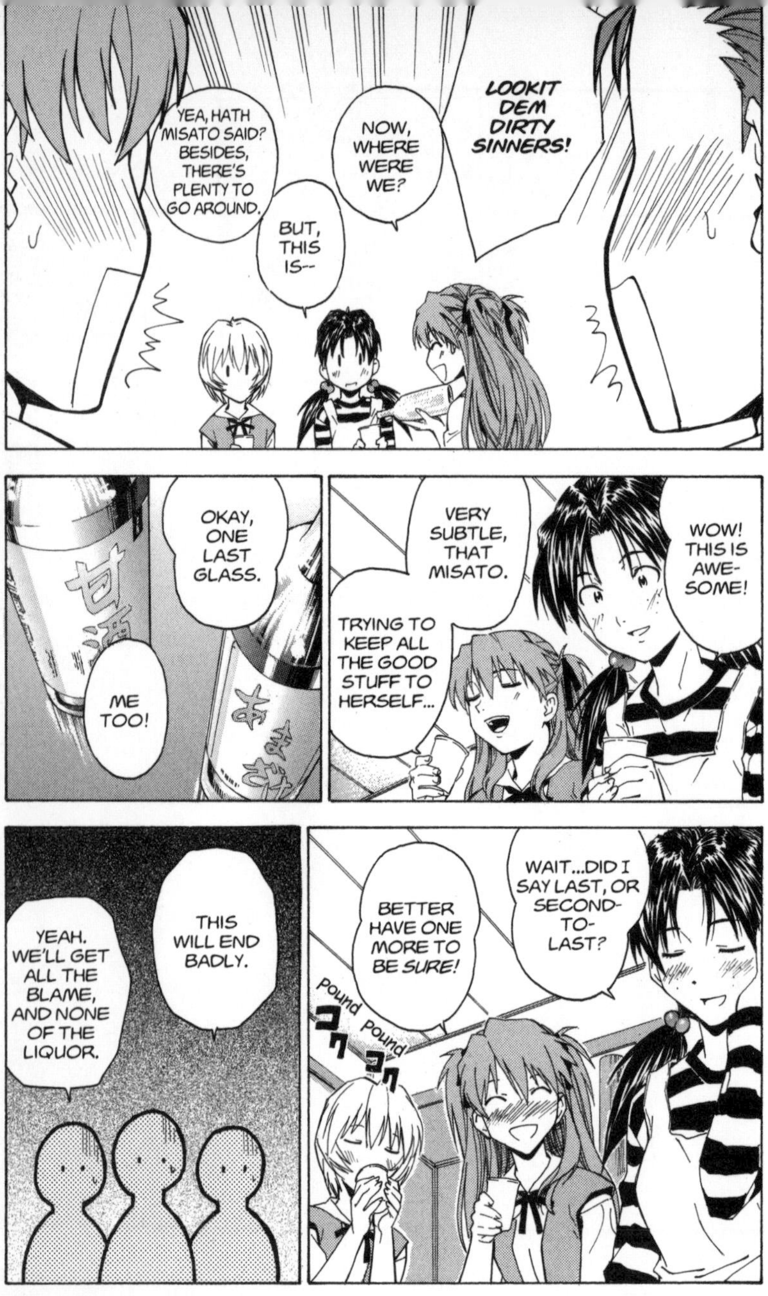
LOOKIT DEM DIRTY SINNERS!
NOW, WHERE WERE WE?
BUT, THIS IS--
YEA, HATH MISATO SAID? BESIDES, THERE'S PLENTY TO GO AROUND.
WOW! THIS IS AWE-SOME!
VERY SUBTLE, THAT MISATO.
TRYING TO KEEP ALL THE GOOD STUFF TO HERSELF...
OKAY, ONE LAST GLASS.
ME TOO!
WAIT...DID I SAY LAST, OR SECOND-TO-LAST?
BETTER HAVE ONE MORE TO BE *SURE*!
Pound Pound
THIS WILL END BADLY.
YEAH. WE'LL GET ALL THE BLAME, AND NONE OF THE LIQUOR.

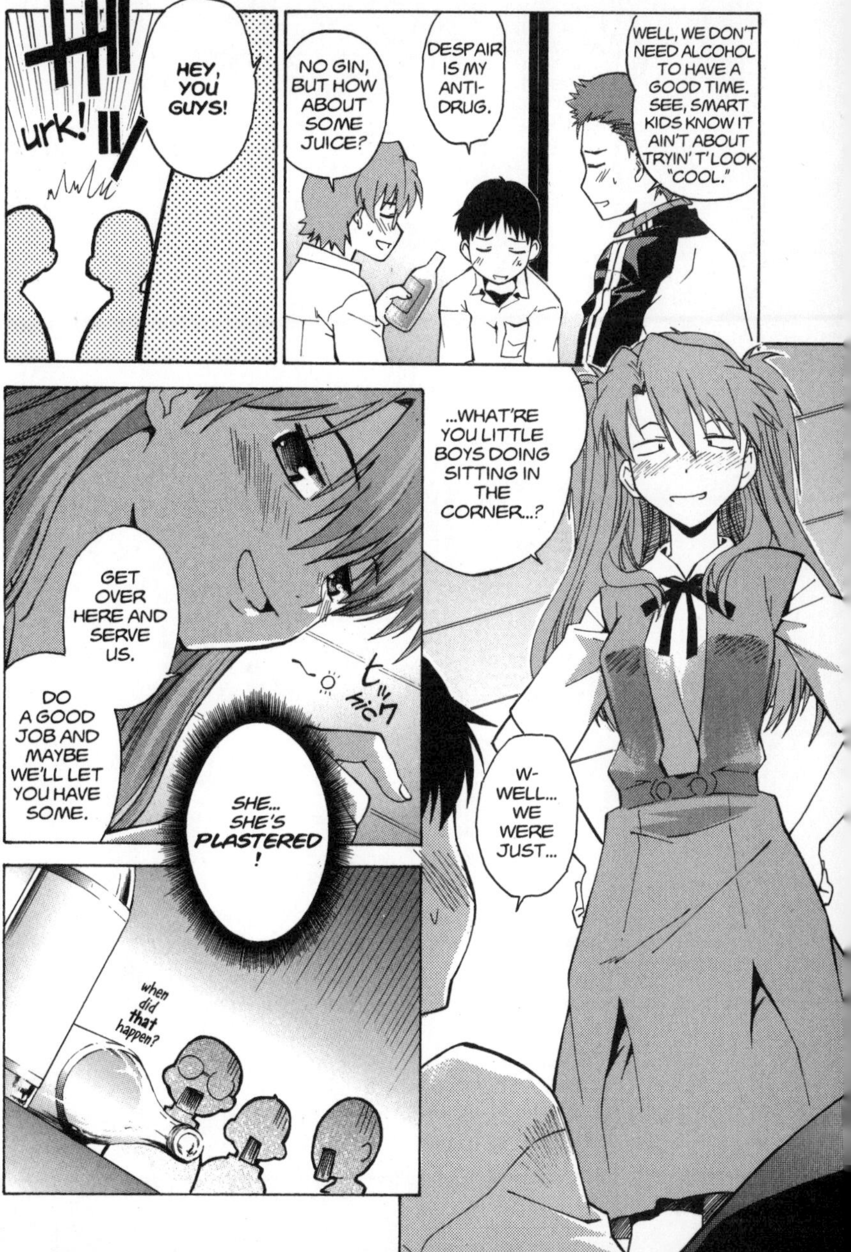

WELL, WE DON'T NEED ALCOHOL TO HAVE A GOOD TIME. SEE, SMART KIDS KNOW IT AIN'T ABOUT TRYIN' T'LOOK "COOL."
DESPAIR IS MY ANTI-DRUG.
NO GIN, BUT HOW ABOUT SOME JUICE?
HEY, YOU GUYS!
urk!
...WHAT'RE YOU LITTLE BOYS DOING SITTING IN THE CORNER...?
W-WELL... WE WERE JUST...
GET OVER HERE AND SERVE US.
DO A GOOD JOB AND MAYBE WE'LL LET YOU HAVE SOME.
hic
SHE... SHE'S PLASTERED!
when did that happen?

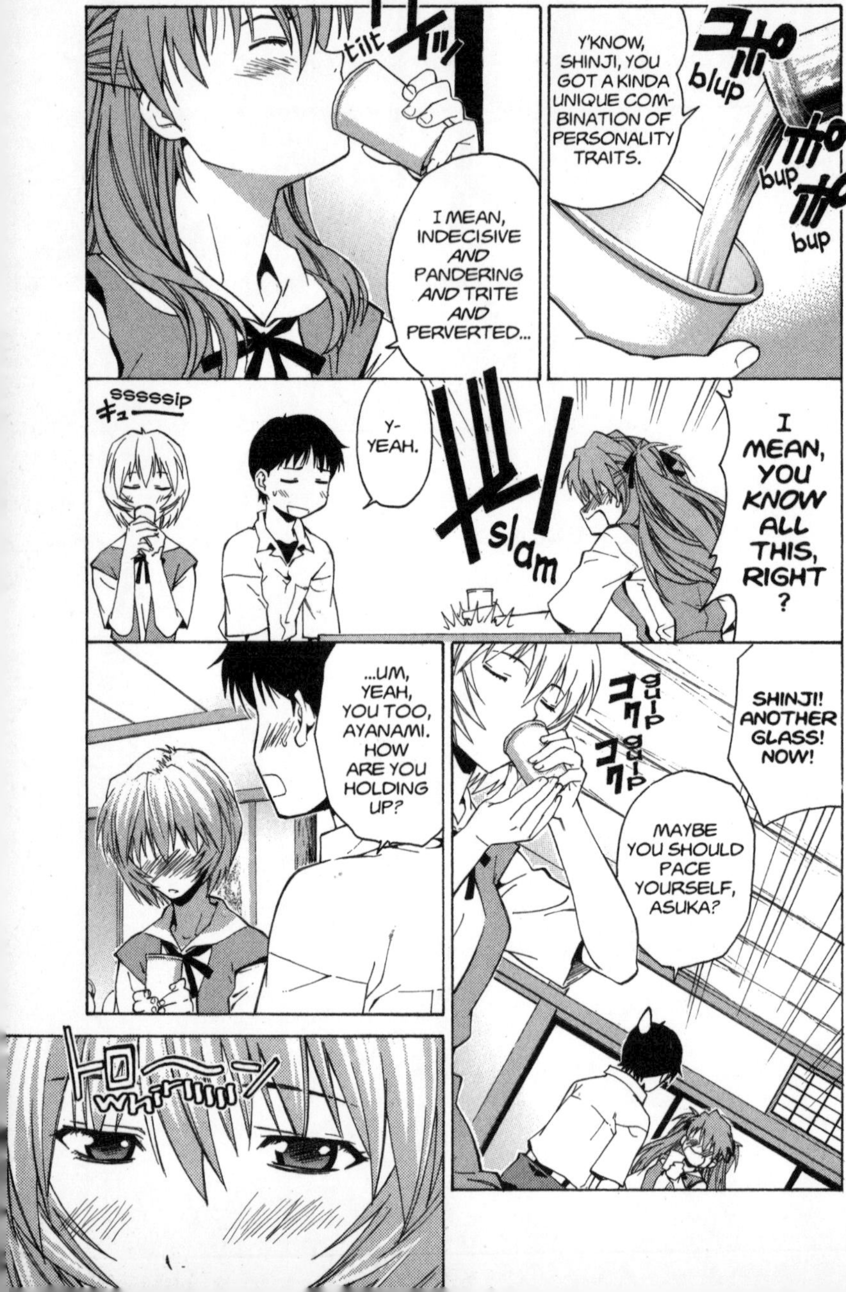
blup
bup
bup
Y'KNOW, SHINJI, YOU GOT A KINDA UNIQUE COMBINATION OF PERSONALITY TRAITS.
tilt
I MEAN, INDECISIVE AND PANDERING AND TRITE AND PERVERTED...
I MEAN, YOU KNOW ALL THIS, RIGHT?
slam
Y-YEAH.
sssssip
SHINJI! ANOTHER GLASS! NOW!
gulp
gulp
MAYBE YOU SHOULD PACE YOURSELF, ASUKA?
...UM, YEAH, YOU TOO, AYANAMI. HOW ARE YOU HOLDING UP?
whirllllll

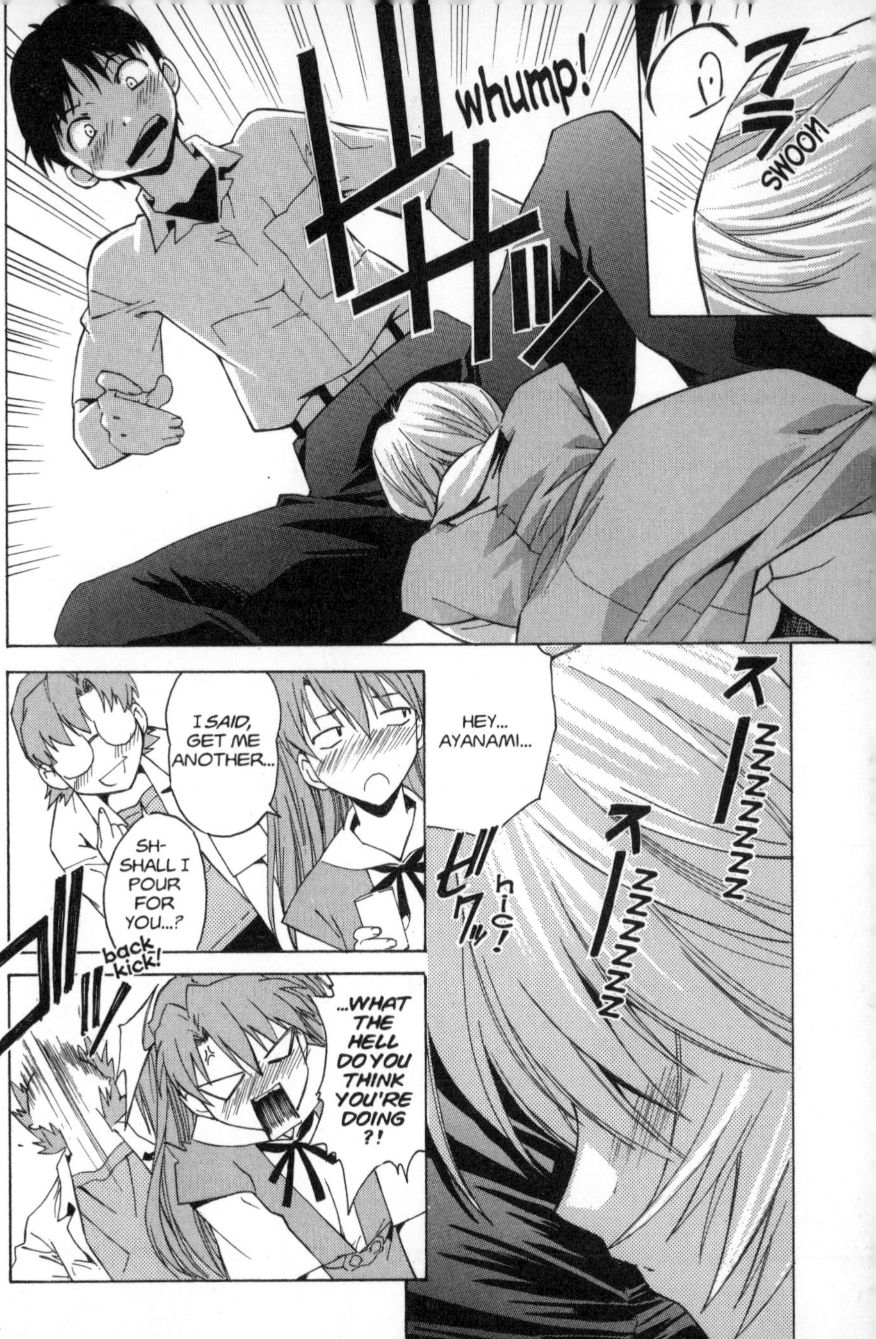
SWOON
whump!
HEY... AYANAMI...
ZZZZZZZZ
ZZZZZZZ
hic!
I SAID, GET ME ANOTHER...
SH- SHALL I POUR FOR YOU...?
back kick!
...WHAT THE HELL DO YOU THINK YOU'RE DOING?!

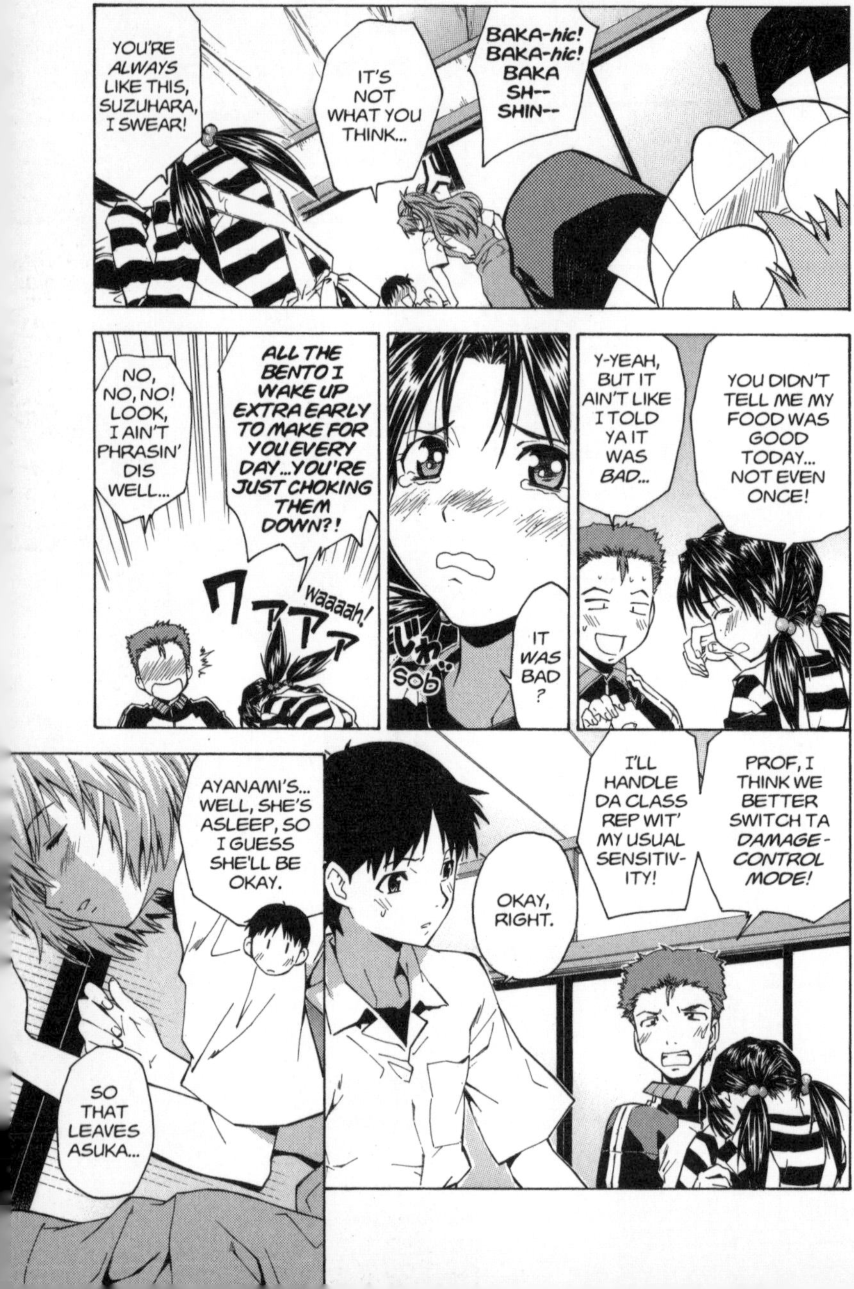
BAKA-*hic!* BAKA-*hic!* BAKA SH-- SHIN--
IT'S NOT WHAT YOU THINK...
YOU'RE *ALWAYS* LIKE THIS, SUZUHARA, I SWEAR!
YOU DIDN'T TELL ME MY FOOD WAS GOOD TODAY... NOT EVEN ONCE!
Y-YEAH, BUT IT AIN'T LIKE I TOLD YA IT WAS *BAD*...
IT WAS BAD?
sob
ALL THE BENTO I WAKE UP EXTRA EARLY TO MAKE FOR YOU EVERY DAY...YOU'RE JUST CHOKING THEM DOWN?!
NO, NO, NO! LOOK, I AIN'T PHRASIN' DIS WELL...
waaaah!
PROF, I THINK WE BETTER SWITCH TA *DAMAGE-CONTROL MODE!*
I'LL HANDLE DA CLASS REP WIT' MY USUAL SENSITIV-ITY!
OKAY, RIGHT.
AYANAMI'S... WELL, SHE'S ASLEEP, SO I GUESS SHE'LL BE OKAY.
SO THAT LEAVES ASUKA...

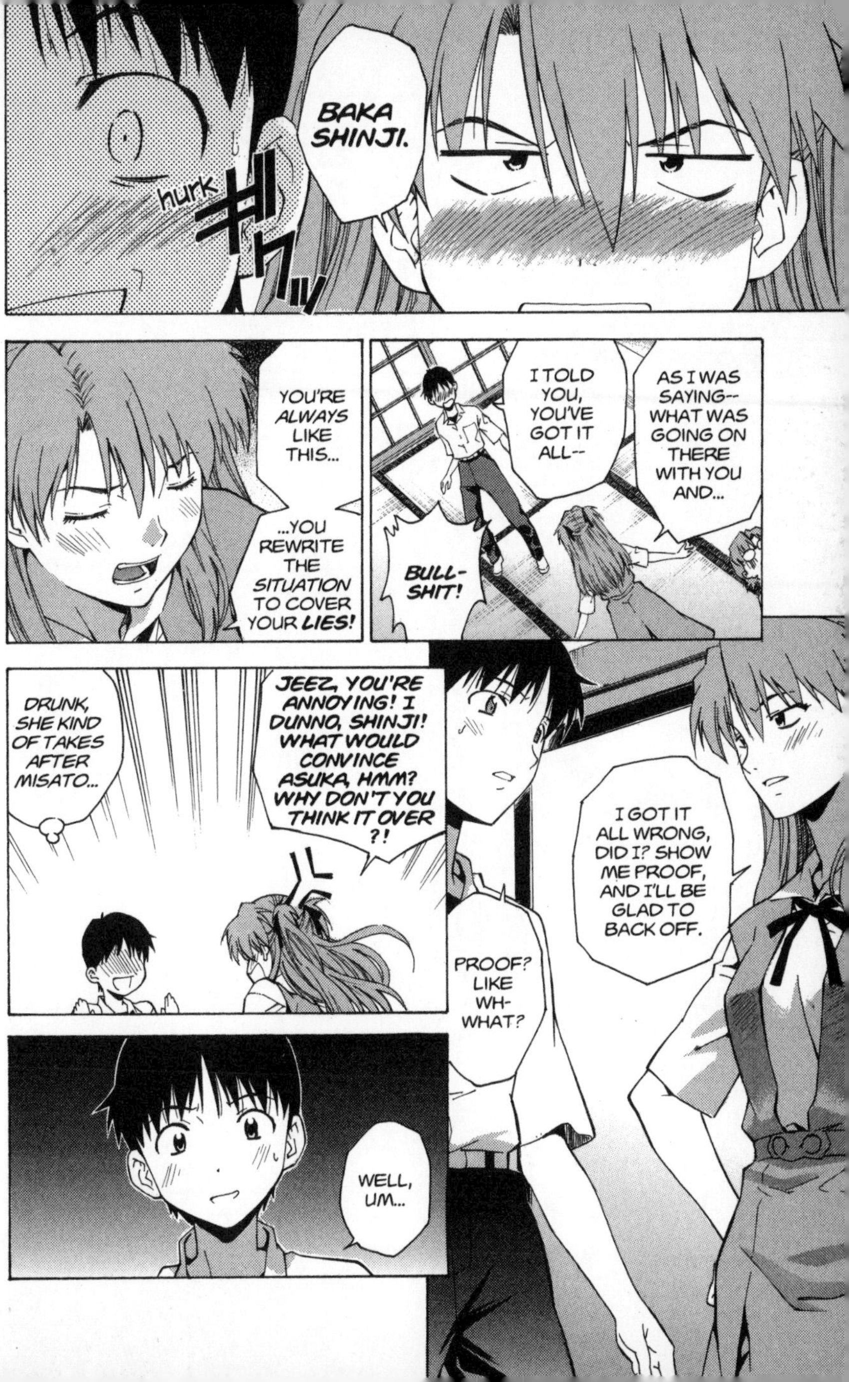
BAKA SHINJI.
hurk
AS I WAS SAYING-- WHAT WAS GOING ON THERE WITH YOU AND...
I TOLD YOU, YOU'VE GOT IT ALL--
BULL-SHIT!
YOU'RE ALWAYS LIKE THIS...
...YOU REWRITE THE SITUATION TO COVER YOUR LIES!
I GOT IT ALL WRONG, DID I? SHOW ME PROOF, AND I'LL BE GLAD TO BACK OFF.
PROOF? LIKE WH-WHAT?
JEEZ, YOU'RE ANNOYING! I DUNNO, SHINJI! WHAT WOULD CONVINCE ASUKA, HMM? WHY DON'T YOU THINK IT OVER ?!
DRUNK, SHE KIND OF TAKES AFTER MISATO...
WELL, UM...

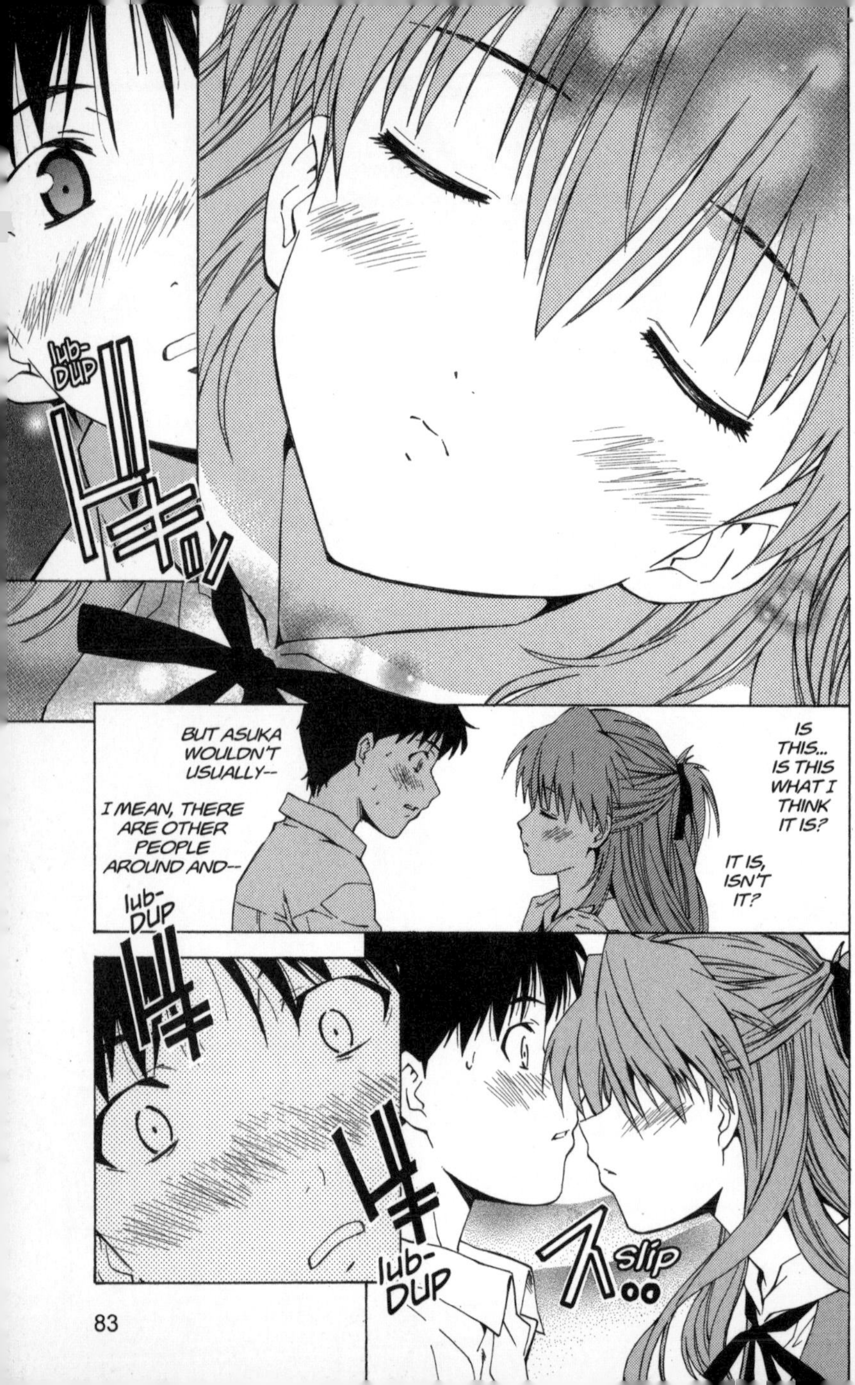
lub-DUP
IS THIS... IS THIS WHAT I THINK IT IS?
IT IS, ISN'T IT?
BUT ASUKA WOULDN'T USUALLY--
I MEAN, THERE ARE OTHER PEOPLE AROUND AND--
lub-DUP
slip
lub-DUP

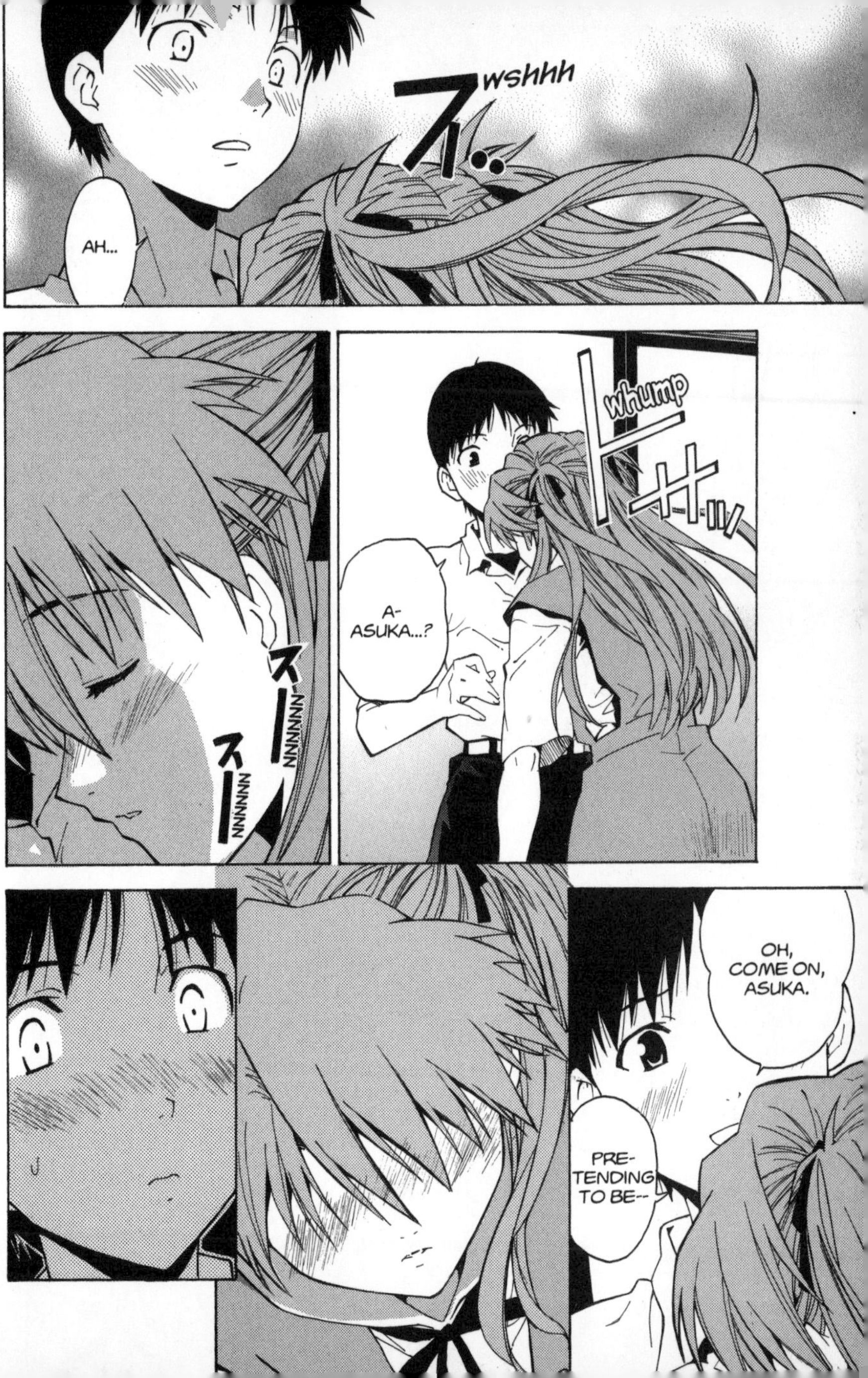
wshhh
AH...
whump
A-ASUKA...?
スー
スー
OH, COME ON, ASUKA.
PRE-TENDING TO BE--

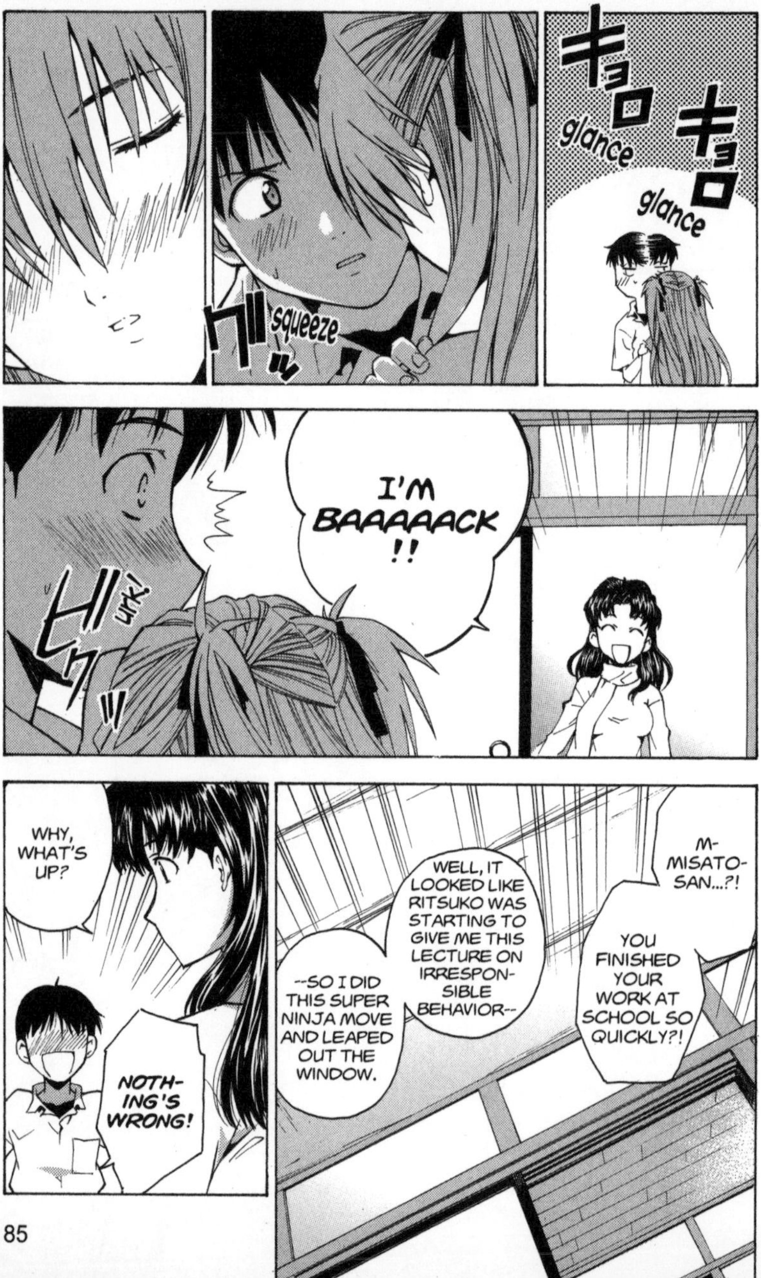
キョロ
glance
キョロ
glance
squeeze
I'M BAAAAACK!!
urk!
M-MISATO-SAN...?!
YOU FINISHED YOUR WORK AT SCHOOL SO QUICKLY?!
WELL, IT LOOKED LIKE RITSUKO WAS STARTING TO GIVE ME THIS LECTURE ON IRRESPONSIBLE BEHAVIOR--
--SO I DID THIS SUPER NINJA MOVE AND LEAPED OUT THE WINDOW.
WHY, WHAT'S UP?
NOTHING'S WRONG!

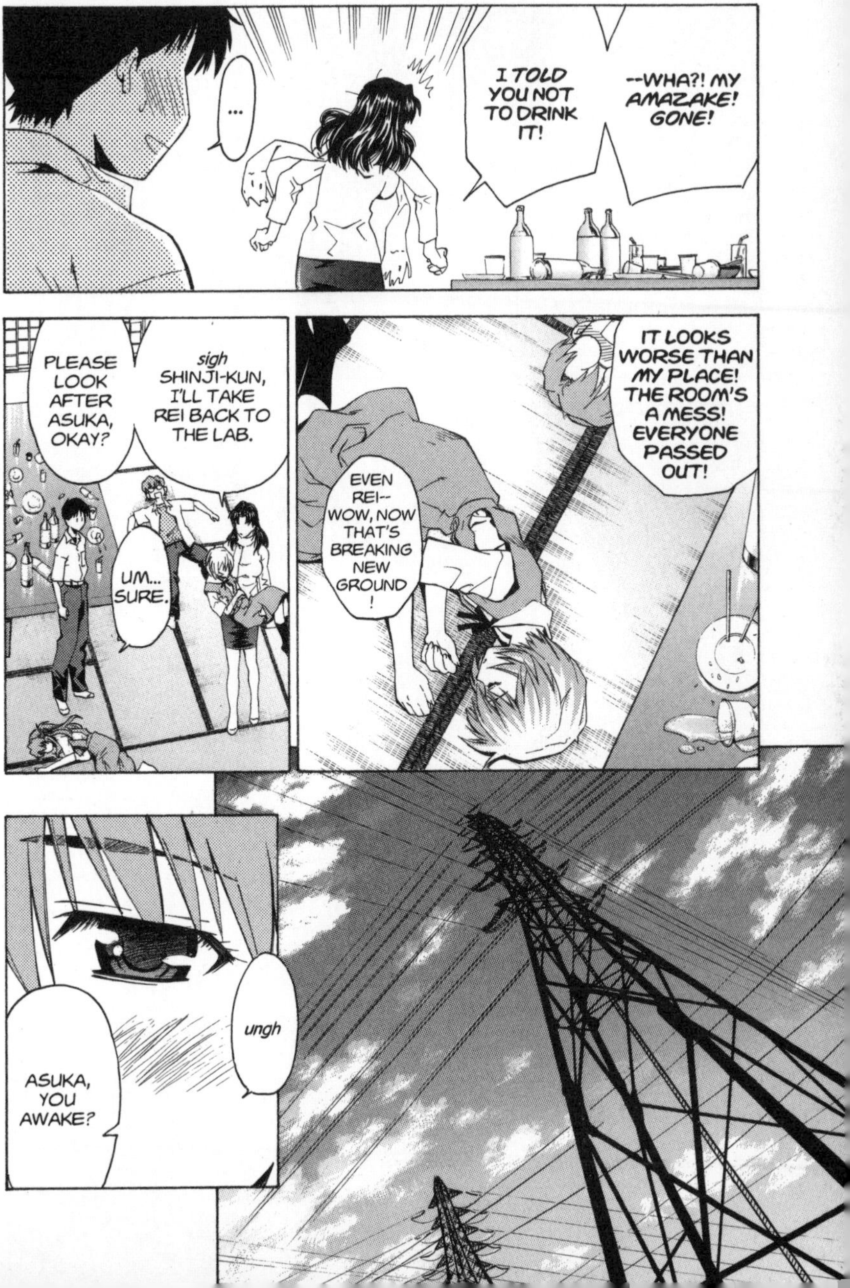
--WHA?! MY AMAZAKE! GONE!
I TOLD YOU NOT TO DRINK IT!
...
IT LOOKS WORSE THAN MY PLACE! THE ROOM'S A MESS! EVERYONE PASSED OUT!
EVEN REI-- WOW, NOW THAT'S BREAKING NEW GROUND!
sigh SHINJI-KUN, I'LL TAKE REI BACK TO THE LAB.
PLEASE LOOK AFTER ASUKA, OKAY?
UM... SURE.
ungh
ASUKA, YOU AWAKE?

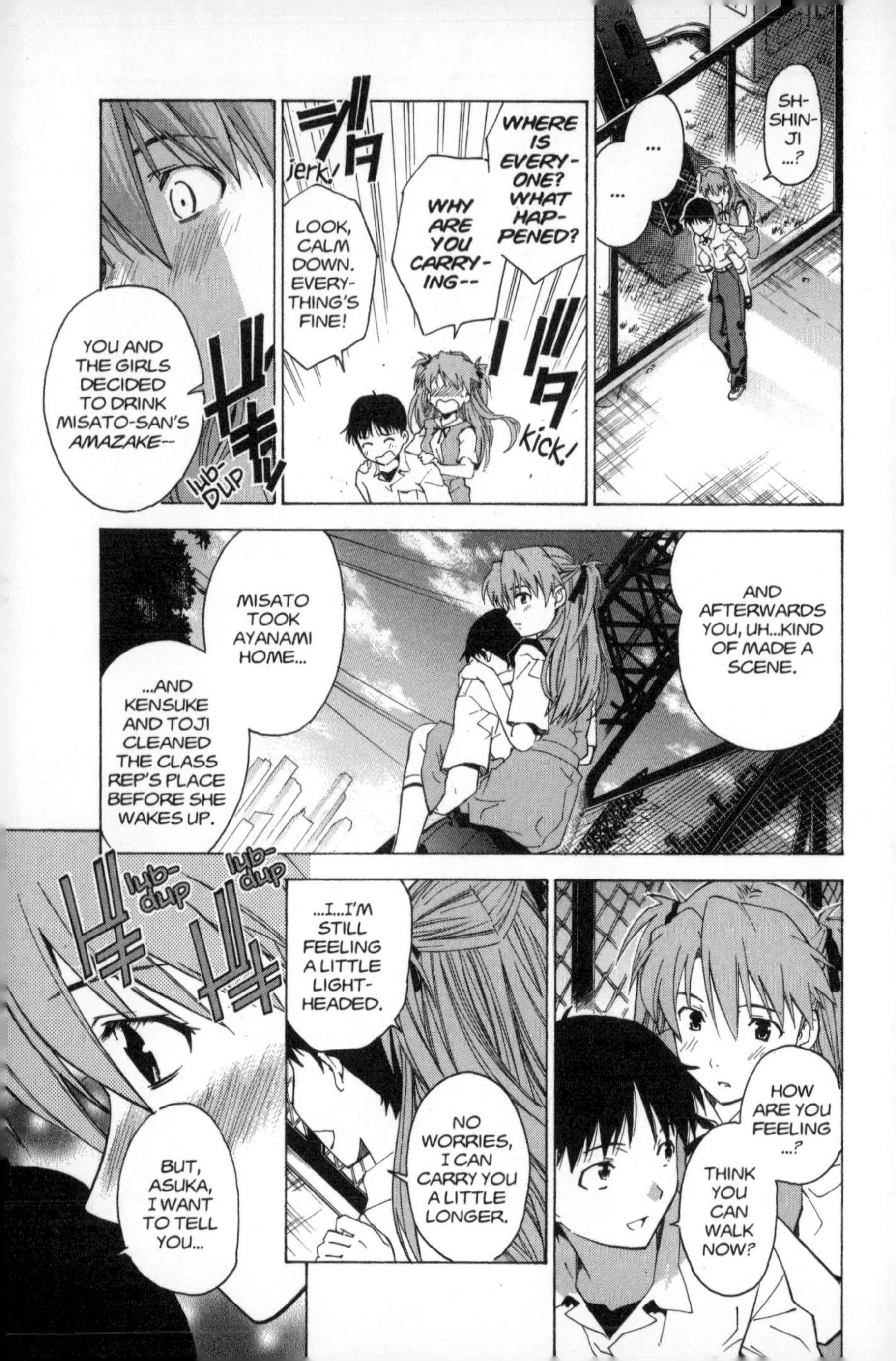
SH-SHIN-JI ...?
...
...
WHERE IS EVERYONE? WHAT HAPPENED?
WHY ARE YOU CARRYING--
jerk!
kick!
LOOK, CALM DOWN. EVERYTHING'S FINE!
YOU AND THE GIRLS DECIDED TO DRINK MISATO-SAN'S AMAZAKE--
lub-DUP
AND AFTERWARDS YOU, UH...KIND OF MADE A SCENE.
MISATO TOOK AYANAMI HOME...
...AND KENSUKE AND TOJI CLEANED THE CLASS REP'S PLACE BEFORE SHE WAKES UP.
HOW ARE YOU FEELING ...?
THINK YOU CAN WALK NOW?
...I...I'M STILL FEELING A LITTLE LIGHT-HEADED.
NO WORRIES, I CAN CARRY YOU A LITTLE LONGER.
lub-dup
lub-dup
BUT, ASUKA, I WANT TO TELL YOU...

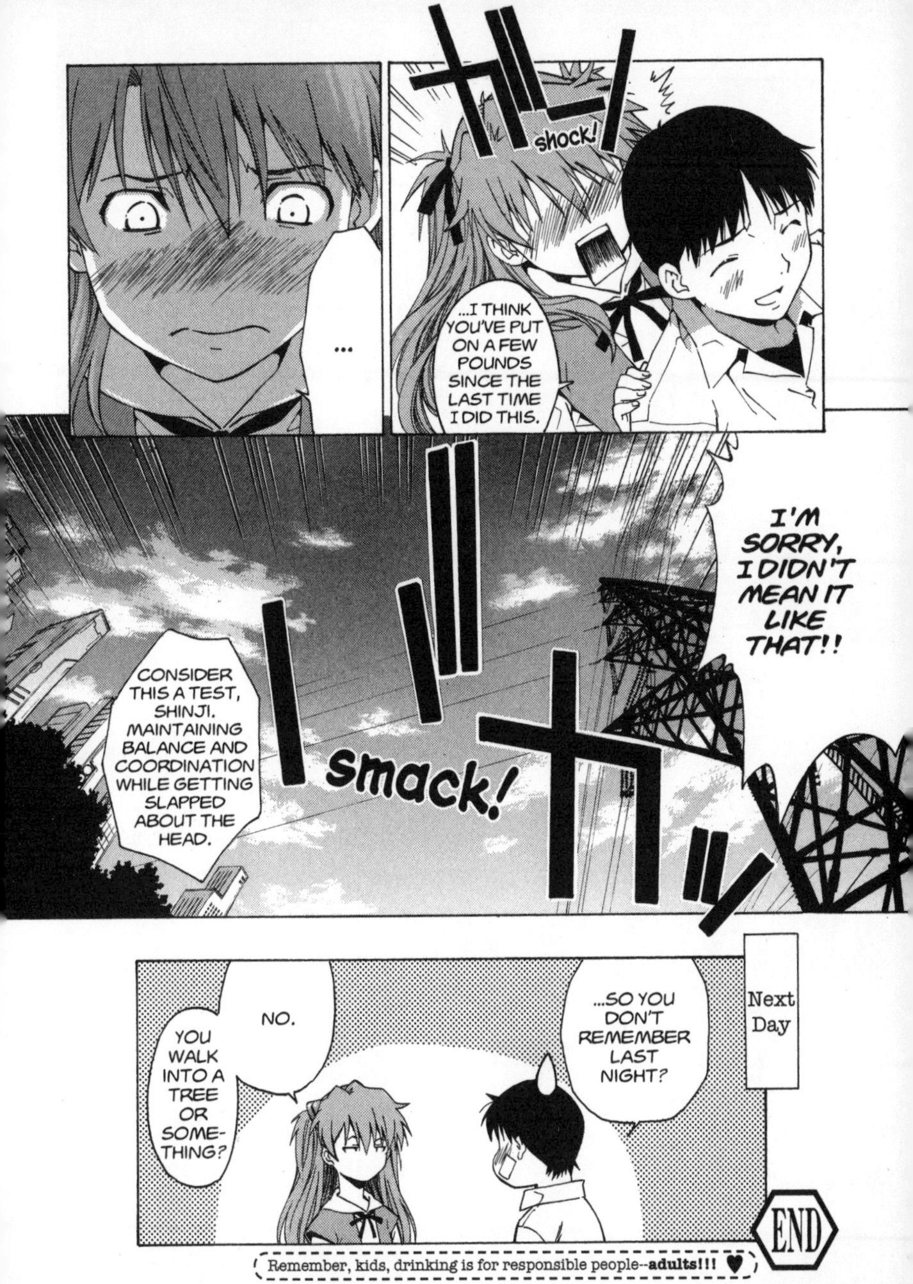
shock!
...I THINK YOU'VE PUT ON A FEW POUNDS SINCE THE LAST TIME I DID THIS.
...
I'M SORRY, I DIDN'T MEAN IT LIKE THAT!!
smack!
CONSIDER THIS A TEST, SHINJI. MAINTAINING BALANCE AND COORDINATION WHILE GETTING SLAPPED ABOUT THE HEAD.
Next Day
...SO YOU DON'T REMEMBER LAST NIGHT?
NO.
YOU WALK INTO A TREE OR SOME-THING?
END

Remember, kids, drinking is for responsible people--**adults!!!** ♥

NEON GENESIS
EVANGELION
THE SHINJI IKARI RAISING PROJECT

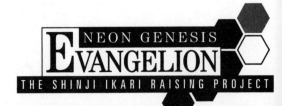

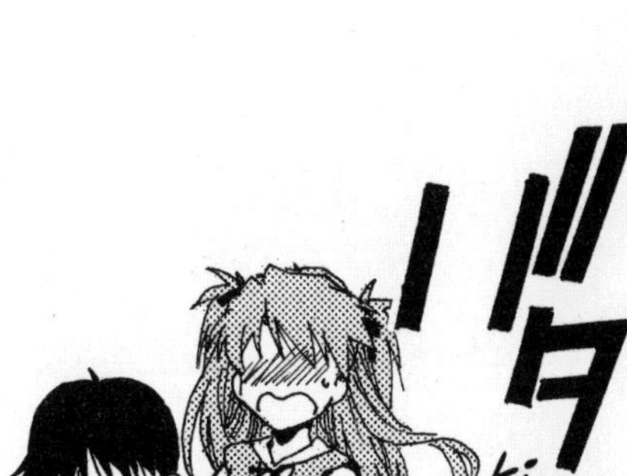
ドタ
KICK!

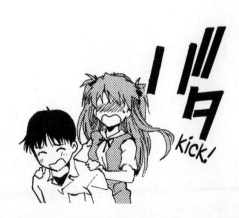

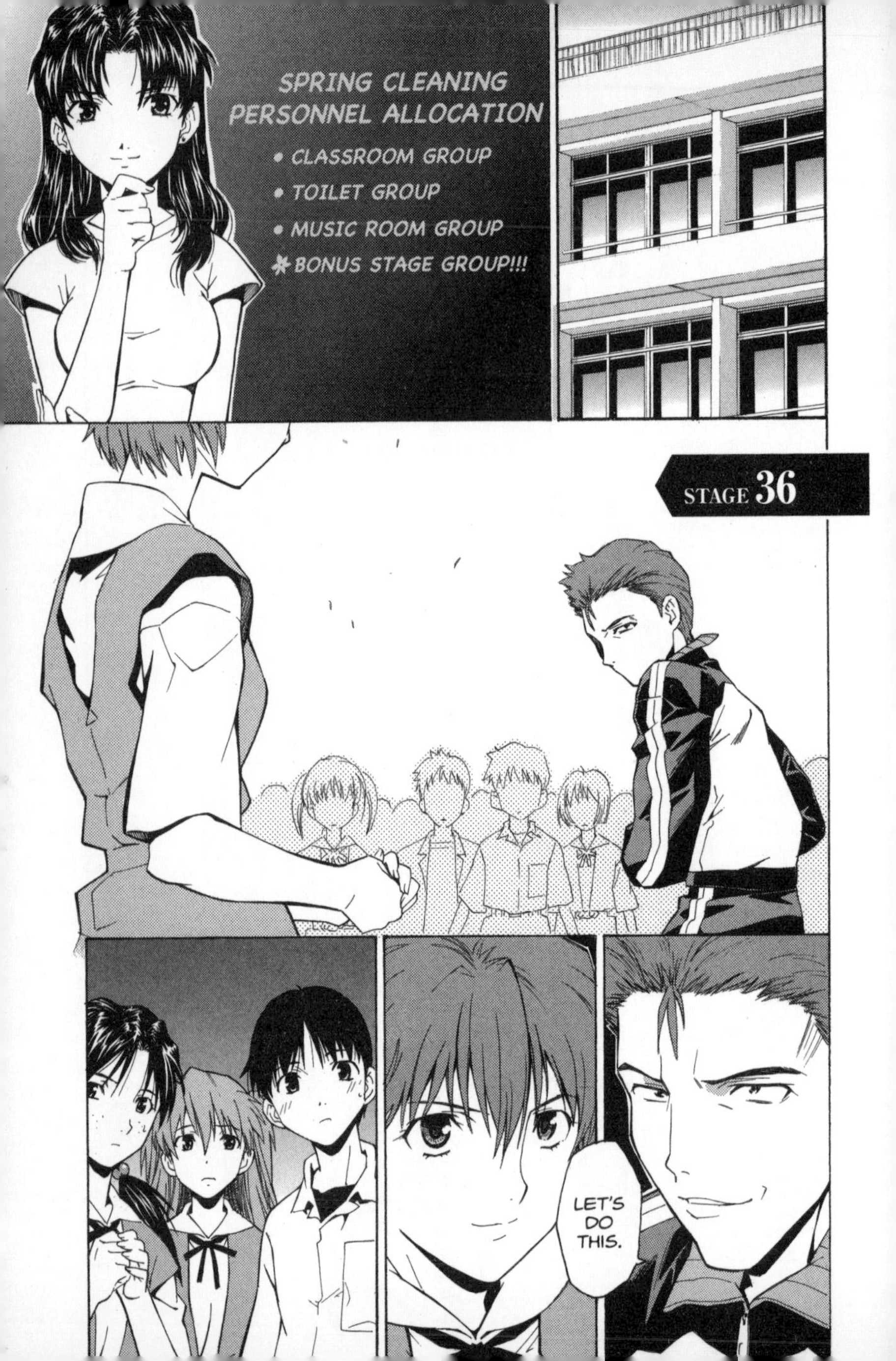
SPRING CLEANING
PERSONNEL ALLOCATION
• CLASSROOM GROUP
• TOILET GROUP
• MUSIC ROOM GROUP
✲ BONUS STAGE GROUP!!!
STAGE 36
LET'S DO THIS.

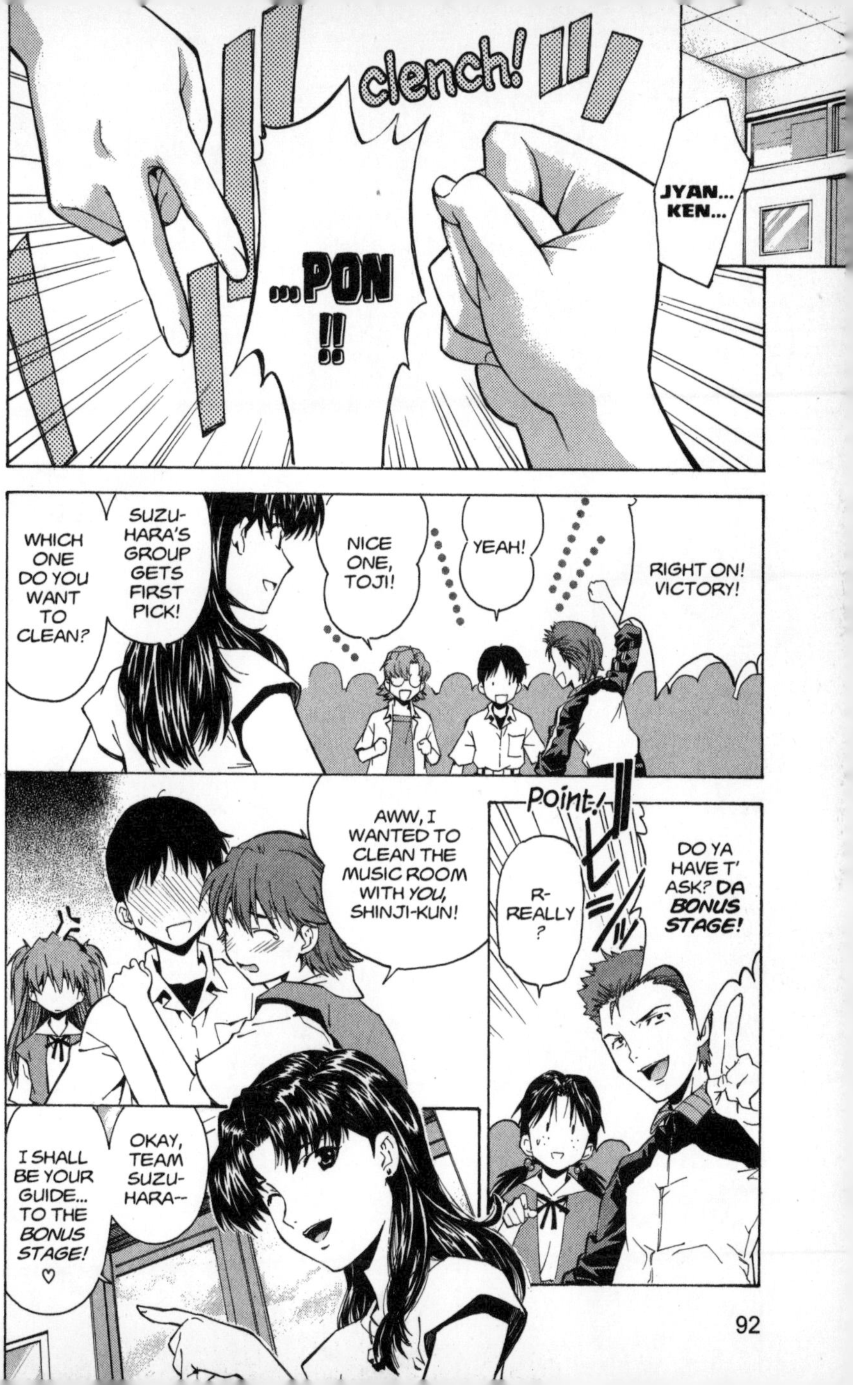

JYAN... KEN...
clench!
...PON !!
RIGHT ON! VICTORY!
YEAH!
NICE ONE, TOJI!
SUZU-HARA'S GROUP GETS FIRST PICK!
WHICH ONE DO YOU WANT TO CLEAN?
DO YA HAVE T' ASK? DA *BONUS STAGE!*
Point!
R-REALLY?
AWW, I WANTED TO CLEAN THE MUSIC ROOM WITH *YOU*, SHINJI-KUN!
OKAY, TEAM SUZU-HARA--
I SHALL BE YOUR GUIDE... TO THE *BONUS STAGE!* ♡

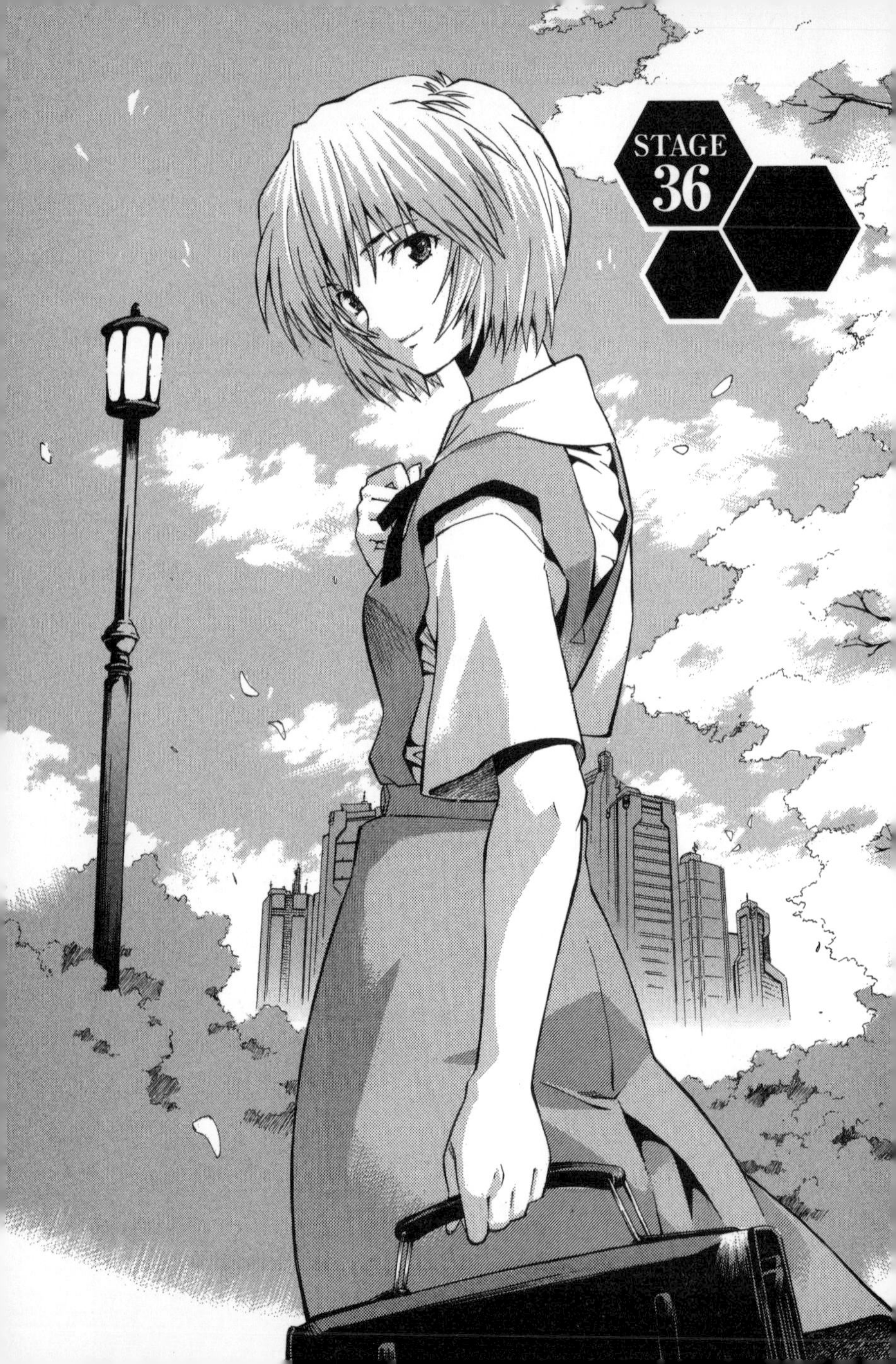
STAGE
36

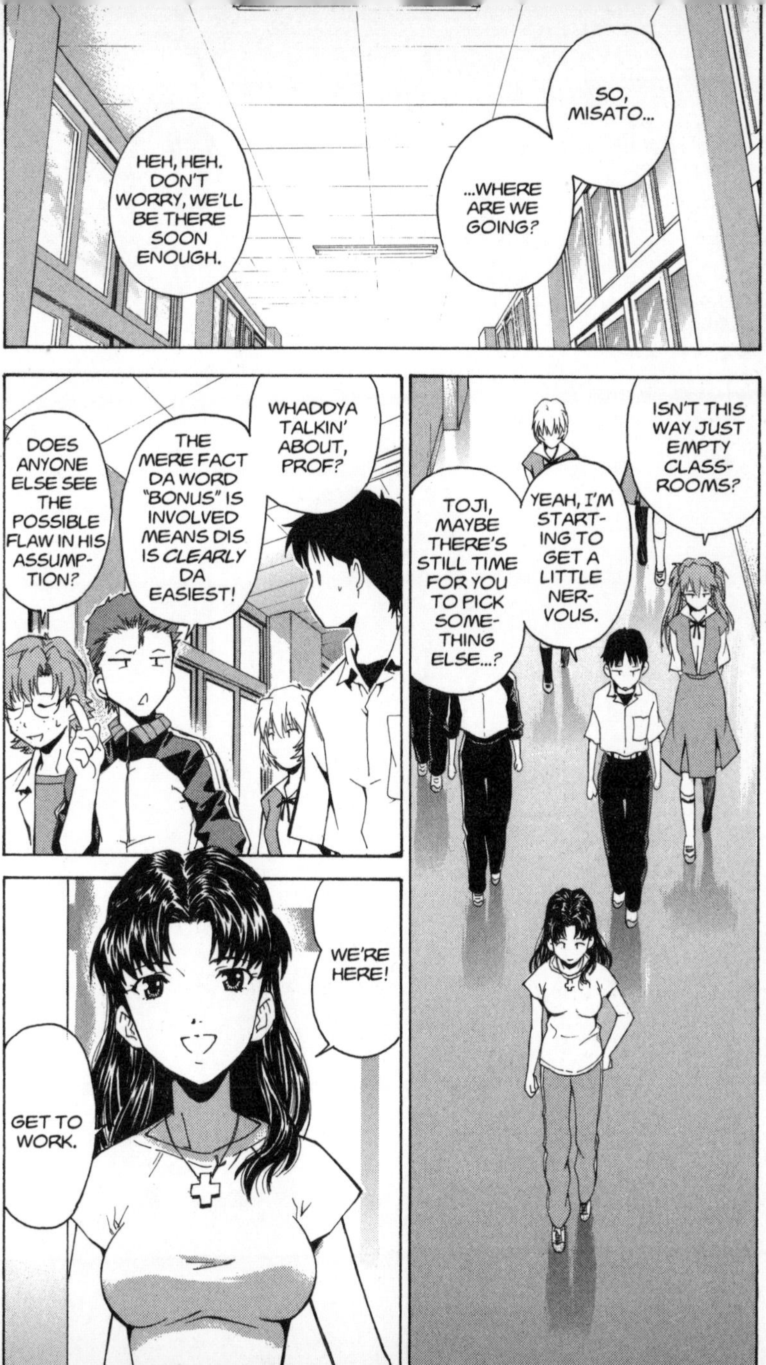
SO, MISATO...
...WHERE ARE WE GOING?
HEH, HEH. DON'T WORRY, WE'LL BE THERE SOON ENOUGH.
ISN'T THIS WAY JUST EMPTY CLASS-ROOMS?
YEAH, I'M START-ING TO GET A LITTLE NER-VOUS.
TOJI, MAYBE THERE'S STILL TIME FOR YOU TO PICK SOME-THING ELSE...?
WHADDYA TALKIN' ABOUT, PROF?
THE MERE FACT DA WORD "BONUS" IS INVOLVED MEANS DIS IS *CLEARLY* DA EASIEST!
DOES ANYONE ELSE SEE THE POSSIBLE FLAW IN HIS ASSUMP-TION?
WE'RE HERE!
GET TO WORK.

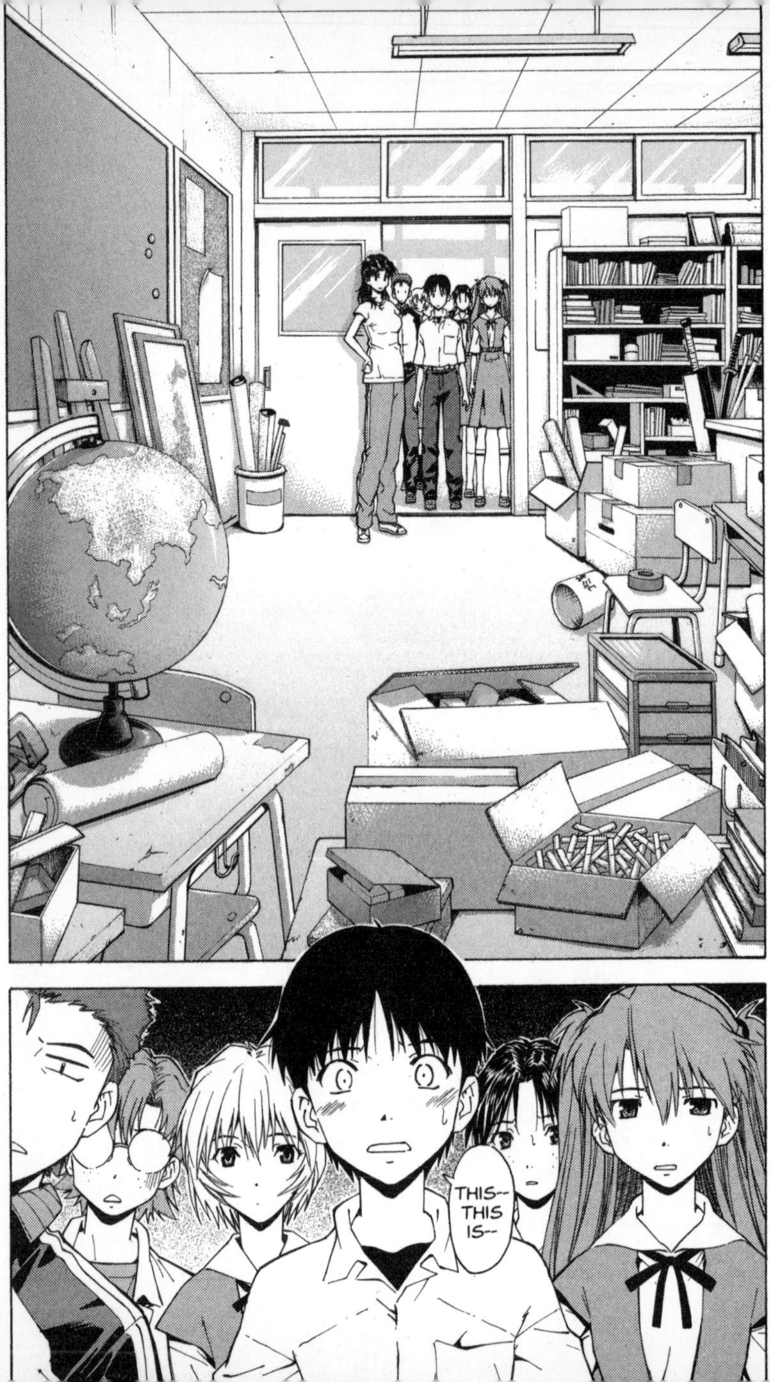
THIS-- THIS IS--

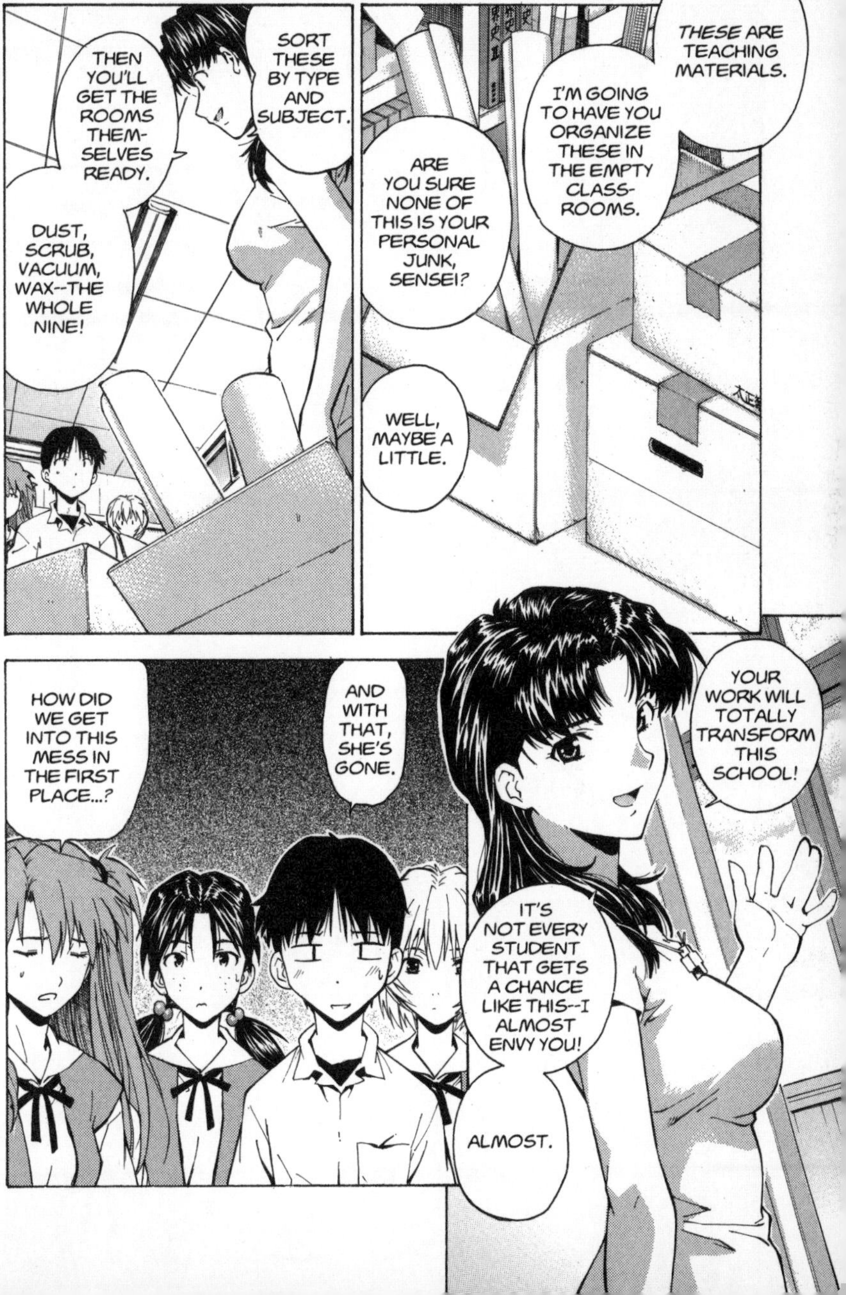
THESE ARE TEACHING MATERIALS.
I'M GOING TO HAVE YOU ORGANIZE THESE IN THE EMPTY CLASSROOMS.
ARE YOU SURE NONE OF THIS IS YOUR PERSONAL JUNK, SENSEI?
WELL, MAYBE A LITTLE.
SORT THESE BY TYPE AND SUBJECT.
THEN YOU'LL GET THE ROOMS THEMSELVES READY.
DUST, SCRUB, VACUUM, WAX--THE WHOLE NINE!
YOUR WORK WILL TOTALLY TRANSFORM THIS SCHOOL!
IT'S NOT EVERY STUDENT THAT GETS A CHANCE LIKE THIS--I ALMOST ENVY YOU!
ALMOST.
AND WITH THAT, SHE'S GONE.
HOW DID WE GET INTO THIS MESS IN THE FIRST PLACE...?

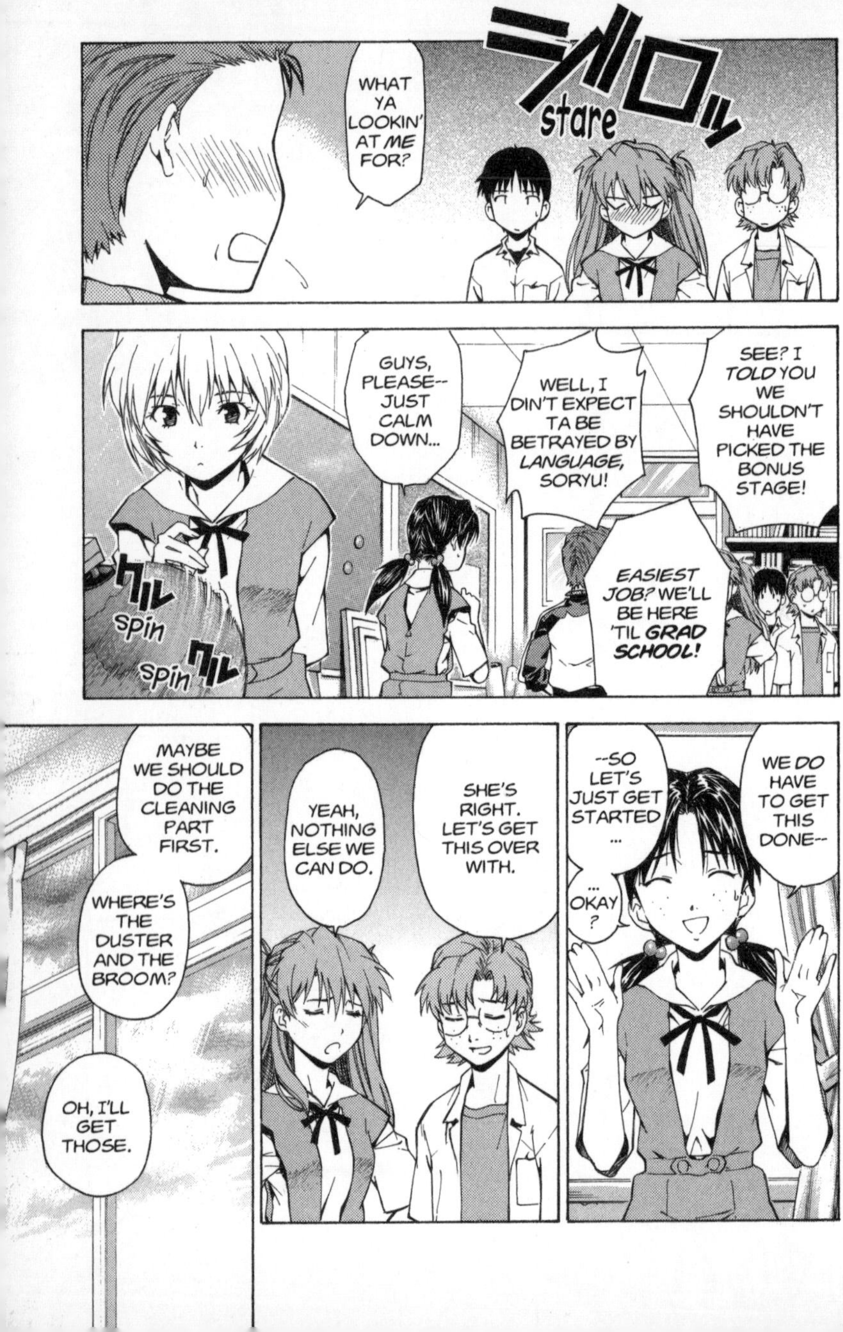
ジロッ
stare
WHAT YA LOOKIN' AT *ME* FOR?
SEE? I *TOLD* YOU WE SHOULDN'T HAVE PICKED THE BONUS STAGE!
EASIEST JOB? WE'LL BE HERE 'TIL *GRAD SCHOOL!*
WELL, I DIN'T EXPECT TA BE BETRAYED BY *LANGUAGE*, SORYU!
GUYS, PLEASE-- JUST CALM DOWN...
spin
spin
WE *DO* HAVE TO GET THIS DONE--
--SO LET'S JUST GET STARTED ...
... OKAY?
SHE'S RIGHT. LET'S GET THIS OVER WITH.
YEAH, NOTHING ELSE WE CAN DO.
MAYBE WE SHOULD DO THE CLEANING PART FIRST.
WHERE'S THE DUSTER AND THE BROOM?
OH, I'LL GET THOSE.

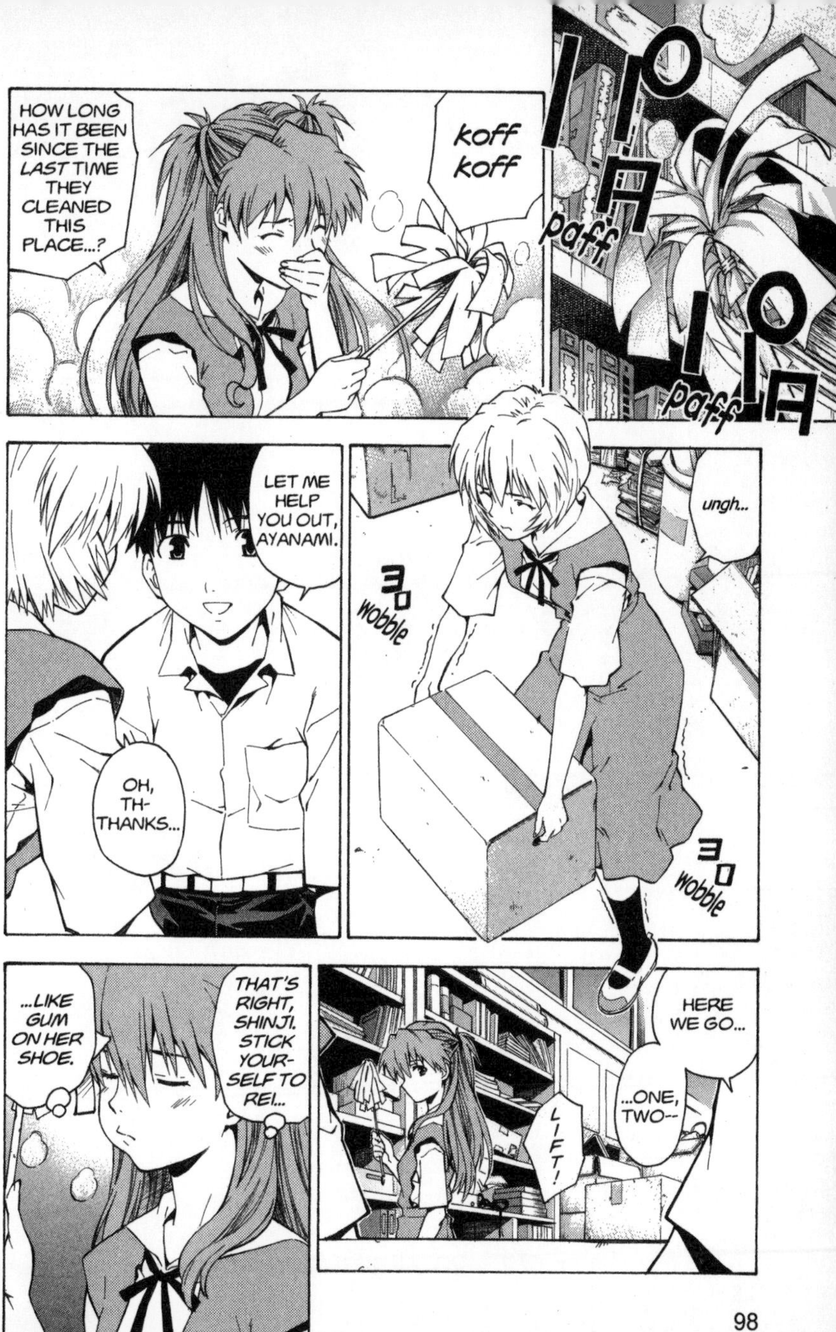
paff
paff
koff koff
HOW LONG HAS IT BEEN SINCE THE LAST TIME THEY CLEANED THIS PLACE...?
ungh...
wobble
wobble
LET ME HELP YOU OUT, AYANAMI.
OH, TH- THANKS...
HERE WE GO...
...ONE, TWO--
LIFT!
THAT'S RIGHT, SHINJI. STICK YOURSELF TO REI...
...LIKE GUM ON HER SHOE.

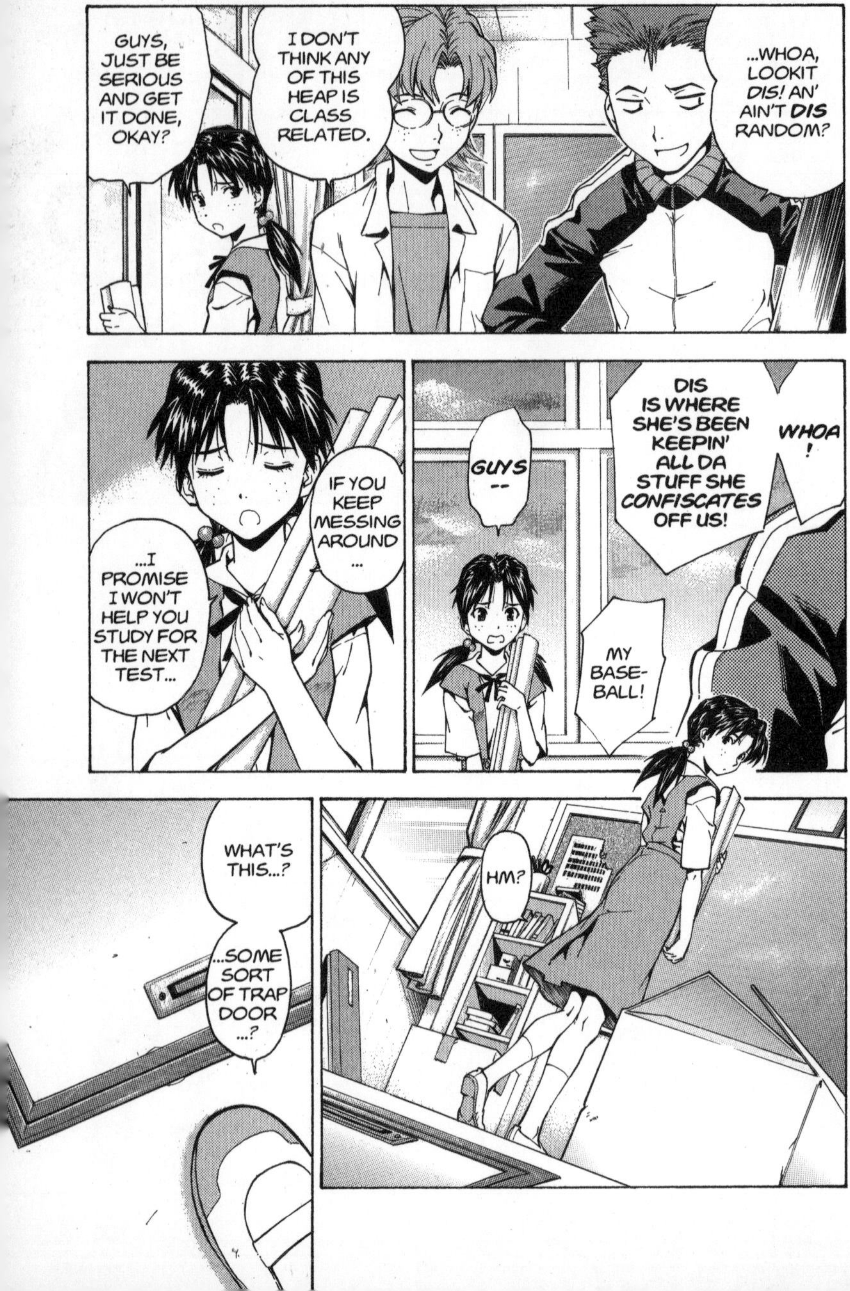
...WHOA, LOOKIT DIS! AN' AIN'T DIS RANDOM?
I DON'T THINK ANY OF THIS HEAP IS CLASS RELATED.
GUYS, JUST BE SERIOUS AND GET IT DONE, OKAY?
WHOA!
DIS IS WHERE SHE'S BEEN KEEPIN' ALL DA STUFF SHE CONFISCATES OFF US!
GUYS --
MY BASEBALL!
IF YOU KEEP MESSING AROUND ...
...I PROMISE I WON'T HELP YOU STUDY FOR THE NEXT TEST...
HM?
WHAT'S THIS...?
...SOME SORT OF TRAP DOOR ...?

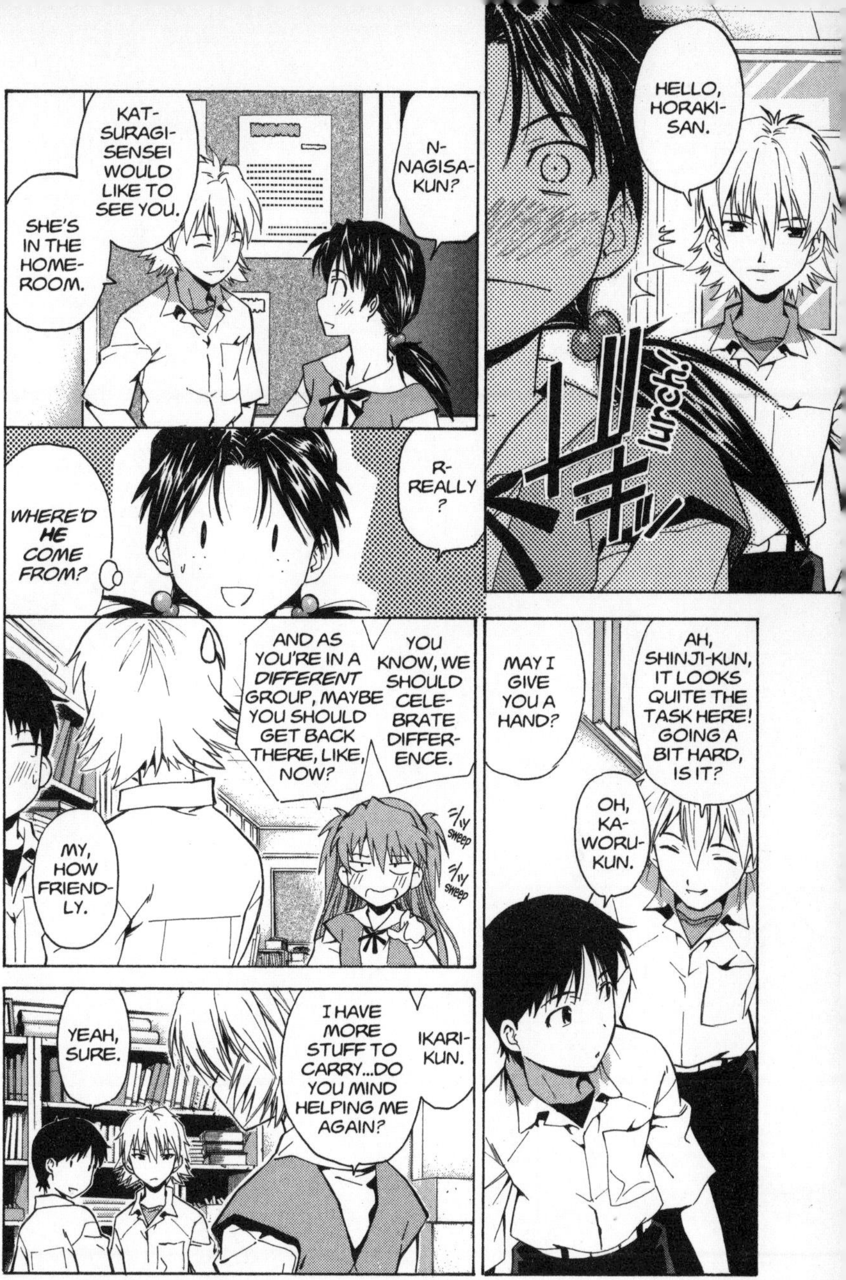
HELLO, HORAKI-SAN.
lurch!
N-NAGISA-KUN?
KAT-SURAGI-SENSEI WOULD LIKE TO SEE YOU.
SHE'S IN THE HOME-ROOM.
R-REALLY?
WHERE'D HE COME FROM?
AH, SHINJI-KUN, IT LOOKS QUITE THE TASK HERE! GOING A BIT HARD, IS IT?
MAY I GIVE YOU A HAND?
OH, KA-WORU-KUN.
YOU KNOW, WE SHOULD CELE-BRATE DIFFER-ENCE.
AND AS YOU'RE IN A *DIFFERENT* GROUP, MAYBE YOU SHOULD GET BACK THERE, LIKE, NOW?
sweep
sweep
MY, HOW FRIEND-LY.
IKARI-KUN.
I HAVE MORE STUFF TO CARRY...DO YOU MIND HELPING ME AGAIN?
YEAH, SURE.

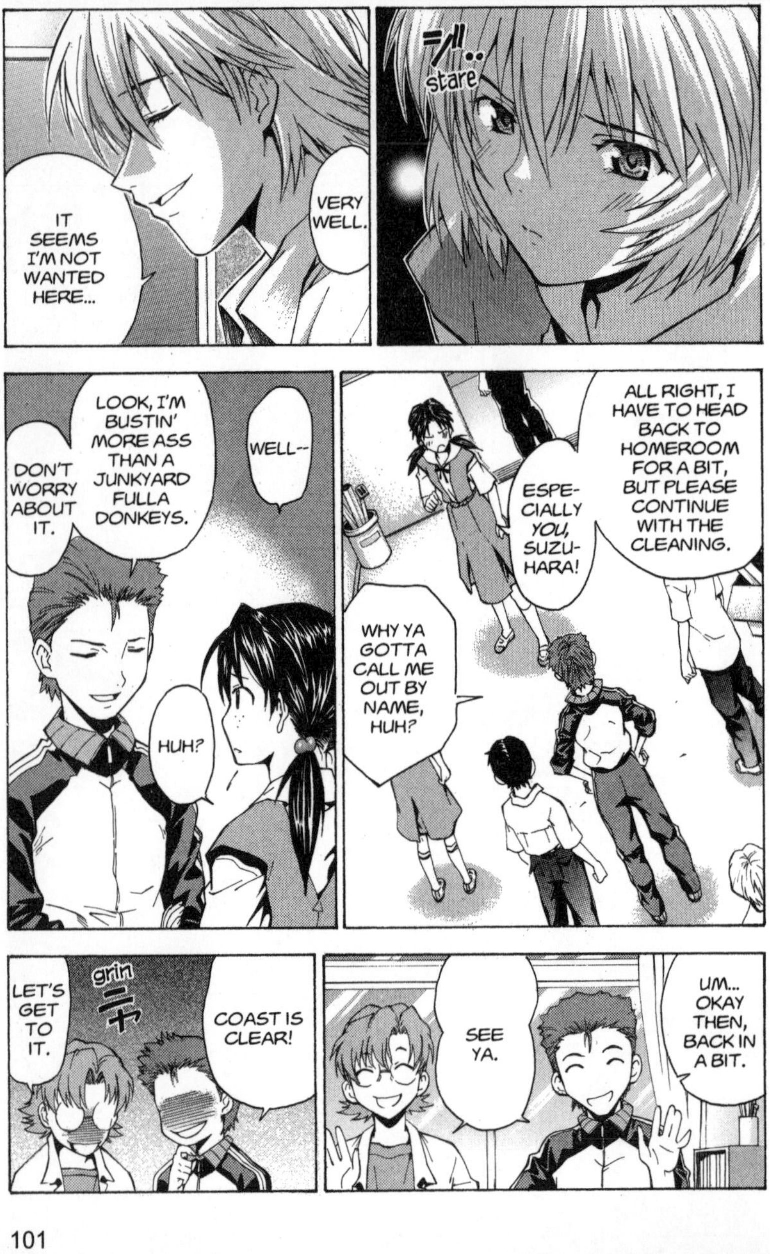
ジッ..
stare
VERY WELL.
IT SEEMS I'M NOT WANTED HERE...
ALL RIGHT, I HAVE TO HEAD BACK TO HOMEROOM FOR A BIT, BUT PLEASE CONTINUE WITH THE CLEANING.
ESPECIALLY *YOU*, SUZUHARA!
WHY YA GOTTA CALL ME OUT BY NAME, HUH?
WELL--
LOOK, I'M BUSTIN' MORE ASS THAN A JUNKYARD FULLA DONKEYS.
DON'T WORRY ABOUT IT.
HUH?
UM... OKAY THEN, BACK IN A BIT.
SEE YA.
COAST IS CLEAR!
grin
ニヤ
LET'S GET TO IT.

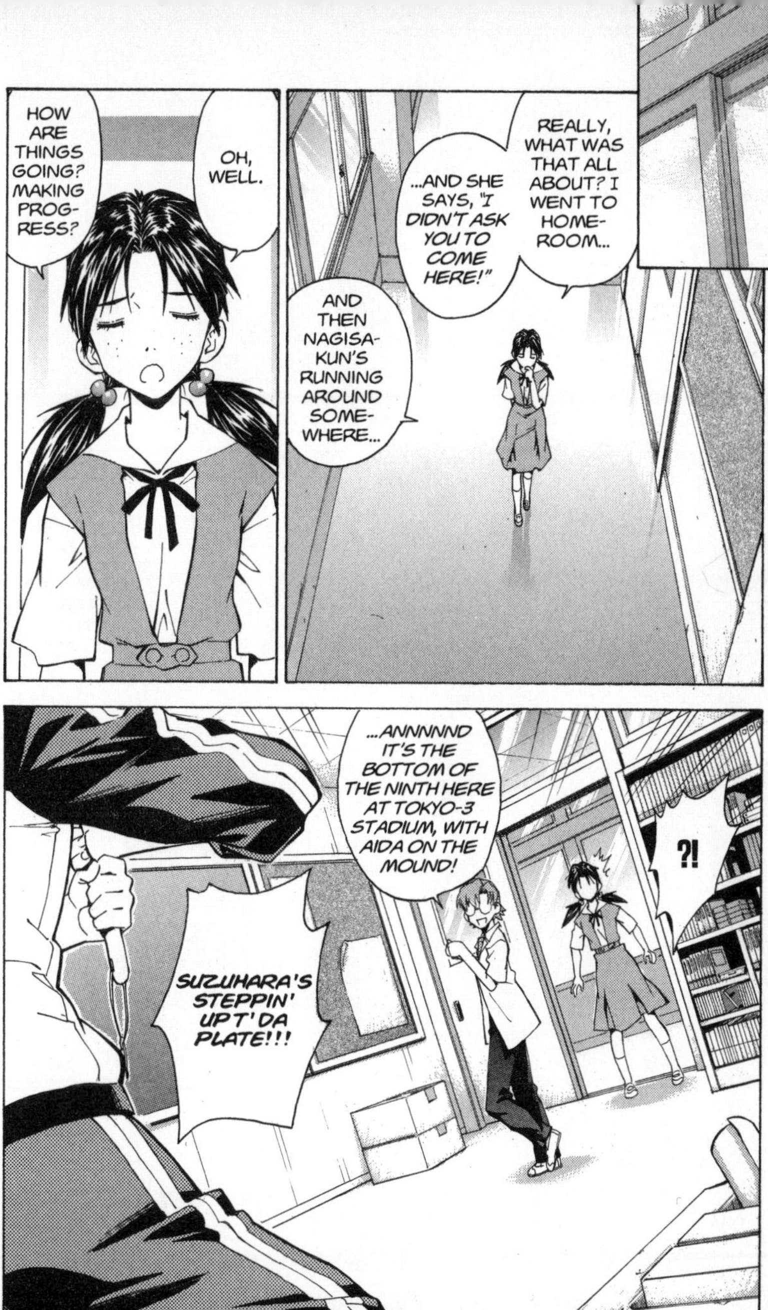
REALLY, WHAT WAS THAT ALL ABOUT? I WENT TO HOME-ROOM...
...AND SHE SAYS, "I DIDN'T ASK YOU TO COME HERE!"
AND THEN NAGISA-KUN'S RUNNING AROUND SOME-WHERE...
OH, WELL.
HOW ARE THINGS GOING? MAKING PROG-RESS?
?!
...ANNNNND IT'S THE BOTTOM OF THE NINTH HERE AT TOKYO-3 STADIUM, WITH AIDA ON THE MOUND!
SUZUHARA'S STEPPIN' UP T' DA PLATE!!!

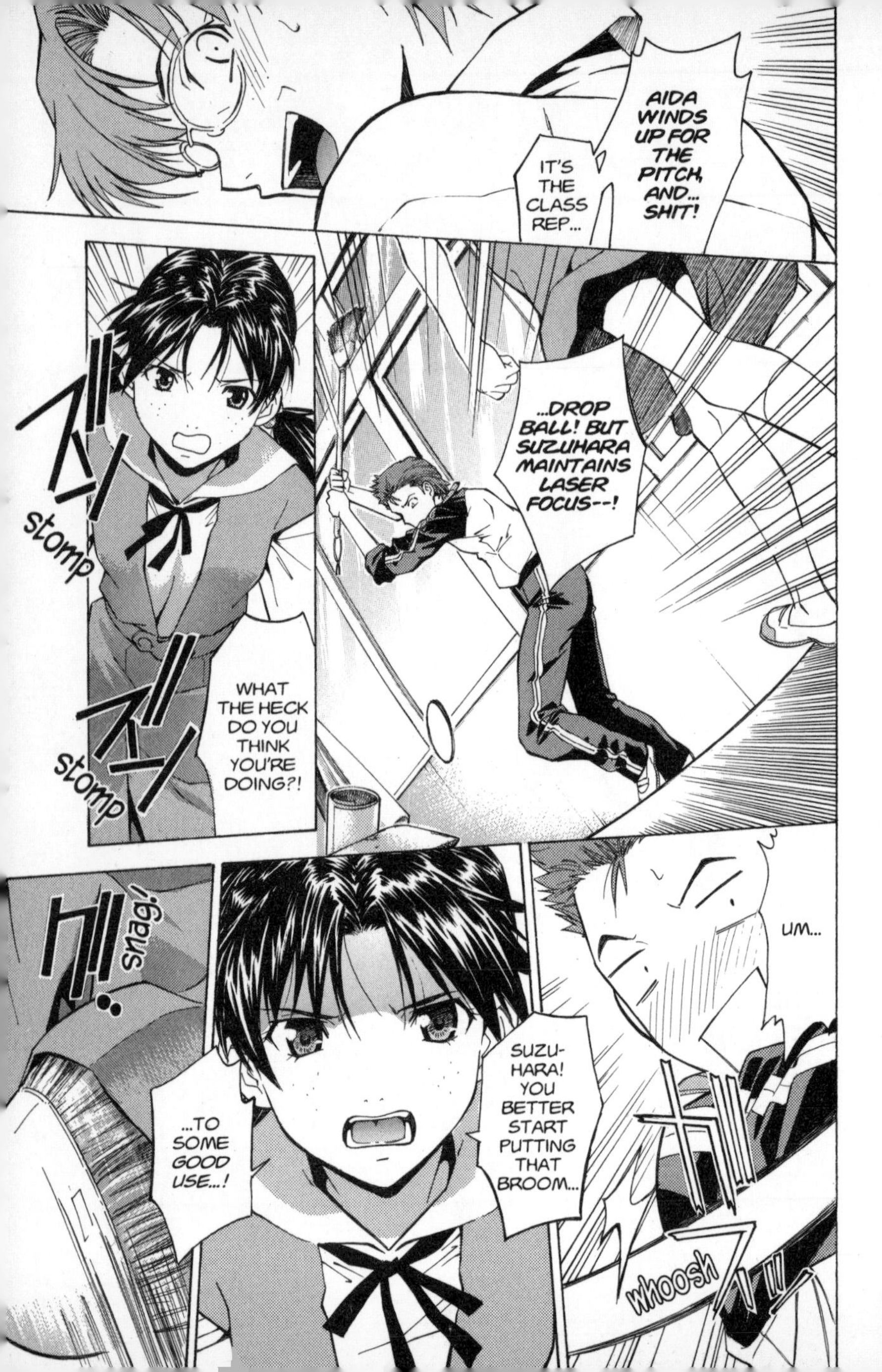
AIDA WINDS UP FOR THE PITCH, AND... SHIT!
IT'S THE CLASS REP...
...DROP BALL! BUT SUZUHARA MAINTAINS LASER FOCUS--!
stomp
stomp
WHAT THE HECK DO YOU THINK YOU'RE DOING?!
UM...
whoosh
snag!
SUZU-HARA! YOU BETTER START PUTTING THAT BROOM...
...TO SOME GOOD USE...!

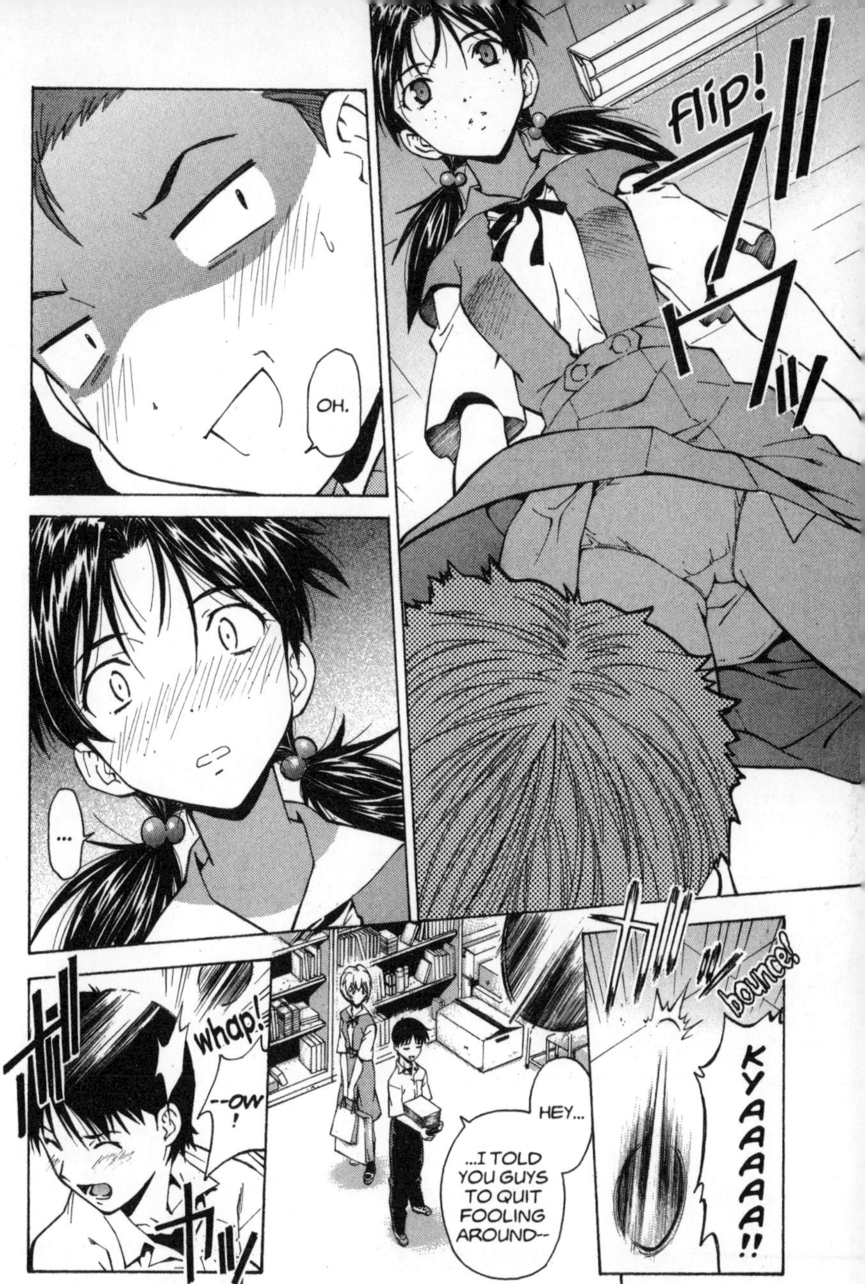
flip!
OH.
...
bounce!
KYAAAAAA!!
HEY...
...I TOLD YOU GUYS TO QUIT FOOLING AROUND--
whap!
--OW!

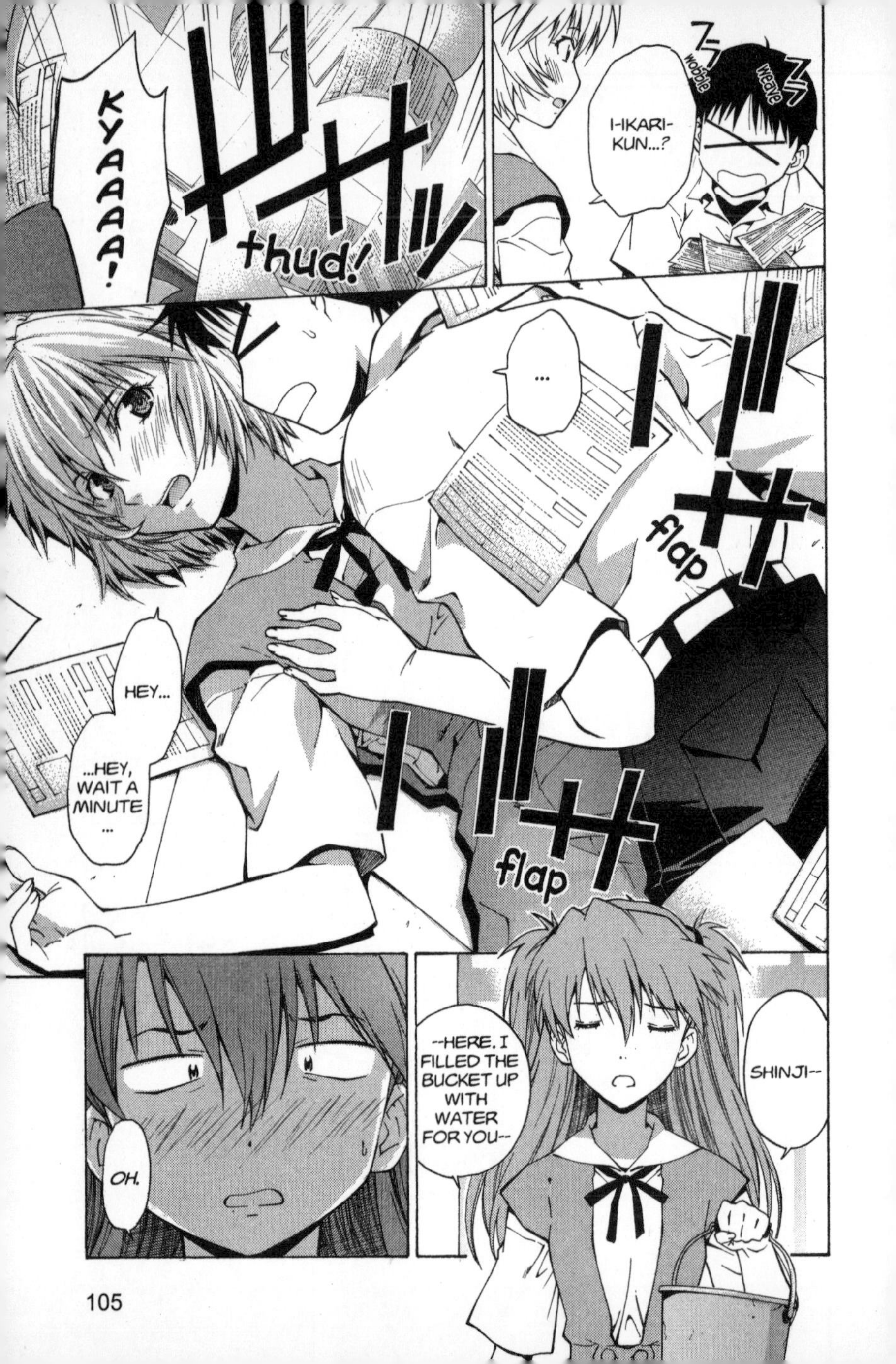
wobble
weave
I-IKARI-KUN...?
KYAAAAA!
thud!
...
flap
flap
HEY...
...HEY, WAIT A MINUTE ...
SHINJI--
--HERE. I FILLED THE BUCKET UP WITH WATER FOR YOU--
OH.

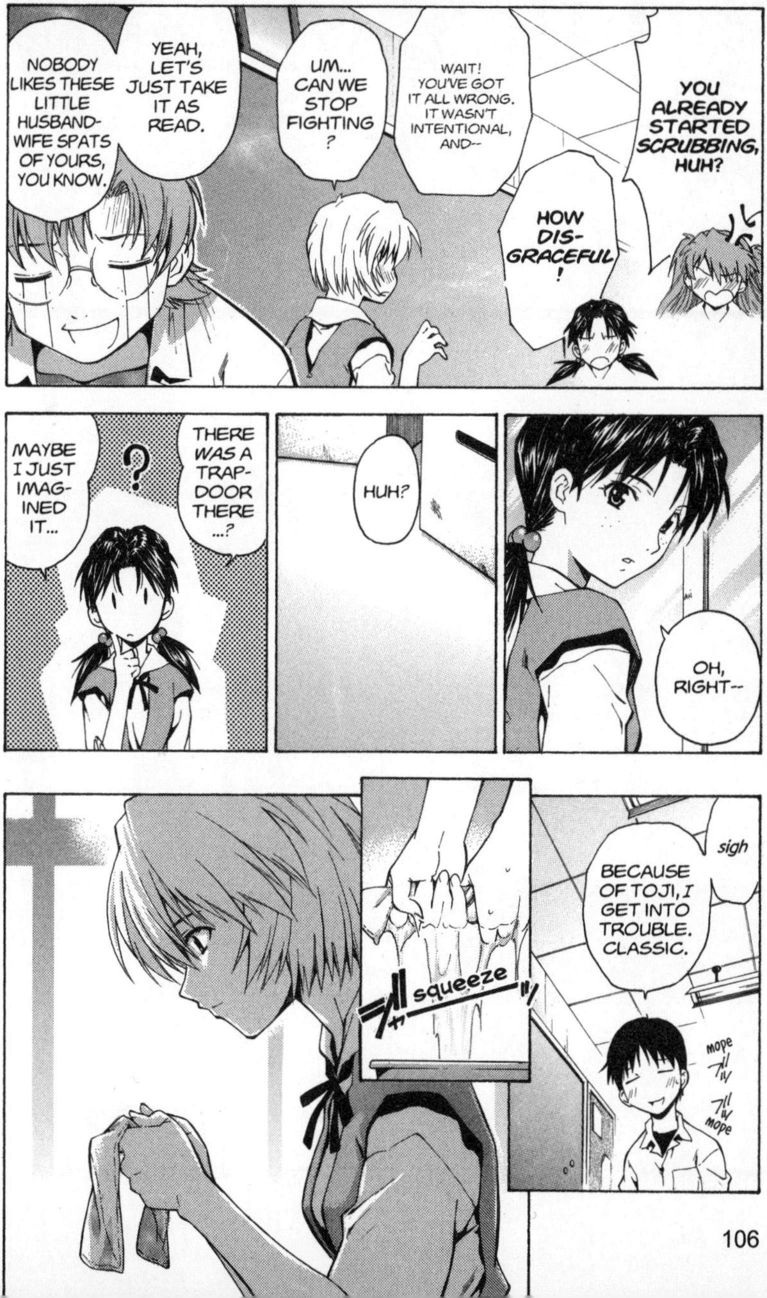
YOU ALREADY STARTED SCRUBBING, HUH?
HOW DIS-GRACEFUL!
WAIT! YOU'VE GOT IT ALL WRONG. IT WASN'T INTENTIONAL, AND--
UM... CAN WE STOP FIGHTING?
YEAH, LET'S JUST TAKE IT AS READ.
NOBODY LIKES THESE LITTLE HUSBAND-WIFE SPATS OF YOURS, YOU KNOW.
OH, RIGHT--
HUH?
THERE WAS A TRAP-DOOR THERE ...?
MAYBE I JUST IMAG-INED IT...
sigh
BECAUSE OF TOJI, I GET INTO TROUBLE. CLASSIC.
mope
mope
squeeze

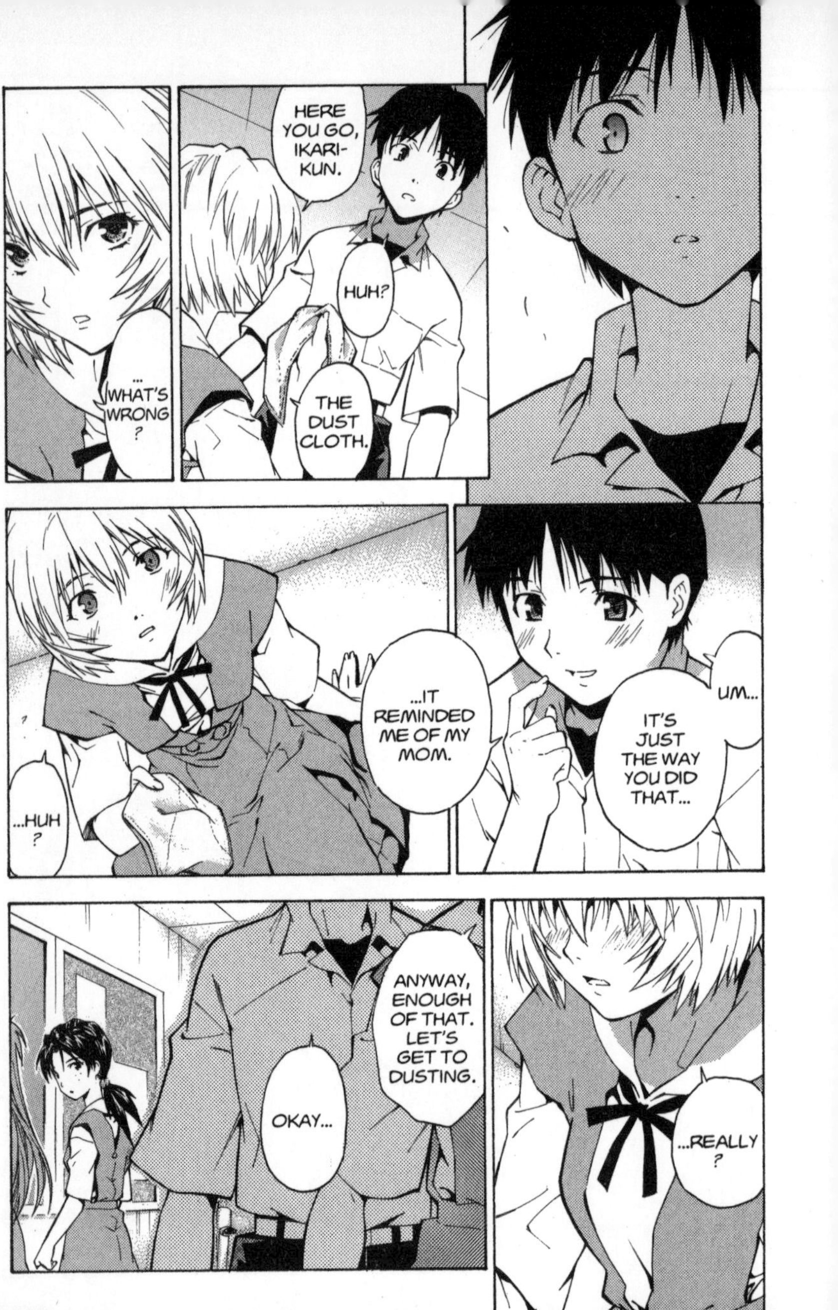
HERE YOU GO, IKARI-KUN.
HUH?
THE DUST CLOTH.
...WHAT'S WRONG?
UM...
IT'S JUST THE WAY YOU DID THAT...
...IT REMINDED ME OF MY MOM.
?
...HUH?
...REALLY?
ANYWAY, ENOUGH OF THAT. LET'S GET TO DUSTING.
OKAY...

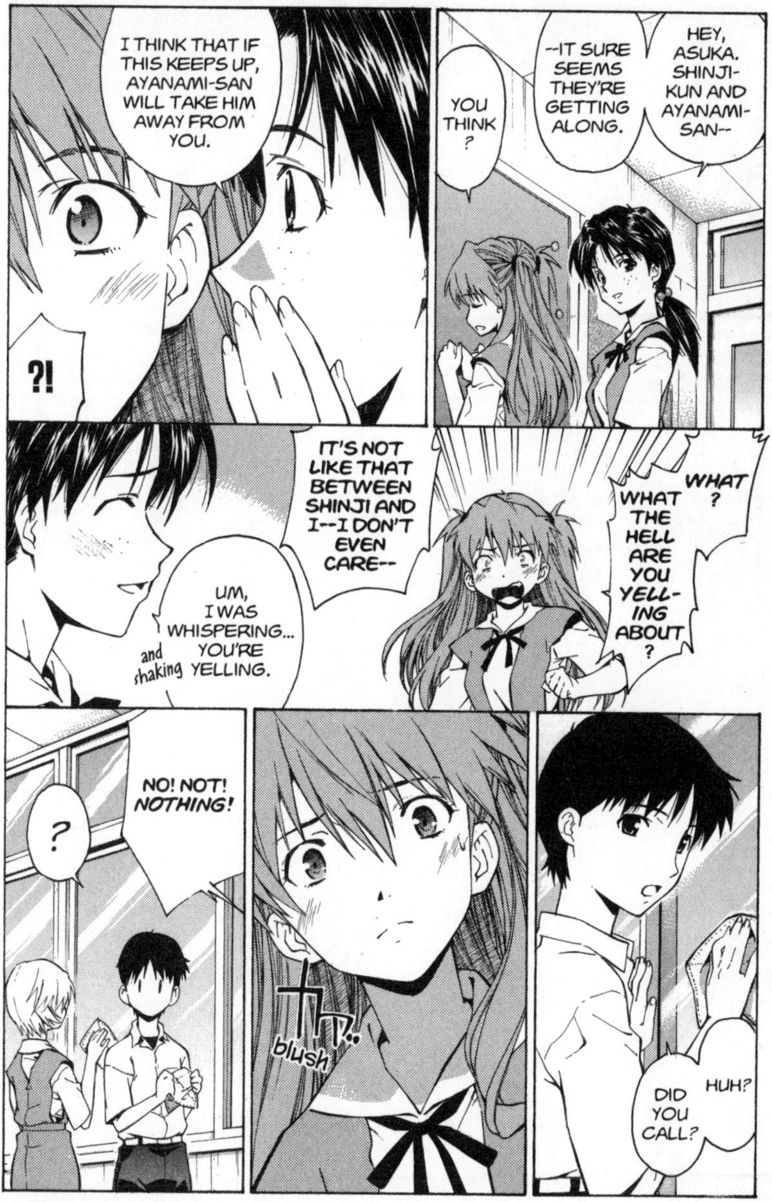
HEY, ASUKA. SHINJI-KUN AND AYANAMI-SAN--
--IT SURE SEEMS THEY'RE GETTING ALONG.
YOU THINK?
I THINK THAT IF THIS KEEPS UP, AYANAMI-SAN WILL TAKE HIM AWAY FROM YOU.
?!
WHAT? WHAT THE HELL ARE YOU YELLING ABOUT?
IT'S NOT LIKE THAT BETWEEN SHINJI AND I--I DON'T EVEN CARE--
UM, I WAS WHISPERING... YOU'RE YELLING.
and shaking
HUH?
DID YOU CALL?
blush
NO! NOT! NOTHING!
?

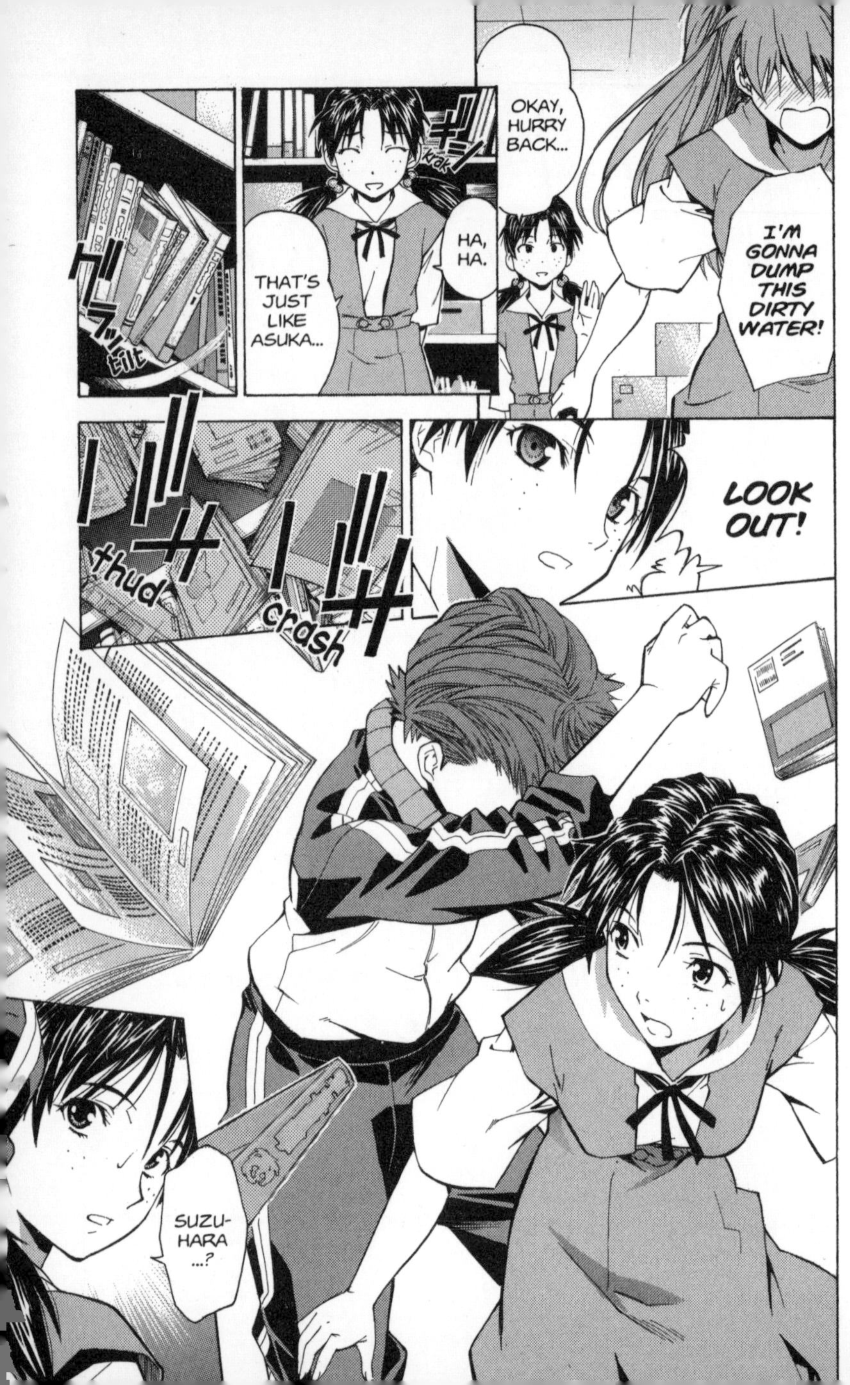
I'M GONNA DUMP THIS DIRTY WATER!
OKAY, HURRY BACK...
krak
HA, HA.
THAT'S JUST LIKE ASUKA...
tilt
LOOK OUT!
thud
crash
SUZU-HARA ...?

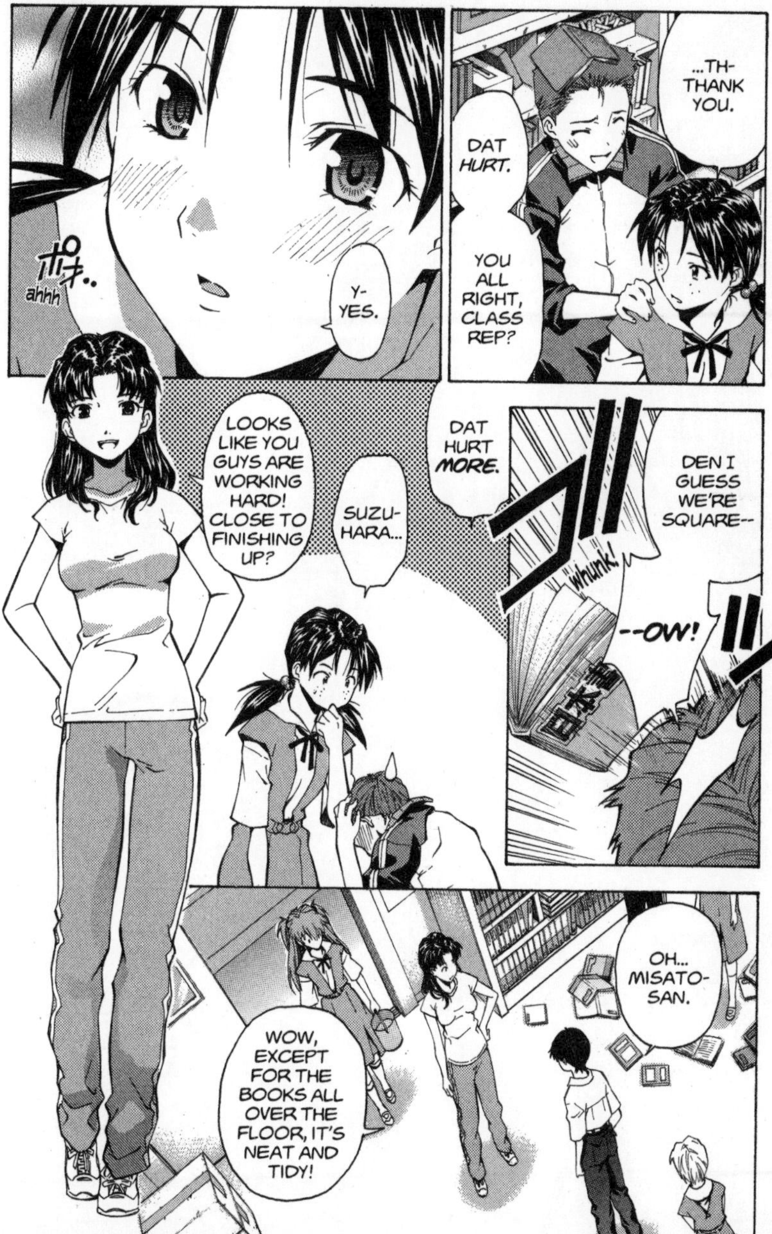
...TH- THANK YOU.
DAT HURT.
YOU ALL RIGHT, CLASS REP?
Y- YES.
ポォ.. ahhh
DEN I GUESS WE'RE SQUARE--
whunk!
--OW!
DAT HURT MORE.
SUZU- HARA...
LOOKS LIKE YOU GUYS ARE WORKING HARD! CLOSE TO FINISHING UP?
OH... MISATO- SAN.
WOW, EXCEPT FOR THE BOOKS ALL OVER THE FLOOR, IT'S NEAT AND TIDY!

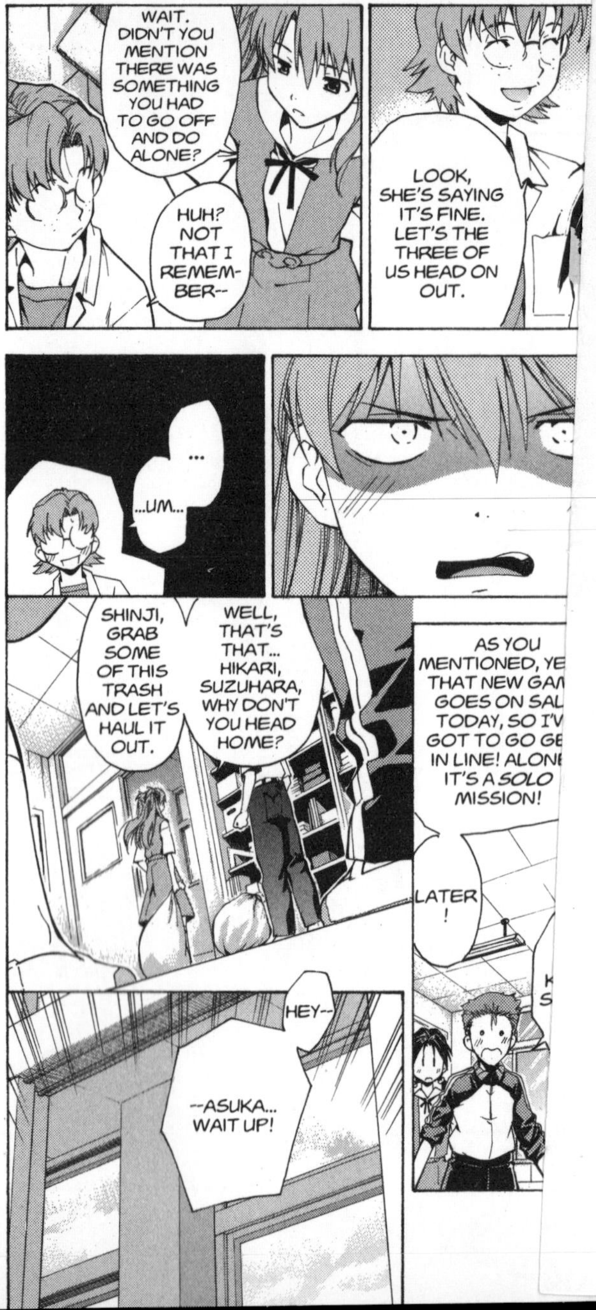
LOOK, SHE'S SAYING IT'S FINE. LET'S THE THREE OF US HEAD ON OUT.
WAIT. DIDN'T YOU MENTION THERE WAS SOMETHING YOU HAD TO GO OFF AND DO ALONE?
HUH? NOT THAT I REMEM-BER--
...
...UM...
AS YOU MENTIONED, YE THAT NEW GAM GOES ON SAL TODAY, SO I'V GOT TO GO GE IN LINE! IT'S A *SOLO* MISSION!
LATER!
WELL, THAT'S THAT... HIKARI, SUZUHARA, WHY DON'T YOU HEAD HOME?
SHINJI, GRAB SOME OF THIS TRASH AND LET'S HAUL IT OUT.
HEY--
--ASUKA... WAIT UP!
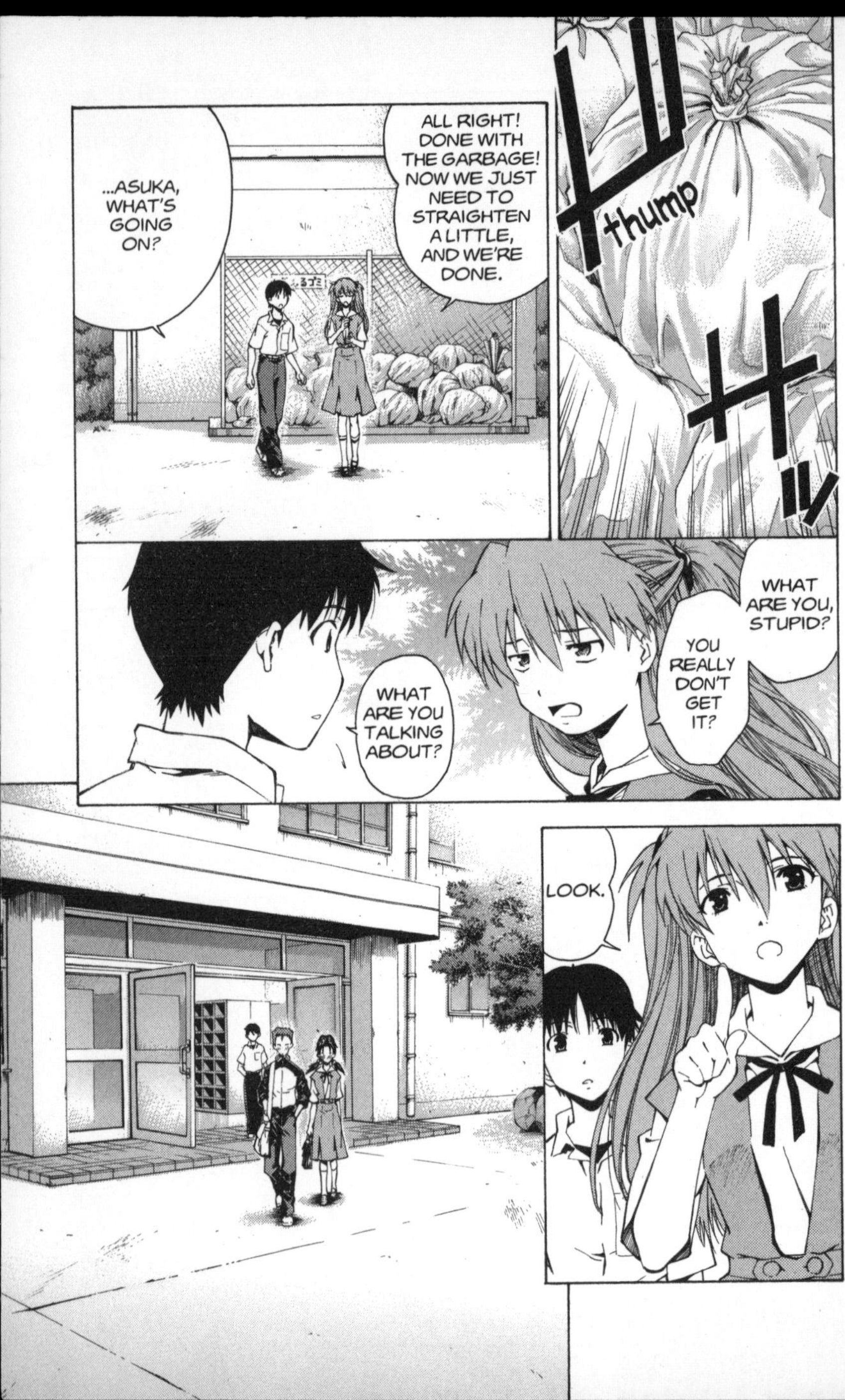
thump
ALL RIGHT! DONE WITH THE GARBAGE! NOW WE JUST NEED TO STRAIGHTEN A LITTLE, AND WE'RE DONE.
...ASUKA, WHAT'S GOING ON?
WHAT ARE YOU, STUPID?
YOU REALLY DON'T GET IT?
WHAT ARE YOU TALKING ABOUT?
LOOK.

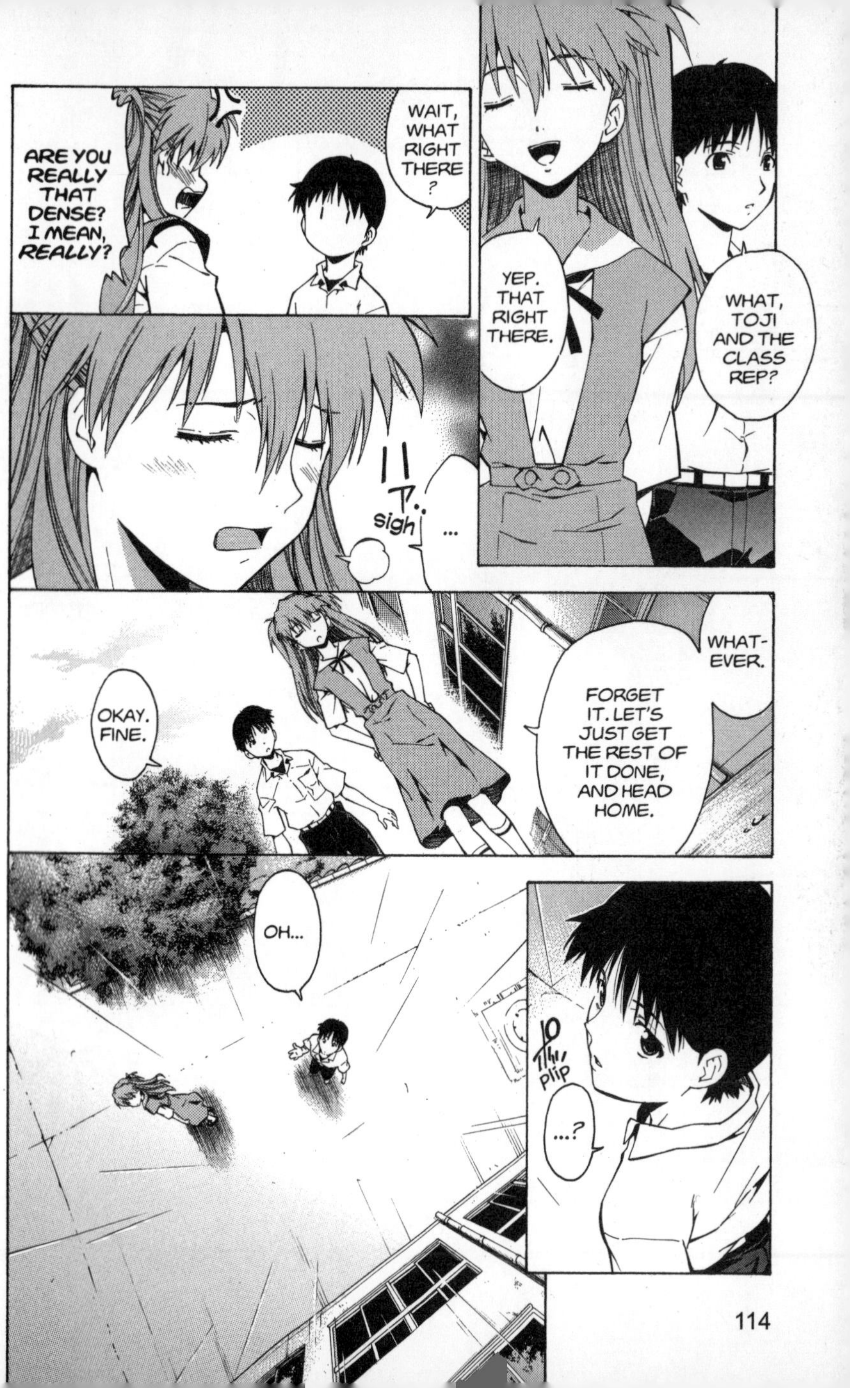
WHAT, TOJI AND THE CLASS REP?
YEP. THAT RIGHT THERE.
WAIT, WHAT RIGHT THERE?
ARE YOU REALLY THAT DENSE? I MEAN, *REALLY*?
...
sigh
WHAT-EVER.
FORGET IT. LET'S JUST GET THE REST OF IT DONE, AND HEAD HOME.
OKAY. FINE.
plip
...?
OH...

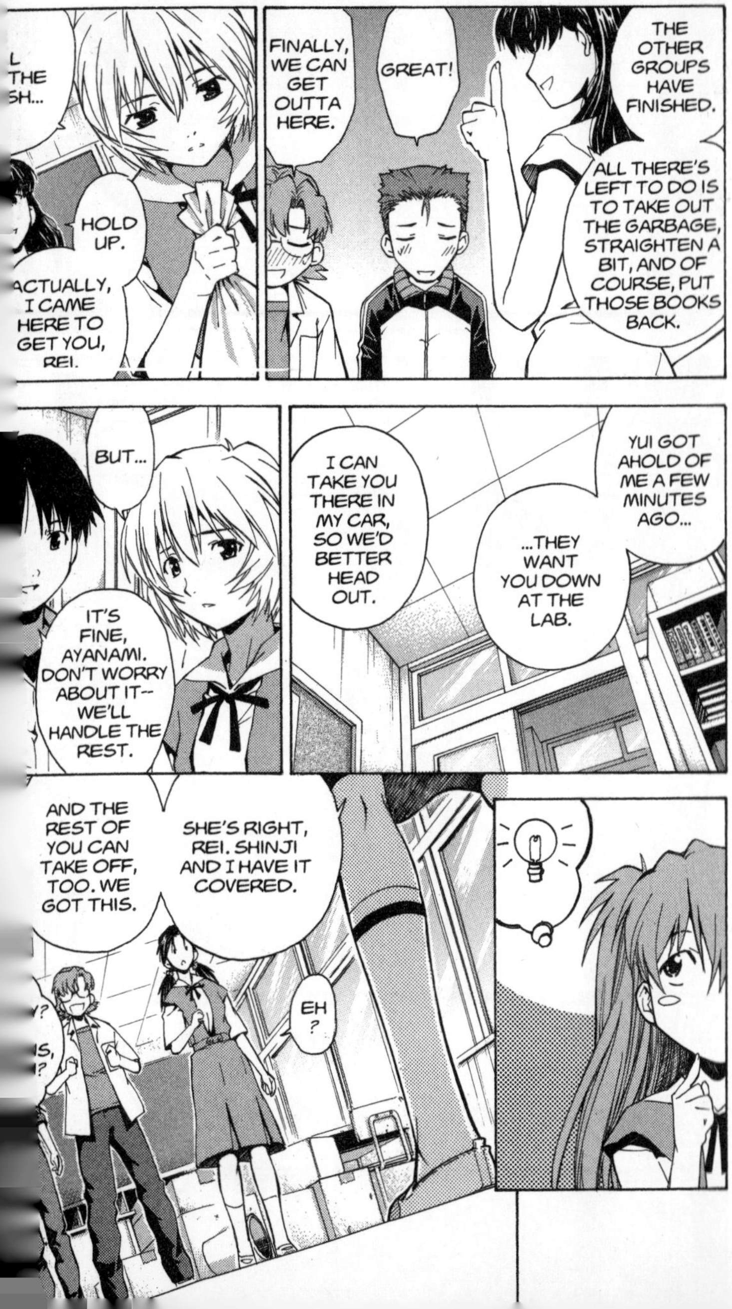
THE OTHER GROUPS HAVE FINISHED.
GREAT!
FINALLY, WE CAN GET OUTTA HERE.
ALL THERE'S LEFT TO DO IS TO TAKE OUT THE GARBAGE, STRAIGHTEN A BIT, AND OF COURSE, PUT THOSE BOOKS BACK.
HOLD UP.
ACTUALLY, I CAME HERE TO GET YOU, REI.
YUI GOT AHOLD OF ME A FEW MINUTES AGO...
...THEY WANT YOU DOWN AT THE LAB.
I CAN TAKE YOU THERE IN MY CAR, SO WE'D BETTER HEAD OUT.
BUT...
IT'S FINE, AYANAMI. DON'T WORRY ABOUT IT-- WE'LL HANDLE THE REST.
SHE'S RIGHT, REI. SHINJI AND I HAVE IT COVERED.
AND THE REST OF YOU CAN TAKE OFF, TOO. WE GOT THIS.
EH?

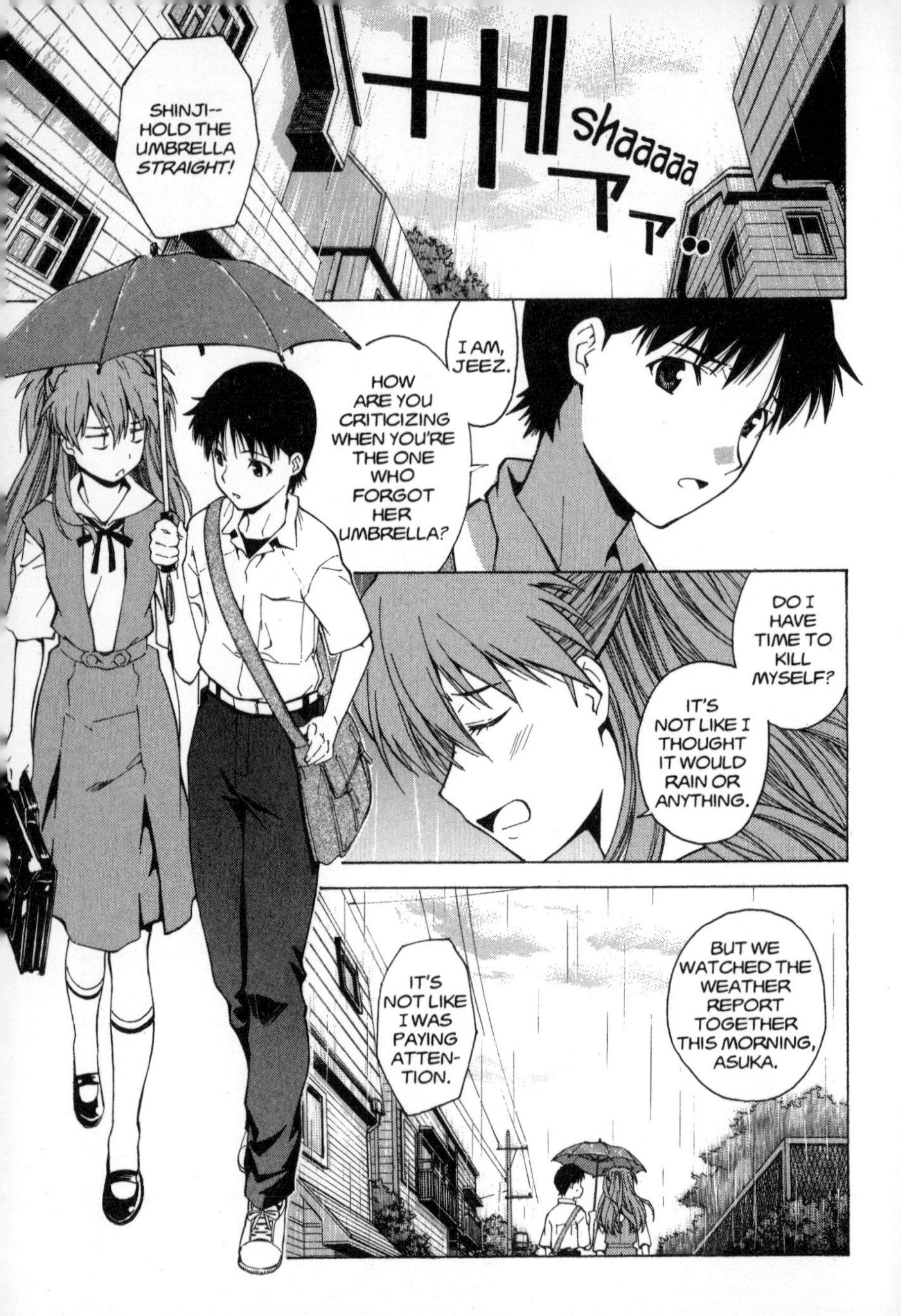
shaaaaaa
SHINJI-- HOLD THE UMBRELLA STRAIGHT!
I AM, JEEZ.
HOW ARE YOU CRITICIZING WHEN YOU'RE THE ONE WHO FORGOT HER UMBRELLA?
DO I HAVE TIME TO KILL MYSELF?
IT'S NOT LIKE I THOUGHT IT WOULD RAIN OR ANYTHING.
BUT WE WATCHED THE WEATHER REPORT TOGETHER THIS MORNING, ASUKA.
IT'S NOT LIKE I WAS PAYING ATTEN-TION.

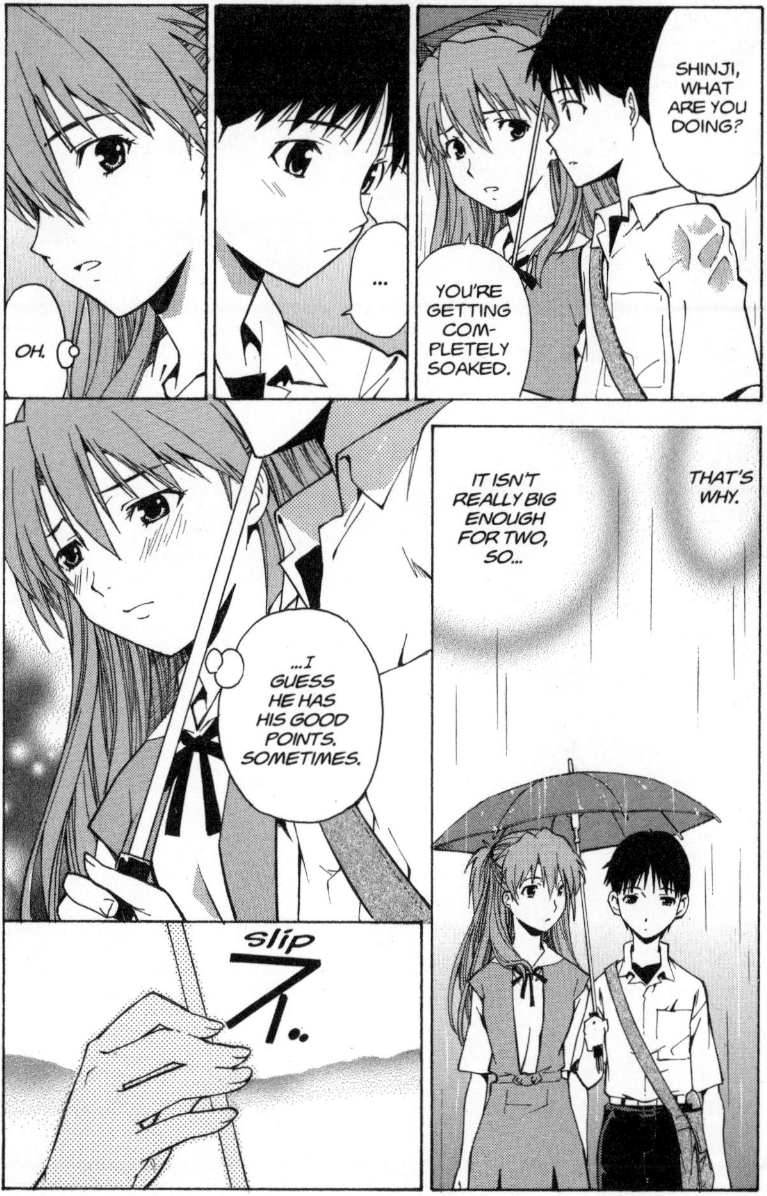
SHINJI, WHAT ARE YOU DOING?
YOU'RE GETTING COM-PLETELY SOAKED.
...
OH.
IT ISN'T REALLY BIG ENOUGH FOR TWO, SO...
THAT'S WHY.
...I GUESS HE HAS HIS GOOD POINTS. SOMETIMES.
slip

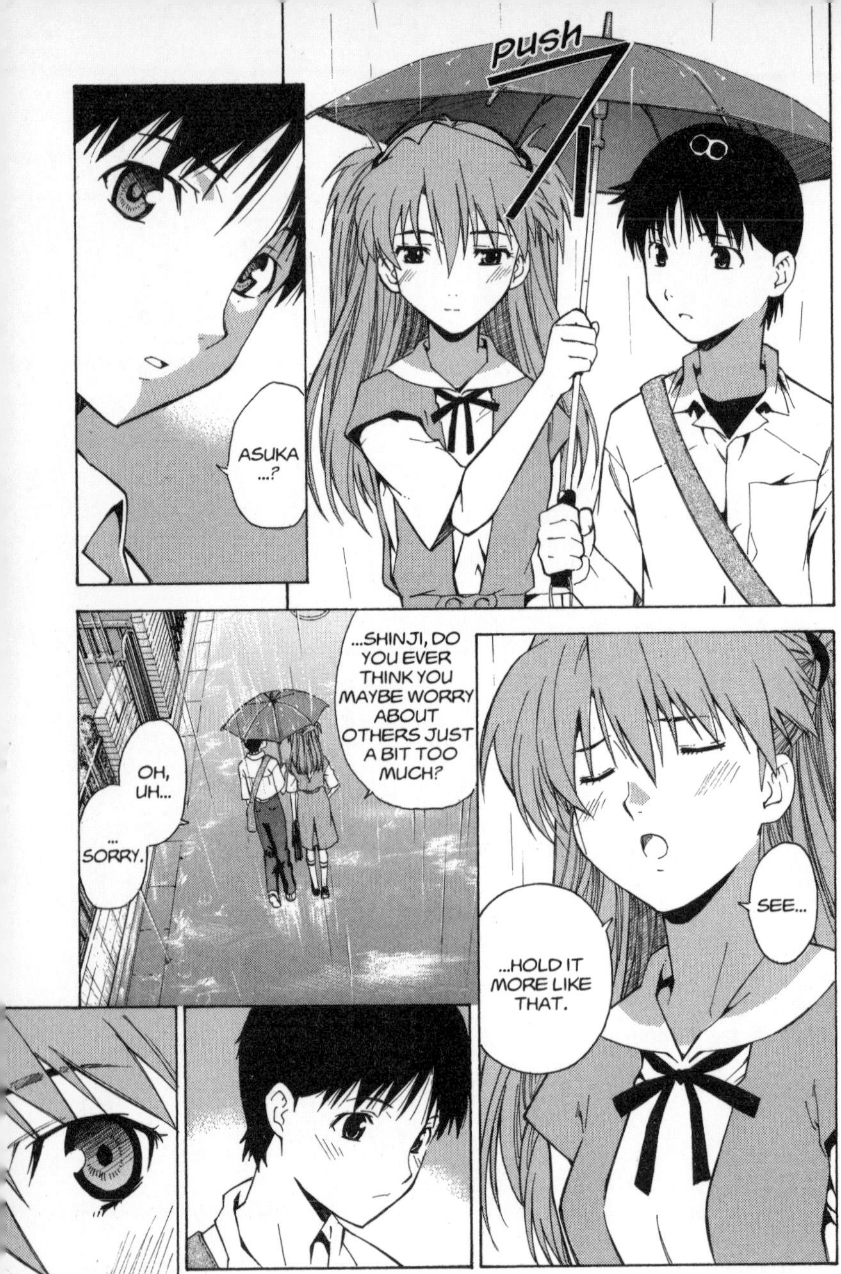
PUSH
ASUKA ...?
SEE...
...HOLD IT MORE LIKE THAT.
...SHINJI, DO YOU EVER THINK YOU MAYBE WORRY ABOUT OTHERS JUST A BIT TOO MUCH?
OH, UH... ... SORRY.

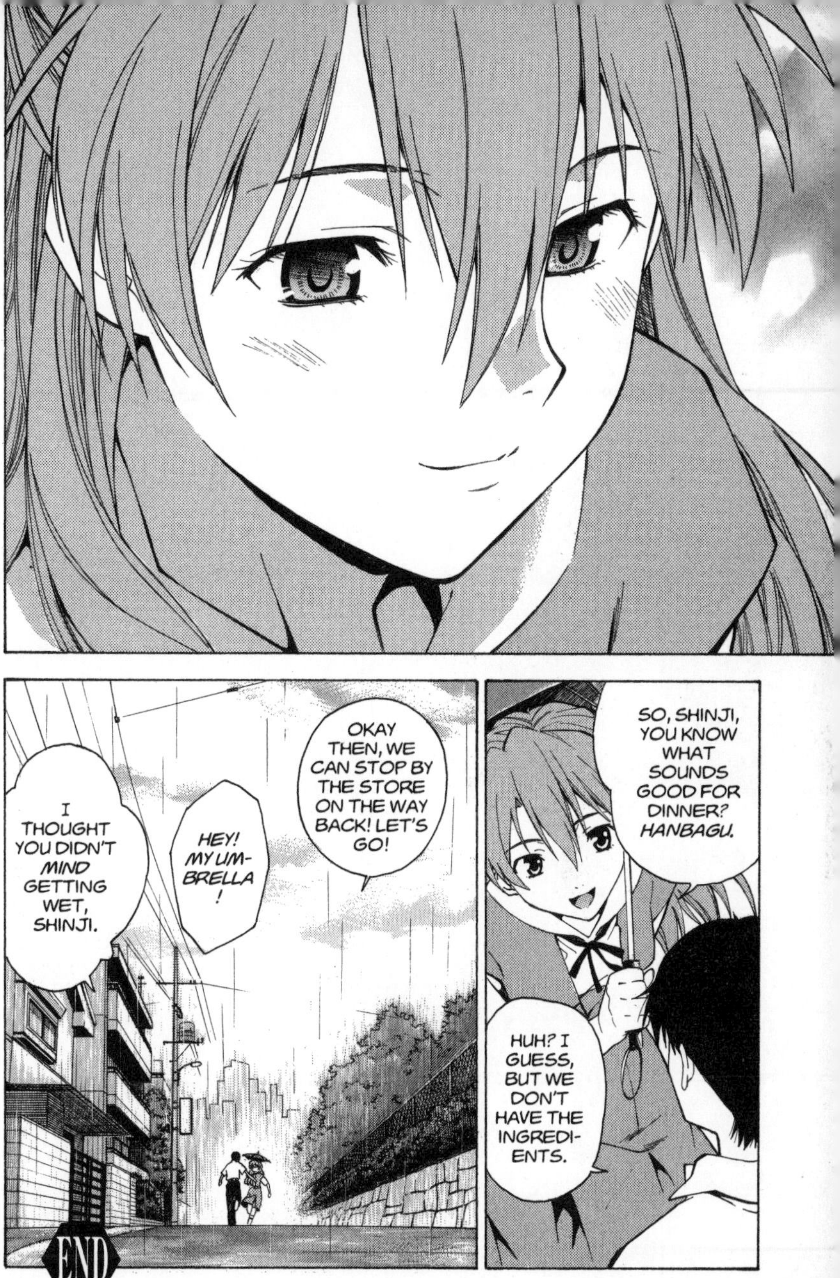
SO, SHINJI, YOU KNOW WHAT SOUNDS GOOD FOR DINNER? *HANBAGU.*
HUH? I GUESS, BUT WE DON'T HAVE THE INGREDIENTS.
OKAY THEN, WE CAN STOP BY THE STORE ON THE WAY BACK! LET'S GO!
HEY! MY UMBRELLA!
I THOUGHT YOU DIDN'T *MIND* GETTING WET, SHINJI.
END

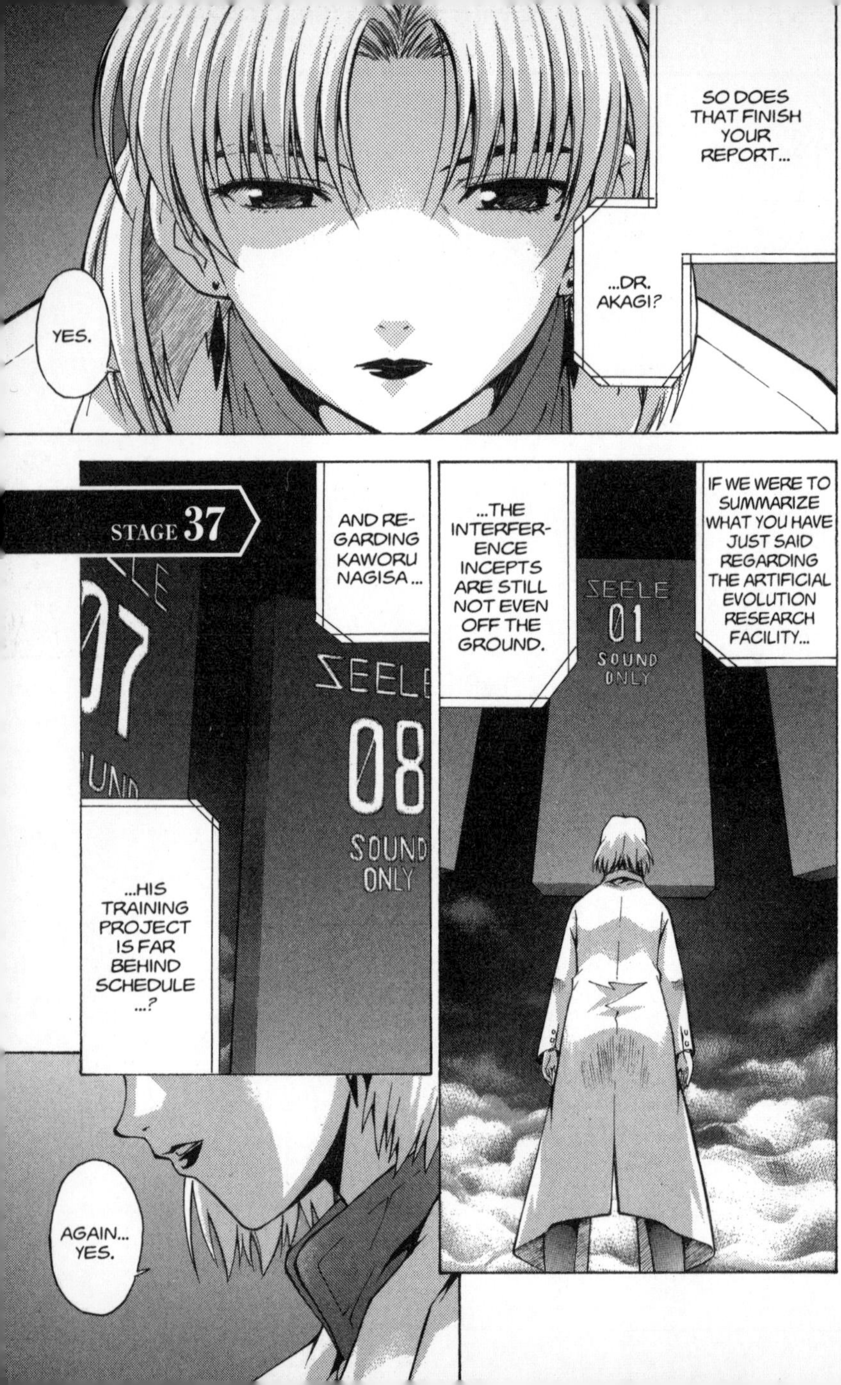
SO DOES THAT FINISH YOUR REPORT...
...DR. AKAGI?
YES.
STAGE 37
IF WE WERE TO SUMMARIZE WHAT YOU HAVE JUST SAID REGARDING THE ARTIFICIAL EVOLUTION RESEARCH FACILITY...
SEELE 01 SOUND ONLY
...THE INTERFERENCE INCEPTS ARE STILL NOT EVEN OFF THE GROUND.
AND REGARDING KAWORU NAGISA...
SEELE 08 SOUND ONLY
...HIS TRAINING PROJECT IS FAR BEHIND SCHEDULE ...?
AGAIN... YES.

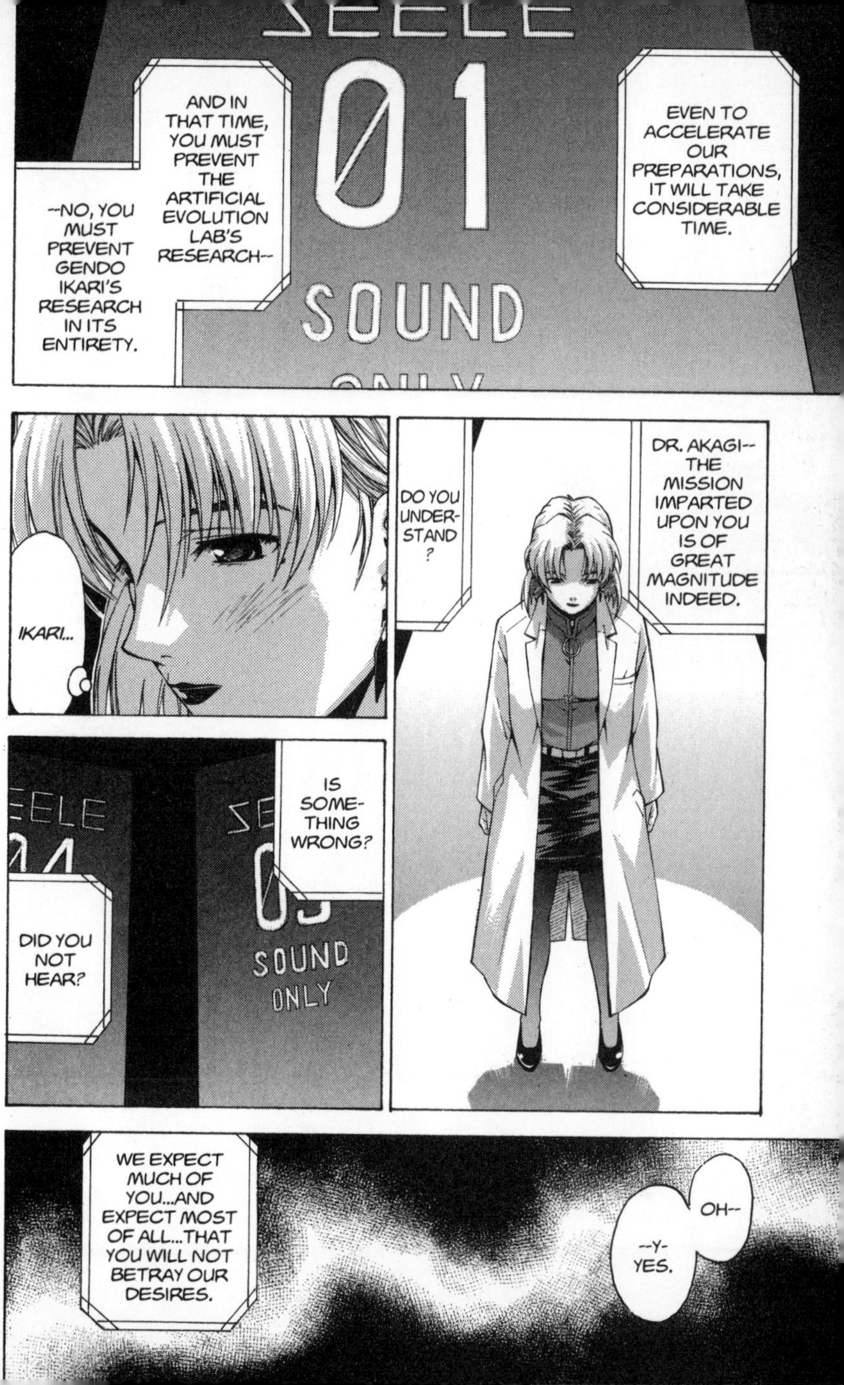
EVEN TO ACCELERATE OUR PREPARATIONS, IT WILL TAKE CONSIDERABLE TIME.
01
SOUND
AND IN THAT TIME, YOU MUST PREVENT THE ARTIFICIAL EVOLUTION LAB'S RESEARCH--
--NO, YOU MUST PREVENT GENDO IKARI'S RESEARCH IN ITS ENTIRETY.
DR. AKAGI-- THE MISSION IMPARTED UPON YOU IS OF GREAT MAGNITUDE INDEED.
DO YOU UNDER-STAND?
IKARI...
IS SOME-THING WRONG?
SOUND ONLY
DID YOU NOT HEAR?
OH--
--Y-YES.
WE EXPECT MUCH OF YOU...AND EXPECT MOST OF ALL...THAT YOU WILL NOT BETRAY OUR DESIRES.

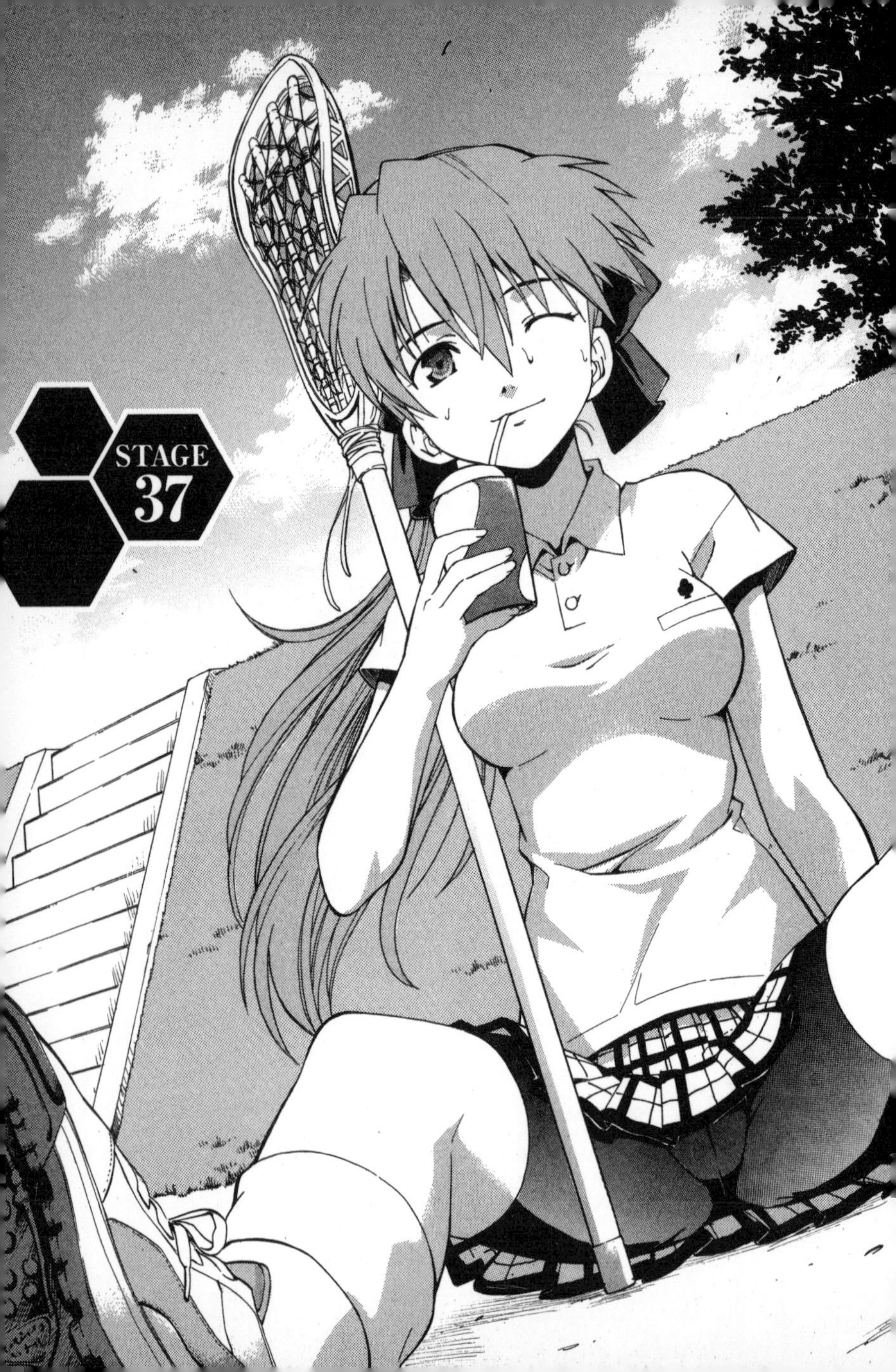
STAGE
37

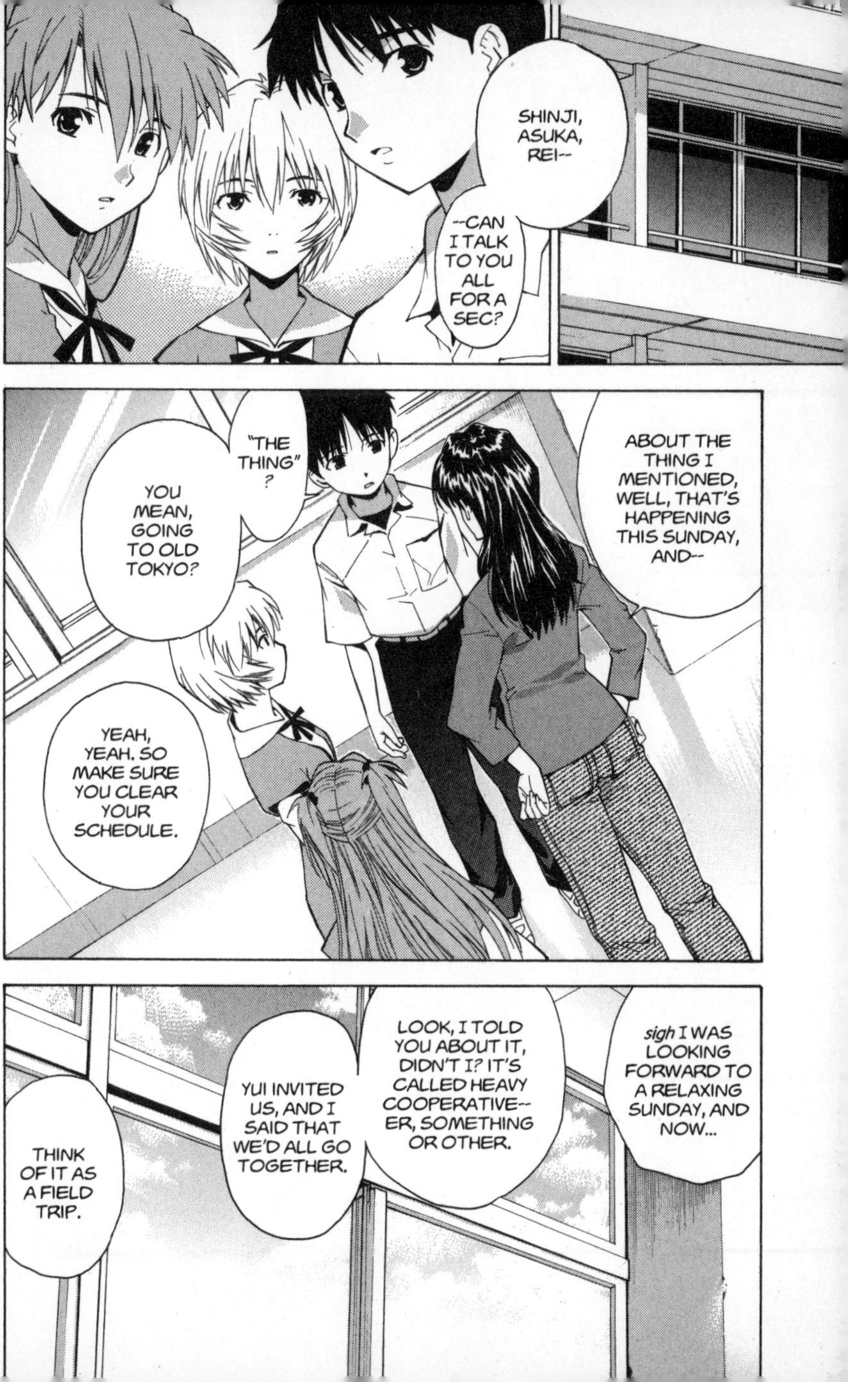
SHINJI, ASUKA, REI--
--CAN I TALK TO YOU ALL FOR A SEC?
ABOUT THE THING I MENTIONED, WELL, THAT'S HAPPENING THIS SUNDAY, AND--
"THE THING"?
YOU MEAN, GOING TO OLD TOKYO?
YEAH, YEAH. SO MAKE SURE YOU CLEAR YOUR SCHEDULE.
sigh I WAS LOOKING FORWARD TO A RELAXING SUNDAY, AND NOW...
LOOK, I TOLD YOU ABOUT IT, DIDN'T I? IT'S CALLED HEAVY COOPERATIVE--ER, SOMETHING OR OTHER.
YUI INVITED US, AND I SAID THAT WE'D ALL GO TOGETHER.
THINK OF IT AS A FIELD TRIP.

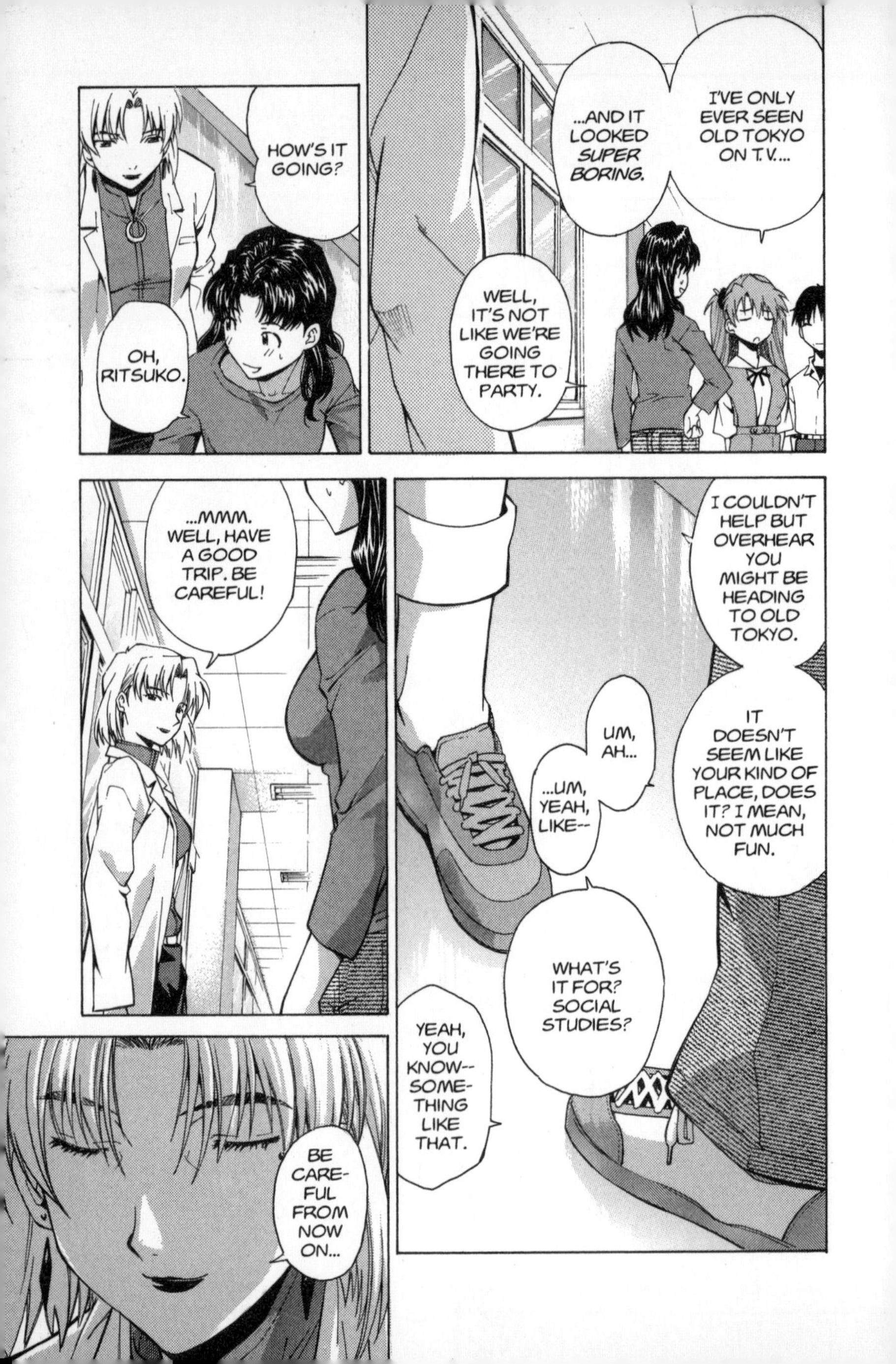
I'VE ONLY EVER SEEN OLD TOKYO ON T.V....
...AND IT LOOKED SUPER BORING.
WELL, IT'S NOT LIKE WE'RE GOING THERE TO PARTY.
HOW'S IT GOING?
OH, RITSUKO.
I COULDN'T HELP BUT OVERHEAR YOU MIGHT BE HEADING TO OLD TOKYO.
IT DOESN'T SEEM LIKE YOUR KIND OF PLACE, DOES IT? I MEAN, NOT MUCH FUN.
UM, AH...
...UM, YEAH, LIKE--
WHAT'S IT FOR? SOCIAL STUDIES?
YEAH, YOU KNOW--SOMETHING LIKE THAT.
...MMM. WELL, HAVE A GOOD TRIP. BE CAREFUL!
BE CAREFUL FROM NOW ON...

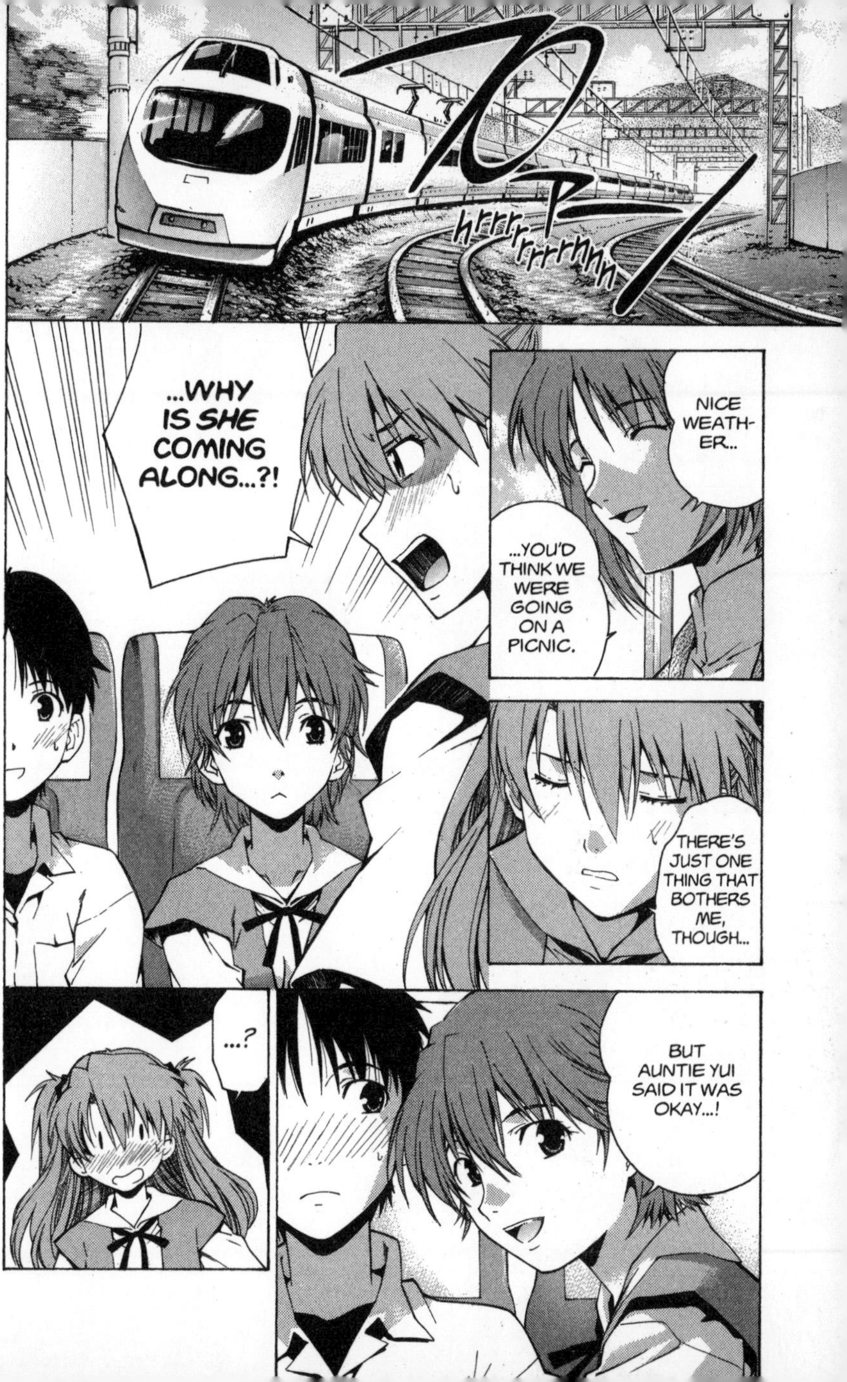
hrrrrrrrrrnnn
NICE WEATHER...
...YOU'D THINK WE WERE GOING ON A PICNIC.
THERE'S JUST ONE THING THAT BOTHERS ME, THOUGH...
...WHY IS SHE COMING ALONG...?!
BUT AUNTIE YUI SAID IT WAS OKAY...!
...?

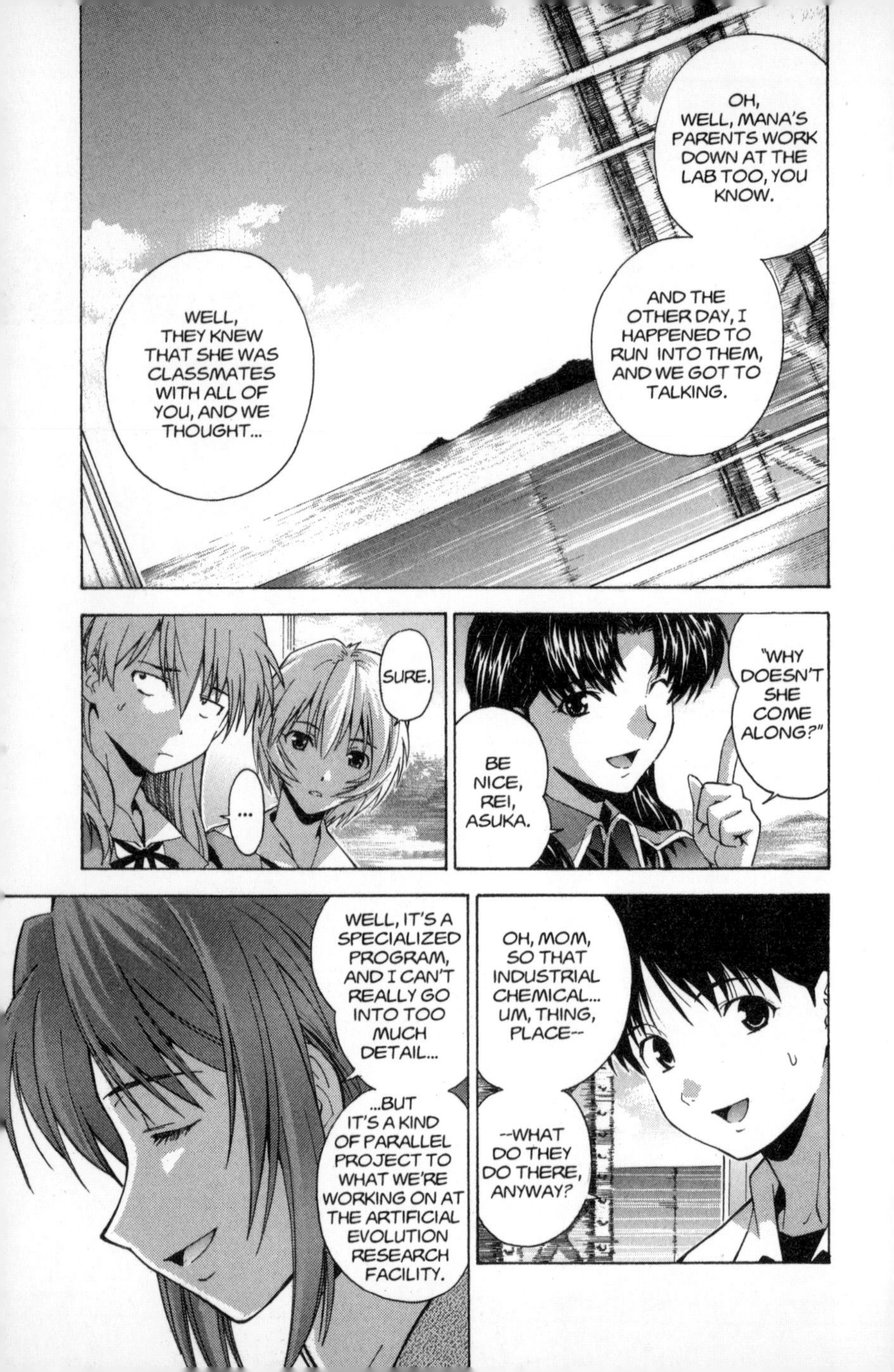
OH, WELL, MANA'S PARENTS WORK DOWN AT THE LAB TOO, YOU KNOW.
AND THE OTHER DAY, I HAPPENED TO RUN INTO THEM, AND WE GOT TO TALKING.
WELL, THEY KNEW THAT SHE WAS CLASSMATES WITH ALL OF YOU, AND WE THOUGHT...
"WHY DOESN'T SHE COME ALONG?"
BE NICE, REI, ASUKA.
SURE.
...
OH, MOM, SO THAT INDUSTRIAL CHEMICAL... UM, THING, PLACE--
--WHAT DO THEY DO THERE, ANYWAY?
WELL, IT'S A SPECIALIZED PROGRAM, AND I CAN'T REALLY GO INTO TOO MUCH DETAIL...
...BUT IT'S A KIND OF PARALLEL PROJECT TO WHAT WE'RE WORKING ON AT THE ARTIFICIAL EVOLUTION RESEARCH FACILITY.

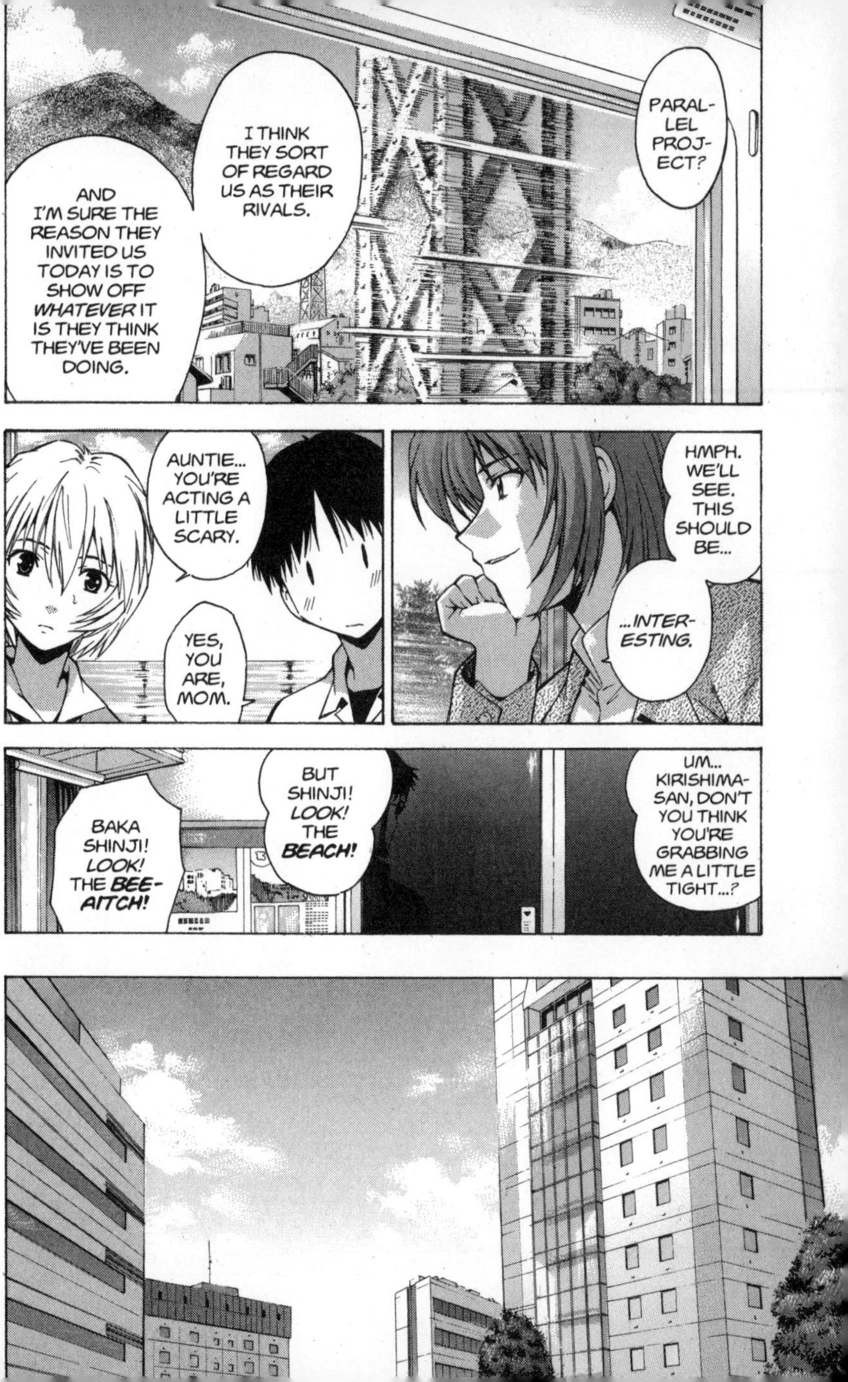
PARALLEL PROJECT?
I THINK THEY SORT OF REGARD US AS THEIR RIVALS.
AND I'M SURE THE REASON THEY INVITED US TODAY IS TO SHOW OFF *WHATEVER* IT IS THEY THINK THEY'VE BEEN DOING.
HMPH. WE'LL SEE. THIS SHOULD BE...
...INTERESTING.
AUNTIE... YOU'RE ACTING A LITTLE SCARY.
YES, YOU ARE, MOM.
UM... KIRISHIMA-SAN, DON'T YOU THINK YOU'RE GRABBING ME A LITTLE TIGHT...?
BUT SHINJI! *LOOK!* THE ***BEACH!***
BAKA SHINJI! *LOOK!* THE ***BEE-AITCH!***

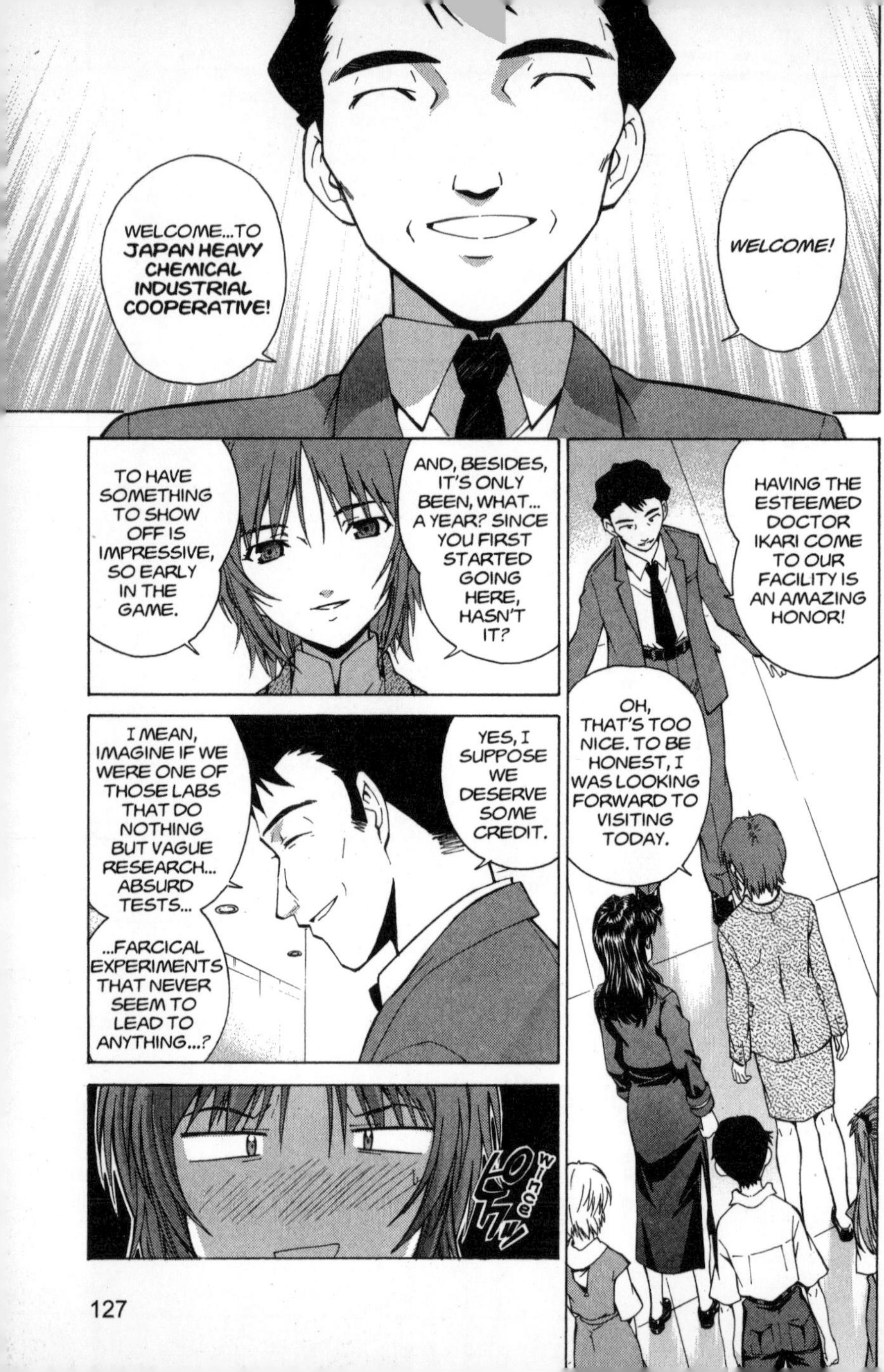
WELCOME!
WELCOME...TO JAPAN HEAVY CHEMICAL INDUSTRIAL COOPERATIVE!
HAVING THE ESTEEMED DOCTOR IKARI COME TO OUR FACILITY IS AN AMAZING HONOR!
OH, THAT'S TOO NICE. TO BE HONEST, I WAS LOOKING FORWARD TO VISITING TODAY.
AND, BESIDES, IT'S ONLY BEEN, WHAT... A YEAR? SINCE YOU FIRST STARTED GOING HERE, HASN'T IT?
TO HAVE SOMETHING TO SHOW OFF IS IMPRESSIVE, SO EARLY IN THE GAME.
YES, I SUPPOSE WE DESERVE SOME CREDIT.
I MEAN, IMAGINE IF WE WERE ONE OF THOSE LABS THAT DO NOTHING BUT VAGUE RESEARCH... ABSURD TESTS...
...FARCICAL EXPERIMENTS THAT NEVER SEEM TO LEAD TO ANYTHING...?
WINCE

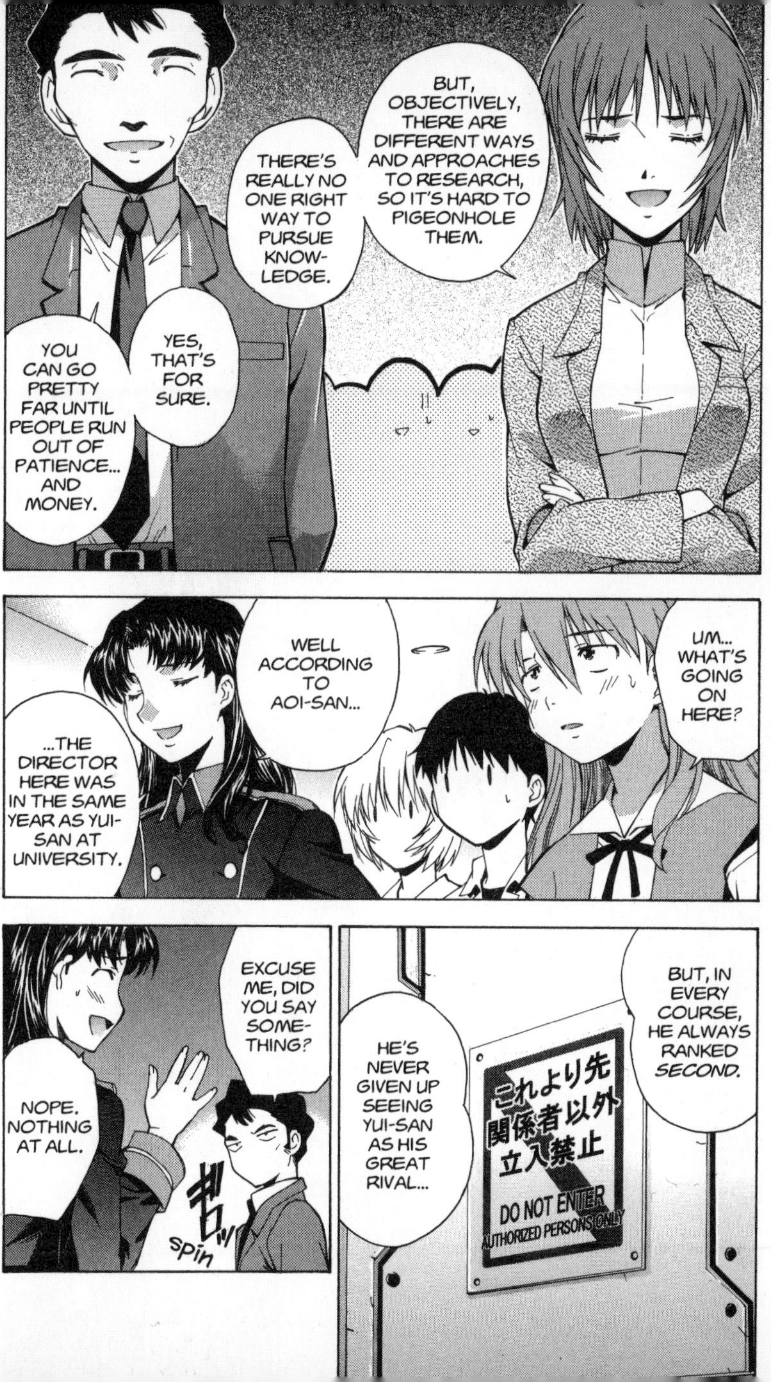
BUT, OBJECTIVELY, THERE ARE DIFFERENT WAYS AND APPROACHES TO RESEARCH, SO IT'S HARD TO PIGEONHOLE THEM.
THERE'S REALLY NO ONE RIGHT WAY TO PURSUE KNOW-LEDGE.
YES, THAT'S FOR SURE.
YOU CAN GO PRETTY FAR UNTIL PEOPLE RUN OUT OF PATIENCE... AND MONEY.
UM... WHAT'S GOING ON HERE?
WELL ACCORDING TO AOI-SAN...
...THE DIRECTOR HERE WAS IN THE SAME YEAR AS YUI-SAN AT UNIVERSITY.
BUT, IN EVERY COURSE, HE ALWAYS RANKED SECOND.
HE'S NEVER GIVEN UP SEEING YUI-SAN AS HIS GREAT RIVAL...
これより先
関係者以外
立入禁止
DO NOT ENTER
AUTHORIZED PERSONS ONLY
EXCUSE ME, DID YOU SAY SOME-THING?
NOPE. NOTHING AT ALL.
spin

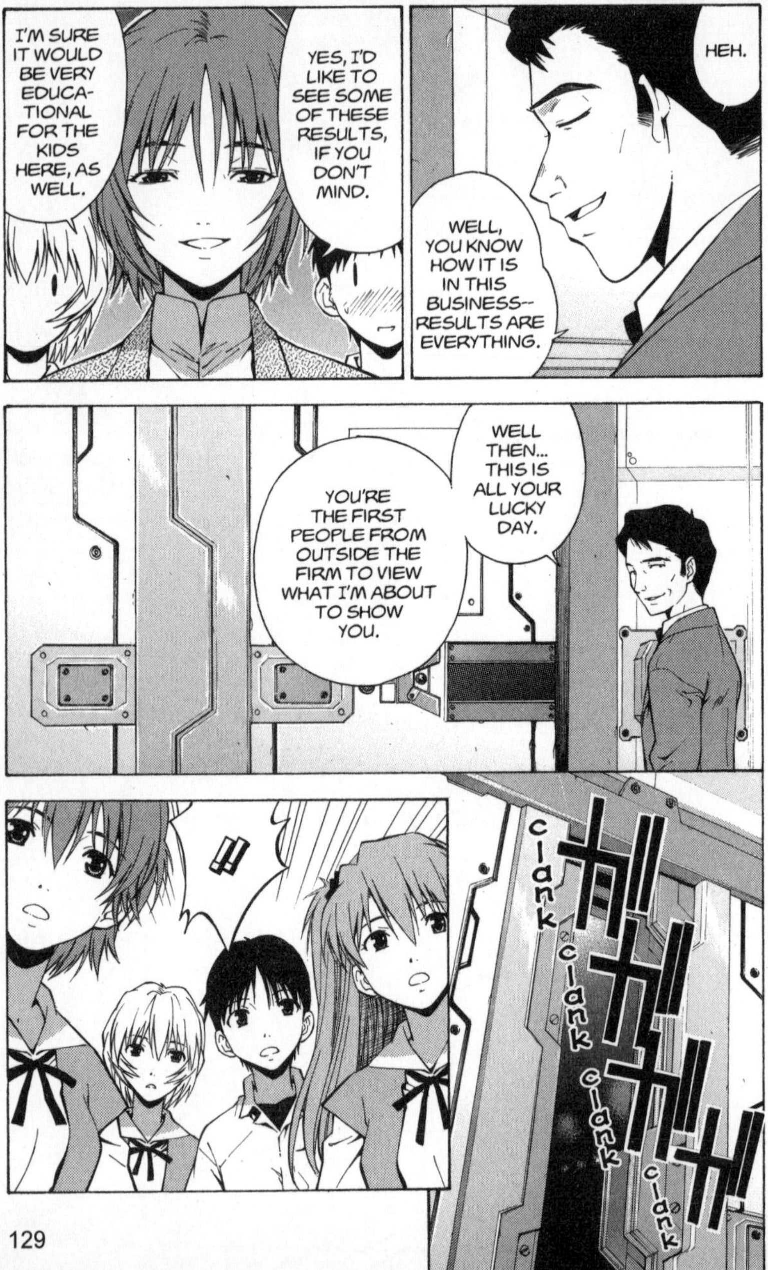
HEH.
WELL, YOU KNOW HOW IT IS IN THIS BUSINESS-- RESULTS ARE EVERYTHING.
YES, I'D LIKE TO SEE SOME OF THESE RESULTS, IF YOU DON'T MIND.
I'M SURE IT WOULD BE VERY EDUCATIONAL FOR THE KIDS HERE, AS WELL.
WELL THEN... THIS IS ALL YOUR LUCKY DAY.
YOU'RE THE FIRST PEOPLE FROM OUTSIDE THE FIRM TO VIEW WHAT I'M ABOUT TO SHOW YOU.
clank
clank
clank
clank
clank
!!

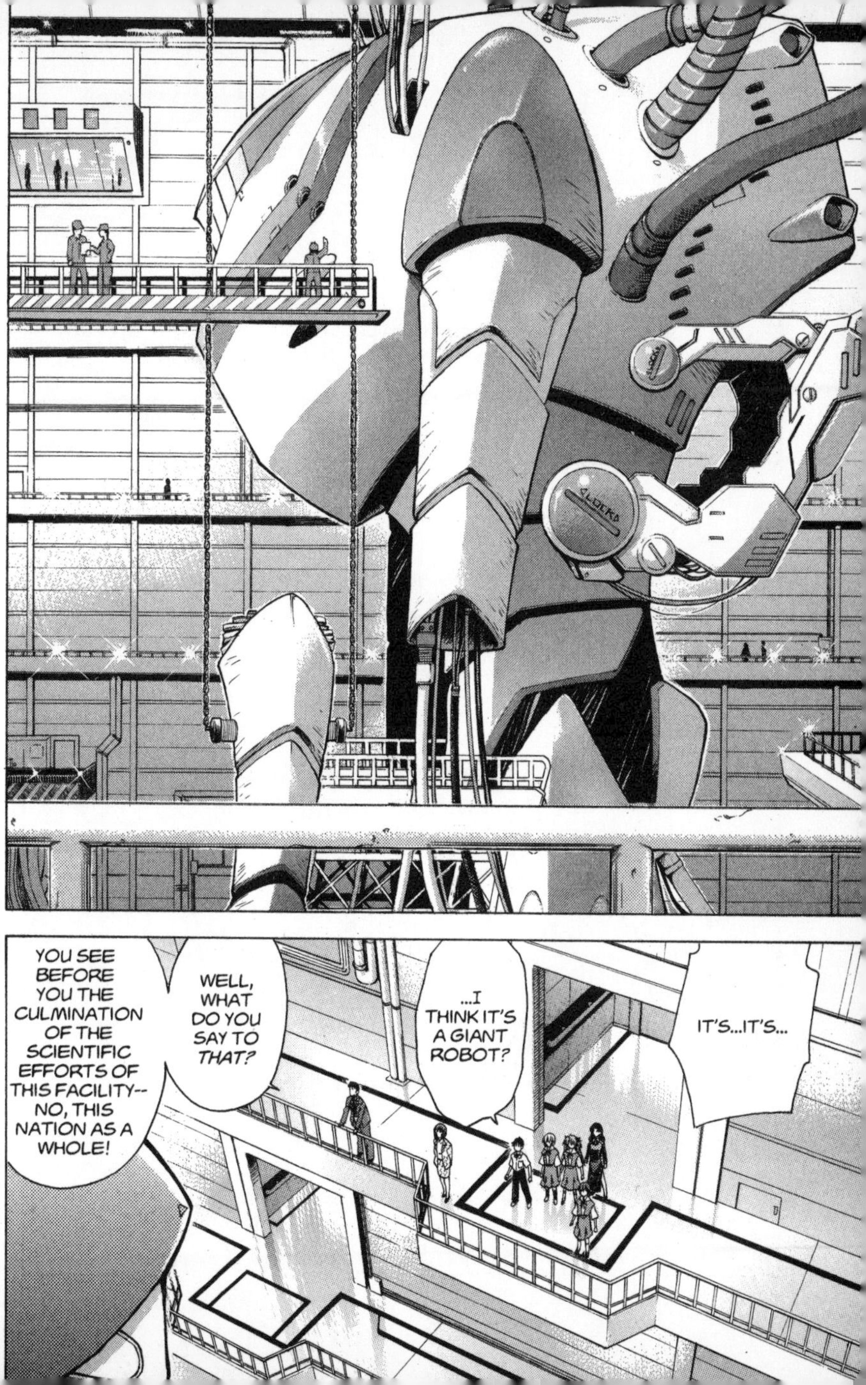
IT'S...IT'S...
...I THINK IT'S A GIANT ROBOT?
WELL, WHAT DO YOU SAY TO *THAT?*
YOU SEE BEFORE YOU THE CULMINATION OF THE SCIENTIFIC EFFORTS OF THIS FACILITY-- NO, THIS NATION AS A WHOLE!

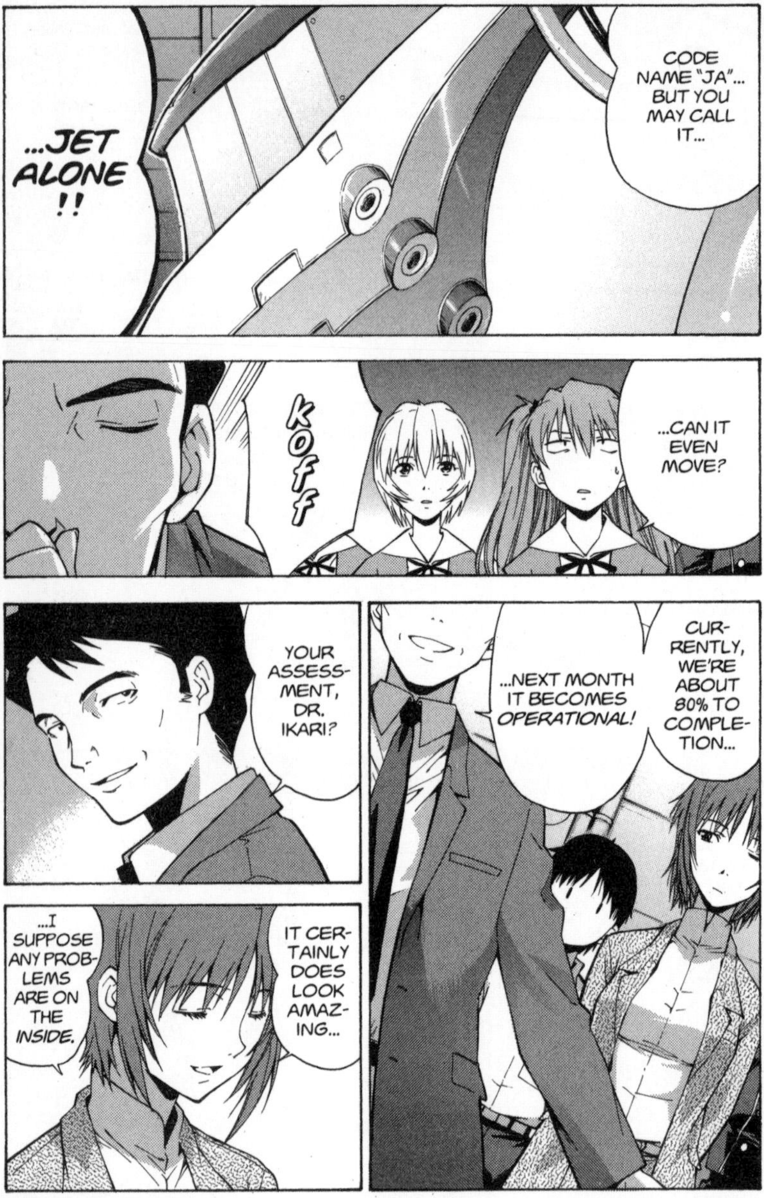
CODE NAME "JA"... BUT YOU MAY CALL IT...
...JET ALONE !!
...CAN IT EVEN MOVE?
KOFF
CURRENTLY, WE'RE ABOUT 80% TO COMPLETION...
...NEXT MONTH IT BECOMES OPERATIONAL!
YOUR ASSESSMENT, DR. IKARI?
IT CERTAINLY DOES LOOK AMAZING...
...I SUPPOSE ANY PROBLEMS ARE ON THE INSIDE.

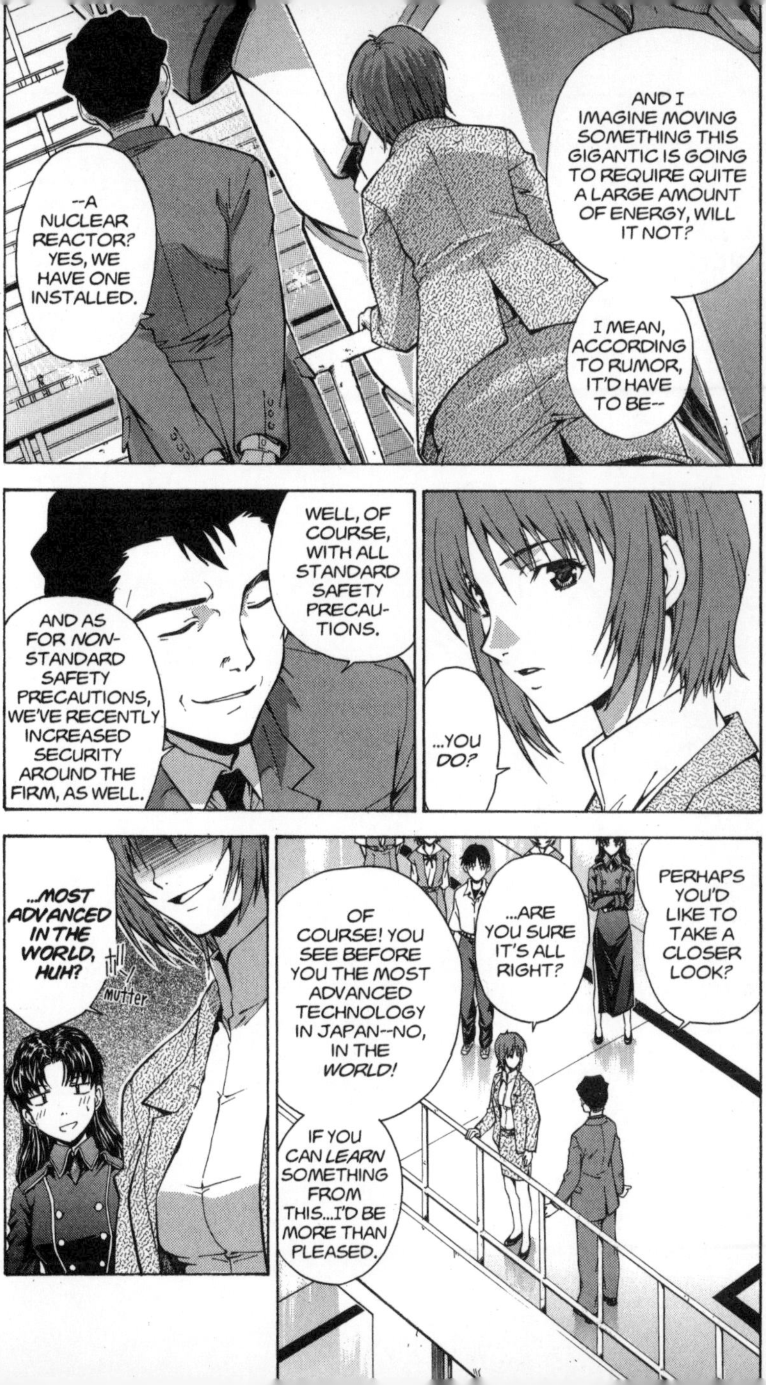
AND I IMAGINE MOVING SOMETHING THIS GIGANTIC IS GOING TO REQUIRE QUITE A LARGE AMOUNT OF ENERGY, WILL IT NOT?
I MEAN, ACCORDING TO RUMOR, IT'D HAVE TO BE--
--A NUCLEAR REACTOR? YES, WE HAVE ONE INSTALLED.
...YOU *DO?*
WELL, OF COURSE, WITH ALL STANDARD SAFETY PRECAU-TIONS.
AND AS FOR *NON*-STANDARD SAFETY PRECAUTIONS, WE'VE RECENTLY INCREASED SECURITY AROUND THE FIRM, AS WELL.
PERHAPS YOU'D LIKE TO TAKE A CLOSER LOOK?
...ARE YOU SURE IT'S ALL RIGHT?
OF COURSE! YOU SEE BEFORE YOU THE MOST ADVANCED TECHNOLOGY IN JAPAN--NO, IN THE *WORLD!*
IF YOU CAN *LEARN* SOMETHING FROM THIS...I'D BE MORE THAN PLEASED.
...MOST ADVANCED IN THE WORLD, HUH?
mutter

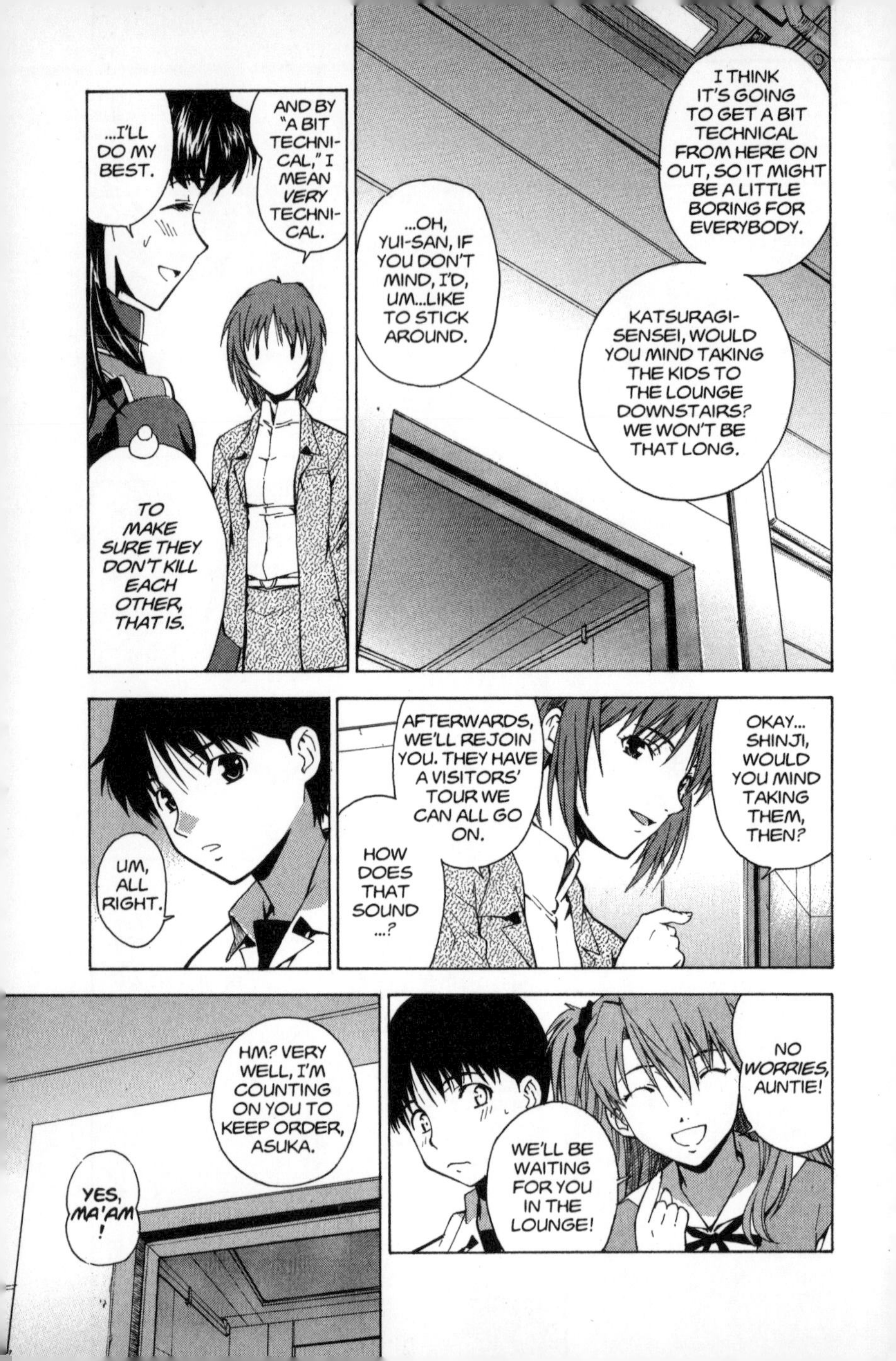
I THINK IT'S GOING TO GET A BIT TECHNICAL FROM HERE ON OUT, SO IT MIGHT BE A LITTLE BORING FOR EVERYBODY.
KATSURAGI-SENSEI, WOULD YOU MIND TAKING THE KIDS TO THE LOUNGE DOWNSTAIRS? WE WON'T BE THAT LONG.
...OH, YUI-SAN, IF YOU DON'T MIND, I'D, UM...LIKE TO STICK AROUND.
AND BY "A BIT TECHNI-CAL," I MEAN *VERY* TECHNI-CAL.
...I'LL DO MY BEST.
TO MAKE SURE THEY DON'T KILL EACH OTHER, THAT IS.
OKAY... SHINJI, WOULD YOU MIND TAKING THEM, THEN?
AFTERWARDS, WE'LL REJOIN YOU. THEY HAVE A VISITORS' TOUR WE CAN ALL GO ON.
HOW DOES THAT SOUND ...?
UM, ALL RIGHT.
NO *WORRIES,* AUNTIE!
WE'LL BE WAITING FOR YOU IN THE LOUNGE!
HM? VERY WELL, I'M COUNTING ON YOU TO KEEP ORDER, ASUKA.
YES, MA'AM!

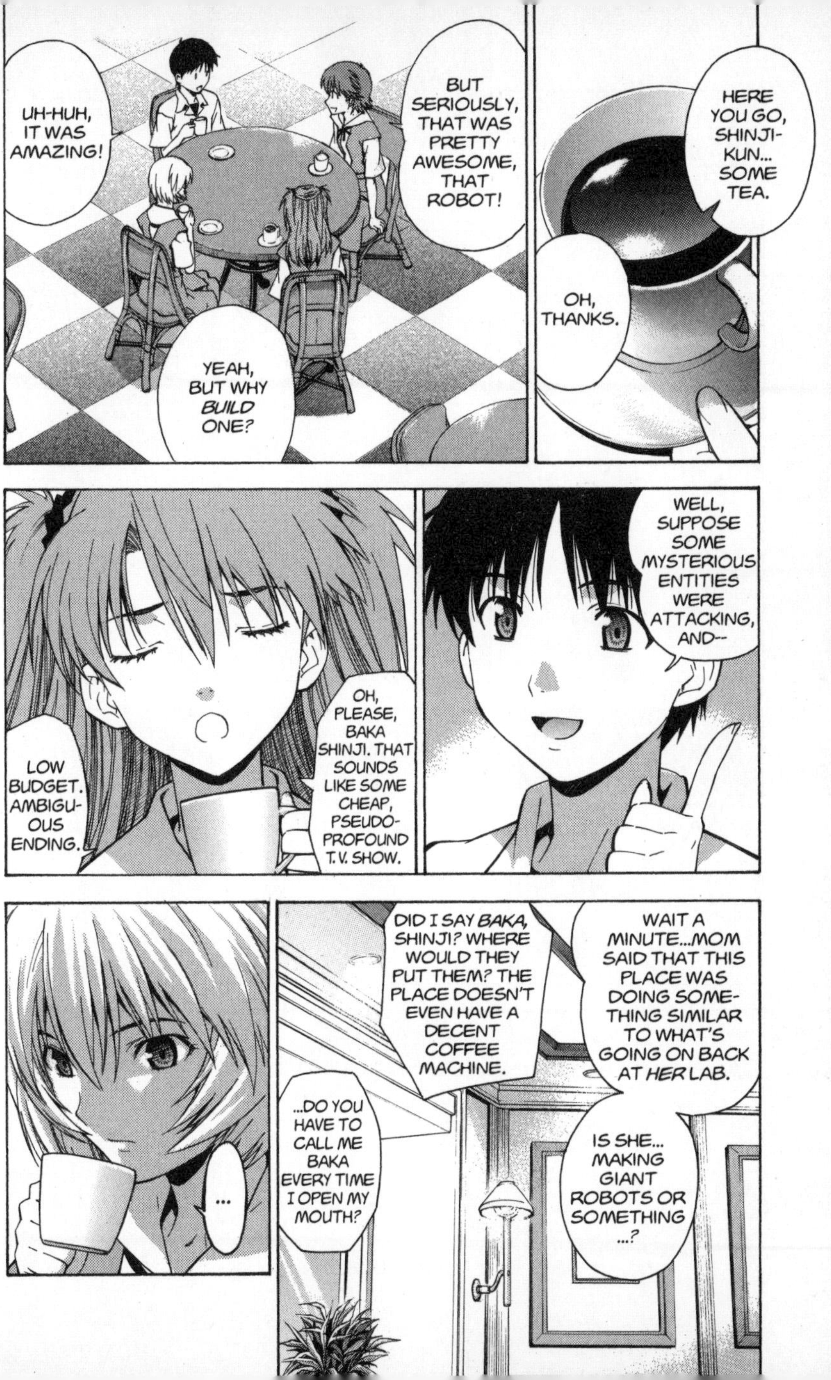
HERE YOU GO, SHINJI-KUN... SOME TEA.
OH, THANKS.
BUT SERIOUSLY, THAT WAS PRETTY AWESOME, THAT ROBOT!
UH-HUH, IT WAS AMAZING!
YEAH, BUT WHY *BUILD* ONE?
WELL, SUPPOSE SOME MYSTERIOUS ENTITIES WERE ATTACKING, AND--
OH, PLEASE, BAKA SHINJI. THAT SOUNDS LIKE SOME CHEAP, PSEUDO-PROFOUND T.V. SHOW.
LOW BUDGET. AMBIGU-OUS ENDING.
WAIT A MINUTE...MOM SAID THAT THIS PLACE WAS DOING SOME-THING SIMILAR TO WHAT'S GOING ON BACK AT *HER* LAB.
DID I SAY *BAKA*, SHINJI? WHERE WOULD THEY PUT THEM? THE PLACE DOESN'T EVEN HAVE A DECENT COFFEE MACHINE.
IS SHE... MAKING GIANT ROBOTS OR SOMETHING ...?
...DO YOU HAVE TO CALL ME BAKA EVERY TIME I OPEN MY MOUTH?
...

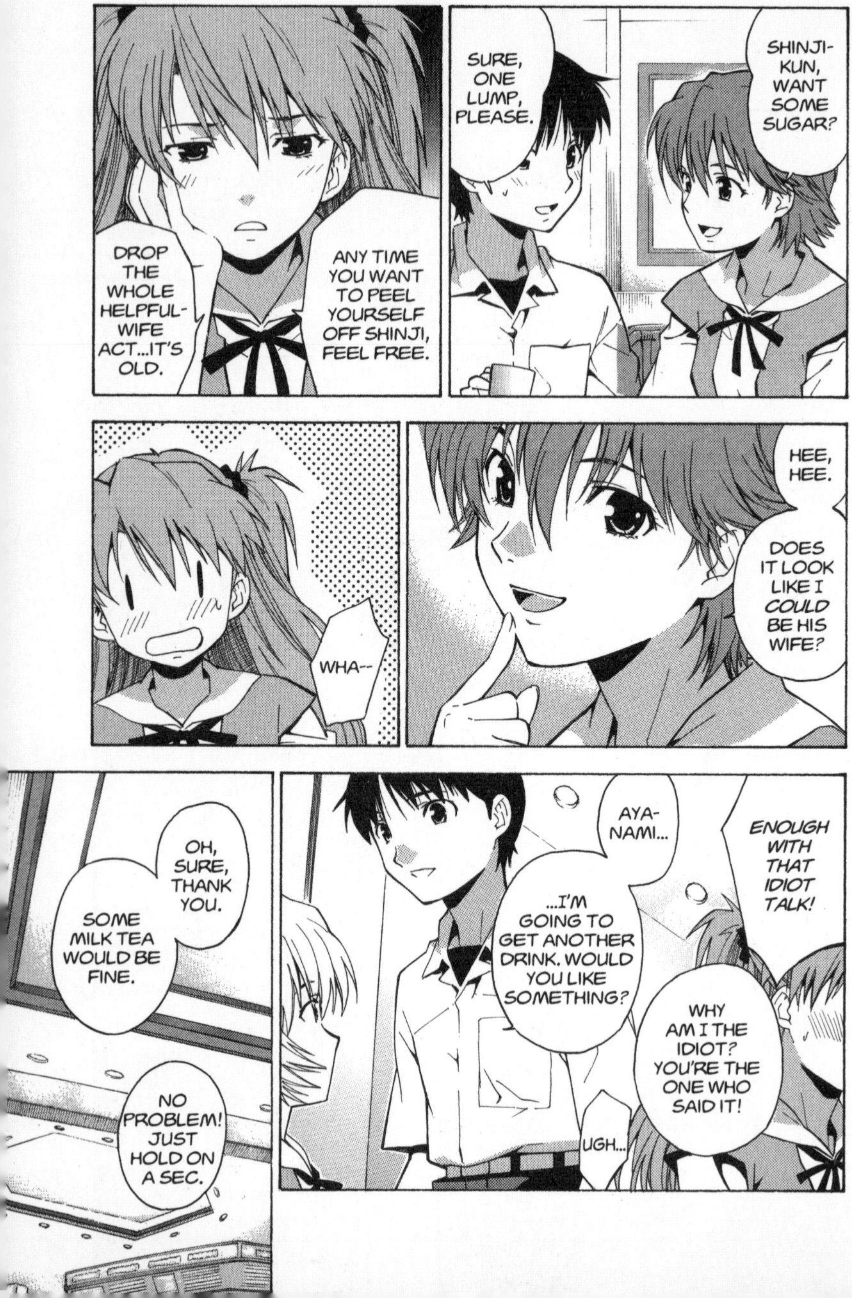
SHINJI-KUN, WANT SOME SUGAR?
SURE, ONE LUMP, PLEASE.
ANY TIME YOU WANT TO PEEL YOURSELF OFF SHINJI, FEEL FREE.
DROP THE WHOLE HELPFUL-WIFE ACT...IT'S OLD.
HEE, HEE.
DOES IT LOOK LIKE I *COULD* BE HIS WIFE?
WHA--
ENOUGH WITH THAT IDIOT TALK!
WHY AM I THE IDIOT? YOU'RE THE ONE WHO SAID IT!
UGH...
AYA-NAMI...
...I'M GOING TO GET ANOTHER DRINK. WOULD YOU LIKE SOMETHING?
OH, SURE, THANK YOU.
SOME MILK TEA WOULD BE FINE.
NO PROBLEM! JUST HOLD ON A SEC.

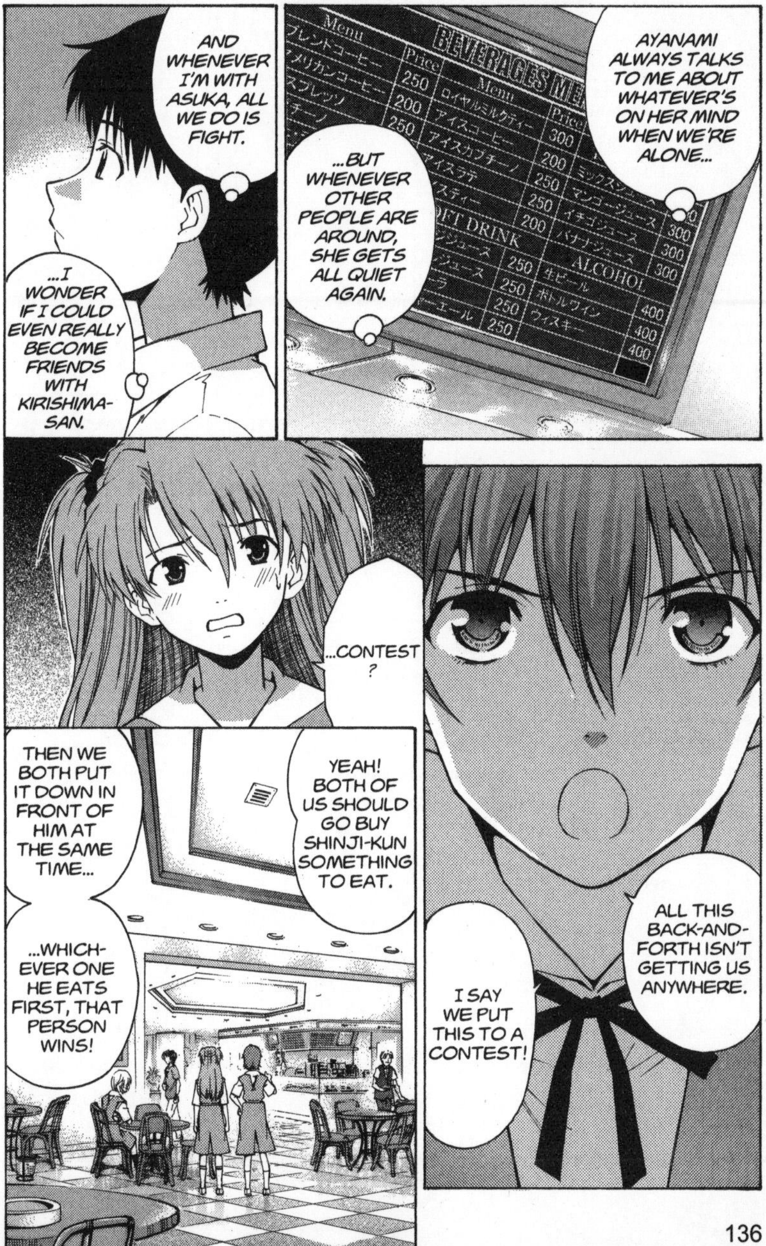
AYANAMI ALWAYS TALKS TO ME ABOUT WHATEVER'S ON HER MIND WHEN WE'RE ALONE...
...BUT WHENEVER OTHER PEOPLE ARE AROUND, SHE GETS ALL QUIET AGAIN.
AND WHENEVER I'M WITH ASUKA, ALL WE DO IS FIGHT.
...I WONDER IF I COULD EVEN REALLY BECOME FRIENDS WITH KIRISHIMA-SAN.
ALL THIS BACK-AND-FORTH ISN'T GETTING US ANYWHERE.
I SAY WE PUT THIS TO A CONTEST!
...CONTEST?
YEAH! BOTH OF US SHOULD GO BUY SHINJI-KUN SOMETHING TO EAT.
THEN WE BOTH PUT IT DOWN IN FRONT OF HIM AT THE SAME TIME...
...WHICH-EVER ONE HE EATS FIRST, THAT PERSON WINS!

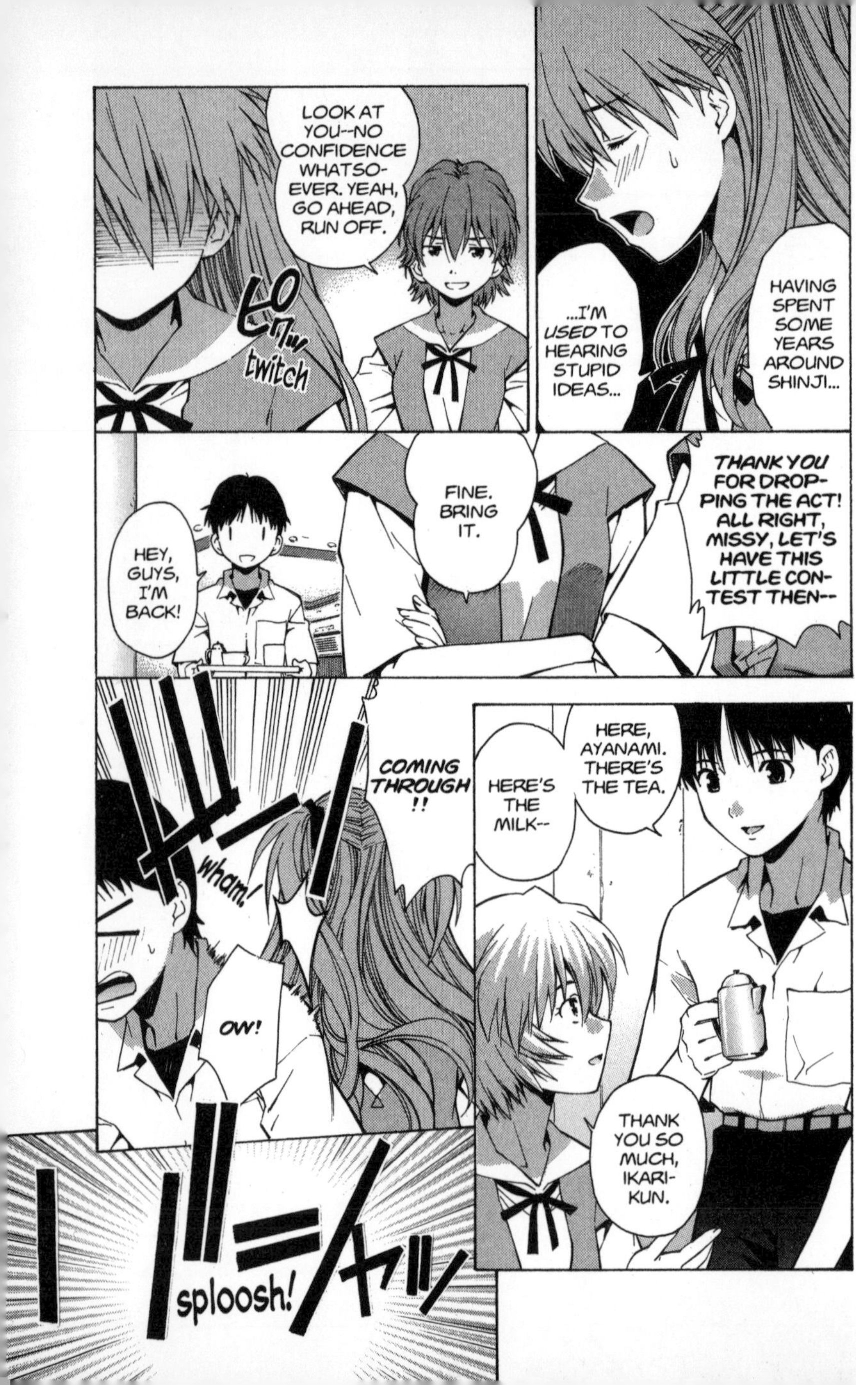
HAVING SPENT SOME YEARS AROUND SHINJI...
...I'M *USED* TO HEARING STUPID IDEAS...
LOOK AT YOU--NO CONFIDENCE WHATSOEVER. YEAH, GO AHEAD, RUN OFF.
twitch
THANK YOU FOR DROPPING THE ACT! ALL RIGHT, MISSY, LET'S HAVE THIS LITTLE CONTEST THEN--
FINE. BRING IT.
HEY, GUYS, I'M BACK!
HERE, AYANAMI. THERE'S THE TEA.
HERE'S THE MILK--
THANK YOU SO MUCH, IKARI-KUN.
COMING THROUGH!!
wham!
OW!
sploosh!

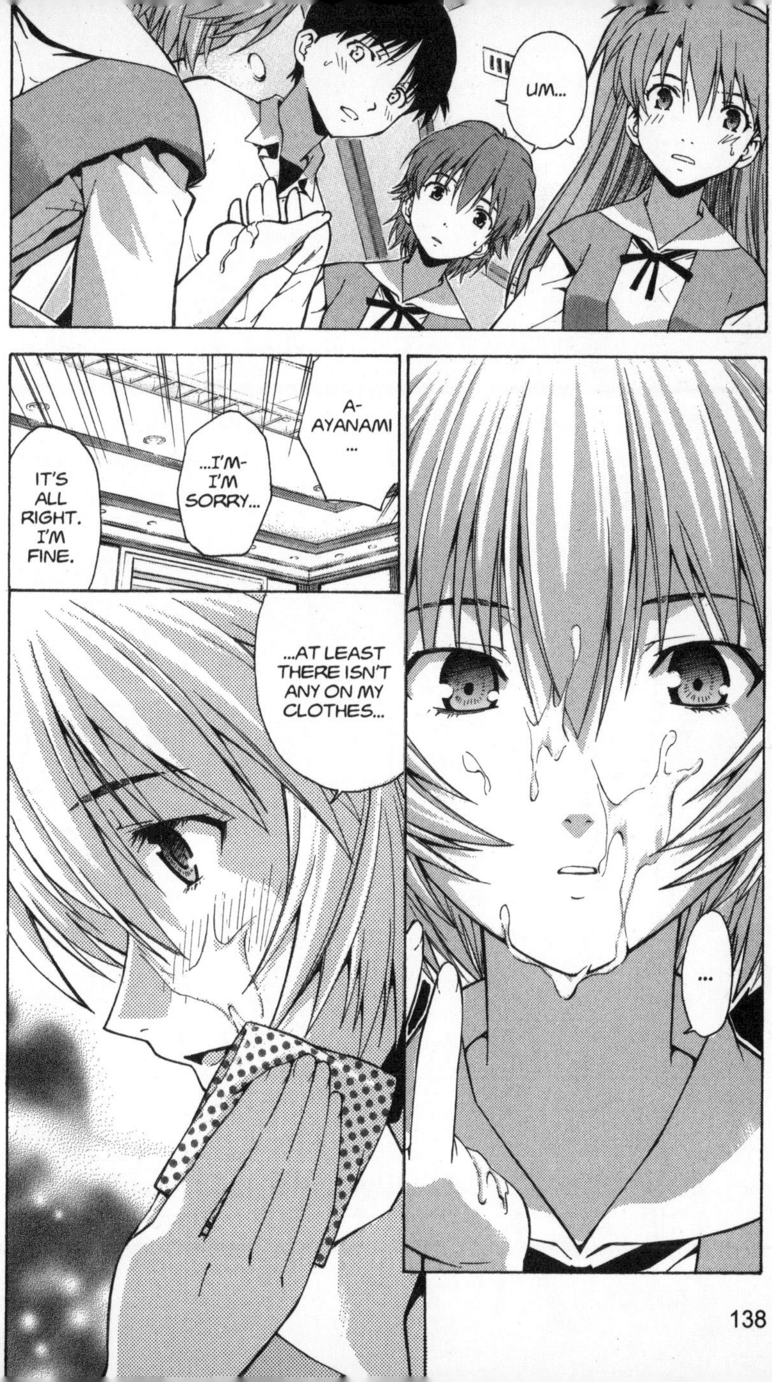
UM...
...
A-AYANAMI...
...I'M-I'M SORRY...
IT'S ALL RIGHT. I'M FINE.
...AT LEAST THERE ISN'T ANY ON MY CLOTHES...

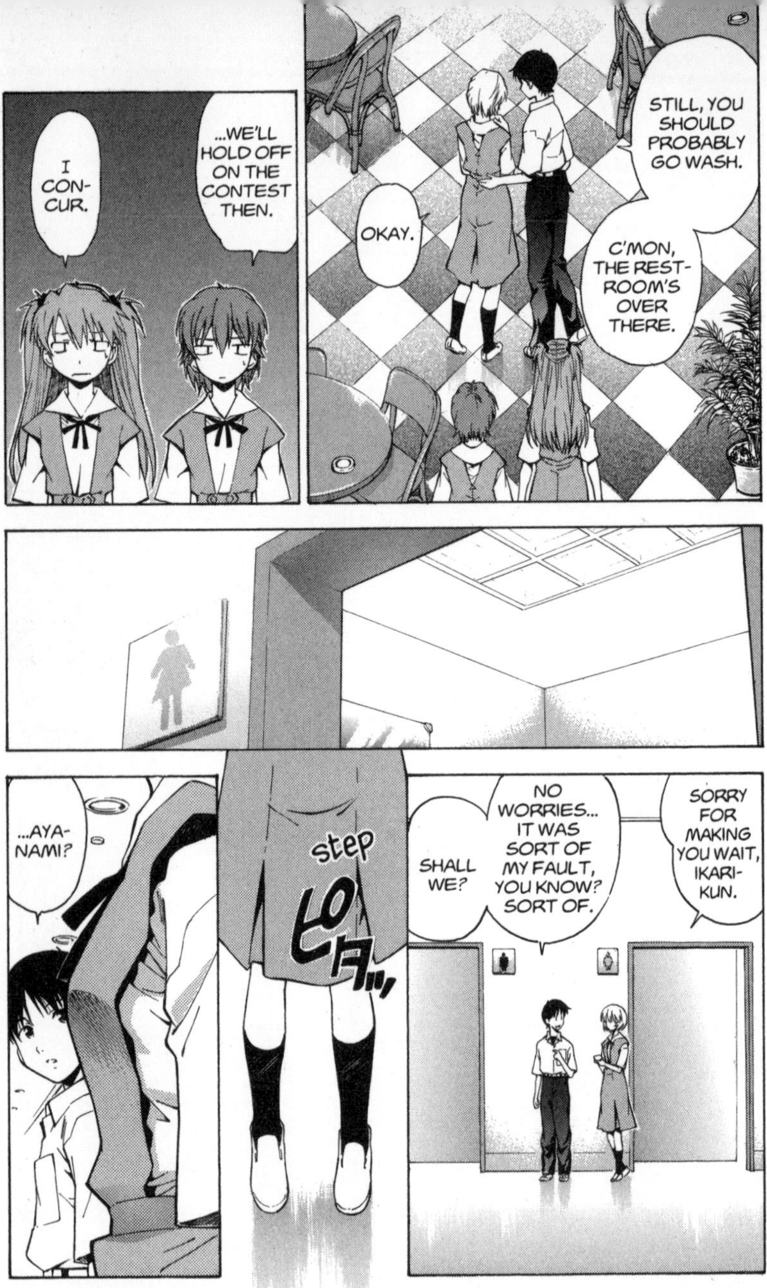
STILL, YOU SHOULD PROBABLY GO WASH.
OKAY.
C'MON, THE REST-ROOM'S OVER THERE.
...WE'LL HOLD OFF ON THE CONTEST THEN.
I CON-CUR.
SORRY FOR MAKING YOU WAIT, IKARI-KUN.
NO WORRIES... IT WAS SORT OF MY FAULT, YOU KNOW? SORT OF.
SHALL WE?
step
...AYA-NAMI?

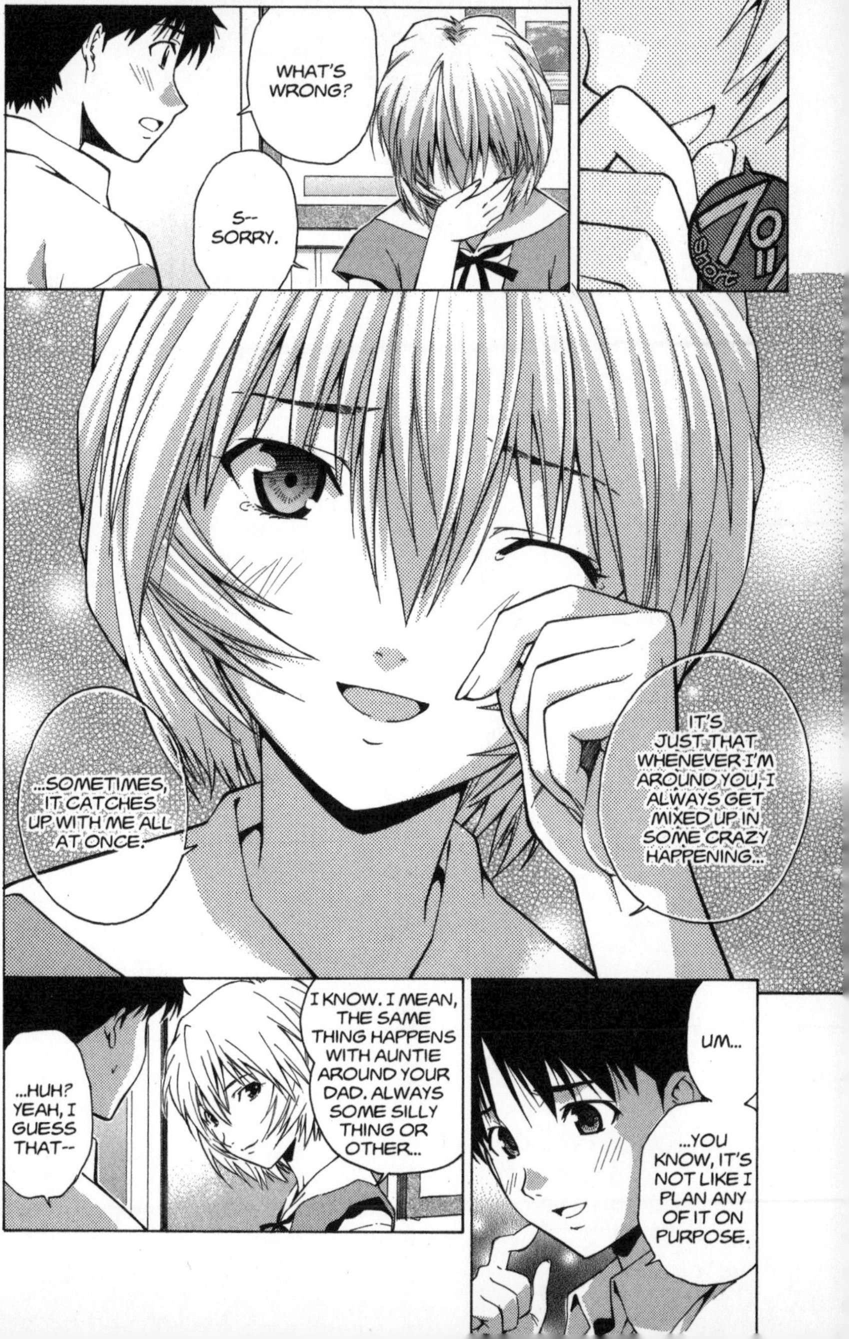
WHAT'S WRONG?
S-- SORRY.
IT'S JUST THAT WHENEVER I'M AROUND YOU, I ALWAYS GET MIXED UP IN SOME CRAZY HAPPENING...
...SOMETIMES, IT CATCHES UP WITH ME ALL AT ONCE.
UM...
...YOU KNOW, IT'S NOT LIKE I PLAN ANY OF IT ON PURPOSE.
I KNOW. I MEAN, THE SAME THING HAPPENS WITH AUNTIE AROUND YOUR DAD. ALWAYS SOME SILLY THING OR OTHER...
...HUH? YEAH, I GUESS THAT--

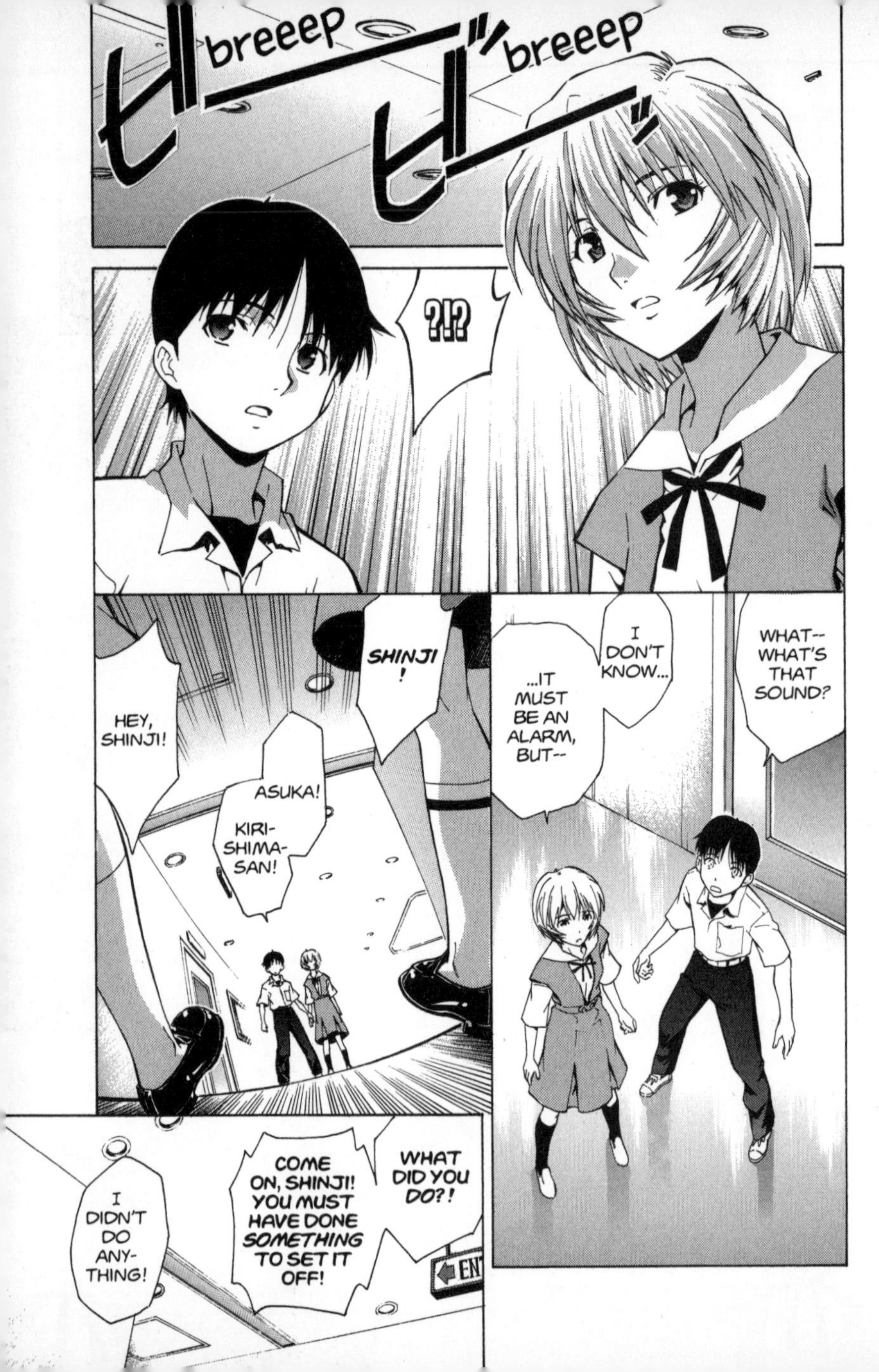
breeep
breeep
?!?
WHAT-- WHAT'S THAT SOUND?
I DON'T KNOW...
...IT MUST BE AN ALARM, BUT--
SHINJI!
HEY, SHINJI!
ASUKA!
KIRI-SHIMA-SAN!
WHAT DID YOU DO?!
COME ON, SHINJI! YOU MUST HAVE DONE SOMETHING TO SET IT OFF!
I DIDN'T DO ANY-THING!

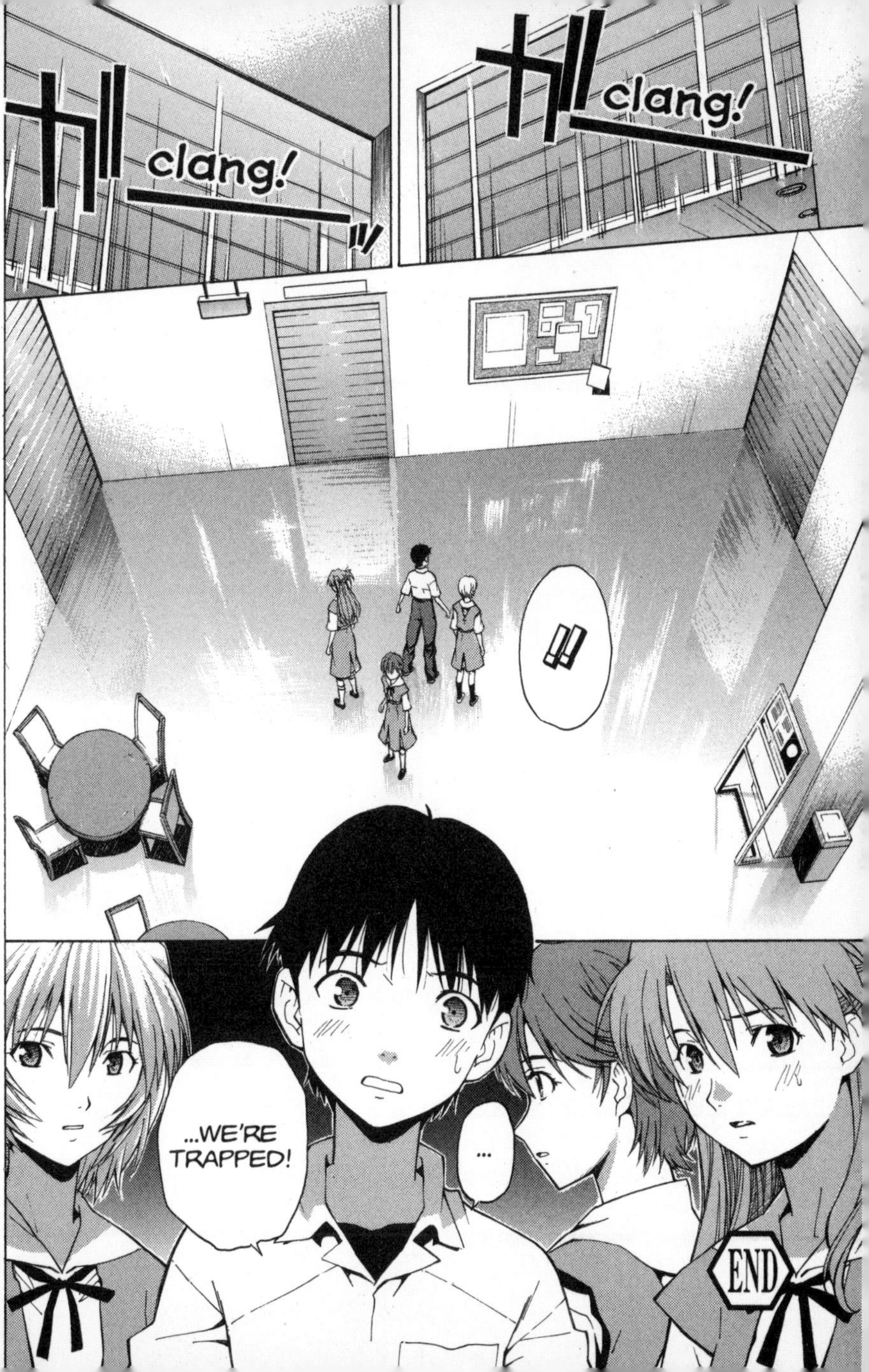
clang!
clang!
!!
...
...WE'RE TRAPPED!
END

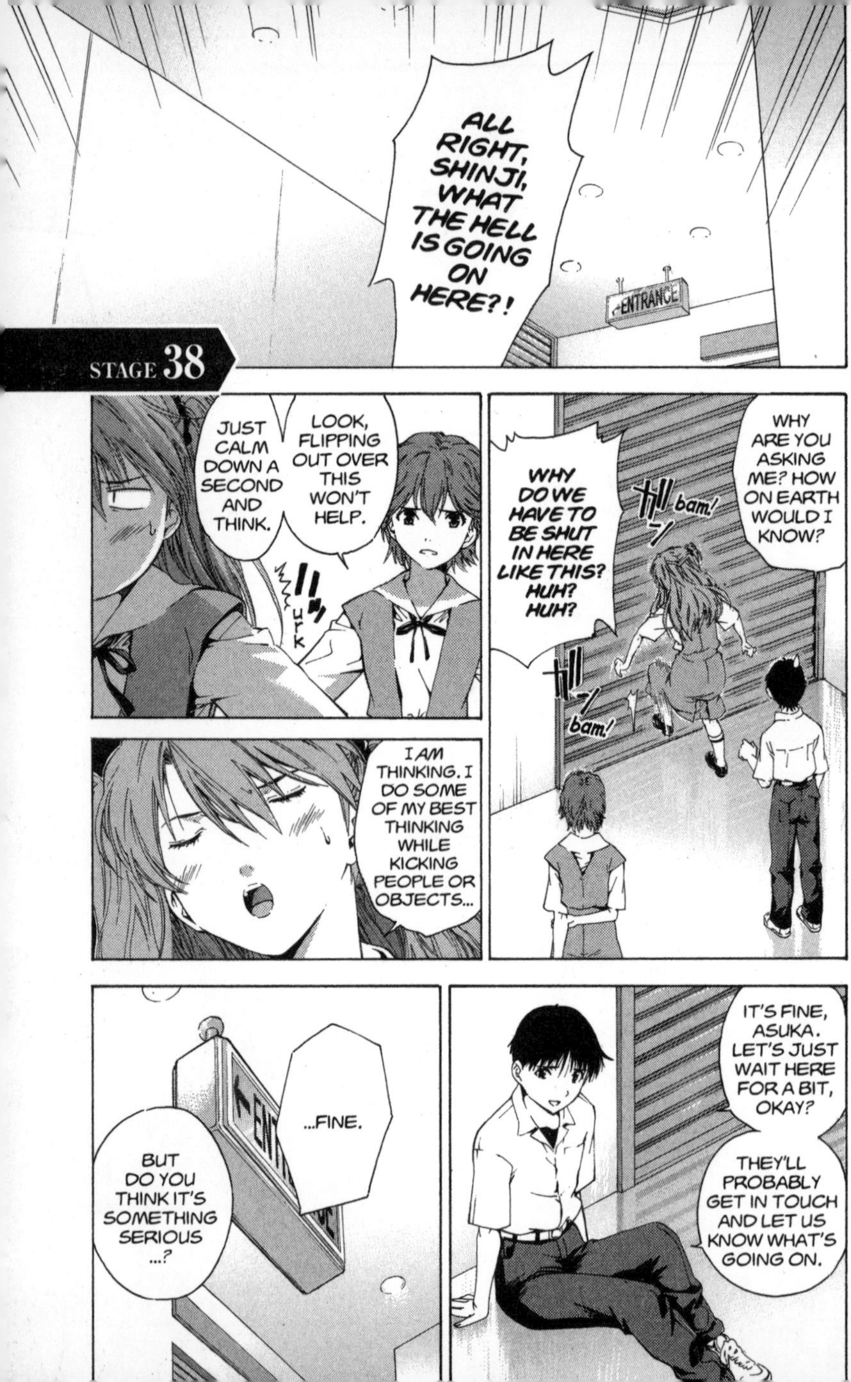
ALL RIGHT, SHINJI, WHAT THE HELL IS GOING ON HERE?!
ENTRANCE
STAGE 38
WHY ARE YOU ASKING ME? HOW ON EARTH WOULD I KNOW?
WHY DO WE HAVE TO BE SHUT IN HERE LIKE THIS? HUH? HUH?
bam!
bam!
LOOK, FLIPPING OUT OVER THIS WON'T HELP.
JUST CALM DOWN A SECOND AND THINK.
urk
I AM THINKING. I DO SOME OF MY BEST THINKING WHILE KICKING PEOPLE OR OBJECTS...
IT'S FINE, ASUKA. LET'S JUST WAIT HERE FOR A BIT, OKAY?
THEY'LL PROBABLY GET IN TOUCH AND LET US KNOW WHAT'S GOING ON.
...FINE.
BUT DO YOU THINK IT'S SOMETHING SERIOUS ...?

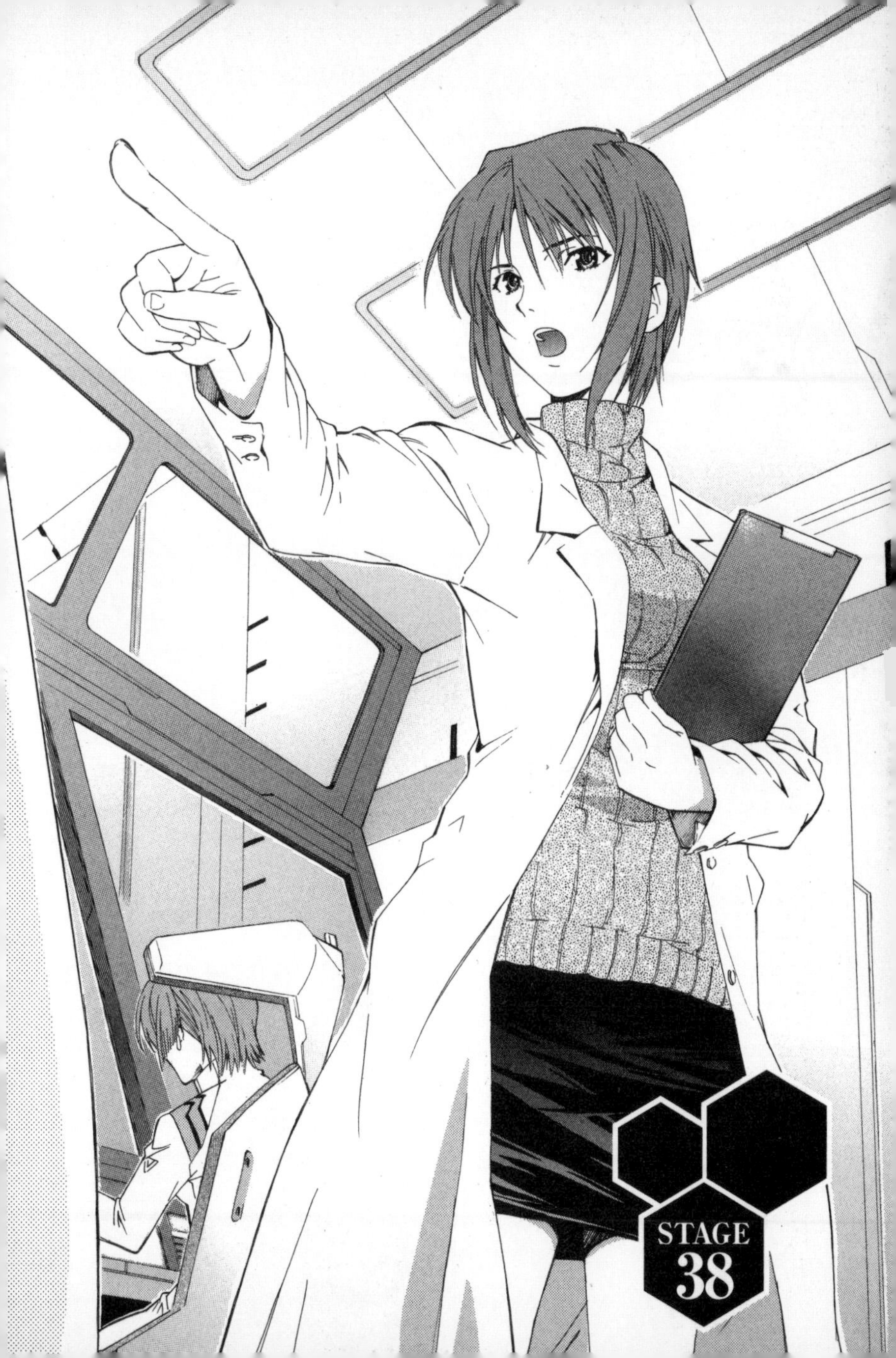
STAGE
38

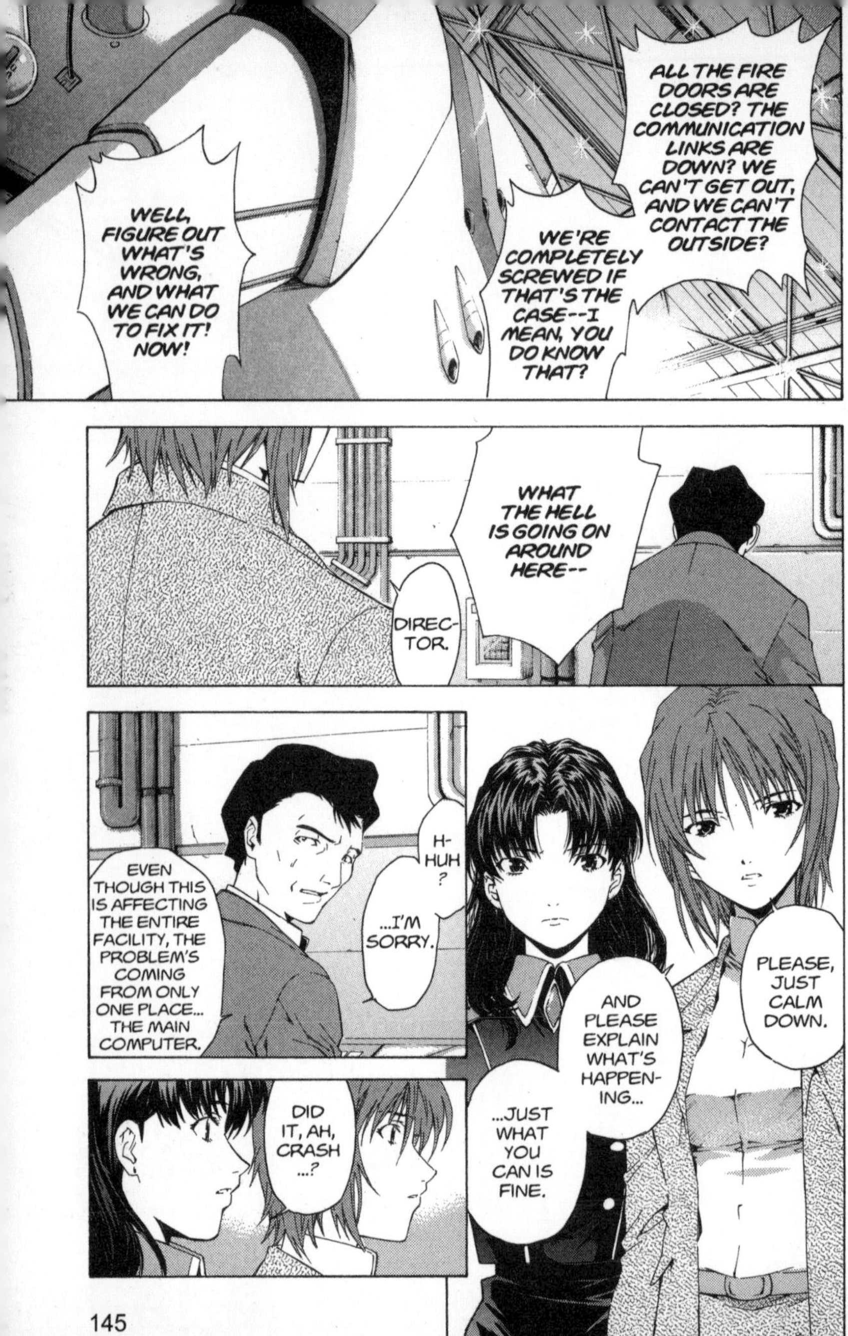
ALL THE FIRE DOORS ARE CLOSED? THE COMMUNICATION LINKS ARE DOWN? WE CAN'T GET OUT, AND WE CAN'T CONTACT THE OUTSIDE?
WE'RE COMPLETELY SCREWED IF THAT'S THE CASE--I MEAN, YOU DO KNOW THAT?
WELL, FIGURE OUT WHAT'S WRONG, AND WHAT WE CAN DO TO FIX IT! NOW!
WHAT THE HELL IS GOING ON AROUND HERE--
DIREC-TOR.
PLEASE, JUST CALM DOWN.
AND PLEASE EXPLAIN WHAT'S HAPPEN-ING...
...JUST WHAT YOU CAN IS FINE.
H-HUH?
...I'M SORRY.
EVEN THOUGH THIS IS AFFECTING THE ENTIRE FACILITY, THE PROBLEM'S COMING FROM ONLY ONE PLACE... THE MAIN COMPUTER.
DID IT, AH, CRASH...?

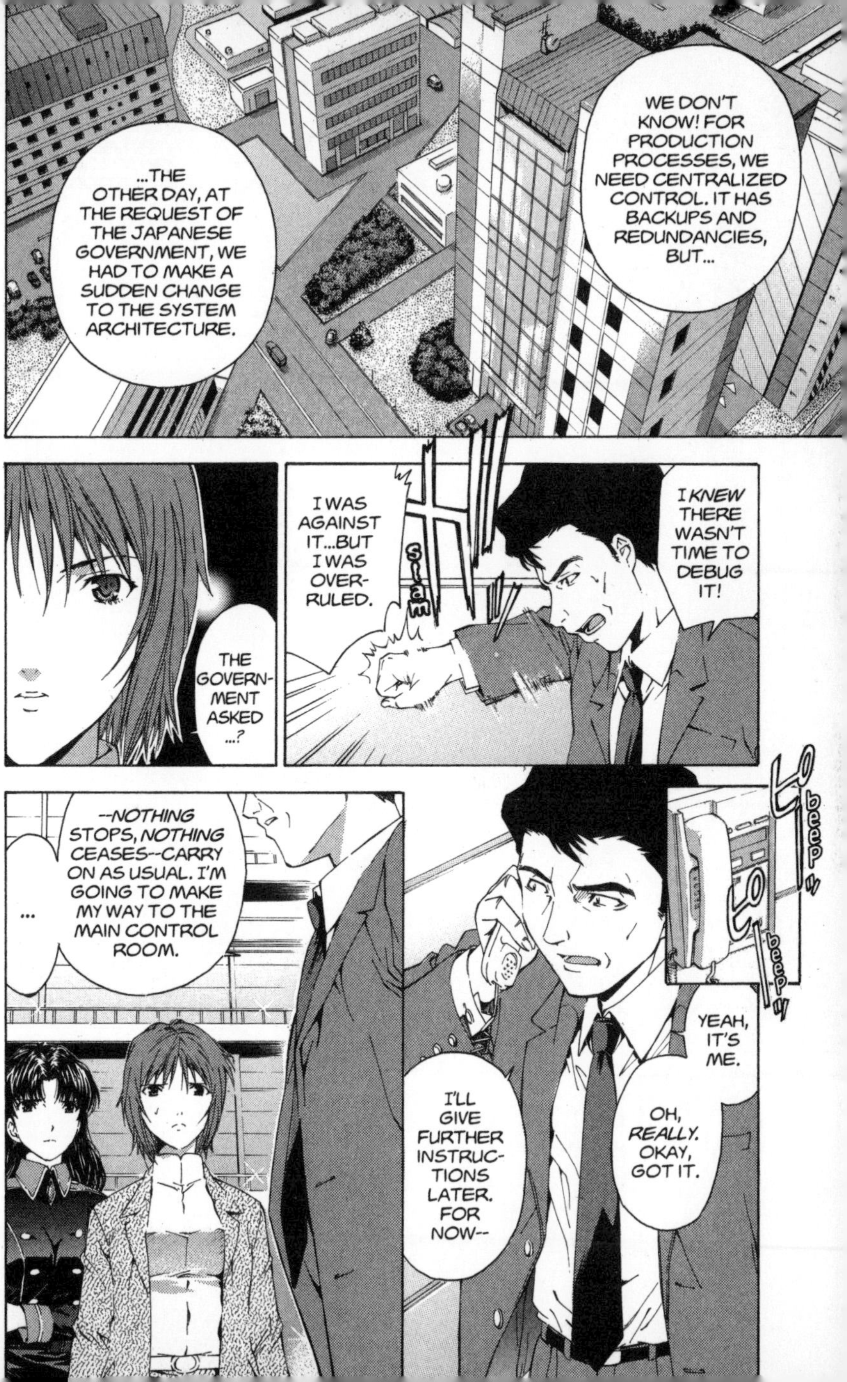

WE DON'T KNOW! FOR PRODUCTION PROCESSES, WE NEED CENTRALIZED CONTROL. IT HAS BACKUPS AND REDUNDANCIES, BUT...
...THE OTHER DAY, AT THE REQUEST OF THE JAPANESE GOVERNMENT, WE HAD TO MAKE A SUDDEN CHANGE TO THE SYSTEM ARCHITECTURE.
I KNEW THERE WASN'T TIME TO DEBUG IT!
slam
I WAS AGAINST IT...BUT I WAS OVER-RULED.
THE GOVERN-MENT ASKED ...?
beep
beep
YEAH, IT'S ME.
OH, REALLY. OKAY, GOT IT.
I'LL GIVE FURTHER INSTRUC-TIONS LATER. FOR NOW--
--NOTHING STOPS, NOTHING CEASES--CARRY ON AS USUAL. I'M GOING TO MAKE MY WAY TO THE MAIN CONTROL ROOM.
...

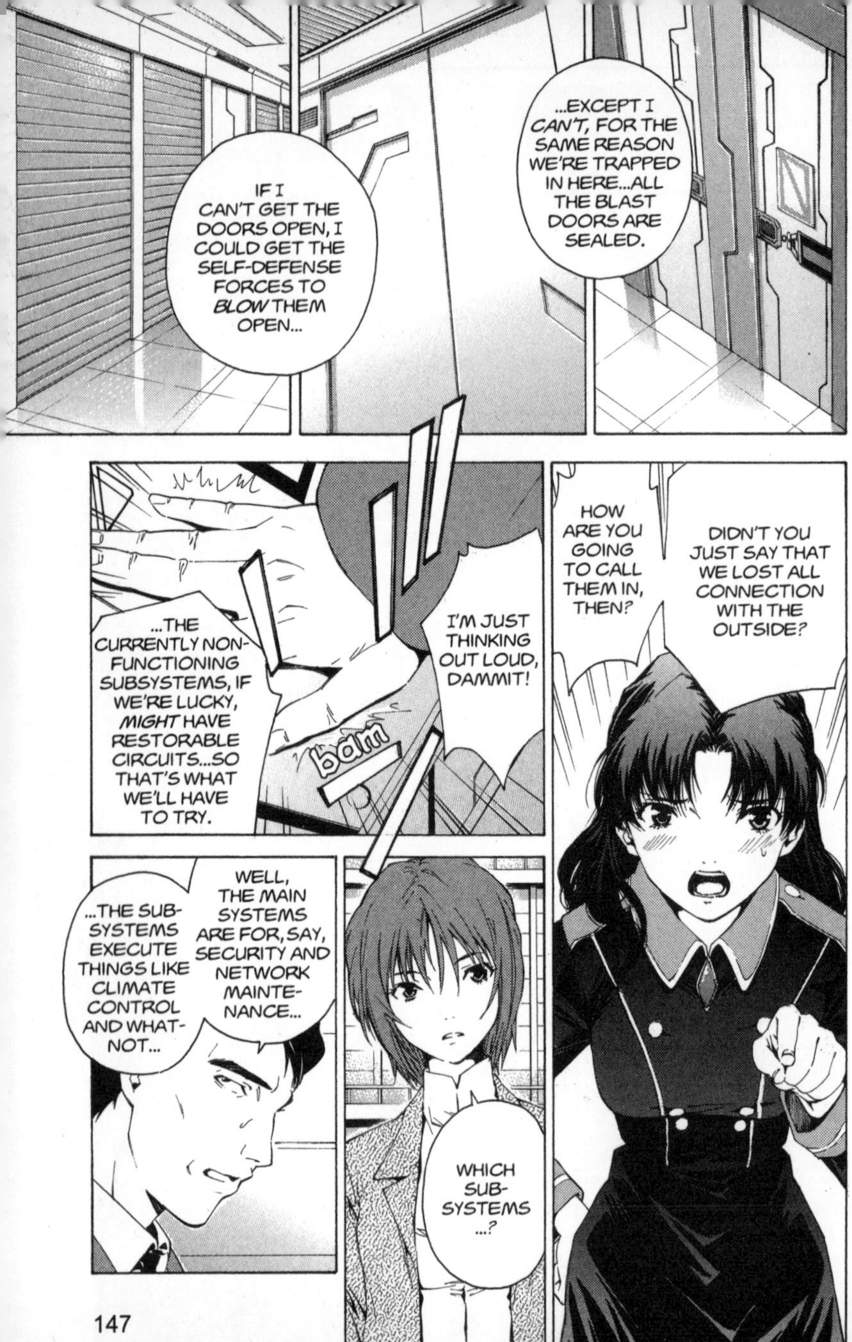
IF I CAN'T GET THE DOORS OPEN, I COULD GET THE SELF-DEFENSE FORCES TO *BLOW* THEM OPEN...
...EXCEPT I *CAN'T*, FOR THE SAME REASON WE'RE TRAPPED IN HERE...ALL THE BLAST DOORS ARE SEALED.
DIDN'T YOU JUST SAY THAT WE LOST ALL CONNECTION WITH THE OUTSIDE?
HOW ARE YOU GOING TO CALL THEM IN, THEN?
I'M JUST THINKING OUT LOUD, DAMMIT!
...THE CURRENTLY NON-FUNCTIONING SUBSYSTEMS, IF WE'RE LUCKY, *MIGHT* HAVE RESTORABLE CIRCUITS...SO THAT'S WHAT WE'LL HAVE TO TRY.
bam
WHICH SUB-SYSTEMS ...?
WELL, THE MAIN SYSTEMS ARE FOR, SAY, SECURITY AND NETWORK MAINTE-NANCE...
...THE SUB-SYSTEMS EXECUTE THINGS LIKE CLIMATE CONTROL AND WHAT-NOT...

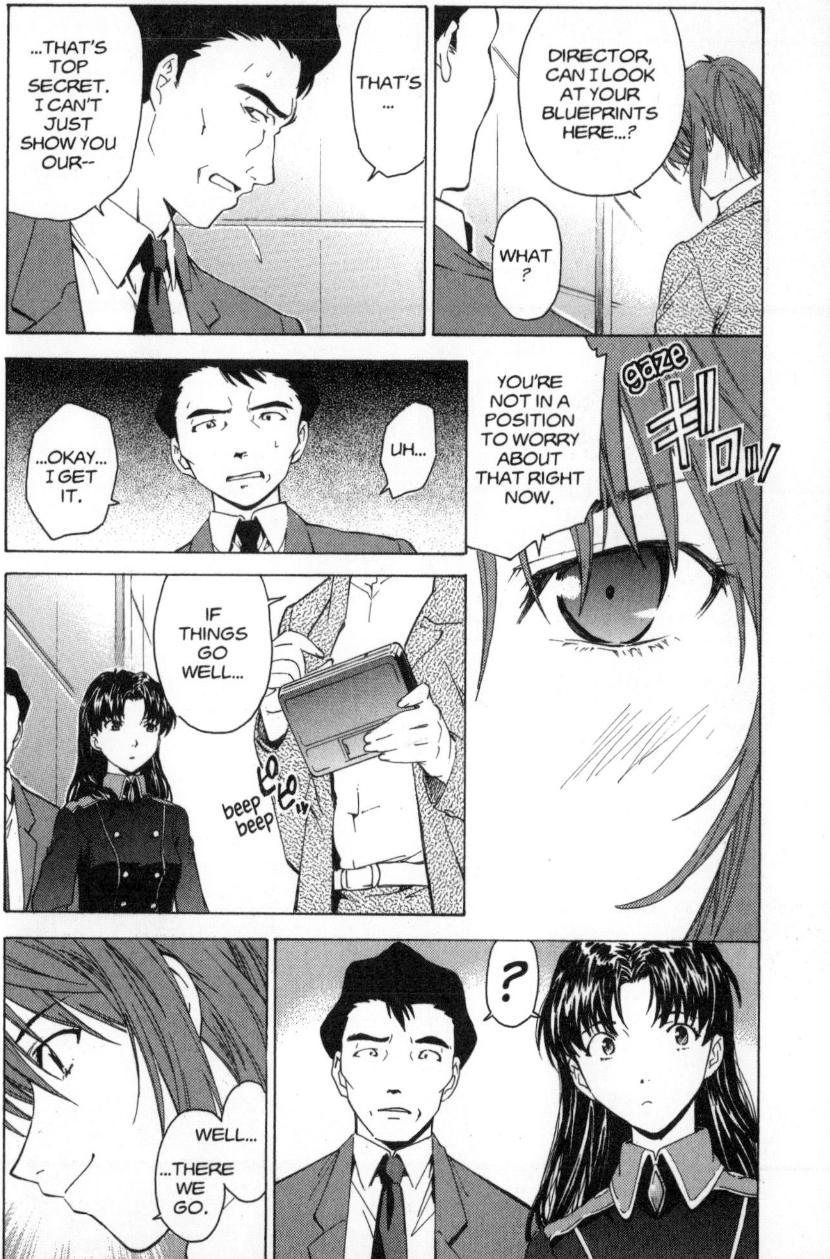
DIRECTOR, CAN I LOOK AT YOUR BLUEPRINTS HERE...?
WHAT?
THAT'S...
...THAT'S TOP SECRET. I CAN'T JUST SHOW YOU OUR--
YOU'RE NOT IN A POSITION TO WORRY ABOUT THAT RIGHT NOW.
gaze
UH...
...OKAY... I GET IT.
IF THINGS GO WELL...
beep beep
?
WELL...
...THERE WE GO.

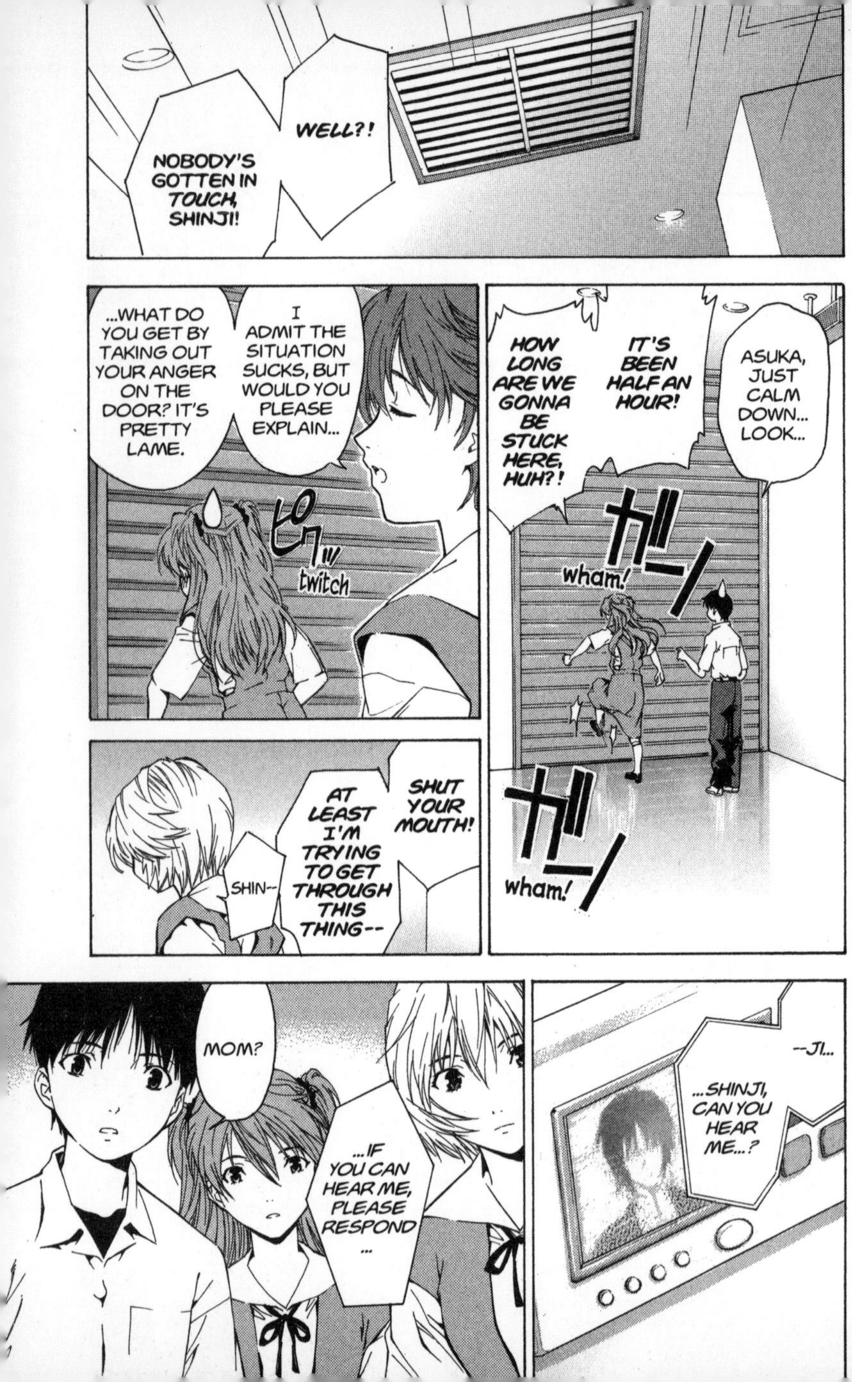
WELL?!
NOBODY'S GOTTEN IN TOUCH, SHINJI!
ASUKA, JUST CALM DOWN... LOOK...
IT'S BEEN HALF AN HOUR!
HOW LONG ARE WE GONNA BE STUCK HERE, HUH?!
ガーン
wham!
ガーン
wham!
I ADMIT THE SITUATION SUCKS, BUT WOULD YOU PLEASE EXPLAIN...
...WHAT DO YOU GET BY TAKING OUT YOUR ANGER ON THE DOOR? IT'S PRETTY LAME.
ピクッ
twitch
SHUT YOUR MOUTH!
AT LEAST I'M TRYING TO GET THROUGH THIS THING--
SHIN--
--JI...
...SHINJI, CAN YOU HEAR ME...?
MOM?
...IF YOU CAN HEAR ME, PLEASE RESPOND ...

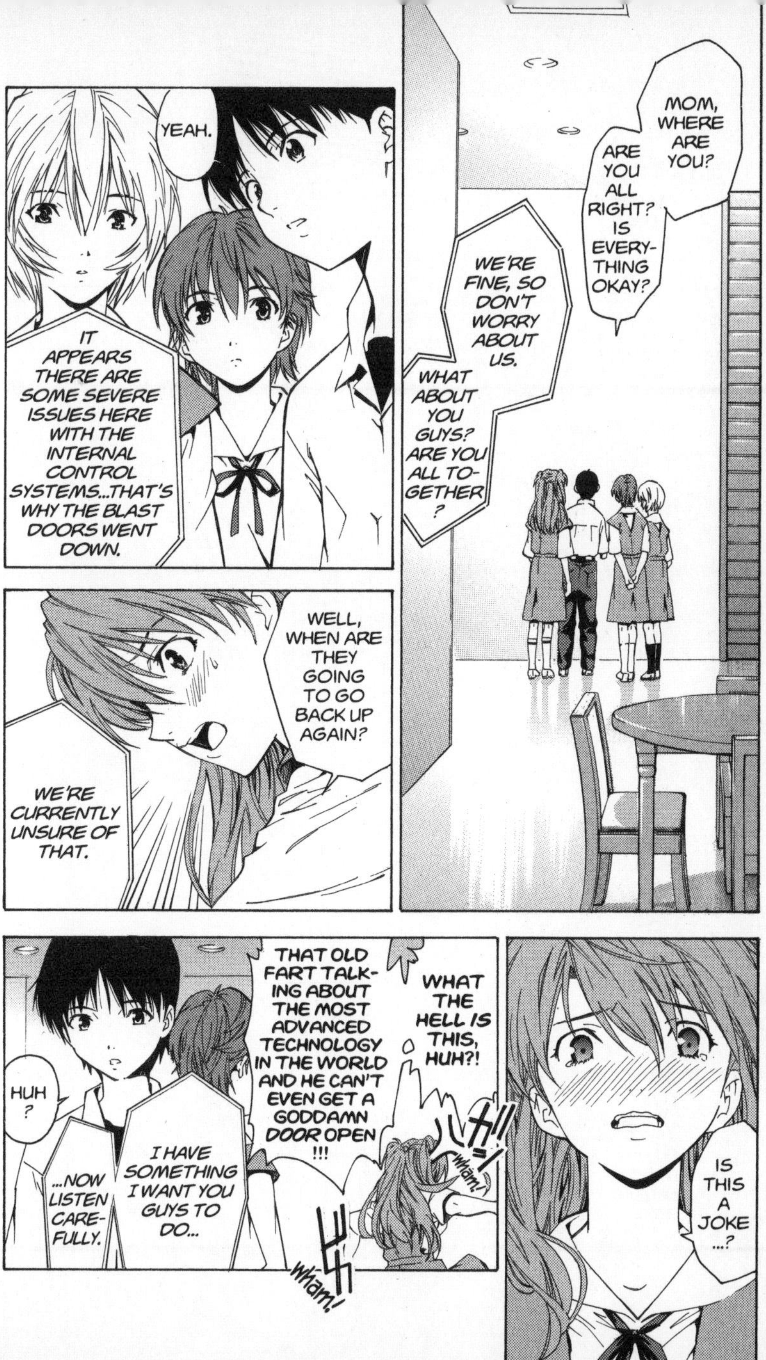
MOM, WHERE ARE YOU?
ARE YOU ALL RIGHT? IS EVERYTHING OKAY?
WE'RE FINE, SO DON'T WORRY ABOUT US.
WHAT ABOUT YOU GUYS? ARE YOU ALL TOGETHER?
YEAH.
IT APPEARS THERE ARE SOME SEVERE ISSUES HERE WITH THE INTERNAL CONTROL SYSTEMS...THAT'S WHY THE BLAST DOORS WENT DOWN.
WELL, WHEN ARE THEY GOING TO GO BACK UP AGAIN?
WE'RE CURRENTLY UNSURE OF THAT.
IS THIS A JOKE...?
WHAT THE HELL IS THIS, HUH?!
THAT OLD FART TALKING ABOUT THE MOST ADVANCED TECHNOLOGY IN THE WORLD AND HE CAN'T EVEN GET A GODDAMN DOOR OPEN!!!
WHAM!
WHAM!
HUH?
I HAVE SOMETHING I WANT YOU GUYS TO DO...
...NOW LISTEN CAREFULLY.

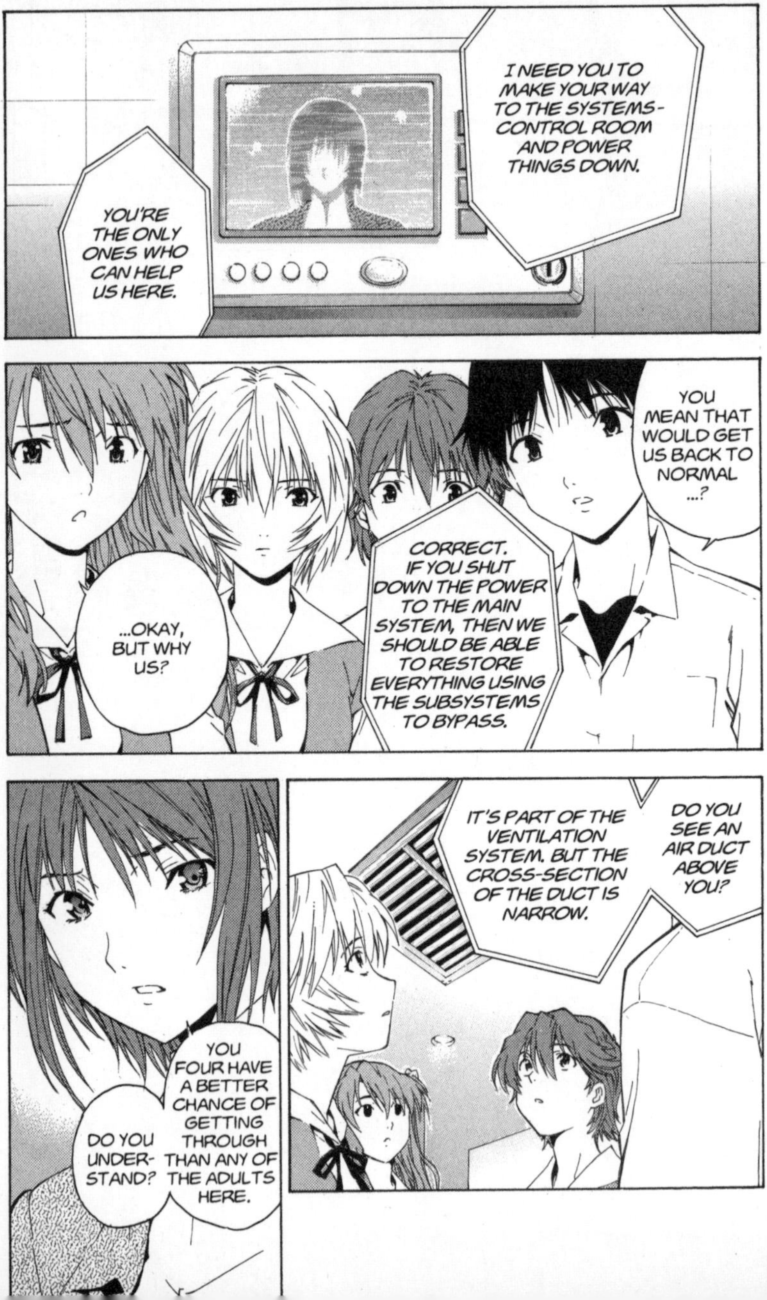
I NEED YOU TO MAKE YOUR WAY TO THE SYSTEMS-CONTROL ROOM AND POWER THINGS DOWN.
YOU'RE THE ONLY ONES WHO CAN HELP US HERE.
YOU MEAN THAT WOULD GET US BACK TO NORMAL ...?
CORRECT. IF YOU SHUT DOWN THE POWER TO THE MAIN SYSTEM, THEN WE SHOULD BE ABLE TO RESTORE EVERYTHING USING THE SUBSYSTEMS TO BYPASS.
...OKAY, BUT WHY US?
DO YOU SEE AN AIR DUCT ABOVE YOU?
IT'S PART OF THE VENTILATION SYSTEM. BUT THE CROSS-SECTION OF THE DUCT IS NARROW.
YOU FOUR HAVE A BETTER CHANCE OF GETTING THROUGH THAN ANY OF THE ADULTS HERE.
DO YOU UNDER-STAND?

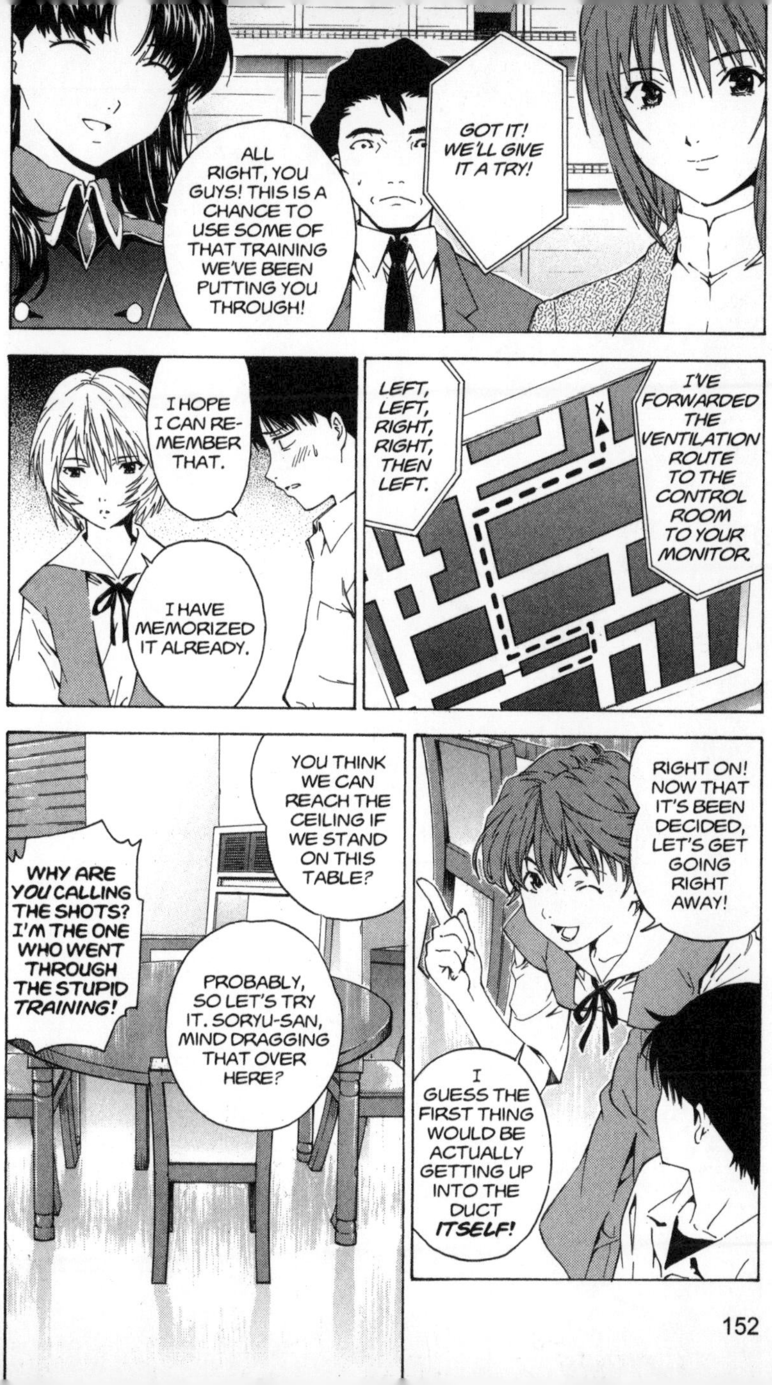
GOT IT! WE'LL GIVE IT A TRY!
ALL RIGHT, YOU GUYS! THIS IS A CHANCE TO USE SOME OF THAT TRAINING WE'VE BEEN PUTTING YOU THROUGH!
I'VE FORWARDED THE VENTILATION ROUTE TO THE CONTROL ROOM TO YOUR MONITOR.
X
LEFT, LEFT, RIGHT, RIGHT, THEN LEFT.
I HOPE I CAN RE-MEMBER THAT.
I HAVE MEMORIZED IT ALREADY.
RIGHT ON! NOW THAT IT'S BEEN DECIDED, LET'S GET GOING RIGHT AWAY!
I GUESS THE FIRST THING WOULD BE ACTUALLY GETTING UP INTO THE DUCT *ITSELF*!
YOU THINK WE CAN REACH THE CEILING IF WE STAND ON THIS TABLE?
WHY ARE *YOU* CALLING THE SHOTS? I'M THE ONE WHO WENT THROUGH THE STUPID *TRAINING*!
PROBABLY, SO LET'S TRY IT. SORYU-SAN, MIND DRAGGING THAT OVER HERE?

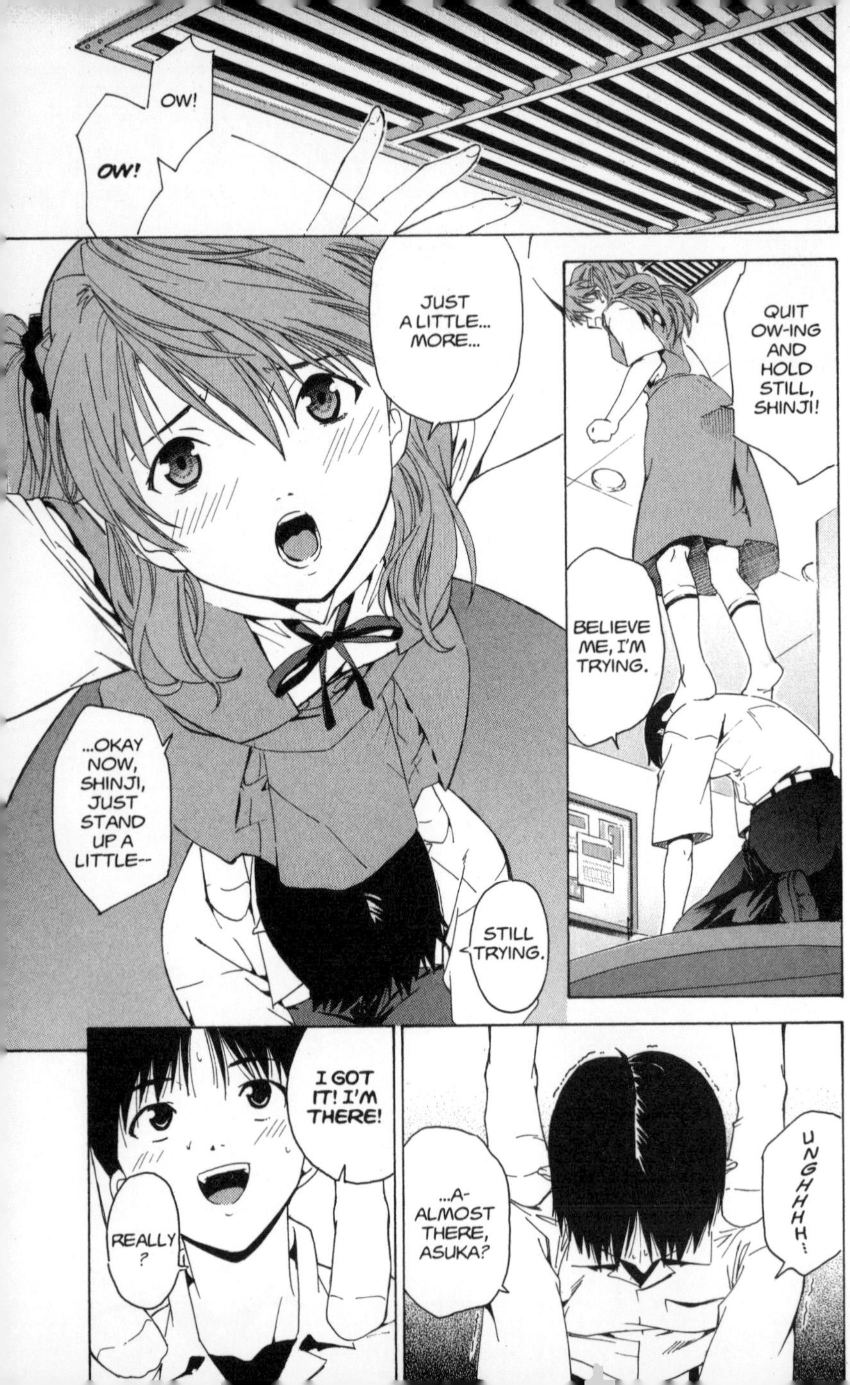
OW!
OW!
QUIT OW-ING AND HOLD STILL, SHINJI!
BELIEVE ME, I'M TRYING.
JUST A LITTLE... MORE...
...OKAY NOW, SHINJI, JUST STAND UP A LITTLE--
STILL TRYING.
UNGHHHH...
...A-ALMOST THERE, ASUKA?
I GOT IT! I'M THERE!
REALLY?

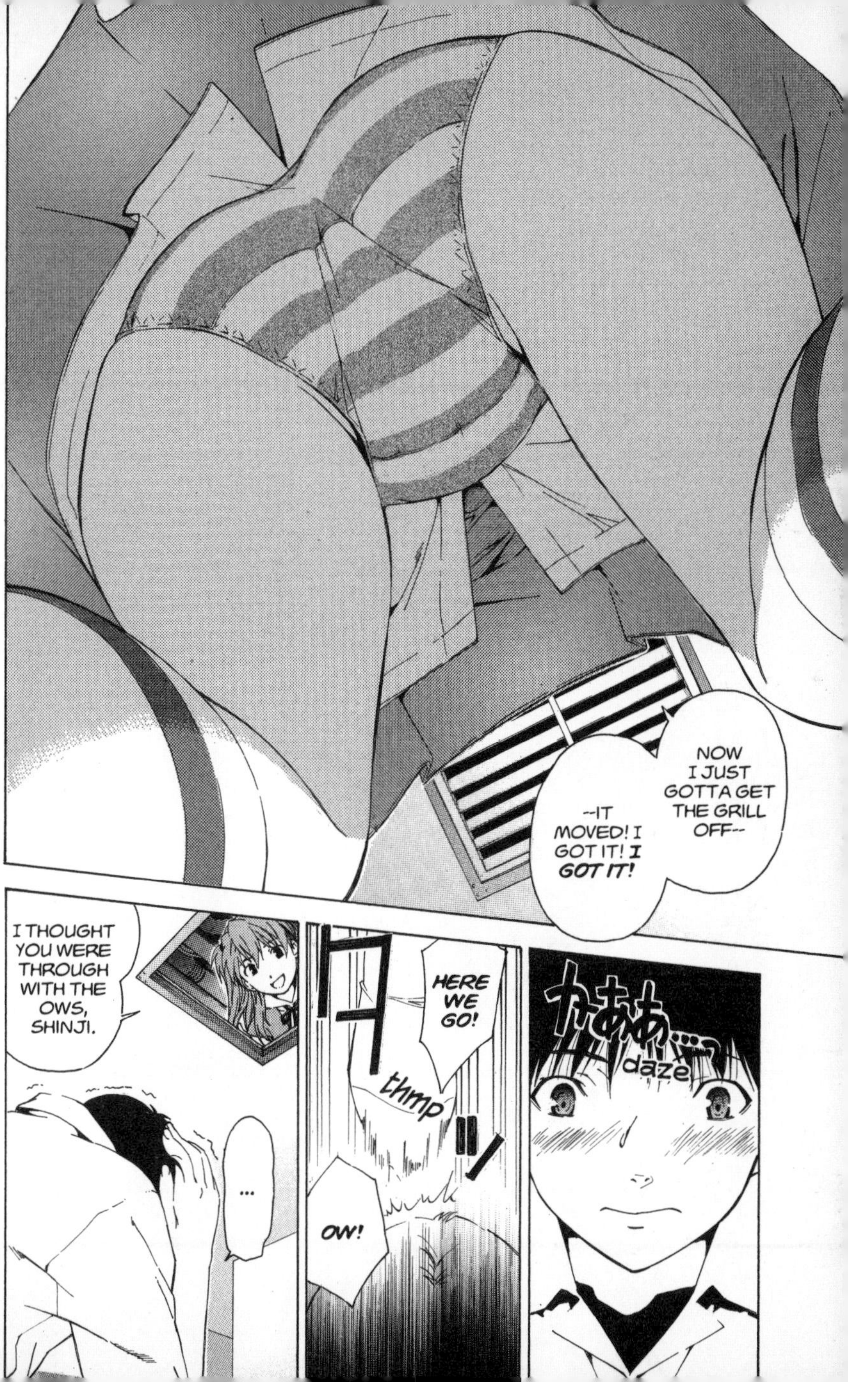
NOW I JUST GOTTA GET THE GRILL OFF--
--IT MOVED! I GOT IT! **I GOT IT!**
daze
HERE WE GO!
thmp
OW!
I THOUGHT YOU WERE THROUGH WITH THE OWS, SHINJI.
...

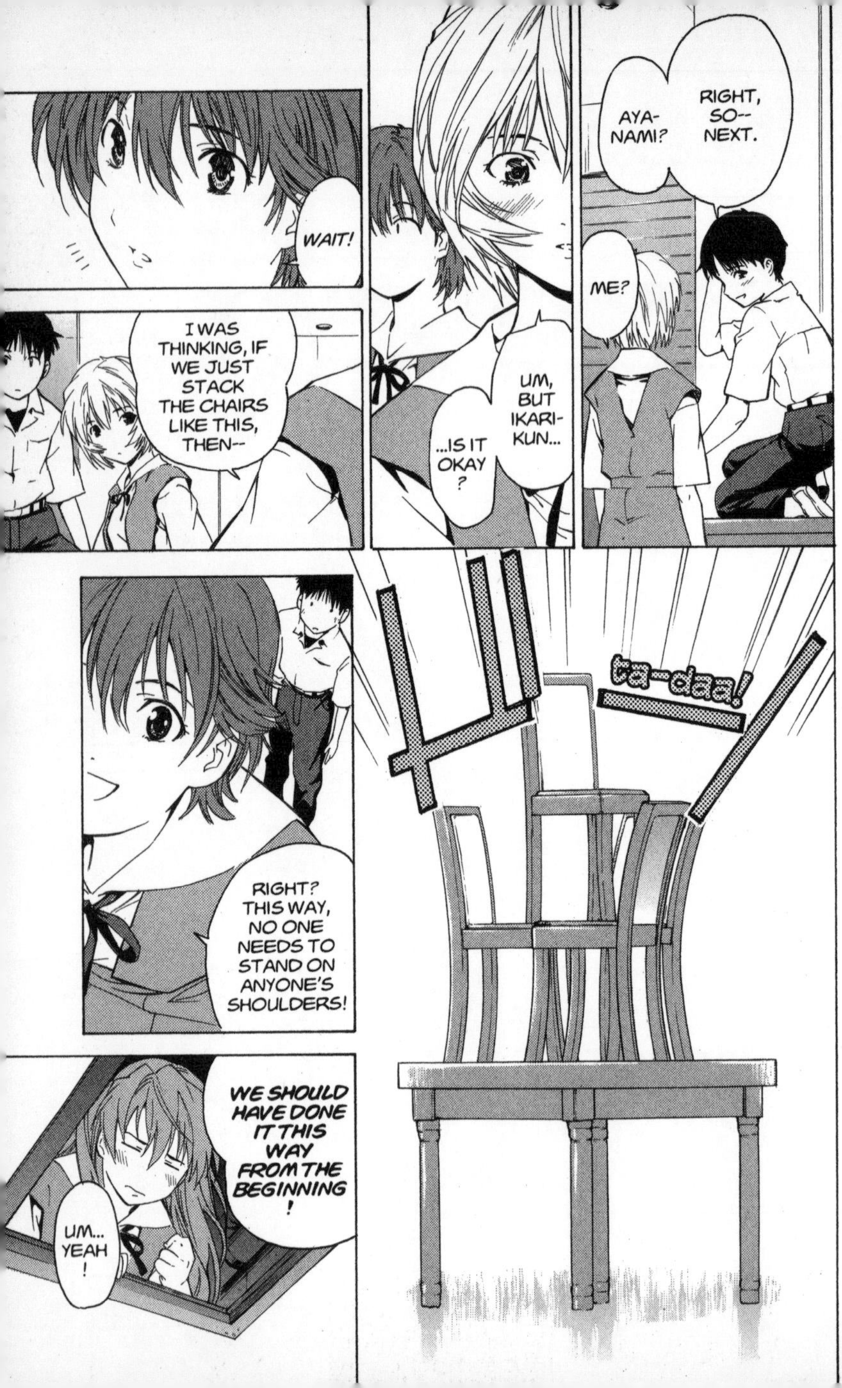
RIGHT, SO-- NEXT.
AYA-NAMI?
ME?
UM, BUT IKARI-KUN...
...IS IT OKAY?
WAIT!
I WAS THINKING, IF WE JUST STACK THE CHAIRS LIKE THIS, THEN--
ta-daa!
RIGHT? THIS WAY, NO ONE NEEDS TO STAND ON ANYONE'S SHOULDERS!
WE SHOULD HAVE DONE IT THIS WAY FROM THE BEGINNING!
UM... YEAH!

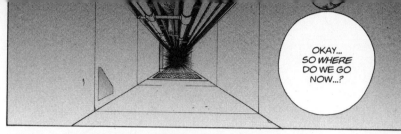

OKAY... SO WHERE DO WE GO NOW...?

DON'T WORRY...AS I SAID, I MEMORIZED IT.

WELL, THAT WAS PRETTY COOL, REMEMBERING IT FROM JUST LOOKING AT IT ONCE!

stare

SHUT UP.

ASUKA, DON'T GO TOO FAST...WAIT FOR AYANAMI'S INSTRUC-TIONS--

?

DO YOU MIND?

156

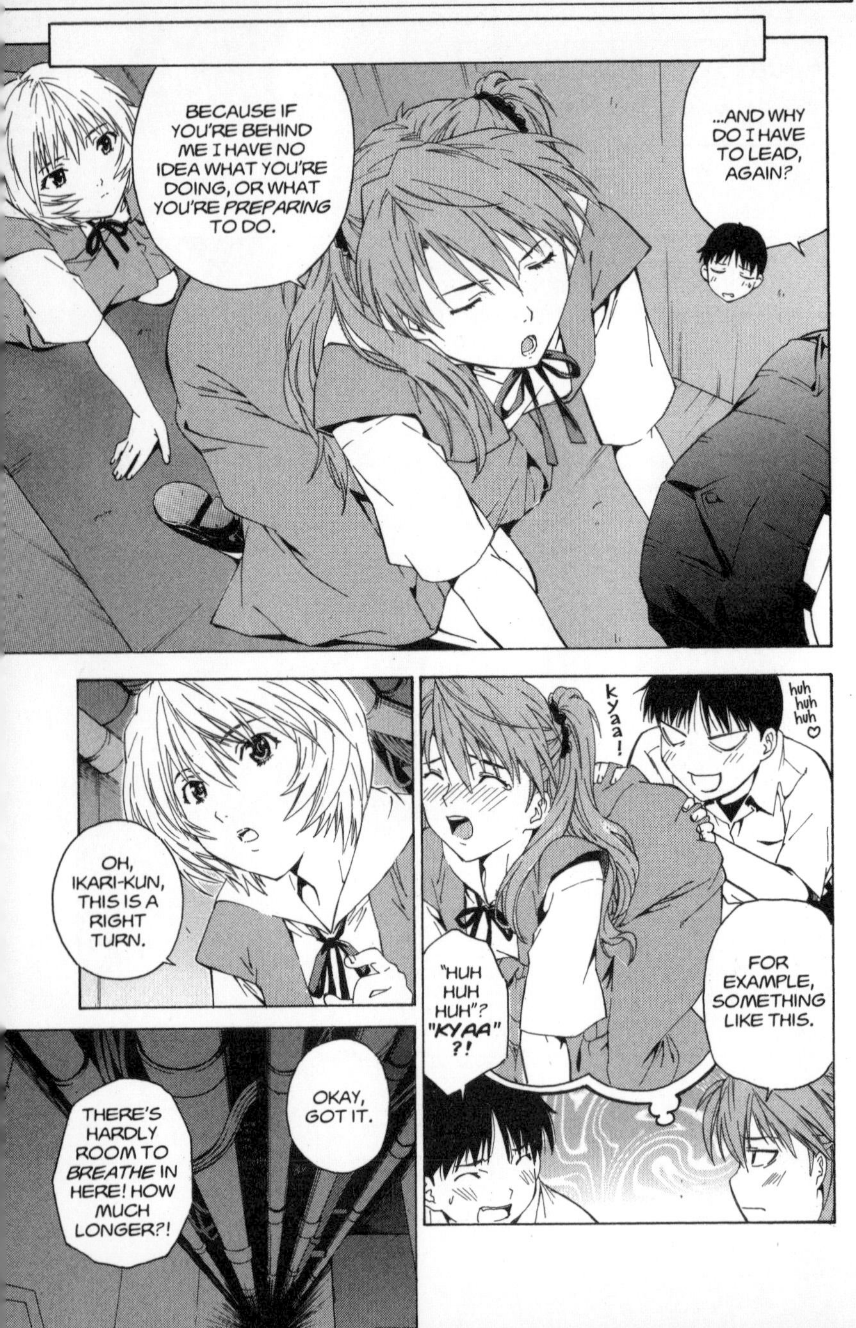
...AND WHY DO I HAVE TO LEAD, AGAIN?
BECAUSE IF YOU'RE BEHIND ME I HAVE NO IDEA WHAT YOU'RE DOING, OR WHAT YOU'RE *PREPARING* TO DO.
huh huh huh ♡
kyaa!
FOR EXAMPLE, SOMETHING LIKE THIS.
"HUH HUH HUH"? ***"KYAA"*** ?!
OH, IKARI-KUN, THIS IS A RIGHT TURN.
OKAY, GOT IT.
THERE'S HARDLY ROOM TO *BREATHE* IN HERE! HOW MUCH LONGER?!

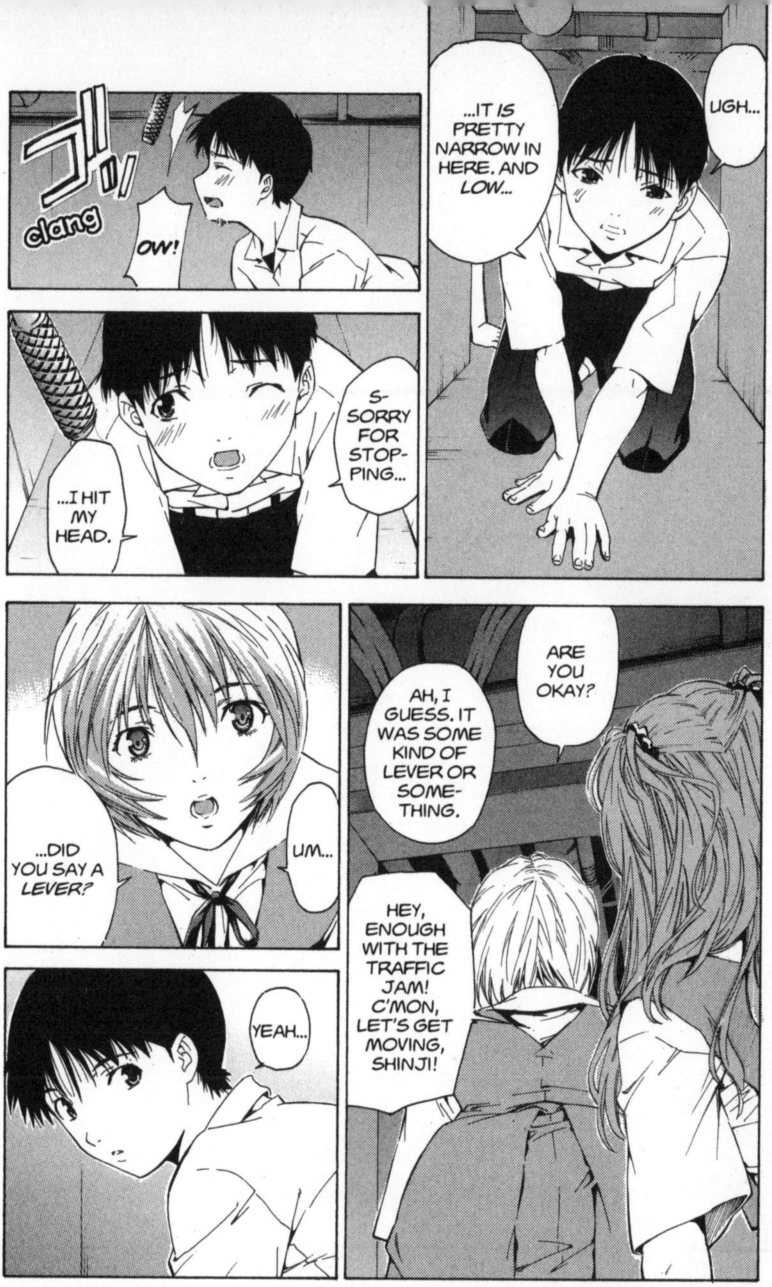
UGH...
...IT IS PRETTY NARROW IN HERE. AND LOW...
clang
OW!
S-SORRY FOR STOPPING...
...I HIT MY HEAD.
ARE YOU OKAY?
AH, I GUESS. IT WAS SOME KIND OF LEVER OR SOMETHING.
HEY, ENOUGH WITH THE TRAFFIC JAM! C'MON, LET'S GET MOVING, SHINJI!
UM...
...DID YOU SAY A LEVER?
YEAH...

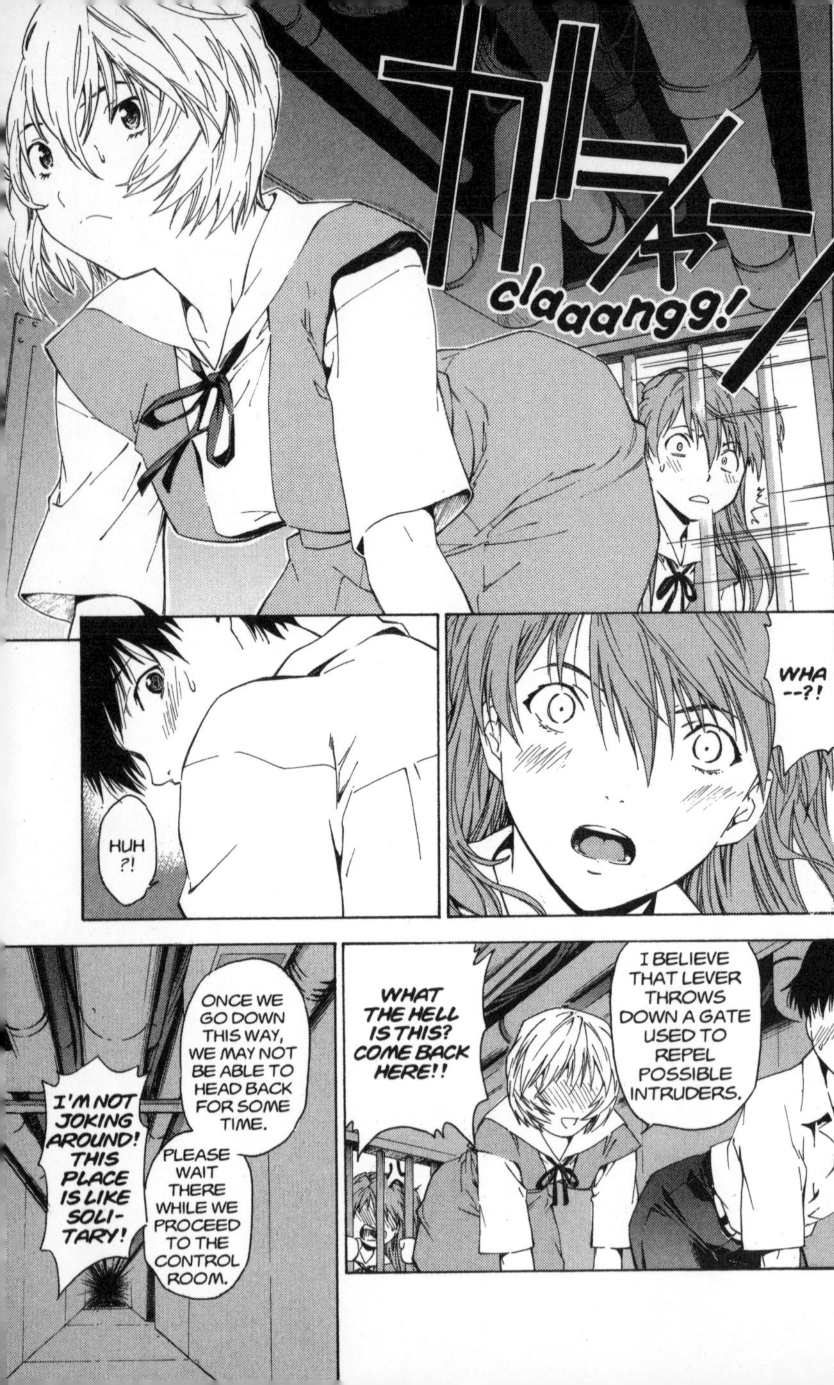
claaangg!
WHA --?!
HUH ?!
I BELIEVE THAT LEVER THROWS DOWN A GATE USED TO REPEL POSSIBLE INTRUDERS.
WHAT THE HELL IS THIS? COME BACK HERE!!
ONCE WE GO DOWN THIS WAY, WE MAY NOT BE ABLE TO HEAD BACK FOR SOME TIME.
PLEASE WAIT THERE WHILE WE PROCEED TO THE CONTROL ROOM.
I'M NOT JOKING AROUND! THIS PLACE IS LIKE SOLI-TARY!

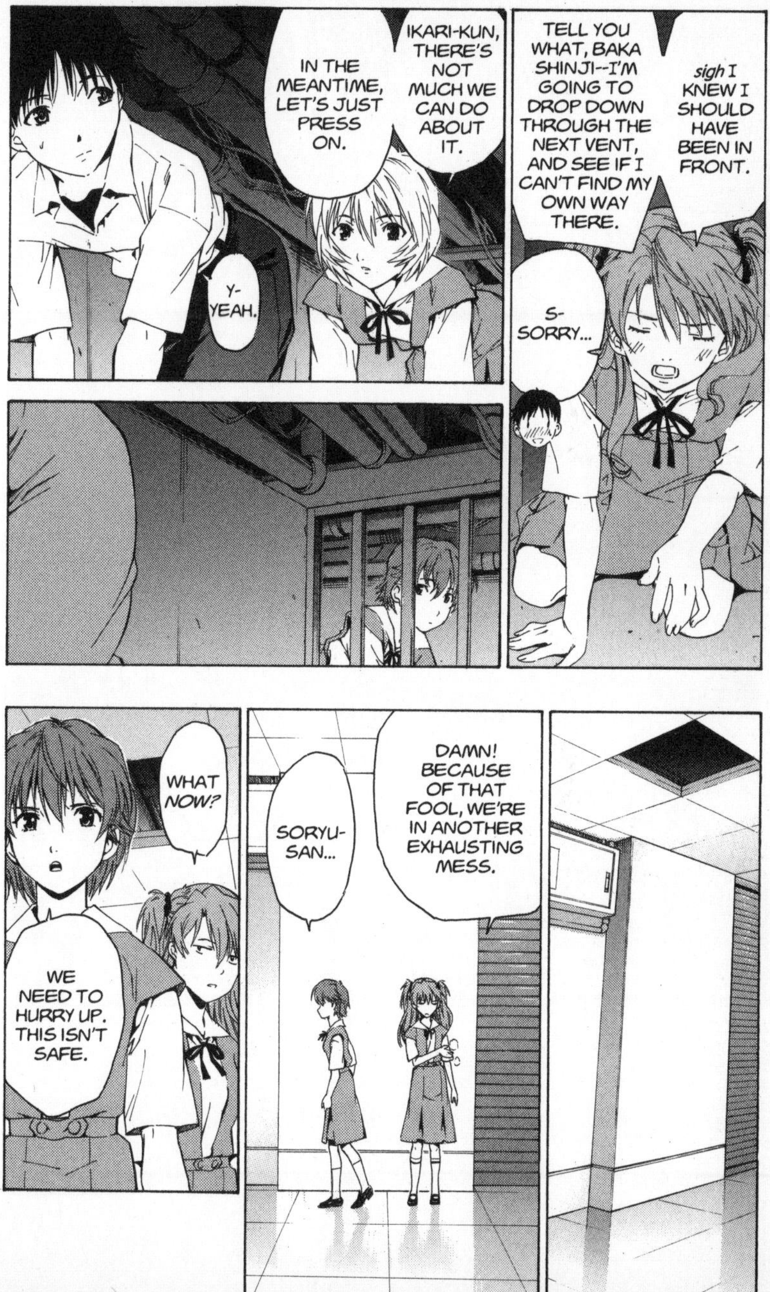
sigh I KNEW I SHOULD HAVE BEEN IN FRONT.
TELL YOU WHAT, BAKA SHINJI--I'M GOING TO DROP DOWN THROUGH THE NEXT VENT, AND SEE IF I CAN'T FIND MY OWN WAY THERE.
S-SORRY...
IKARI-KUN, THERE'S NOT MUCH WE CAN DO ABOUT IT.
IN THE MEANTIME, LET'S JUST PRESS ON.
Y-YEAH.
DAMN! BECAUSE OF THAT FOOL, WE'RE IN ANOTHER EXHAUSTING MESS.
SORYU-SAN...
WHAT *NOW?*
WE NEED TO HURRY UP. THIS ISN'T SAFE.

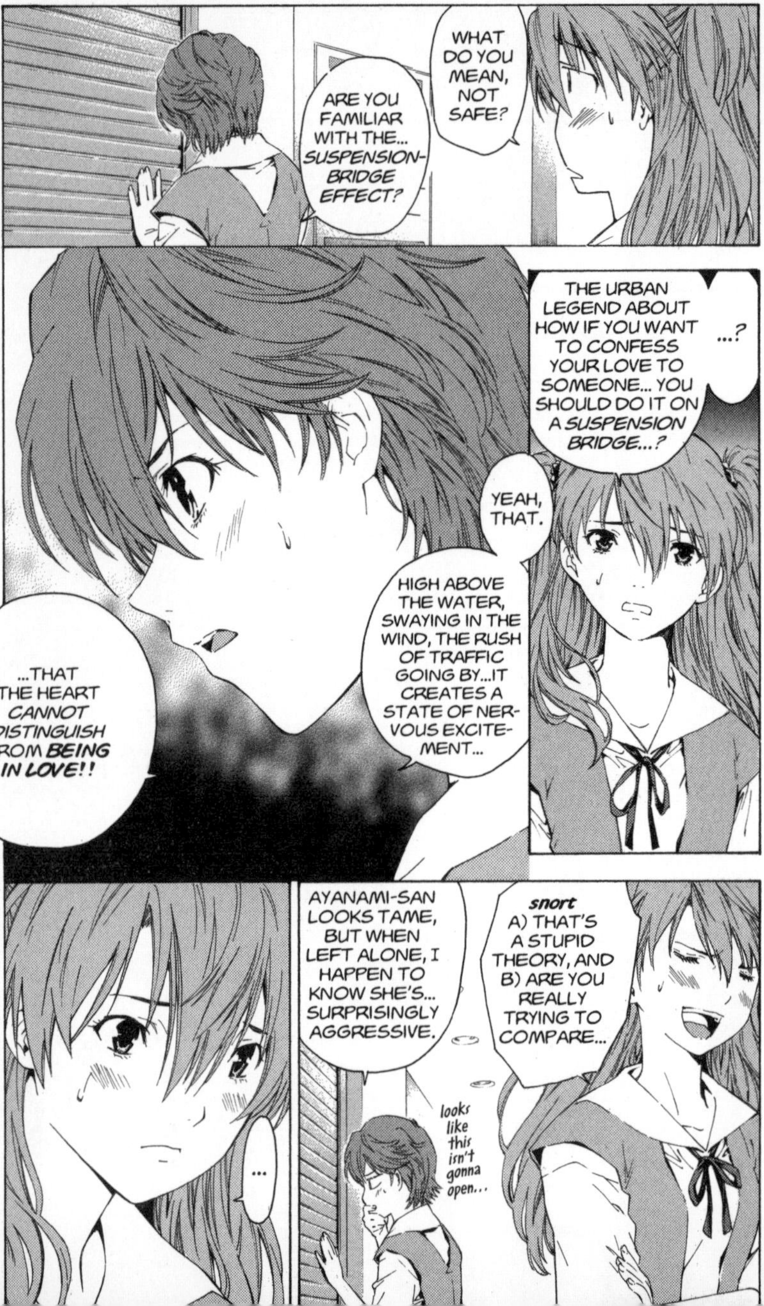
WHAT DO YOU MEAN, NOT SAFE?
ARE YOU FAMILIAR WITH THE... *SUSPENSION-BRIDGE EFFECT?*
THE URBAN LEGEND ABOUT HOW IF YOU WANT TO CONFESS YOUR LOVE TO SOMEONE... YOU SHOULD DO IT ON A *SUSPENSION BRIDGE...?*
...?
YEAH, THAT.
HIGH ABOVE THE WATER, SWAYING IN THE WIND, THE RUSH OF TRAFFIC GOING BY...IT CREATES A STATE OF NERVOUS EXCITEMENT...
...THAT THE HEART *CANNOT* DISTINGUISH FROM ***BEING IN LOVE!!***
snort A) THAT'S A STUPID THEORY, AND B) ARE YOU REALLY TRYING TO COMPARE...
AYANAMI-SAN LOOKS TAME, BUT WHEN LEFT ALONE, I HAPPEN TO KNOW SHE'S... SURPRISINGLY AGGRESSIVE.
looks like this isn't gonna open...
...

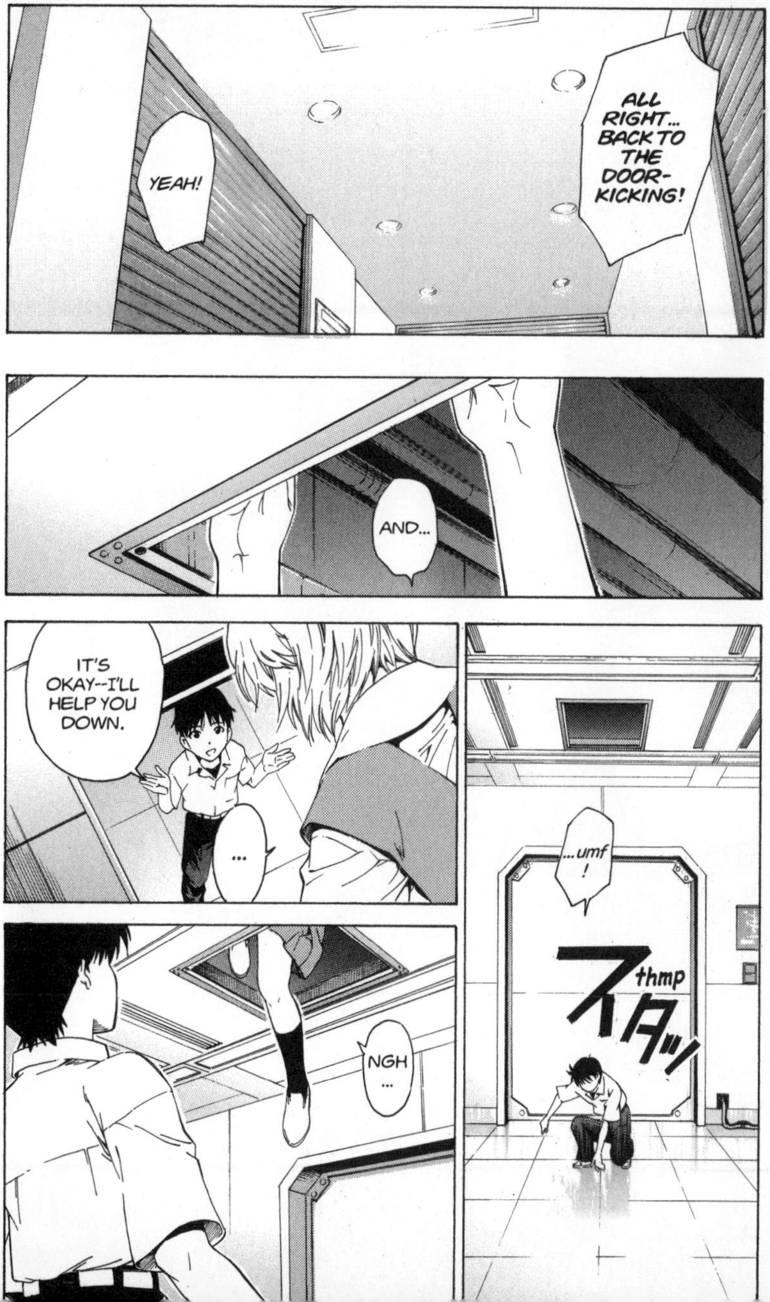
ALL RIGHT... BACK TO THE DOOR-KICKING!
YEAH!
AND...
...umf !
スタッ
thmp
IT'S OKAY--I'LL HELP YOU DOWN.
...
NGH ...

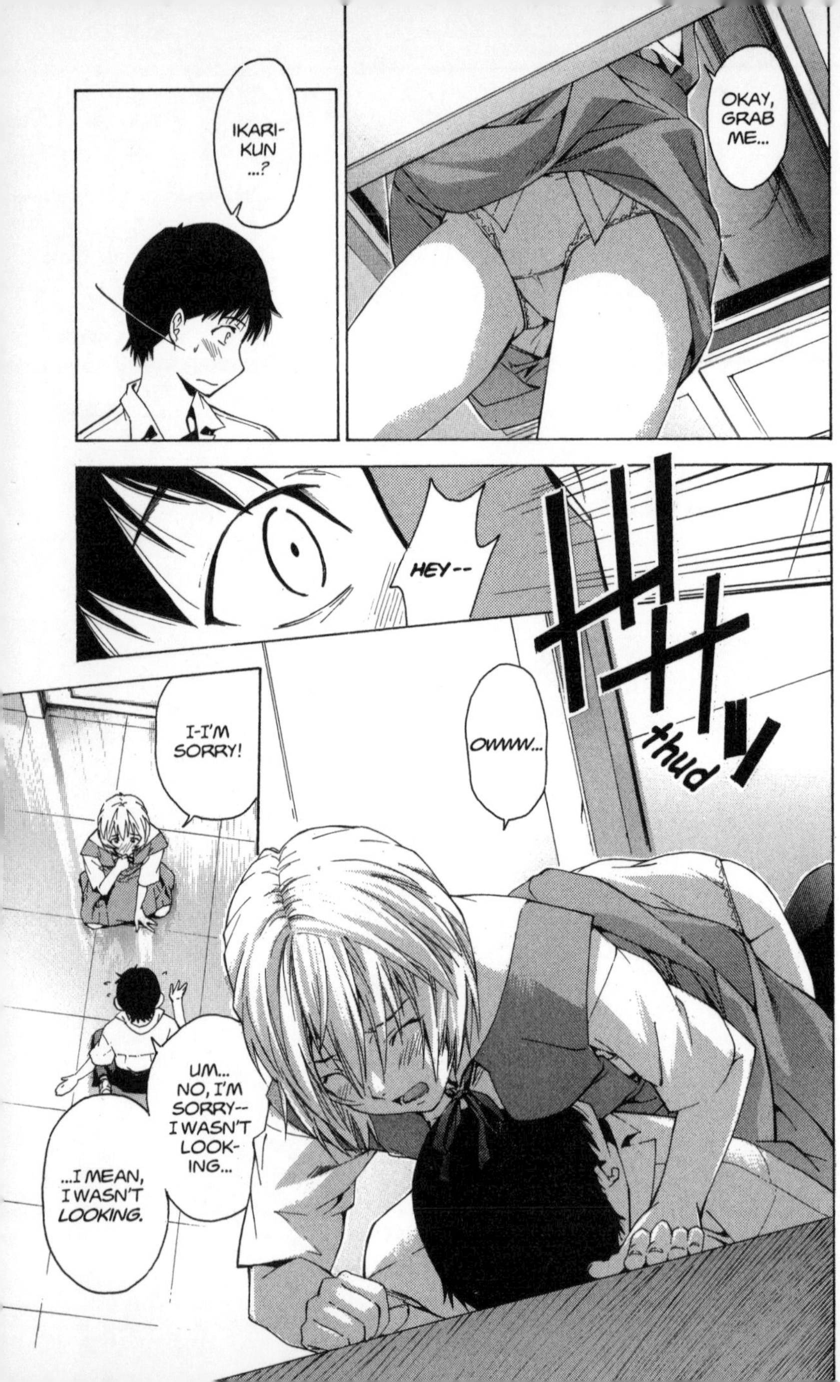
OKAY, GRAB ME...
IKARI-KUN ...?
HEY--
thud
OWWW...
I-I'M SORRY!
UM... NO, I'M SORRY-- I WASN'T LOOKING...
...I MEAN, I WASN'T LOOKING.

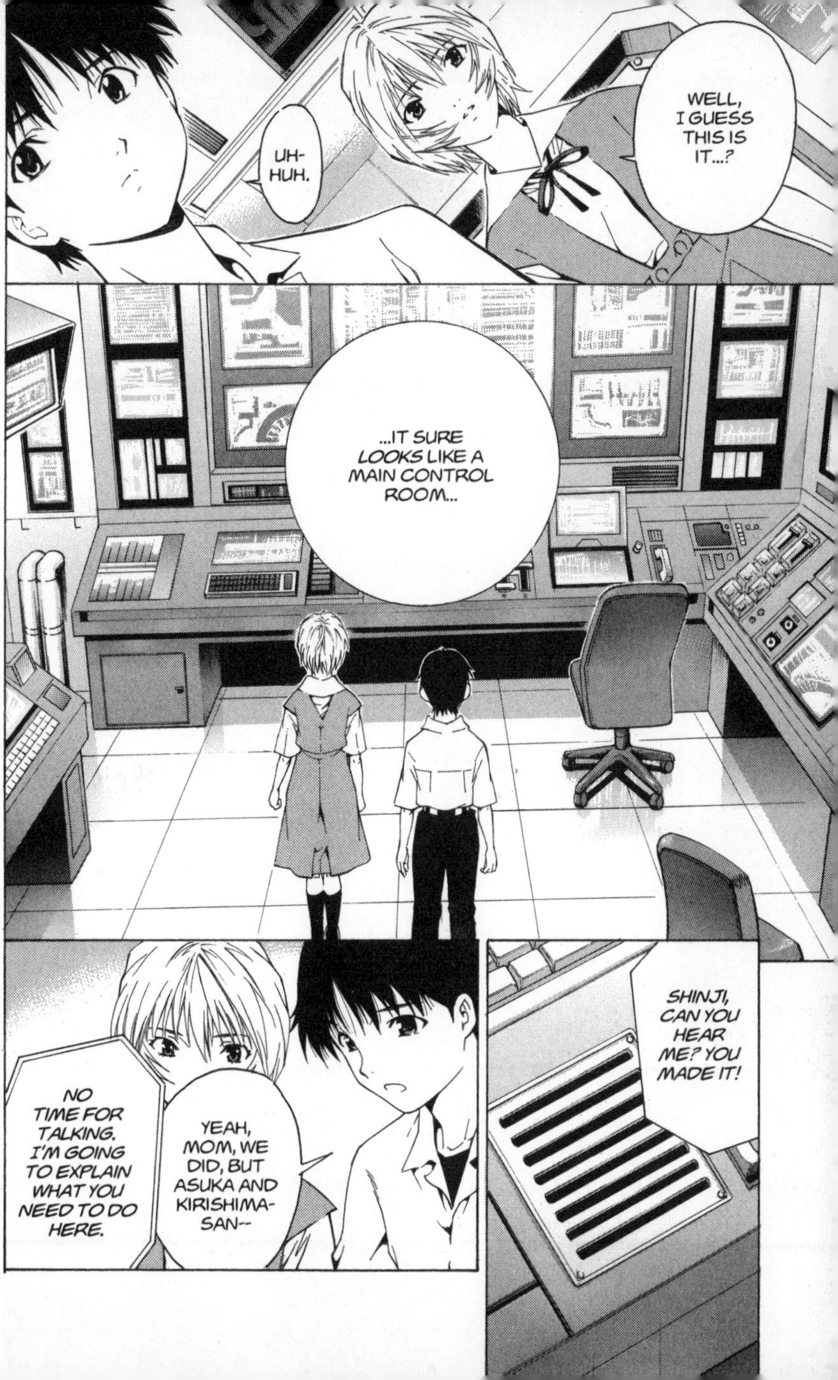
WELL, I GUESS THIS IS IT...?
UH-HUH.
...IT SURE *LOOKS* LIKE A MAIN CONTROL ROOM...
SHINJI, CAN YOU HEAR ME? YOU MADE IT!
YEAH, MOM, WE DID, BUT ASUKA AND KIRISHIMA-SAN--
NO TIME FOR TALKING. I'M GOING TO EXPLAIN WHAT YOU NEED TO DO HERE.

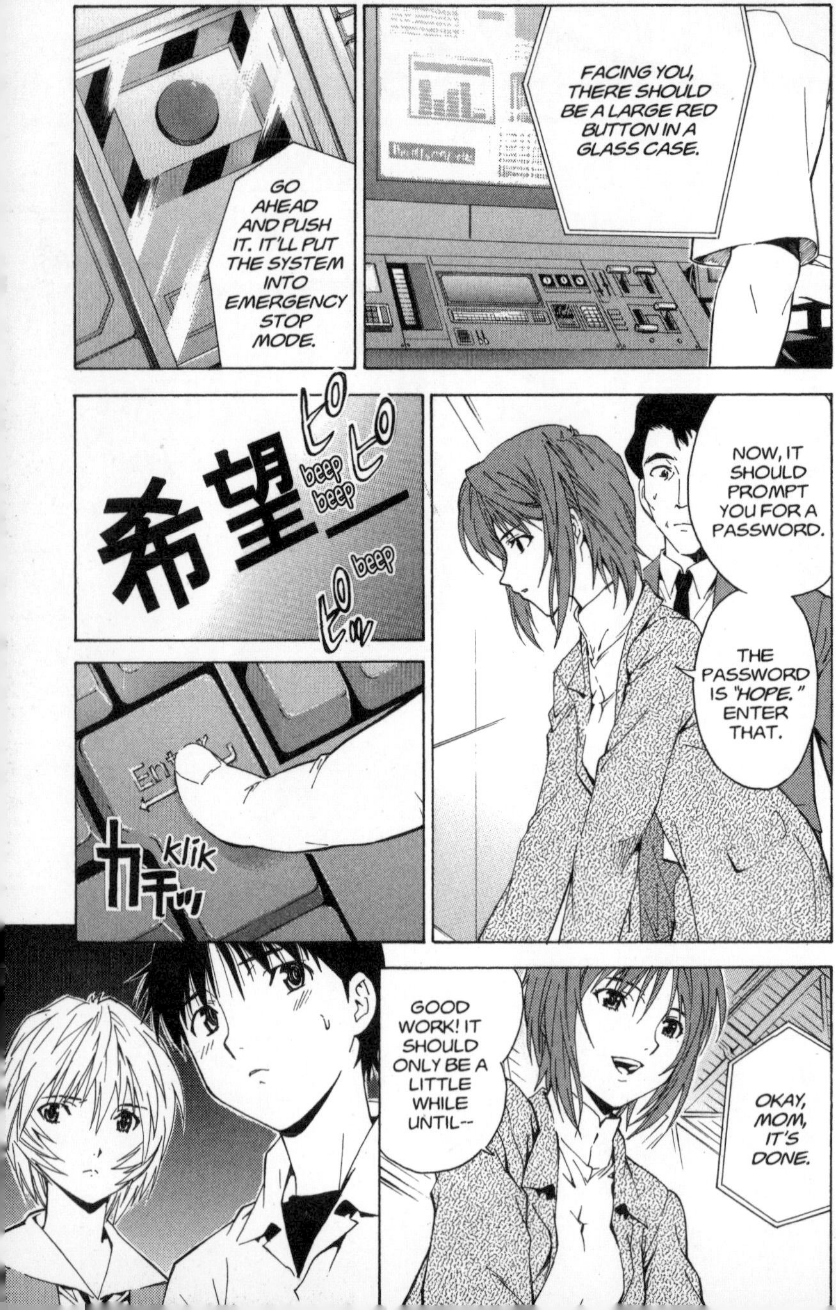

FACING YOU, THERE SHOULD BE A LARGE RED BUTTON IN A GLASS CASE.
GO AHEAD AND PUSH IT. IT'LL PUT THE SYSTEM INTO EMERGENCY STOP MODE.
NOW, IT SHOULD PROMPT YOU FOR A PASSWORD.
THE PASSWORD IS "HOPE." ENTER THAT.
ピポ ピポ
beep beep
希望—
ピッ
beep
カチッ
klik
Enter
OKAY, MOM, IT'S DONE.
GOOD WORK! IT SHOULD ONLY BE A LITTLE WHILE UNTIL--

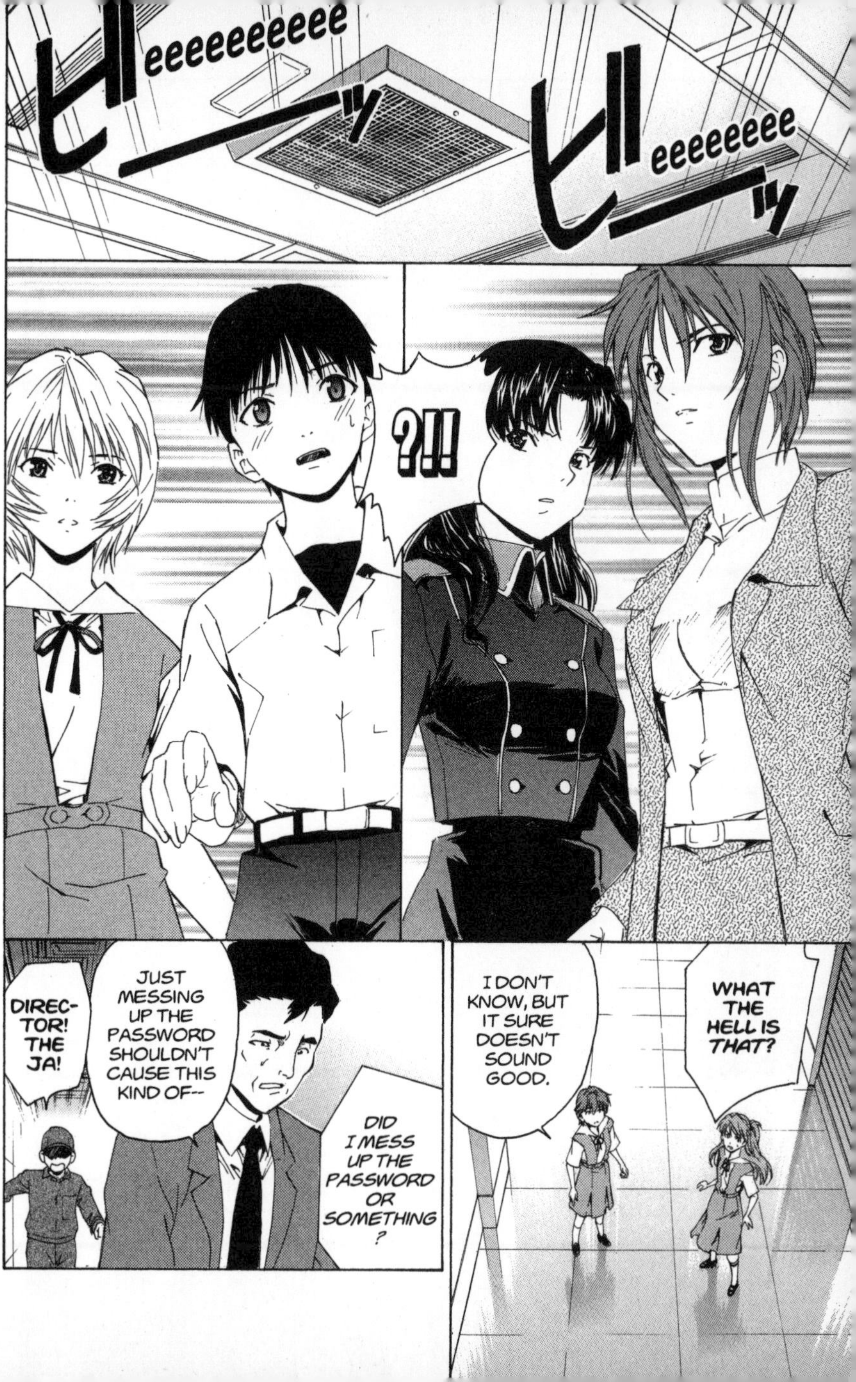
ビeeeeeeeeeeーッ
ビeeeeeeeeーッ
?!!
WHAT THE HELL IS THAT?
I DON'T KNOW, BUT IT SURE DOESN'T SOUND GOOD.
JUST MESSING UP THE PASSWORD SHOULDN'T CAUSE THIS KIND OF--
DIRECTOR! THE JA!
DID I MESS UP THE PASSWORD OR SOMETHING?

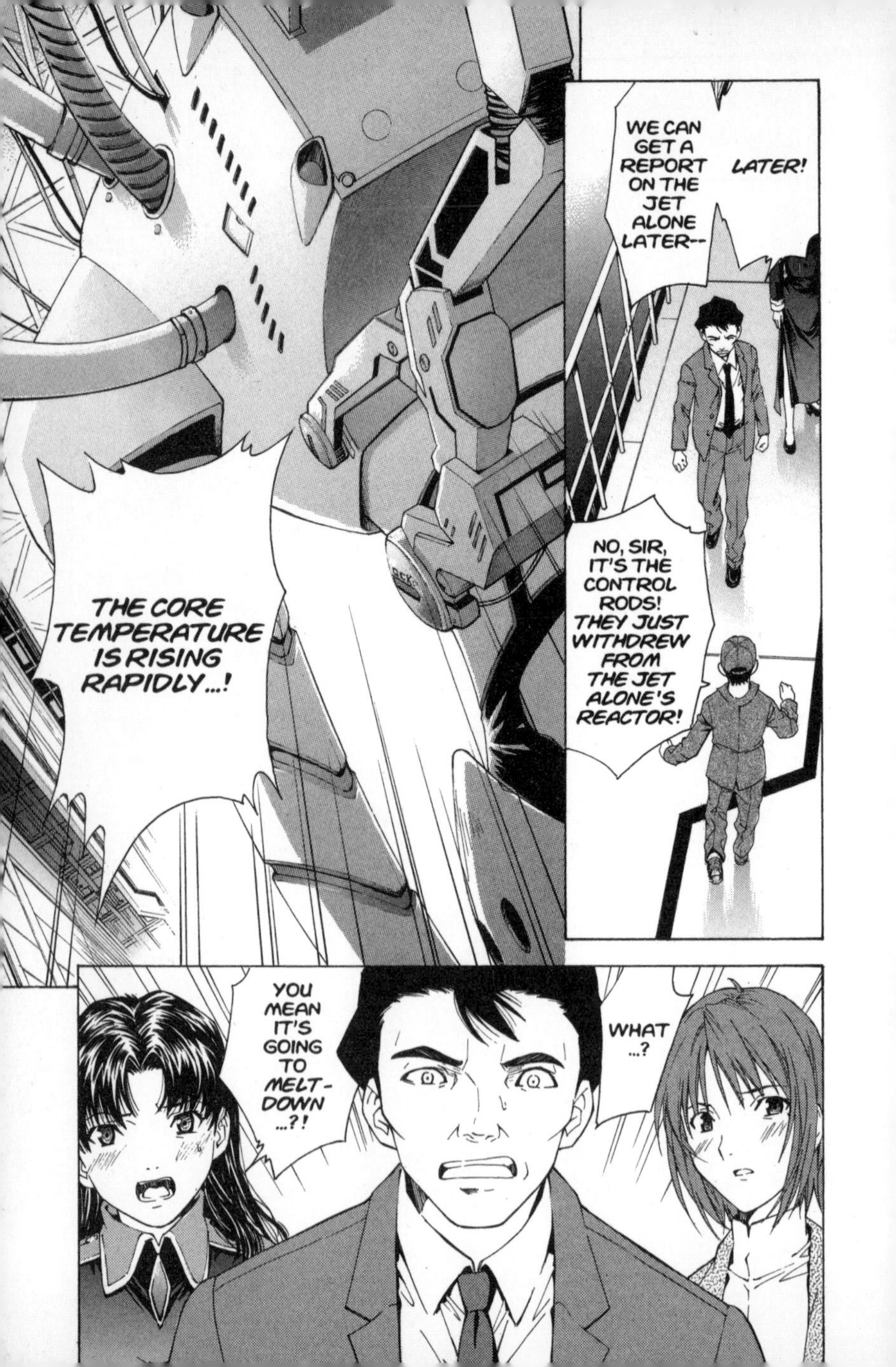
WE CAN GET A REPORT ON THE JET ALONE LATER--
LATER!
NO, SIR, IT'S THE CONTROL RODS! THEY JUST WITHDREW FROM THE JET ALONE'S REACTOR!
THE CORE TEMPERATURE IS RISING RAPIDLY...!
WHAT ...?
YOU MEAN IT'S GOING TO MELT-DOWN ...?!

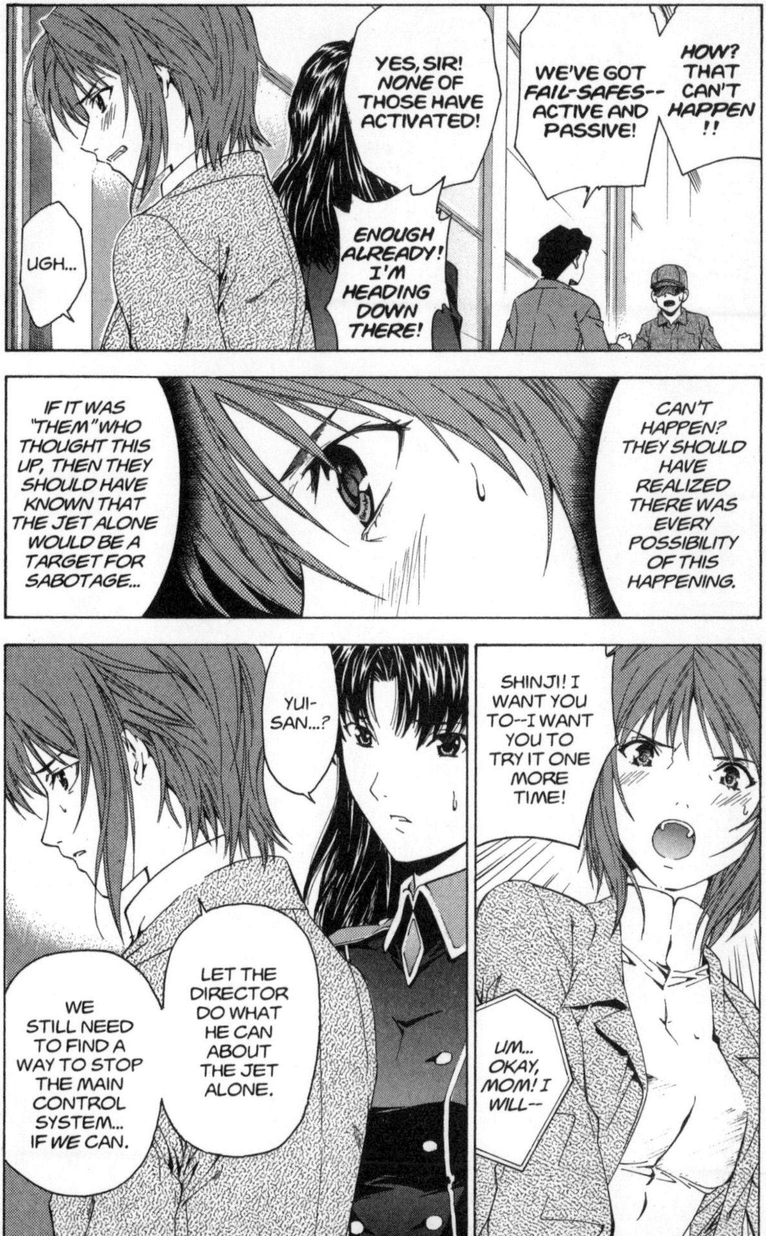
HOW? THAT CAN'T HAPPEN!!
WE'VE GOT FAIL-SAFES-- ACTIVE AND PASSIVE!
YES, SIR! NONE OF THOSE HAVE ACTIVATED!
ENOUGH ALREADY! I'M HEADING DOWN THERE!
UGH...
CAN'T HAPPEN? THEY SHOULD HAVE REALIZED THERE WAS EVERY POSSIBILITY OF THIS HAPPENING.
IF IT WAS "THEM" WHO THOUGHT THIS UP, THEN THEY SHOULD HAVE KNOWN THAT THE JET ALONE WOULD BE A TARGET FOR SABOTAGE...
SHINJI! I WANT YOU TO--I WANT YOU TO TRY IT ONE MORE TIME!
UM... OKAY, MOM! I WILL--
YUI-SAN...?
LET THE DIRECTOR DO WHAT HE CAN ABOUT THE JET ALONE.
WE STILL NEED TO FIND A WAY TO STOP THE MAIN CONTROL SYSTEM... IF WE CAN.

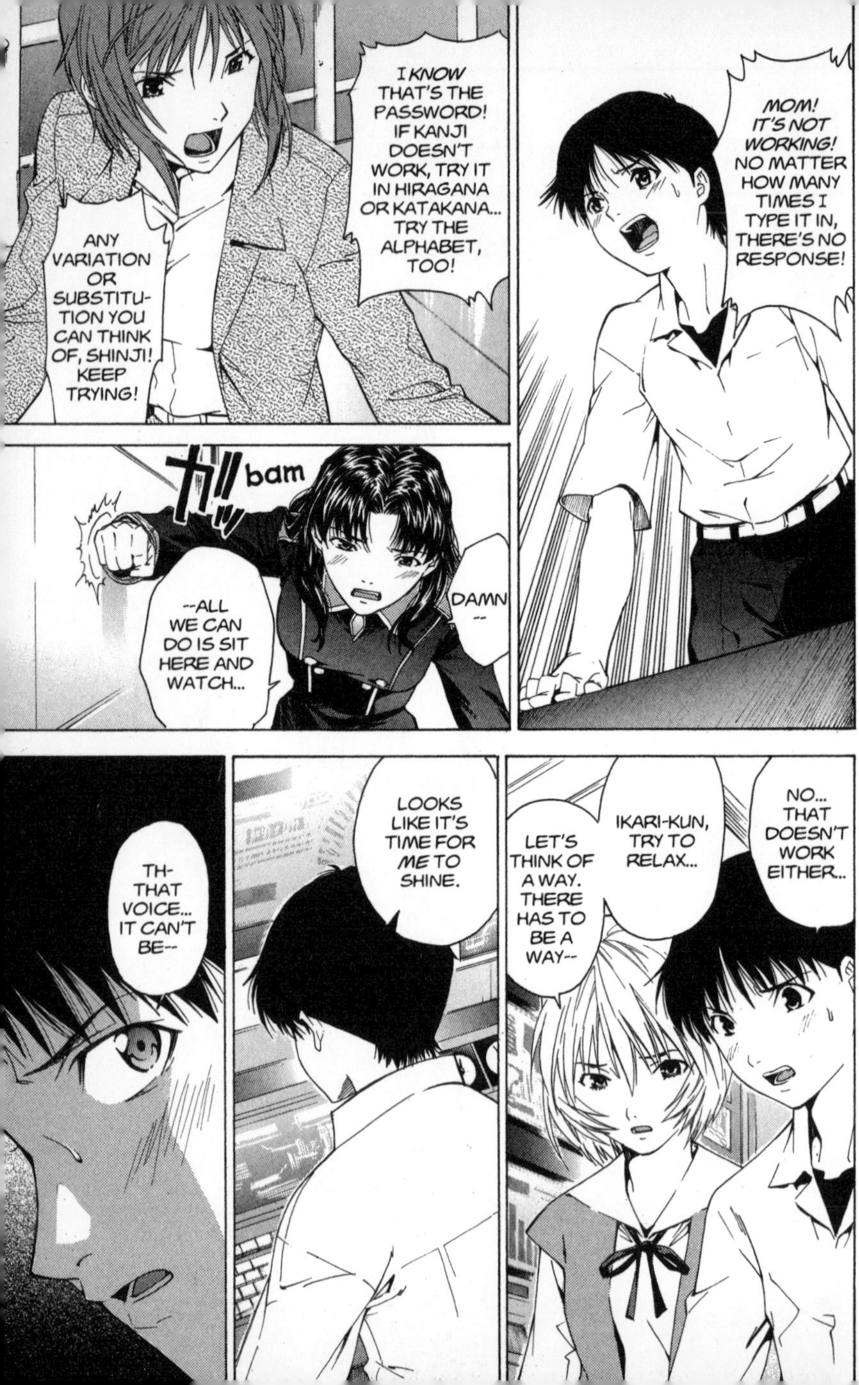
MOM! IT'S NOT WORKING! NO MATTER HOW MANY TIMES I TYPE IT IN, THERE'S NO RESPONSE!
I KNOW THAT'S THE PASSWORD! IF KANJI DOESN'T WORK, TRY IT IN HIRAGANA OR KATAKANA... TRY THE ALPHABET, TOO!
ANY VARIATION OR SUBSTITU-TION YOU CAN THINK OF, SHINJI! KEEP TRYING!
ガッ
bam
DAMN --
--ALL WE CAN DO IS SIT HERE AND WATCH...
NO... THAT DOESN'T WORK EITHER...
IKARI-KUN, TRY TO RELAX...
LET'S THINK OF A WAY. THERE HAS TO BE A WAY--
LOOKS LIKE IT'S TIME FOR *ME* TO SHINE.
TH-THAT VOICE... IT CAN'T BE--

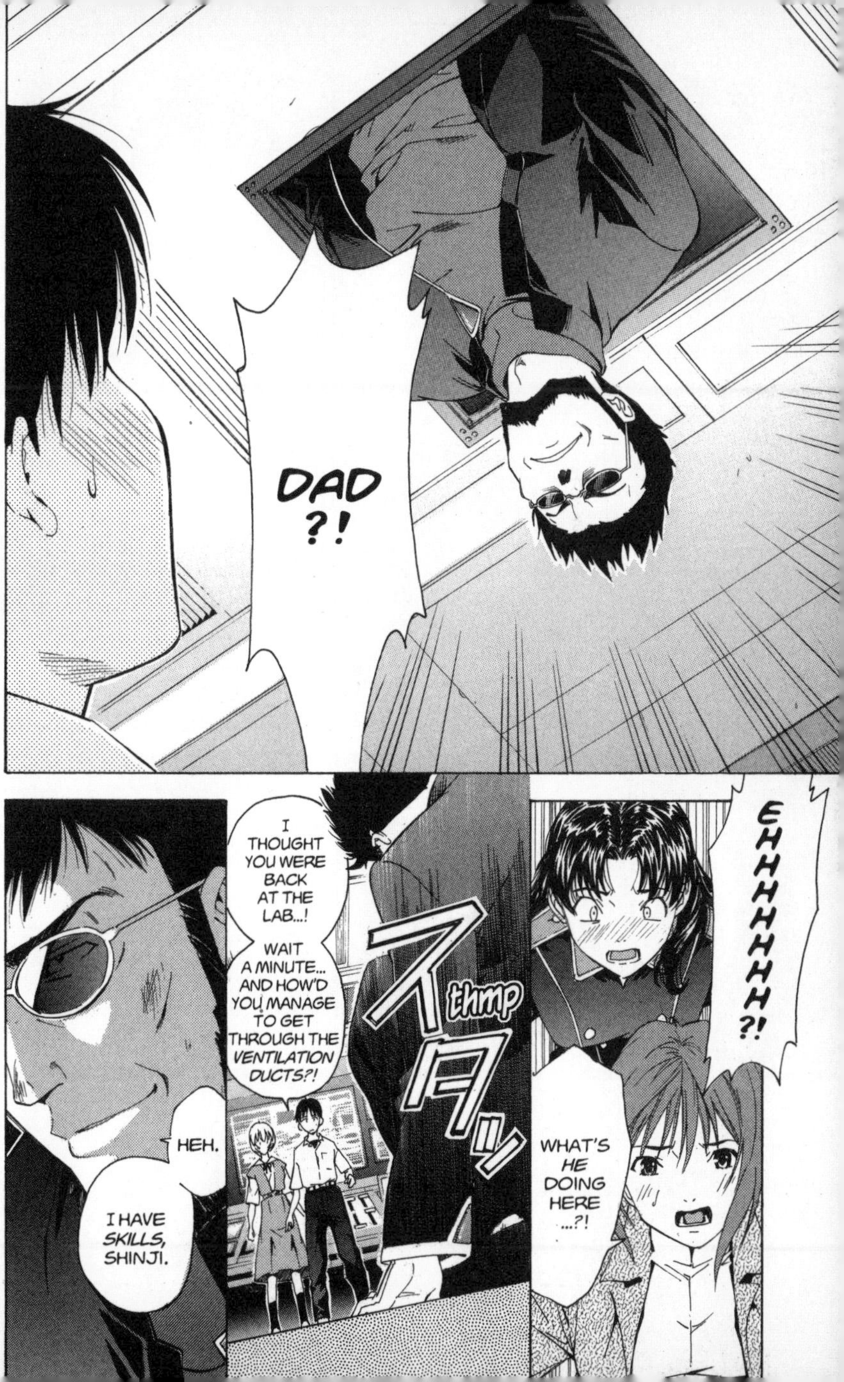
DAD ?!
EHHHHHHHH?!
WHAT'S HE DOING HERE ...?!
I THOUGHT YOU WERE BACK AT THE LAB...!
WAIT A MINUTE... AND HOW'D YOU MANAGE TO GET THROUGH THE VENTILATION DUCTS?!
thmp
HEH.
I HAVE SKILLS, SHINJI.

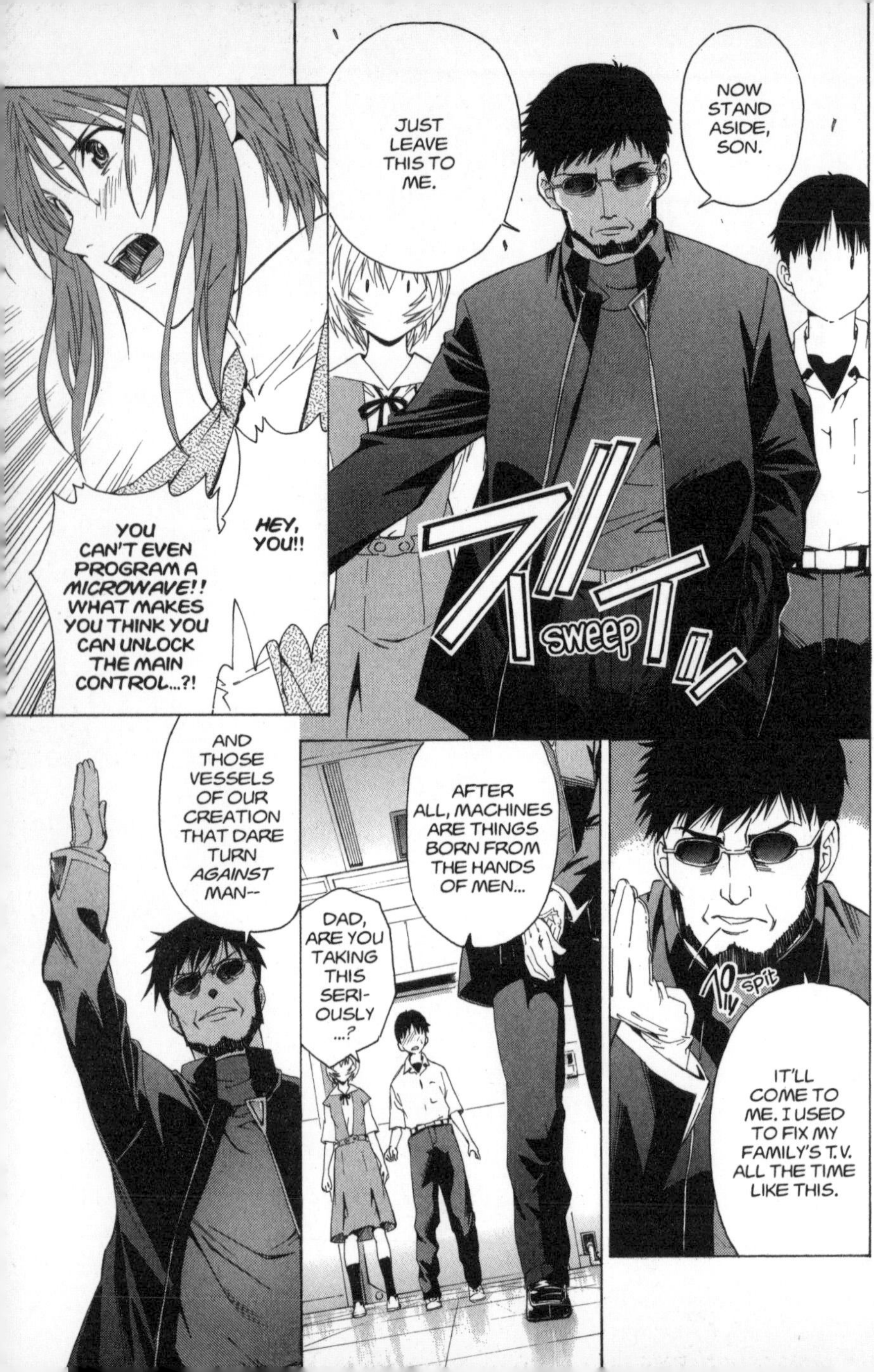
NOW STAND ASIDE, SON.
JUST LEAVE THIS TO ME.
SWEEP
HEY, YOU!!
YOU CAN'T EVEN PROGRAM A *MICROWAVE!!* WHAT MAKES YOU THINK YOU CAN UNLOCK THE MAIN CONTROL...?!
SPIT
IT'LL COME TO ME. I USED TO FIX MY FAMILY'S T.V. ALL THE TIME LIKE THIS.
AFTER ALL, MACHINES ARE THINGS BORN FROM THE HANDS OF MEN...
DAD, ARE YOU TAKING THIS SERIOUSLY ...?
AND THOSE VESSELS OF OUR CREATION THAT DARE TURN *AGAINST* MAN--

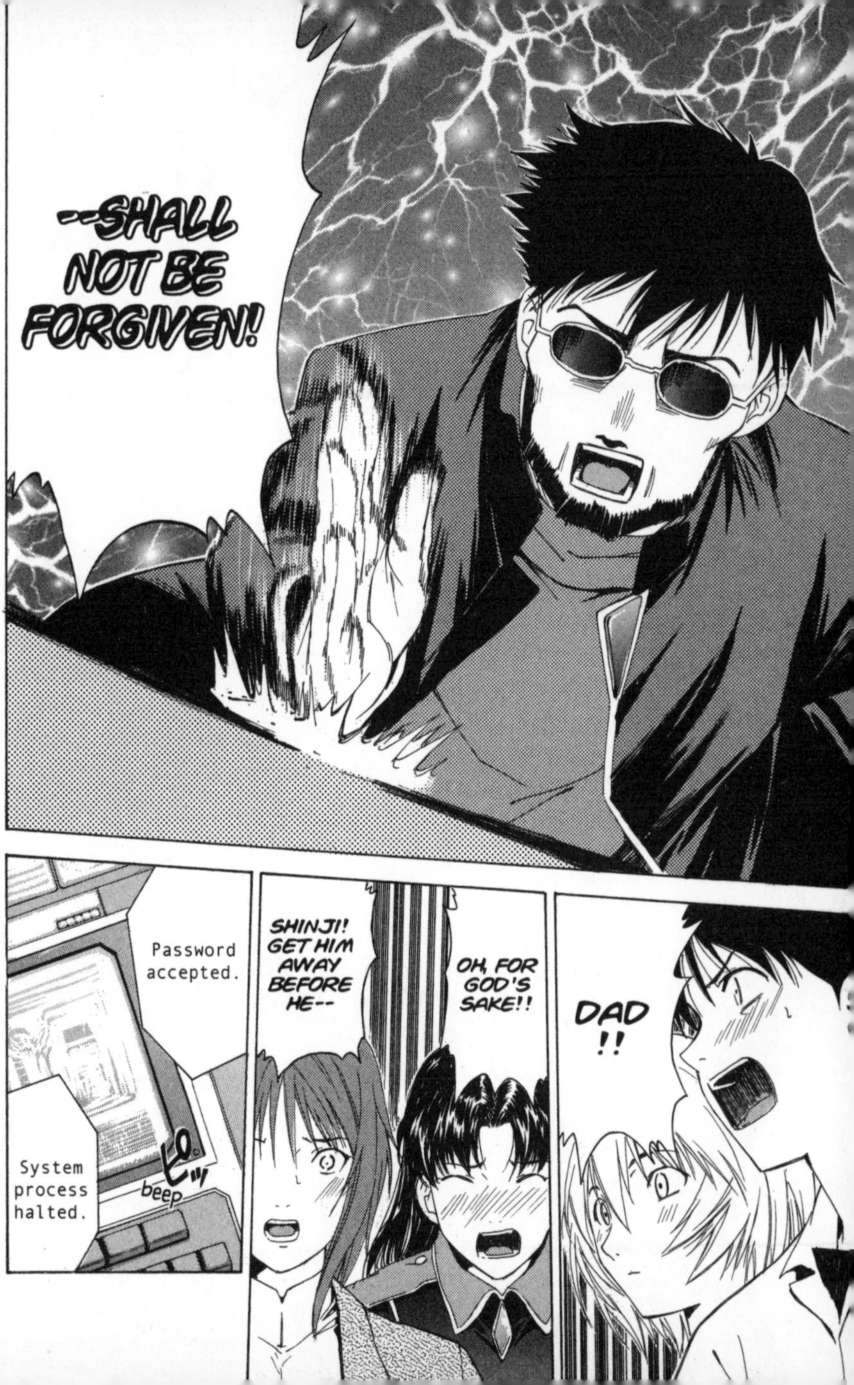
--SHALL NOT BE FORGIVEN!
DAD!!
OH, FOR GOD'S SAKE!!
SHINJI! GET HIM AWAY BEFORE HE--
Password accepted.
beep
System process halted.

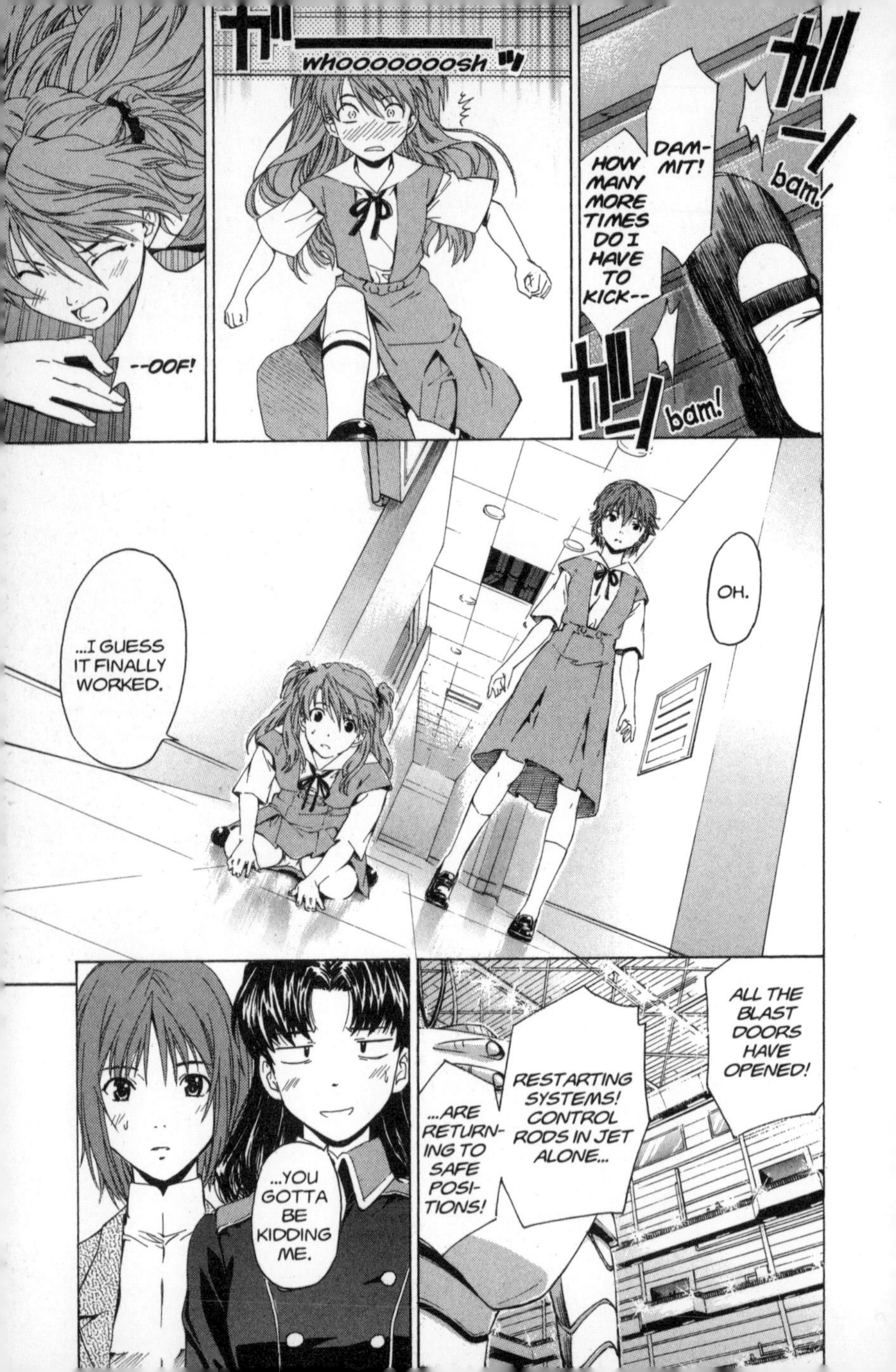

bam!
bam!
DAM-MIT! HOW MANY MORE TIMES DO I HAVE TO KICK--
whoooooooosh
--OOF!
OH.
...I GUESS IT FINALLY WORKED.
ALL THE BLAST DOORS HAVE OPENED!
RESTARTING SYSTEMS! CONTROL RODS IN JET ALONE...
...ARE RETURNING TO SAFE POSITIONS!
...YOU GOTTA BE KIDDING ME.

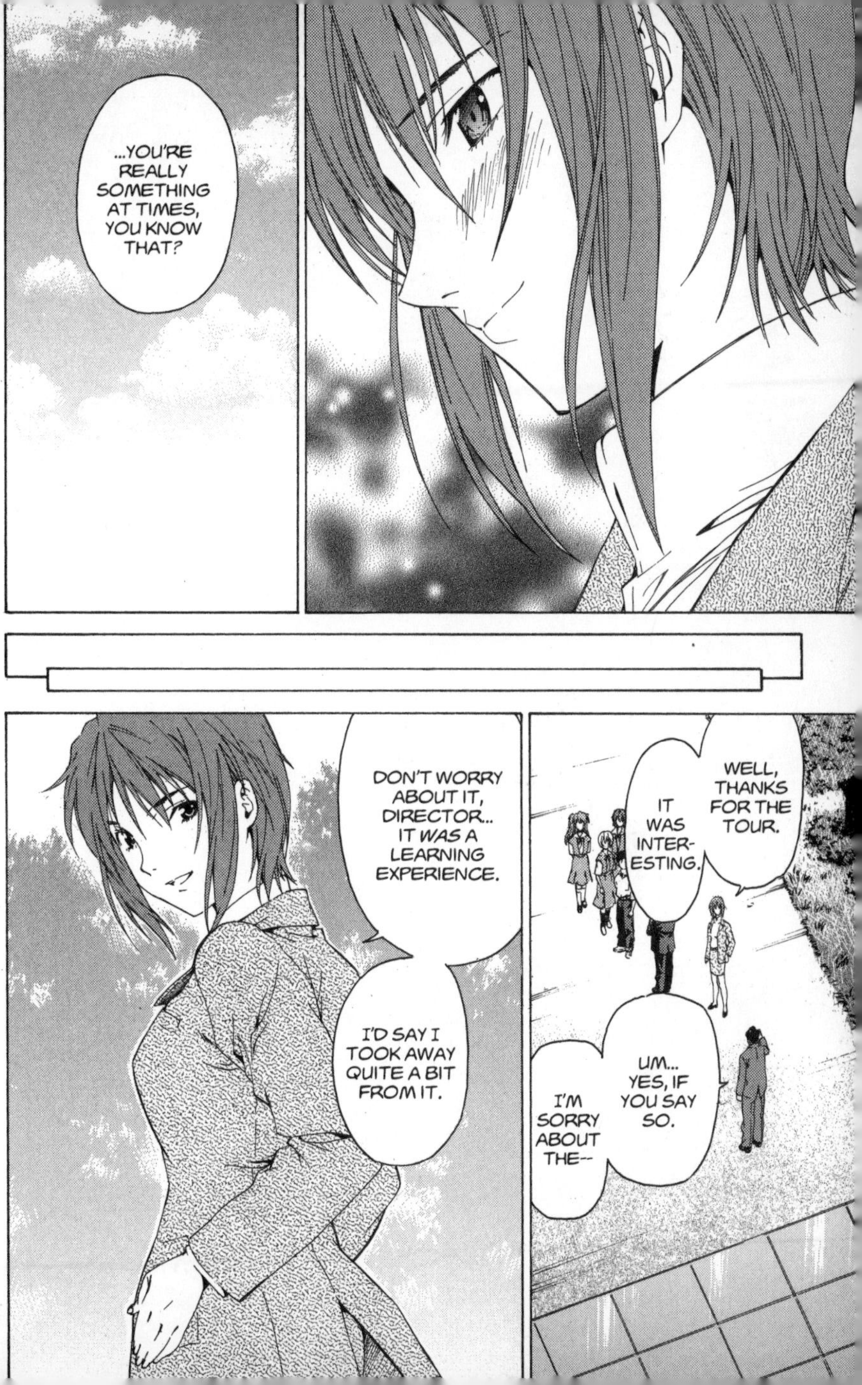
...YOU'RE REALLY SOMETHING AT TIMES, YOU KNOW THAT?
WELL, THANKS FOR THE TOUR.
IT WAS INTERESTING.
UM... YES, IF YOU SAY SO.
I'M SORRY ABOUT THE--
DON'T WORRY ABOUT IT, DIRECTOR... IT *WAS* A LEARNING EXPERIENCE.
I'D SAY I TOOK AWAY QUITE A BIT FROM IT.

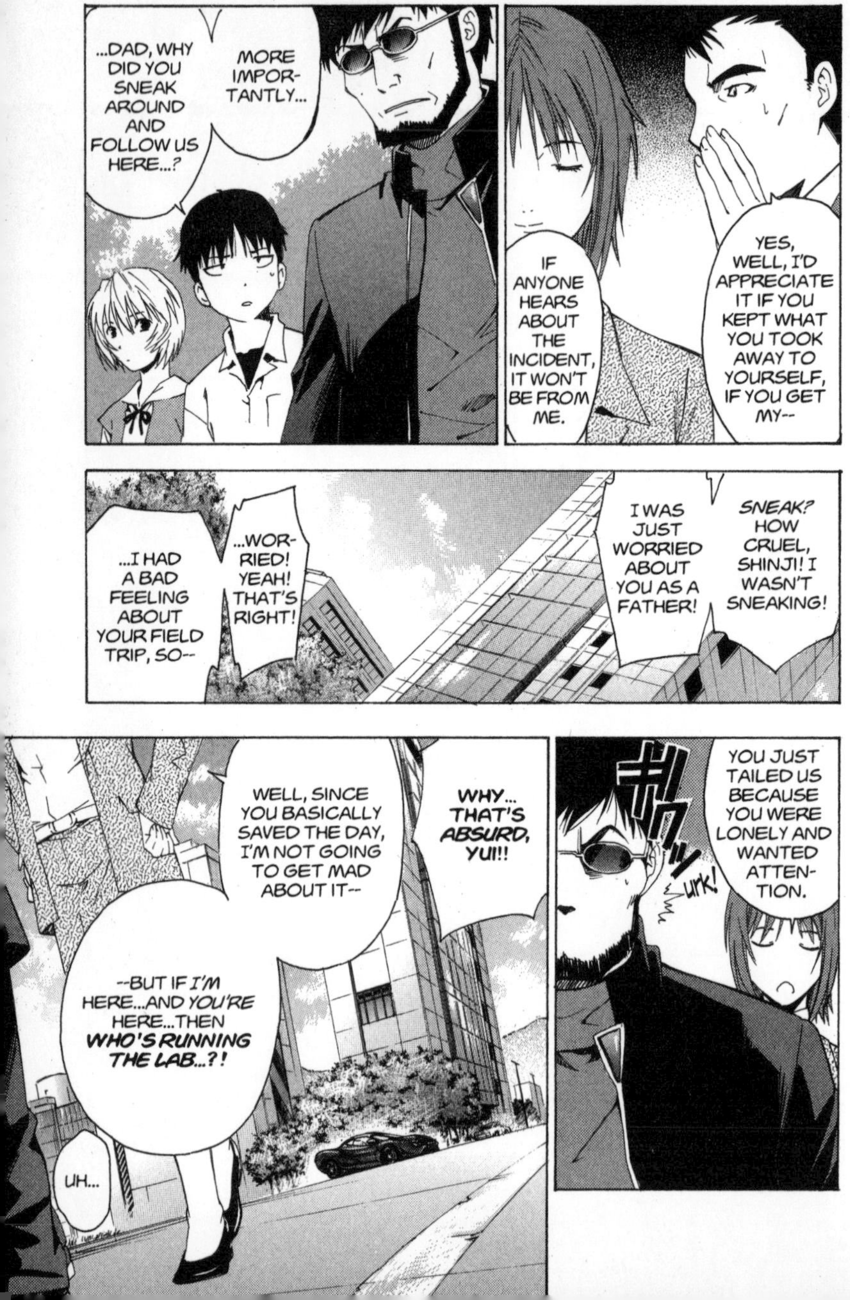
YES, WELL, I'D APPRECIATE IT IF YOU KEPT WHAT YOU TOOK AWAY TO YOURSELF, IF YOU GET MY--
IF ANYONE HEARS ABOUT THE INCIDENT, IT WON'T BE FROM ME.
MORE IMPORTANTLY...
...DAD, WHY DID YOU SNEAK AROUND AND FOLLOW US HERE...?
SNEAK? HOW CRUEL, SHINJI! I WASN'T SNEAKING!
I WAS JUST WORRIED ABOUT YOU AS A FATHER!
...WORRIED! YEAH! THAT'S RIGHT!
...I HAD A BAD FEELING ABOUT YOUR FIELD TRIP, SO--
YOU JUST TAILED US BECAUSE YOU WERE LONELY AND WANTED ATTENTION.
urk!
WHY... THAT'S *ABSURD,* YUI!!
WELL, SINCE YOU BASICALLY SAVED THE DAY, I'M NOT GOING TO GET MAD ABOUT IT--
--BUT IF *I'M* HERE...AND *YOU'RE* HERE...THEN ***WHO'S RUNNING THE LAB...?!***
UH...

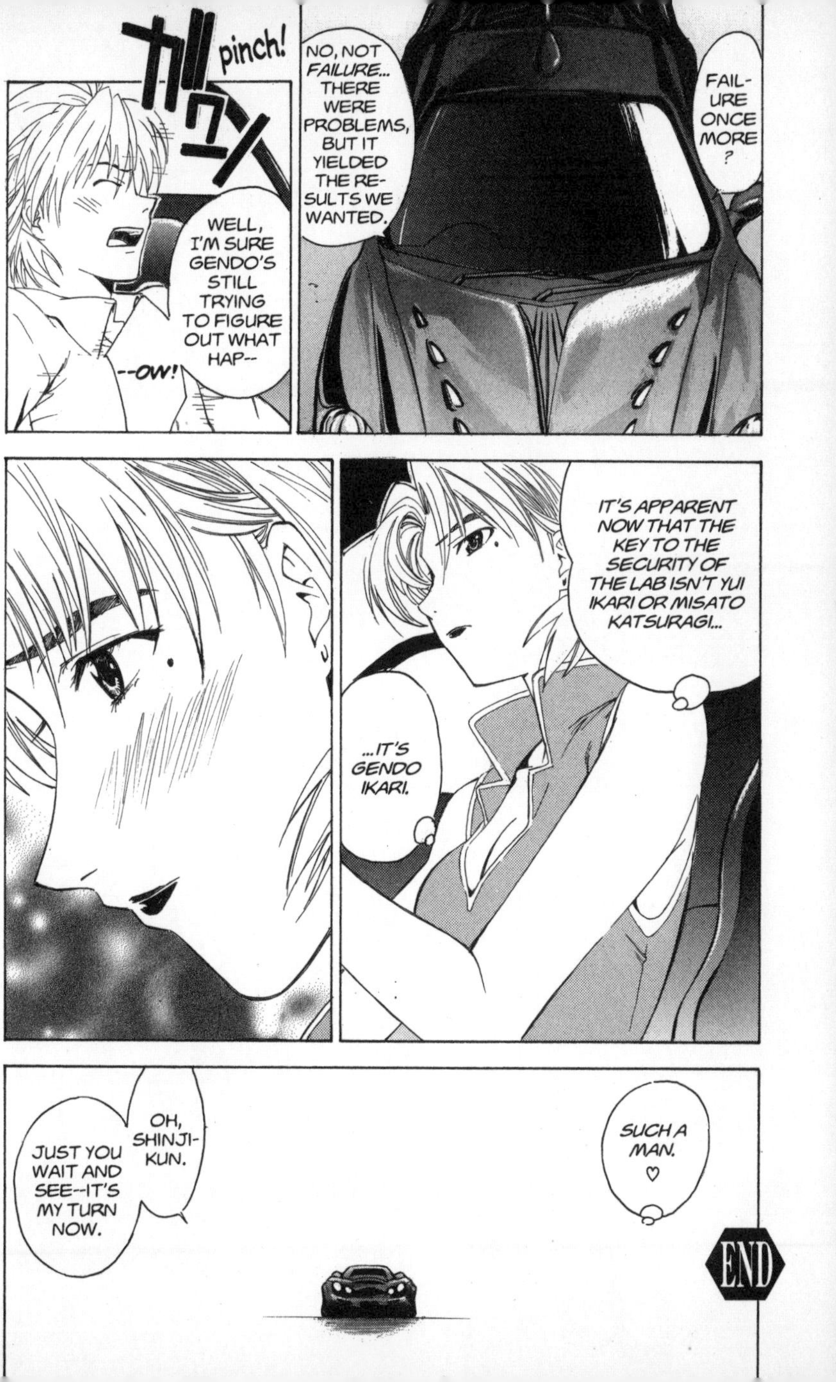
FAIL-URE ONCE MORE?
NO, NOT FAILURE... THERE WERE PROBLEMS, BUT IT YIELDED THE RE-SULTS WE WANTED.
pinch!
WELL, I'M SURE GENDO'S STILL TRYING TO FIGURE OUT WHAT HAP--
--OW!
IT'S APPARENT NOW THAT THE KEY TO THE SECURITY OF THE LAB ISN'T YUI IKARI OR MISATO KATSURAGI...
...IT'S GENDO IKARI.
SUCH A MAN. ♡
OH, SHINJI-KUN.
JUST YOU WAIT AND SEE--IT'S MY TURN NOW.
END

AFTERWORD

You know, the thing that gets me the most are those author/creator comments you see all the time in magazines and so forth. I mean, seriously, we spend most of our time at home all day—working—so it's not like there's tons of stuff happening that warrants writing about.

And even after I let them know that (every time!), they still come to me and ask, "so, isn't anything interesting happening?" And, after all, there really isn't anything interesting happening. [uneasy laughter]

-Osamu Takahashi

~STAFF~

Kasumiryo

Miki

Takuji

Keiji Watarai

Michio Morikawa

COVER DESIGN

Seki Shindo

see you in vol. 7 . . .

EDITOR
CARL GUSTAV HORN

EDITORIAL ASSISTANT
ANNIE GULLION

DESIGNER
STEPHEN REICHERT

PUBLISHER
MIKE RICHARDSON

English-language version produced by Dark Horse Comics

Neon Genesis Evangelion: The Shinji Ikari Raising Project Vol. 6
First published in Japan as NEON GENESIS EVANGELION IKARI-SHINJI IKUSEI KEIKAKU Volume 6. © OSAMU TAKAHASHI 2008 © GAINAX •
khara. First published in Japan in 2008 by KADOKAWA SHOTEN Publishing Co., Ltd., Tokyo. English translation rights arranged with KADOKAWA
SHOTEN Publishing Co., Ltd., Tokyo, through TOHAN CORPORATION, Tokyo. This English-language edition © 2010 by Dark Horse Comics, Inc.
All other material © 2010 by Dark Horse Comics, Inc. All rights reserved. No portion of this publication may be reproduced or transmitted, in any
form or by any means, without the express written permission of the copyright holders. Names, characters, places, and incidents featured in this
publication either are the product of the author's imagination or are used fictitiously. Any resemblance to actual persons (living or dead), events,
institutions, or locales, without satiric intent, is coincidental. Dark Horse Manga™ is a trademark of Dark Horse Comics, Inc. All rights reserved.

Published by
Dark Horse Manga
A division of Dark Horse Comics, Inc.
10956 SE Main Street
Milwaukie, OR 97222

darkhorse.com

To find a comics shop in your area, call the Comic Shop Locator Service toll-free at 1-888-266-4226

First edition: October 2010
ISBN 978-1-59582-580-3

1 3 5 7 9 10 8 6 4 2
Printed at Transcontinental Gagné, Louisville, QC, Canada

MISATO'S FAN SERVICE CENTER

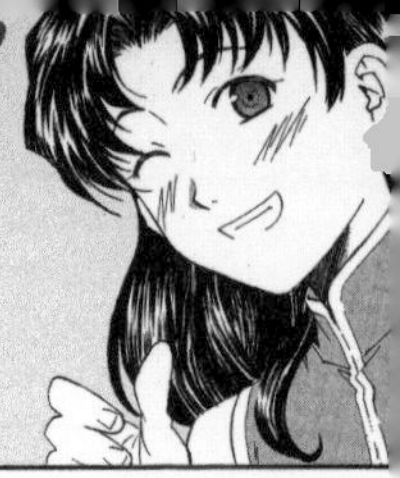

c/o Dark Horse Comics • 10956 SE Main Street • Milwaukie, OR 97222 • evangelion@darkhorse.com

Alex West, via e-mail, writes into MFSC with a very personal story about *Evangelion*:

The first time I saw Eva *was the movie* Evangelion: Death and Rebirth, *about three weeks after my mother attempted suicide. She's doing a lot better now, thank you. But picture the scene: there I was, alone and pretty messed up, and about to watch the two original* Evangelion *films.*

I had almost no idea what I was going to see, other than that my friend Mark had recommended it to me and praised how good it was (at this point Ghost in the Shell *was both my favorite anime and movie—by the end of this movie session, I would have a new one). So I slipped in* Death.

I pressed "play" (you can probably guess where I'm going with this, but please bear with me) and about five minutes in, of course, is the scene where Asuka finds her mom hanging from the ceiling. The expression on her face mirrored my own, or at least, what I felt sure my expression had been when I found my mother.

My mother's method was different and she thankfully survived, but still, the emotion was the same I also had the nightmare of finding my mom. For the past several weeks, I had been devouring movies, novels, manga and comics—anything that dealt with suicide, but nothing had the impact of that little red headed girl, running into that room.

As the movie continued, I found the same sense of confusion, and also isolation—my older sisters, I'm sure, were going through the same experience, but I found myself unable to relate to them. The inability to understand the world I had been forced into was just like a certain character in a certain story...we've been discussing. I lost myself in their pain, or maybe, found myself waiting there, as I switched discs to The End of Evangelion.

I witnessed a boy decide to die and cast off the world he was part of—is that what my mom felt? Is that what Asuka's mom felt? Needless to say, the next day I rushed out, emptied my bank account, and picked up the entire series (the Australian box set—the single most expensive anime purchase of my life). In the TV show, I learned more of Asuka's plight; her desire to hurl herself into something terrifying to be better than what she was.

I understood this, and the hurt it caused her—this tale; it was not just Asuka's or Shinji's story. The whole thing hit home hard, and I connected with it on a level I've never experienced before or after. I also believe that Eva *helped me through that point in my life, by witnessing its characters express and articulate how I felt, even if their story wasn't directly related to my own*

It's strange to think how a Japanese director and writer whom I've never met (but would love to), in expressing his own soul, would help me sort out my own. So when I watch Evangelion: Rebuild, *what I see is Anno looking back at those same emotions that drove* Eva *in the first place, and declaring that he survived them. Which, in a way, is what I get from it too (another reason I love the*

Shinji Ikari Raising Project *is it's super cool to see Shinji, Asuka and Rei just being kids).*

Carl, you once wrote—in reference to the early volumes of Sadamoto's Evangelion *manga, and the comments that were made there by the staff of the series "in real time," that is, while the original anime was still coming out–that the only way* Evangelion *can ever mean anything real is if you make its meaning for yourself. Well, I agree, and this is what* Evangelion *has meant to me.*

Anyhow on a lighter note (!)—back to Evangelion 2.0 *(God I wish I could talk more about, but my anime club is sick of listening to me). Mari is pretty awesome and it seems like it would be easier to get behind Asuka Langley Shikinami then it was for Asuka Langley Soryu (maybe that's why they changed her name to highlight her character's differences, and not just for the merchandise; i.e., the "Soryu" version vs. the "Shikinami" version).*

Alex sends in this panoramic illustration of the cast of the recent *Evangelion 2.0: You Can (Not) Advance* film, noting that "*the colour scheme I used for the pic was inspired by an image of Rei done by Kazuya Tsurumaki in the booklet for the* Refrain of Evangelion *CD. Oh, and is it just me, or does Asuka look kinda frumpy next to that super-skinny Rei and Mari (I did it this way on purpose, inspired by Toji's analyses of Rei and Asuka in vol. 1—but she looks frumpier than I intended).*" I actually do like the color very much, but unfortunately, since this is a b/w section of

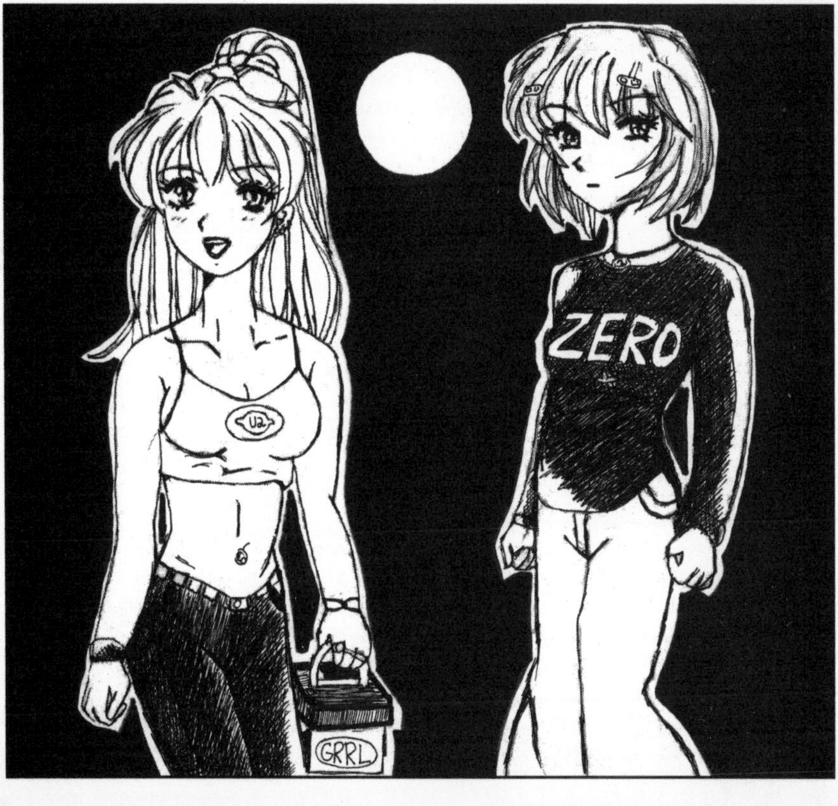
ZERO
GRRL

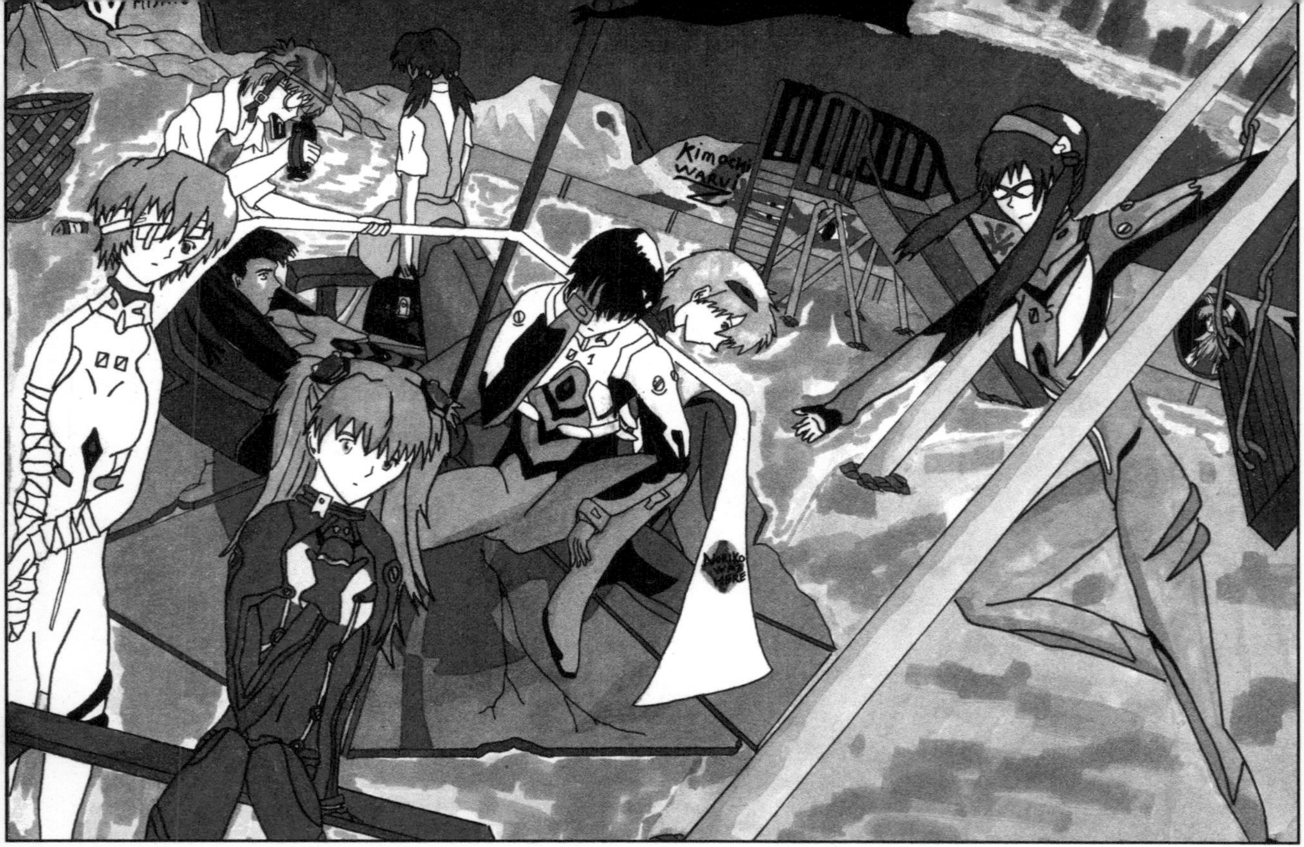
Kimochi WARUI
NORIKO WAS HERE

the book, I have to quote *Spinal Tap*: "You would, though, if it were playing." ^_^

Since I'm about to head down to Gainax's main hangout in America—namely, San Jose, CA's Fanime Con—I thought I'd highlight two MSFC contributions by some Fanime people! The super-retro 90s mallrat rendition of Asuka and Rei (what were those little square purses called, anyway?) on p. 180 is courtesy of Danielle Tokunaga. I say "super-retro 90s," but honestly, isn't that the place *Evangelion* comes from? ^_^

And here's Justin Hernandez, aka DJ Kino Senshi (the best *senshi*, of course—well, her and my intellectual role model, Usagi), who is often found spinning house/tribal at Fanime—showing off the one *Evangelion* item I don't have that I wish I did. Naturally, like my *Eva* mug (see vol. 1's MFSC), this t-shirt is what you might call an American *doujinshi*. It was a limited edition, but Justin made sure that Gainax's president Hiroyuki Yamaga got one.

We're looking forward to seeing you (and your letters and art) in vol. 7 of *The Shinji Ikari Raising Project*... but don't forget, vol. 1 of our *new* series, *Neon Genesis Evangelion: Campus Apocalypse* is out now, with vol. 2 coming soon! Check out the cover illustration of *Campus Apocalypse* on the next page—we want your letters there too, you know! ^_^

—CGH

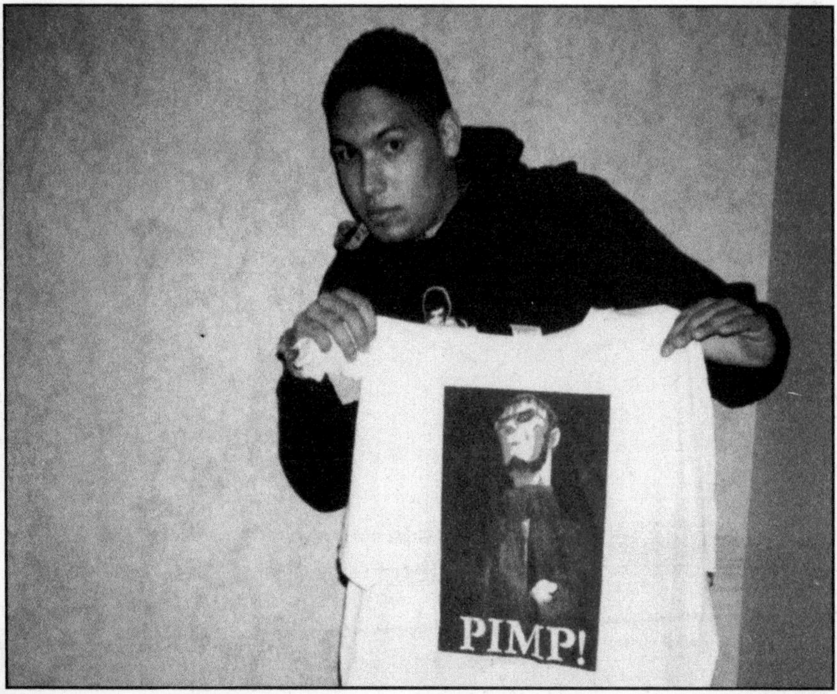
PIMP!

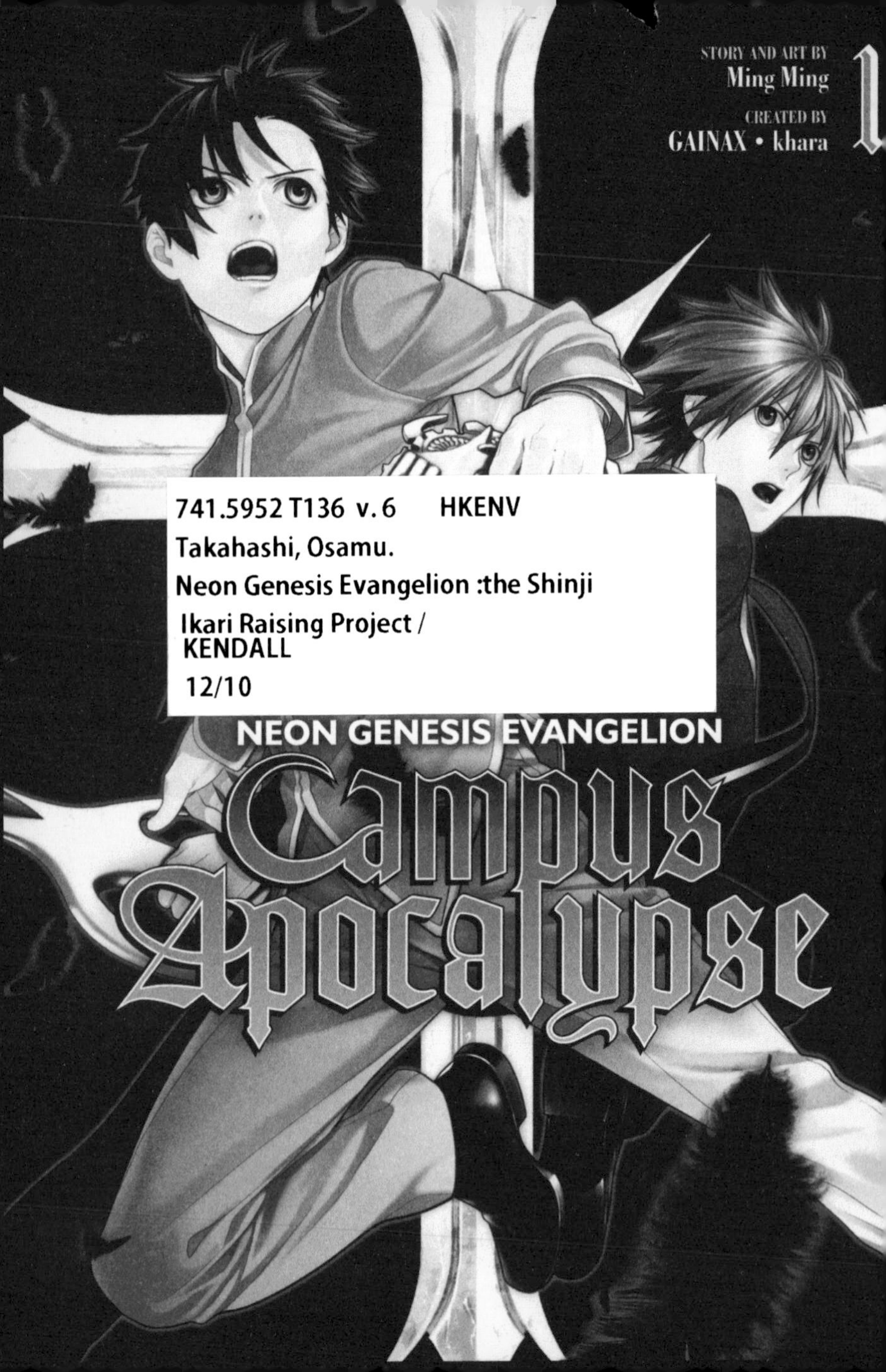

STORY AND ART BY
Ming Ming
CREATED BY
GAINAX • khara

1

NEON GENESIS EVANGELION

Campus Apocalypse

STO

止まれ

THIS IS THE BACK OF THE BOOK!

This manga collection is translated into English, but arranged in right-to-left reading format to maintain the artwork's visual orientation as originally drawn and published in Japan. If you've never read comics this way before, take a look at the diagram below to give yourself an idea of how to go about it. Basically, you'll be starting in the upper-right-hand corner, and will read each word balloon and panel moving right to left. It may take a little getting used to, but you should get the hang of it very quickly. Have fun! If this is the millionth manga you've read this way, never mind.

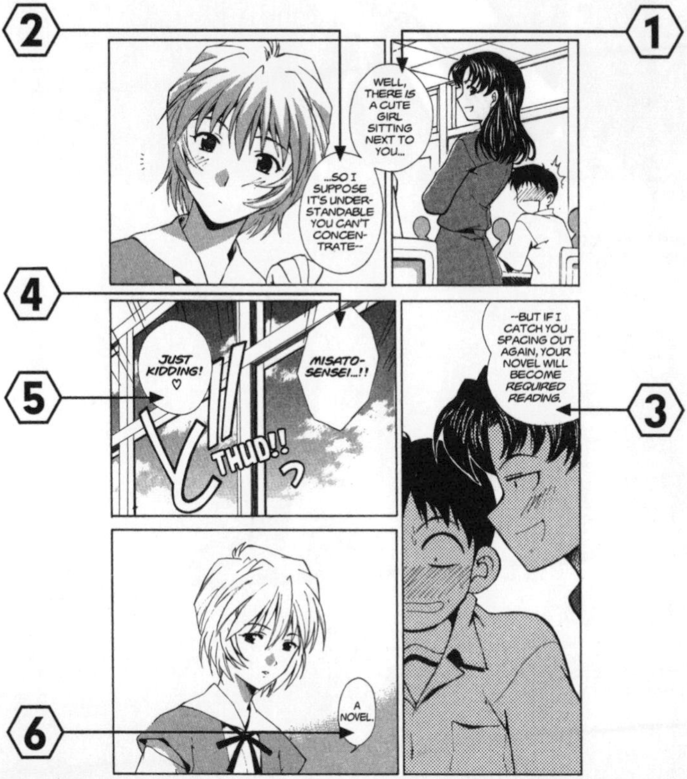
1
WELL, THERE IS A CUTE GIRL SITTING NEXT TO YOU...
2
...SO I SUPPOSE IT'S UNDERSTANDABLE YOU CAN'T CONCENTRATE--
3
--BUT IF I CATCH YOU SPACING OUT AGAIN, YOUR NOVEL WILL BECOME REQUIRED READING.
4
MISATO-SENSEI...!!
5
JUST KIDDING! ♡
THUD!!
6
A NOVEL.